Chief Umpire Reference Manual V4.0

컬링 심판 규정집

V 4.0

양재봉

학력

- 동국대학교 체육교육학과 졸업
- 동국대학교 체육학 석사(체육학 전공)
- 동국대학교 이학 박사(체육학 전공)

경력

- 現 서울시컬링연합회 사무국장
- 現 대한컬링경기연맹 1급 심판
- 煎 한국외국어대학교 컬링 외래교수
- World Curling Federation Advanced Umpire
- World Curling Federation Instructors of Curling
- World Curling Federation Level 1 Technical Instructor
- World Curling Federation Advanced Course for Caches

컬링 심판 규정집 V 4.0

발행일 2018년 9월 14일

지은이 세계컬링연맹
옮긴이 양 재 봉
펴낸이 손 형 국
펴낸곳 (주)북랩
편집인 선일영 편집 권혁신, 오경진, 최승헌, 최예은, 김경무
디자인 이현수, 김민하, 한수희, 김윤주, 허지혜 제작 박기성, 황동현, 구성우, 정성배
마케팅 김회란, 박진관, 조하라
출판등록 2004. 12. 1(제2012-000051호)
주소 서울시 금천구 가산디지털 1로 168, 우림라이온스밸리 B동 B113, 114호
홈페이지 www.book.co.kr
전화번호 (02)2026-5777 팩스 (02)2026-5747

ISBN 979-11-6299-303-3 13690(종이책) 979-11-6299-304-0 15690(전자책)

이 도서의 국립중앙도서관 출판예정도서목록(CIP)은 서지정보유통지원시스템 홈페이지(http://seoji.nl.go.kr)와 국가자료공동목록시스템(http://www.nl.go.kr/kolisnet)에서 이용하실 수 있습니다.
(CIP제어번호: CIP2018029107)

CURLING

세계컬링연맹 지음 • 양재봉 옮김

Chief Umpire Reference Manual V 4.0

컬링 심판 규정집 V 4.0

북랩book Lab

세계컬링연맹 번역서 출간 승인서

To: Dear officials

On 2 July 2015 at 04:23,

Republic of Korea, Seoul, Curling Federation
I am the Managing Director
Many data were collected and I collected several materials.
Five years ago created the foundation curling book
i hope used manual and curling want to translate educational books.
the book is WCF Chief Umpire Reference Manual (V4.0)
Can I translate the manual and use that information?
And I would like to write a curling book. Use the Manual (V4.0)
Curling Manual(V4.0) manuscript preparation available?
Please answer if you can use.

from: WCF Info 〈info@worldcurling.org〉
15.07.03 00:01 GMT +0900
Re: Republic of Korea, Seoul, Curling Federation
Dear Jae-Bong,
Thank you for your enquiry.
I have asked our Director of Competitions and Development about this: You are welcome to use the Chief Umpire Reference Manual in any way you like, for example translating it or copying it.
The WCF is trying to do a complete update of the manual after this year's WCF Congress (September), because there will probably be new rules and policies approved at that time. If you would prefer to wait, the WCF will send you the latest version as soon as it is finished.

Kind regards,

Gill Amatt
World Curling Federation

추천사

컬링의 불모지나 다름없던 대한민국이 컬링으로 우뚝 서게 된 계기는 2018 평창 동계올림픽이라고 생각합니다. 영미~ 감동의 여운이 가시지 않은 지금 벌써 한여름의 중턱에 와 있습니다.

안녕하십니까? 컬링을 사랑하고 즐기시는 여러분들 반갑습니다. 제가 컬링을 알게 된 계기도 여러분들과 비슷합니다. 빙판 위에서 빗자루질을 하는 종목인 컬링은 독특하고 신기함으로 다가왔습니다. 거기에 매료되어 컬링 종목에 발로 뛰어다니며 컬링을 알리고자 한 지 10여 년이 지난 지금의 컬링은 격세지감을 느끼고 있습니다. 동계스포츠에서 신기한 종목이었던 컬링이 보다 전문적이고 체계적으로 변화하고 있습니다. 이런 변화에 부응하여 보다 전문적 교재가 필요합니다.

『컬링 심판 규정집 V 4.0』은 지도자와 심판이면 누구나 기존에 알고 있던 정보를 올바르게 제시한다는 것과 다양한 지도방법 및 행동 방법 등이 소개되고 있어 전문서적으로서 정확한 정보를 제공하고 있습니다.

이러한 교재가 출판됨에 따라 대한민국의 모든 컬링인들은 더 쉽고 체계적으로 컬링을 이해하실 수 있을 거라 생각됩니다. 이런 의미에서 본 교재는 지도자, 심판들이 내실 있는 프로그램을 통해 컬링을 처음 접하는 선수들에게 의미 있는 교본으로서 이론과 실제를 제공할 수 있다고 봅니다.

2018 평창 동계올림픽에서의 컬링의 성공에는 많은 지도자와 전문가들이 함께 이룩한 결과물입니다. 이러한 결과물은 새로운 스포츠에 대한 붐업 조성과 생활스포츠로 이어지게 됩니다. 앞으로의 컬링은 생활체육의 중요한 한 자리를 차지할 것이며 많은 생활체육동호회와 클럽, 전문가들이 함께 즐기는 스포츠로 자리매김해야 할 것입니다.

끝으로 양재봉 박사의 이번『컬링 심판 규정집 V 4.0』출간을 진심으로 축하하며, 대한장애인컬링협회 관계자를 대표하여 인사를 전합니다.
감사합니다.

대한장애인컬링협회 회장 최종길

머 리 말

2018 대한민국의 겨울은 어느 때보다 뜨겁고 역동적이었습니다. 삼수 끝에 찾아온 평창의 기적은 컬링을 만나는 순간 더 뜨겁게 활활 타올랐습니다. 2018 평창올림픽 조직위원회 컬링 공식해설위원으로 활동하면서 그동안 준비해오던 심판집을 이번에는 꼭 마무리 지으리라! 다짐하면서 폐막식을 지켜보았습니다. 하지만 쉽지 않았습니다. 이 책은 마치 작은 나무인형을 잘 만들기 위해 준비하는 것처럼 책 쓰기 위한 조각칼을 하나하나 준비해야 했고 오랜 시간 원목을 찾아 헤매다니는 것처럼 정확한 번역을 위해 오랜 시간 공을 들인 끝에 세상에 나올 수 있었습니다. 끝내 이런저런 시간들이 쌓여 다행히도 오늘 또 한 권의 머리말을 글 앞에 올려놓을 수 있게 되었습니다. 완벽한 마무리를 위해 시간을 더 보내기보다는 화장기 없는 여인의 민낯을 보이는 것처럼 조금은 부끄럽지만 덜 정리된 글이지만 마무리하려 합니다. 번역본의 한계를 벗어나지 못하는 이유와 변명 뒤에 숨는 것을 비겁한 사람이라 나무라지만 마시고 좋은 의견과 지적을 통해 한 걸음 더 나아갈 수 있도록 조언해 주시면 다음 매뉴얼에서는 반영하도록 노력하겠습니다.

이 책은 세계컬링연맹 WCF(World Curling Federation)에서 제공하는 심판 매뉴얼 Version 4.0(October 2012)의 번역본으로 우선 컬링 심판에게 가장 먼저 읽어보기를 권합니다. 컬링은 심판교육 수료 후 심판자격증이 공인되기 때문에 더 깊은 공부가 어렵고 그것이 규정 내에서 합당한지 알기 어렵기 때문입니다. 다음으로는 세계대회에 출전하는 지도자와 선수에게 권합니다. 국내대회에서 시시비비를 가리기 위해 많은 논쟁이 있어 왔지만 이번『컬링 심판 규정집 V 4.0』이 해결의 실마리를 제공해 주는 단초가 되기를 바랍니다. 그리고 조금은 어렵겠지만, 컬링에 관심을 갖고 공부하는 선수나 동호인들에게 좀 더 심도 있는 컬링인으로 거듭날 수 있는 계기를 제공하는 교과서가 될 수 있기를 희망합니다.

여러분! 저의 글이 부족하다면 원문과 함께 공부하시길 바라고 2013년부터 시작해온 부끄럽고 아쉬운 몇 년간의 퍼즐 맞추기를 이제야 끝내니 용서 바랍니다. 1급 심판이 될 때까지 동지처럼 잘 이끌어주신 길태오 前심판장님께 고개 숙여 인사드리고 끝까지 밀어주시겠다고 응원해주시는 대한장애인컬링협회 최종길 회장님과 휠체어컬링 부분을 잘 정리해주신 김정훈 사무국장님께 감사드립니다. 마지막으로, 컬링을 사랑하는 가족 양우진과 양진, 특히 어려운 길 함께 걸어 주는 아내 김현주에게 고마움을 전합니다.

기상관측 이후 111년 만에 가장 뜨거운 날로 기록된(서울 39.6℃) 한여름의 8월

대한컬링경기연맹 1급 심판 양재봉

TABLE OF CONTENTS

1. ROLE OF THE UMPIRE/OFFICIAL 12
2. OFFICIALS: ENFORCERS OR LEGISLATORS? 12
3. WCF TECHNICAL OFFICIAL'S AGREEMENT 14
4. CHIEF UMPIRE – DUTIES & RESPONSIBILITIES 18
5. CHIEF UMPIRE'S CHECK LIST 22
6. ON-ICE PRE-COMPETITION CHECK 26
7. UMPIRE EQUIPMENT 28
8. TEAM MEETING AGENDA 30
9. TEAM MEETING DOCUMENT(SAMPLE) 34
10. POST ROUND ROBIN STONE SELECTION 58
11. HANDLING OF HEALTH INFORMATION FORMS 60
12. CHIEF UMPIRE'S REPORT 62
13. GAME UMPIRES 68
14. END-ICE OBSERVER 72
15. END-ICE OBSERVER – MIXED DOUBLES CURLING 76
16. ICE PLAYER ASSISTANT(IPA) - WHEELCHAIR CURLING 82
17. HAND-OUT: ICE PLAYER ASSISTANT(IPA) 84
18. CHIEF TIMER 90
19. CurlTime INSTRUCTIONS 98
20. TIME CLOCK OPERATOR 110
21. PROCEDURE WHEN A TEAM IS LOW ON TIME 114
22. PROCEDURES FOR TIME-OUTS 116
23. TIMING BETWEEN ENDS 118
24. TIME CLOCK ADJUSTMENTS 120
25. TIMING - MIXED DOUBLES CURLING 122
26. TIMING - WHEELCHAIR CURLING(See also Sections: 20 - 24 & 27) 124
27. WHEELCHAIR CURLING - TIMING RELATED SCENARIOS 126
28. HAND-OUT: TIMING - WHEELCHAIR CURLING 130
29. HAND-OUT: TIMERS 140
30. HOG LINE OBSERVER 142
31. EYE ON THE HOG – HOG LINE VIOLATION DETECTION SYSTEM 144
32. EYE ON THE HOG MALFUNCTION PROCEDURES 148
33. CHIEF STATISTICIAN 150

목차

추천사 5

머리말 7

1. 심판/관계자의 역할 13

2. 심판: 진행자인가, 입법자인가? 13

3. 세계컬링연맹 기술 심판의 역할 15

4. 주심 - 의무와 책임 19

5. 주심의 확인 사항 23

6. 빙판 위에서의 경기 전 확인 목록 27

7. 심판 장비 29

8. 팀 회의 의제 31

9. 팀 회의 문서(양식) 35

10. 라운드 로빈 이후의 스톤 선택 59

11. 건강 정보 양식 관리 61

12. 주심 보고서 63

13. 경기 심판들 69

14. 엔드 아이스 관찰자 73

15. 혼합복식(믹스더블) 컬링에서의 엔드 아이스 관찰자 77

16. 빙상 선수 보조자(빙상 선수 보조자) - 휠체어 컬링 83

17. 유인물: 빙상 선수 보조자(빙상 선수 보조자) 85

18. 시간 계측 담당자 91

19. CurlTime 지시사항들 99

20. 시간 기록계 오퍼레이터 111

21. 팀이 시간이 모자랄 때의 절차 115

22. 타임아웃을 위한 절차 117

23. 엔드 중간의 시간 측정 119

24. 시간 조정 121

25. 시간 측정 - 혼합복식(믹스더블) 컬링 123

26. 시간 측정 - 휠체어 컬링(세션 20-24 & 27도 보아라.) 125

27. 휠체어 컬링 - 시간 측정과 관련된 양식 127

28. 핸드아웃: 휠체어 컬링 타임 계측 131

29. 핸드 아웃: 타이머들(시간 계측자들) 141

30. 호그 라인 관찰자 143

31. EYE ON THE HOG - 호그 라인 위반 검출 시스템 145

32. 호그 라인 위반 탐지 시스템 오작동 시 대처 방안 149

33. 대표 통계 전문가 151

34. STATISTICS SYTEM 152
35. MEASURING PROCEDURES 154
36. LAST STONE DRAW(LSD) 158
37. DRAW SHOT CHALLENGE(DSC) 162
38. ACCESS TO FIELD OF PLAY(FOP) 164
39. COACH BENCH 166
40. RULE CLARIFICATION – Late start 168
41. RULE CLARIFICATION – Hand or Body Prints 170
42. TEAM PARTICIPATION IN CEREMONIES 172
43. SPORTSMANSHIP BALLOTS 172
44. OPENING CEREMONIES – WCF EVENTS 174
45. CLOSING CEREMONIES – WCF EVENTS 176
46. PROCEDURES FOR BLOOD and HEAD INJURIES 186
47. COMPETITOR'S GUIDE(SAMPLE) 192
48. WCF ICE TECHNICIAN'S AGREEMENT 220
49. CARE OF CURLING STONES 226
50. DEALING WITH THE MEDIA 228
51. MEDIA INTERVIEWS 230
52. WCF CODE OF CONDUCT FOR PHOTOGRAPHERS 232
53. PHOTOGRAPHING - THINGS TO WATCH FOR 234
54. SOCIAL MEDIA COMMUNICATIONS 236
55. CURLING 238
56. CURLING HISTORY 240
57. LIST OF FORMS 248
58. ENTRY FORMS(WCF Office 250
59. COMPETITION FORMS 282

If you find any errors or omissions, or can suggest ways to improve the contents, please send comments to:

Keith Wendorf
WCF Director of Competitions & Development
keith.wendorf@worldcurling.org

34. 통계 시스템 ······ 153
35. 측정 절차 ······ 155
36. 라스트 스톤 드로우(LSD) ······ 159
37. 드로우 샷 챌린지(DSC) ······ 163
38. 경기장 접근(입장, FOP) ······ 165
39. 코치석 ······ 167
40. 규칙 명확화 - 늦은 시작 ······ 169
41. 규칙 명확화 - 손이나 몸 자국 ······ 171
42. 개막/폐막식의 팀 참여 ······ 173
43. 스포츠맨십 투표 용지 ······ 173
44. 개회식 ······ 175
45. 폐회식 - 세계컬링연맹 행사들 ······ 177
46. 혈액과 머리부상 대처 ······ 187
47. 참가자 안내서(샘플) ······ 193
48. 세계컬링연맹 경기 기술자 동의서 ······ 221
49. 컬링 스톤 관리 ······ 227
50. 언론 통제(관리) ······ 229
51. 언론 인터뷰 ······ 231
52. 세계컬링연맹의 사진사에 대한 행동강령 ······ 233
53. 촬영 - 주의점 ······ 235
54. 소셜 미디어 커뮤니케이션 ······ 237
55. 컬링 ······ 239
56. 컬링의 역사 ······ 241
57. 양식 리스트 ······ 249
58. 세계컬링연맹 공식 참가 신청서 ······ 251
59. 대회 양식 ······ 283

부록 The_Rules_of_Curling_(October_2017) ······ 347

1. ROLE OF THE UMPIRE/OFFICIAL

1. In curling, as in most sports, umpiring is performed by dedicated volunteers without whom the sport could not progress.

2. The role of the Umpire has been established to ensure fair play between two or more teams in any competition. Umpires act as a complement to the game, working with the teams in a fair and neutral manner within the rules of the game, doing measurements and intervening only to make a correction or following a breach of the rules.

3. Umpires' decisions must be made in fairness and sound judgement relative to the rules in the World Curling Federation "Rules of Curling and Rules of Competition" booklet.

4. All Umpires must have a thorough knowledge of the rules, their interpretation and implementation. Within the umpiring system, dependent on the assignment, the Umpire should have a sound knowledge of the record sheets, scoreboards, measuring devices, hog line discipline, statistics and time clocks. All play an important part in the smooth running of any competition while allowing an Umpire to "specialise" within a preferred area.

5. The game is first, and foremost, for the curlers and the role of the Umpire is secondary.

2. OFFICIALS: ENFORCERS OR LEGISLATORS?

Extracts from an article by Kevin Merkle (Associate Director Minnesota State High School)

Officials must remember that their job is one of enforcers, much like a police officer. When officials decide what rules to enforce they become legislators – or rule makers – and that is not their role. Just as it is not the role of the police officer to decide whether or not to enforce a particular law, or to "make up" the laws that they will enforce.

There will always be some inconsistency, but when officials decide which rules to enforce they are manipulating the game and creating much more inconsistency. This causes frustrations for players, coaches, and fans and leads to problems with sportsmanship and criticism of officials.

The interpretation of rules cannot be dependent upon the opinion of an individual official or even a group of officials. Coaches, players, and fans deserve to know how the rules will be enforced and should see little variance from game to game.

Consistently enforcing the rules as they are written will lead to events that will be better and more enjoyable for players, coaches, fans – and officials!

1. 심판/관계자의 역할

1. 대부분의 스포츠처럼, 컬링에서도 심판은 헌신적인 자원봉사자에 의해 수행된다. 이런 자원봉사자 없이 스포츠는 진보할 수 없다.
2. 심판의 역할은 어느 경기에서나 두 팀 혹은 그 이상의 팀들 간의 공정한 경기를 보장하도록 규정되어있다. 따라서 심판은 경기 규칙 이내에서 공정하고 중립적으로 팀을 돕고, 잘못을 바로잡거나 규칙을 위반할 때만 측정과 개입을 하는 보조자로서 행동한다.
3. 심판의 결정은 반드시 세계컬링연맹의『컬링 규칙과 대회 규정』책자의 규정에 관련되어 공정하고 현명한 판단으로 이어져야 한다.
4. 모든 심판들은 반드시 규정에 대한 이해와 실행을 바탕으로 규칙 전체(내용)를 알고 있어야 한다. 심판 규정 하에, 심판은 의무에 충실하여 반드시 경기 기록지, 점수판, 계측기기, 호그 라인 규칙, 점수 및 시간 측정에 대한 정통한 지식을 가지고 있어야 한다. 정해진 범위 내에서 전문화된 심판의 관할 내의 모든 경기는 대회의 원활한 운영에 있어 중요하다.
5. 선수에게 있어 경기(규칙)가 최우선이며, 심판 규정이 그다음이다.

2. 심판은 집행자인가, 입법자인가?

Kevin Merkle(미네소타 주 고등학교의 교감)이 쓴 기사에서 발췌

심판(officier)들은 그들의 직업이 경찰관과 같은 일종의 집행자라는 것을 기억해야 한다. 심판들이 어떤 규칙을 적용시켜야 한다고 판단한다면 그들은 입법자 또는 법률 창조자가 된다. 그러나 그것이 그들의 역할은 아니다. 특정한 법률의 집행 여부를 결정하는 것 혹은 그들이 집행할 법을 "만드는 것"이 경찰관의 역할이 아니듯이 말이다.

언제나 비일관성(불일치; 충돌)은 존재할 것이다. 그러나 심판들이 어떠한 규칙을 집행할지 결정하게 되면, 그들은 경기를 조작하고 더욱 심한 비일관성을 창조해낸다. 이것은 선수들과 코치, 그리고 팬들에게 좌절감을 안겨주고, 스포츠맨 정신의 문제와 위원들에 대한 비난으로 이어질 것이다.

규칙에 대한 해석은 개인 심판의 의견이나 여러 명의 심판들의 의견에 의존되어서는 안 된다. 감독, 선수, 그리고 팬들은 어떻게 규칙들이 적용되는지 알 자격이 있고 경기와 경기 사이의 변화를 최소한으로 느껴야 한다.

일관적으로 적혀있는 규정에 따라 경기를 진행하게 되면 선수, 코치진, 팬들 - 그리고 심판들에게도 훨씬 즐길 수 있는 경기로 이어질 것이다.

3. WCF TECHNICAL OFFICIAL'S AGREEMENT

Role of the Technical Official (Umpire, Timer and Statistician):

- It is of vital importance that all Technical Officials are professional and dedicated to providing and maintaining fair and equitable playing conditions in order to allow the sport to be played to the highest level.

- Technical Officials must have an extensive knowledge of the rules and treat all those involved with a competition with courtesy and respect.

- Everyone must commit to the competition the required number of working hours to ensure an equal workload for all Technical Officials.

- It must be remembered that a competition may be judged by how competent the officials are. All Technical Officials are vitally important members of the Officiating team and as such it is their responsibility to ensure they fulfil all of their obligations and responsibilities including fair play and impartiality throughout the competition.

Code of Conduct for the Technical Official:

Technical Officials are in a position of trust and responsibility and as such the following code of ethics should be followed:

- Technical Officials must be impartial in respect of all participating athletes. They should be prepared to converse with athletes and coaches on a general level (i.e. non-specific information) and with the Chief Umpire and WCF Director of Competitions / Technical Delegate on matters regarding rules and officiating.

- The Chief Umpire is the only person to answer questions from the media about officiating decisions and rulings. Remember that there is no such thing as an "off the record" comment, so be careful what is said.

- Good working relationships between the athletes, coaches, other officials, ice technicians, media and site personnel are expected. Respect everyone's job assignment, roles and duties.

- All decisions shall be made quickly and fairly, in accordance with the rules, without being officious. At no time will score, individuals, or biased spectators influence any decisions. Never put yourself in a position, real or perceived, of being partial in any situation

- Never become involved in any betting in a competition where you are a Technical Official.

- Consumption of alcoholic beverages during a competition should be done in moderation. Alcoholic beverages may not be consumed within 6 hours prior to, or during any game that you are working. After discussions (e.g. – the person involved, the Chief Umpire, etc.) the WCF Director of Competitions, or the WCF Technical Delegate, may suspend from the competition any Technical Official for violating basic common sense with alcohol.

- Comments about any aspect of the competition, officiating decisions or the rules of curling should only be discussed amongst the Technical Officials – not in the presence of other people or media.

3. 세계컬링연맹 기술 심판의 역할

기술위원의 규정 (심판, 타이머 및 통계원) :

- 모든 기술 심판들이 전문적이고 헌신적인 자세로 공정하고 평등한 경기 환경을 조성하는 것은 경기가 최상의 상태로 진행되기 위해 가장 중요하다.
- 기술 심판들은 규칙에 대한 광범위한 지식을 가지고 있어야 하며, 시합에 관련된 모든 사람들에게 공손하고 정중한 태도로 행동하여야 한다.
- 모든 기술 심판들은 동등한 작업량을 보장하기 위해, 요구되는 만큼의 활동시간 동안 대회를 위해 최선을 다해야 한다.
- 대회는 반드시 기술 심판들이 얼마나 유능한지에 의해 평가되었는지 인지되어야 한다. 기술 심판은 직무팀 내에서 필수적인 인물들이며, 경기 전반에 걸쳐 공평•공정한 플레이를 포함하여 모든 의무와 책임감을 이행할 것을 약속하는 것이 그들의 책임이다.

기술위원들이 지켜야 할 행동 규칙:

기술위원들은 신뢰와 책임감의 자리에 있는 만큼 다음과 같은 도덕적 규칙을 지켜야 한다. :

- 기술위원들은 반드시 대회에 참가한 모든 선수들에 대하여 공평한 존경심을 가지고 있어야 한다. 그들은 선수와 코치들과 일반적인 수준(즉, 구체적이지 않은 정보)에 관하여, 혹은 주심과 세계컬링연맹 소속의 시합 관계자, 기술 관련 대표자들과 규정과 심판에 관련하여 대화를 나눌 수 있도록 준비되어야 한다.
- 주심만이 매체로부터의 심판의 판단에 관한 질문에 답할 수 있는 유일한 사람이다. "비공개의" 논평 따위는 존재하지 않으므로 말하는 것을 조심해야 함을 기억하라.
- 선수들, 코치진, 기타 관계자, 경기 관계자, 언론, 장소 관계들 간의 좋은 관계가 요구된다. 모든 사람들의 직무, 역할, 의무를 존중해야 한다.
- 모든 결정은 신속하고 공정하게, 룰에 따라서, 권위를 내세우지 않으면서 이뤄져야 할 것이다. 결코 점수, 개개인, 또는 편향된 관중에 어떠한 판단에도 영향을 받아서는 안 된다. 어떠한 상황에서도 절대 실질적으로 혹은 느끼기에 편파적인 위치에 자신을 두지 말라.
- 기술위원직에 있으면서 절대로 시합에 관한 도박에 관여되어서는 안 된다.
- 경기 중 알코올성 음료를 섭취하는 것은 절제해야 한다. 알코올성 음료는 경기 전 6시간 혹은 (일하고 있는) 경기 도중 섭취해서는 안 된다. 음주 상태로 상식 밖의 폭력을 행사한 모든 관계자들은 세계컬링연맹 경기 감독 혹은 기술 심사위원(예-관계자, 주심, 등)과의 논의 후에 경기로부터 정직당할 수 있다.
- 어떤 경쟁의 측면을 집행하는 결정이나 컬링의 규칙에 대한 의견은 다른 관계자 혹은 언론 매체가 아닌 기술 심판들 사이에서만 논의되어야 한다.
- 세계컬링연맹과 주심은 모든 기술 관련 관계자들을 위해 복장 규정을 정해야 한다. 기술 심사위원들은 모든 경기 동안 적합한 복장을 하고 있어야 한다(예-청바지는 허용되지 않는다). 경기 중 복장은 관리위원회나 세계컬링연맹으로부터 제공받은 검정 바지와 특별한 윗옷이 될 것이다. 경기장에서 숙소로 바로 향하는 경우

- The WCF and Chief Umpire will set the dress code for all Technical Officials. An official should wear appropriate attire at all Event functions (i.e. – no blue jeans). The Field of Play clothing shall be black pants and a special jacket (supplied by the Organising Committee or the WCF). Outside the curling facility (public places) the official clothing should not be worn, unless it is to go directly from the venue to the place of residence.

- A neat and clean personal appearance and proper conduct is essential at all times

- Technical Officials should ensure that they have had enough rest so that their minds are fresh and alert. Umpires, in order to present the best impression during games, should be seated or standing, not leaning against the boards. Technical Officials should not be in the Field of Play without reason during games (e.g. - should not be in the Field of Play taking pictures).

- Technical Officials should uphold the principles of the officiating system and the philosophies of the WCF at all times, but maintain a degree of flexibility to avoid confrontation with the Organising Committee, teams, WCF Executive Board and the media.

- Technical Officials should never become more than casually involved socially with any specific team or athletes during the competition. There should be full disclosure to the WCF if there is a personal or business relationship with an athlete or coach. It is acceptable to speak with and be around teams socially, but Technical Officials should be careful not to be found in a position of spending an excessive amount of time with one team or athlete.

- During the competition the Chief Umpire and all other Technical Officials should be at the venue in enough time to prepare for every practice and game. All of the Technical Officials assigned to the competition must abide by the work schedule approved by the Chief Umpire. In the absence of the Chief Umpire, the Deputy Chief Umpire will be in charge and assume the duties of the Chief Umpire.

- When holding a Chief position (Umpire, Timer, Statistician), a report must be submitted to the WCF Director of Competitions within 30 days of the conclusion of the competition.

- Disciplinary action of a Technical Official will be determined and administered by the WCF Discipline Committee (minimum of three persons: WCF President or Vice President; one Executive Board Member or Secretary General; and the WCF Director of Competitions or WCF Competition Technical Delegate). Technical Officials who do not follow these rules of conduct may not be considered for future WCF competitions.

The above conditions apply throughout the duration of the competition and its functions (arrival to departure).

Agreement Points:

1) I accept the assigned role and agree to follow the Code of Conduct.
2) I agree to fulfil all my obligations and responsibilities including fair play and impartiality throughout the competition.
3) I understand that the WCF must provide the proper support so that I can fulfil the duties and responsibilities of the position.

Competition(s) & Position: ______________________________

Read and agreed Name: ______________________________

Signature: ______________________________

Date: ______________________________

가 아니라면, 경기장을 제외한 곳(공적 장소)의 바깥에서 공적 의복을 착용해서는 안 된다.

• 깔끔하고 단정한 외형과 적절한 처신은 항상 필수적이다.

• 기술 기관자들은 그들의 정신이 맑고 민첩하기 위하여 충분한 휴식을 취하고 있어야 한다. 심판들, 경기 도중 최상의 인상을 보여주기 위하여, 착석하고 있거나 서 있어야 하며, 판에 기대어 있어서는 안 된다. 기술 기관자들은 시합 중 이유 없이 경기장에 나가 있으면 안 된다. (예를 들어- 사진을 찍기 위해 경기장에 나가 있어서는 안 된다)

• 기술위원들은 항상 직무 집행 원칙과 세계컬링연맹의 원칙을 잊어서는 안 된다. 하지만 관리위원회, 팀, 세계컬링연맹 집행기관이나 매체들과의 직면하는 것을 피하기 위해 어느 정도의 유연성은 가지고 있어야 한다.

• 기술위원들은 대회 동안에 어떠한 팀이나 선수와도 임시로 연관된 것 이상이 되어서는 안 된다. 만약 선수나 코치와 개인적이거나 사업적인 관계가 있다면, 세계컬링연맹에 의해 완전히 차단될 것이다. 팀과 사회적인 목적의 대화나 어울림은 허용되지만, 기술위원들은 어떠한 팀이나 선수와 과도하게 많은 시간을 함께 보내는 것이 목격되지 않기 위해 조심하여야 한다.

• 경기 도중 주심과 다른 모든 기술위원들은 모든 연습과 게임의 준비를 위해 충분한 시간 동안 경기장에 있어야 한다. 경기에 지정된 모든 기술 기관자들은 주심으로부터 주어진 일정에 따라 움직여야 한다. 주심의 부재 시, 부주심이 담당자가 되어 주심의 의무를 맡는다.

• 주된 직위(심판, 시간 측정자, 통계가)를 맡고 있다면, 세계컬링연맹 주관대회 임원에게 보고서를 경기 종료 30일 전까지 제출해야 한다.

• 기술위원의 징계 행위는 세계컬링연맹 징계협회(최소 세 명: 세계컬링연맹 회장 혹은 부회장; 경영 간부 이사 혹은 사무총장 한 명; 그리고 세계컬링연맹 경기 관계자 혹은 세계컬링연맹 기술위원)에서 결정되고 관리된다. 이 행동규칙을 따르지 않는 기술위원은 차기 세계컬링연맹 주관대회에 발탁되지 못할 것이다.

위의 조항들은 경기 도중과 대회 기간(입국할 때부터 출국할 때까지) 동안 쭉 적용된다.

동의 사항 :

1) 나는 지정된 역할들을 순응하며 행동 수칙들에 동의한다.

2) 나는 경기 내내 나의 의무와 공평한 경기와 공정성을 포함한 나의 책임을 다할 것에 대하여 동의한다.

3) 나는 내가 나의 위치에서 의무와 책임을 다하기 위하여 세계컬링연맹에서 그에 적합한 지원을 해주어야 한다는 데에 동의한다.

경기(들)와 지위:

읽었으며 동의함 ______________________ 이름: ______________________

서명: ______________________

날짜: ______________________

4. CHIEF UMPIRE – DUTIES & RESPONSIBILITIES

The position of Chief Umpire is one that should receive respect from players, coaches, other Umpires, host committee, and representatives of the organisation governing the competition. In order to gain and retain this respect, Chief Umpires must be aware of their conduct 24 hours a day during the time of the competition and must keep the following points in mind:

1. The Chief Umpire must demonstrate qualities of leadership and the ability to negotiate and arbitrate effectively.
2. The Chief Umpire sets the dress code for the Umpire team. Designated officiating clothing is required during the time of the competition. At all other times, dress in an appropriate manner when in public.
3. Never become more than casually involved socially with any specific teams or players for the duration of the competition. It is important to remember that appearance of bias or conflict of interest must be avoided.

DUTIES

PRE-COMPETITION

1. Prepare the Team Meeting Document and submit to the WCF Director of Competitions for review prior to the WCF office sending it out to the teams. Have additional copies available at the team meeting if a team wants a printed copy.
2. Contact host committee well in advance of the competition to confirm transportation arrangements between hotel and arena for the Umpires and to arrange a time and location for meeting with the timers and observers.
3. Confirm with the WCF and host committee that lunch and dinner will be available at the arena for the Umpires at a reasonable cost.
4. Prepare a working schedule for the Umpires and make it available to them in advance of the competition.
5. Confirm receipt of the WCF Competitors' Guide for the event.
6. Confirm with the Umpires their arrival times, and advise of any social functions they must attend and the dress requirements.
7. Set up the Umpires' room with the help of the Umpires.
8. Ensure there are sufficient copies of all necessary forms.
9. Oversee the Pre-competition Check of the ice and facilities. Liaise with Ice Technicians regarding stone and ice conditions.
10. Meet with the timers and observers to review rules and game procedures.
11. Meet with the Umpires to review rules and game procedures.
12. Assign tasks to the Umpires for the Team Meeting and the pre-competition practices.
13. Confirm colour of teams' light and dark clothing.
14. Confirm persons sitting on coach bench.
15. Conduct the Team Meeting.

4. 주심 - 의무와 책임

주심은 선수, 감독, 다른 심판, 사회자 위원회, 경기 운영의 대표자들 모두로부터 존경을 받아야 하는 위치에 있다. 이러한 존경을 얻고 유지하기 위해서 심판은 경기하는 24시간 내내 긴장을 놓치면 안 될 것이며 다음에 명시된 몇 가지 사항들을 명심하여야 한다.

1. 주심은 리더십과 협상하는 능력, 효율적으로 중재하는 모습을 보여주어야 한다.
2. 주심은 심판 팀들의 복장 규정을 정해야 한다. 대회 중에는 정해진 공식 복장을 착용해야 한다. 나머지 시간에는 사회에서 예의를 지킬 수 있는 적당한 복장을 착용해야 한다.
3. 경기 도중에는 어떠한 팀이나 선수와도 일상 속에서 어울리면 안 된다. 편견의 여지나 관심은 피해야 할 것이라는 것을 기억해야 한다.

의무

시합 전

1. 세계컬링연맹 사무실에서 팀들에게 나누어 주기 전에 팀 만남 자료를 준비하여 세계컬링연맹 경기 관리자에게 제출해야 한다. 팀이 복사본을 원할 경우를 위해 여분의 복사본을 가지고 있어야 한다.
2. 주최 위원회와 경기 전에 미리 연락해서 호텔과 심판들을 위한 공간 사이의 교통 상황이 어떤지 확인하고, 시간 측정자들과 참관인들과의 만남 시간과 장소를 정해야 한다.
3. 세계컬링연맹과 주최 위원회에게 심판들을 위한 공간에 점심과 저녁이 합리적인 가격에 제공될 것이라는 것을 확인시켜야 한다.
4. 심판들을 위한 근무 일정을 준비하고, 시합 전에 일정이 가능하도록 준비해야 한다.
5. 대회를 위한 세계컬링연맹 선수 지침서 수령증을 확인해야 한다.
6. 심판들의 출국 시간, 사회적 역할에 대한 권고, 그리고 복장, 주의사항들을 확인해야 한다.
7. 심판들의 도움을 받아 심판 대기실을 만들어야 한다.
8. 모든 필수적인 양식에 대한 충분한 복사본이 있는지 확인해야 한다.
9. 대회 전에 빙판과 시설 검사를 감독해야 하고, 스톤과 빙판 상태를 담당하는 얼음 기술자들과 연락을 취하여야 한다.
10. 규칙과 경기 절차를 검토하기 위해 타이머(시간 재는 사람)와 참관인과 만난다.
11. 규칙과 시합 과정을 검토하기 위하여 심판들을 만나야 한다.
12. 팀 회의와 경기 전 연습을 대비해 심판들에게 일을 배정해야 한다.
13. 팀별 의상이 밝은지 어두운지 확인해야 한다.
14. 코치석에 앉을 사람을 확인해야 한다.
15. 팀 만남을 추진해야 한다.

DURING THE COMPETITION

1. Be available to the coaches and teams at least 45 minutes before draw time.
2. Collect team line-up changes (if any) and communicate changes to Chief Statistician and Media Co-ordinator.
3. Update LSD database for each draw.
4. Be an extra pair of eyes for the Game Umpires and time clock operators.
5. Monitor players' and coaches' uniforms and crests to ensure they conform to guidelines.
6. Monitor movements and conduct of all persons in the Field of Play and on the coaches' bench during the entire competition.
7. Render decisions when Umpire rulings have been appealed.
8. Keep a record of all umpiring activity.
9. Resolve issues as they arise.
10. Before the last round robin draw, ensure there is a live microphone available to announce the playoff scenarios.
11. Prepare script for announcement of playoff scenarios at the end of the round robin and deliver the announcement if required.
12. Assign ice for playoff games in consultation with the Chief Ice Technician and the WCF Director of Competitions if not predetermined by television.
13. Meet with representatives of the playoff teams after the last round robin game to discuss stone selection, sheet assignments, special practice times, etc. for the playoff games. This process will be repeated after each game.
14. Assign Umpires to the playoff games and special practices.
15. Oversee the placing of selected stones on to the game sheet for playoff games.
16. Oversee doping control and liaise with Medical Officer, if required.
17. Oversee media requests in conjunction with the WCF Media Relations Officer.
18. Distribute Sportsmanship ballots to all players at their last round robin game. Ballots are to be returned to the Chief or Deputy Chief Umpire on site before the teams leave the venue that day.

POST COMPETITION

1. Ensure health information documents are shredded.
2. Prepare and submit Chief Umpire's Report to the WCF Director of Competitions within 30 days of the conclusion of the event.
3. Analyse situations that occurred at the event and make recommendations if they may be better handled at future events.
4. Report to Director of Competitions regarding individual Umpire performances, which were noteworthy either for deficiencies or excellence.

경기 중

1. 코치와 팀들은 경기 시간 최소 45분 전에 대기하고 있어야 한다.
2. (만약 있다면) 선수명단의 변화를 모아 대표 통계가, 그리고 매체 조정자에게 보고하여야 한다.
3. 드로우마다 LSD정보를 갱신해야 한다.
4. 경기 심판과 시간 측정자들의 또 다른 눈이 되어 주어야 한다.
5. 선수들과 심판들의 유니폼과 장식들을 지켜보고 그것들이 규정에 맞는지 확인하여야 한다.
6. 경기 내내 경기의 모든 사람들과 감독 의자에 위치한 사람들의 움직임을 지켜보고 지휘하여야 한다.
7. 심판의 결정에 반박이 들어왔을 때 결정을 내려 주어야 한다.
8. 심판들의 행동 모두를 녹화하고 있어야 한다.
9. 문제가 일어나면 즉시 일을 해결해야 한다.
10. 마지막 로빈 라운드에서 스톤이 멈추기 전에, 결승 경기를 발표해 줄 마이크가 있는지 확인해야 한다.
11. 로빈 라운드 끝에 결승 경기 발표를 위한 대본을 만들어 놓고, 발표를 위해 전달하여야 한다.
12. 만약 미리 텔레비전에 예정되어 있지 않았다면 대표 얼음 기술자와 경기의 세계컬링연맹 감독자와의 의논을 통해 결승 경기를 위한 빙판을 배정한다.
13. 결승전 경기를 위한 스톤 선별, 시트 과제, 특별 연습 시간 등을 의논하기 위하여 마지막 로빈 라운드 시합 후에 결승 경기 참가 팀 대표를 만난다. 이러한 과정은 매 경기 반복된다.
14. 결승전 경기와 특별 연습을 위한 심판을 정해야 한다.
15. 결승전 경기를 위해 정해진 스톤 위치 선정을 감독하여야 한다.
16. 약물 사용 통제를 감독하고, 필요하다면 의료 담당자와 연락을 취해라.
17. 세계컬링연맹 언론 관련 담당자와 함께 언론의 요구를 감독하라.
18. 마지막 리그전의 모든 선수들에게 스포츠맨십 투표용지를 나누어 주어라.
    투표용지는 현장에서 팀이 그 날 그 장소를 떠나기 전에 주심 혹은 부심에게 돌려줄 것이다.

경기 후

1. 건강 정보 문서가 파쇄되었는지 확인하여야 한다.
2. 대회가 끝난 후, 30일 이내로 세계컬링연맹 대회임원에게 주심의 보고서를 준비하여 제출해야 한다.
3. 시합에서 일어난 일들을 정리하고 보다 나은 미래의 시합을 위한 권고를 해야 한다.
4. 대회 관계자에게 심판 개인의 행동에 대하여 보고할 것, 부족한 점이든 잘한 점이든 기록할 만할 것은 무엇이든 보고한다.

5. CHIEF UMPIRE'S CHECK LIST

Prior to competition

Obtain the following contact information

______ Doctor / Hospital
______ Dentist
______ Physiotherapist
______ Ambulance
______ Team hotel
______ Umpire hotel
______ Chief Ice Technician
______ WCF Director of Competition and/or WCF Technical Delegate
______ Contact of the OC
______ Transportation

Stones

______ Which stones are to be used at the event
______ Stone information & numbers in TMD or distributed at the Team Meeting

Additional items to check with the appropriate source

______ Date, time and venue (suitable size) for Team Meeting, scheduled during or prior to Team Practice day, equipped with suitable PA system or microphone
______ Assist (if required) the WCF office to list arrival/departure dates and times for Umpires and accommodation in single rooms with bath/shower and W.C.
______ Accreditation for all Umpires allowing them entry to all necessary areas of the arena
______ Transportation to and from place of arrival and hotel, and to and from arena and hotel
______ Make initial contact with members of umpiring crew
______ Determine source and items which will be supplied for Umpire's on-ice uniforms, obtain uniform sizes if required
______ Make arrangements for lunch and dinner at the venue for Umpires
______ Opening and Closing Banquet tickets for each Umpire
______ Event pin and programme for each Umpire
______ Confirm per diem and travel expenses arrangements
______ Public address system available for arena, with roving microphone
______ Ensure arena staff is aware that one hour evening practice ice is available for teams during the round robin stage. (i.e. lights on and emergency phone lines reachable by Umpire in charge of practice). Also transportation has to be available for teams and Umpires after practice if hotel is not within walking distance. Local medical service in attendance if possible
______ Availability of water within the Field of Play

Umpires' Room

______ Large enough to accommodate all Umpires comfortably
______ Sufficient hanging space for Umpires' clothing
______ 2 good-sized tables, chair for each Umpire
______ Waste bins
______ Lockers for personal belongings if possible (specify if Umpires need to provide locks)
______ Refreshments available (hot and cold)
______ Minimum 2 keys for room (preferably one key per Umpire)
______ Radios and earpieces, batteries and chargers
______ Umpire work schedule prepared and posted
______ Draw posted
______ Sufficient copies of all forms
______ Internet connection

5. 주심의 확인 사항

시합 전
위 연락망들을 가지고 있을 것

_____ 의사/병원
_____ 치과
_____ 물리치료사
_____ 구급차
_____ 선수들의 호텔
_____ 심판들의 호텔
_____ 얼음 전문가
_____ 세계컬링연맹 대회 관계자 및 또는 세계컬링연맹 기술위원들
_____ 조직위원회 연락망
_____ 교통

스톤
_____ 대회에서 사용될 스톤
_____ 팀 회의 자료 또는 팀 회의에서 배포한 스톤의 정보(색깔)와 숫자

적합한 요소들과 함께 확인되어야 할 부수적인 물품들
_____ 적합한 장내 방송 설비 혹은 마이크 장비를 갖춰서 팀 미팅을 위한 날짜, 시간, (적합한 규모의) 장소를 팀 연습 기간 혹은 그 이전에 예정해라.
_____ 필요하다면, 세계컬링연맹 사무국이 심판을 위한 도착/떠나는 날짜와 시간, 하나의 방 안에 욕조와 샤워 시설, 그리고 화장실이 있는 숙소를 정하는 것을 도와라.
_____ 모든 심판들이 경기장의 필요한 모든 장소에 입장하는 것을 허락하는 인증 수단을 마련해라.
_____ 도착지에서 호텔까지의 왕복 교통, 경기장과 호텔을 오고 가는 교통을 확인해라.
_____ 심판들과의 첫 만남을 마련해라.
_____ 심판에게 제공될 빙판 위에서의 유니폼의 공급처와 물품을 결정하고, 필요하다면 유니폼 치수를 확인해라.
_____ 심판 대기실에 심판들의 점심과 저녁을 준비해라.
_____ 심판을 위한 개회식, 폐회식 티켓을 준비해라.
_____ 각각의 주심에게 경기(시트) 번호와 일정을 전달해라.
_____ 일일 이동 경비가 준비되었는지 확인해라.
_____ 무선 마이크를 포함하여, 장내 방송 설비가 경기장에서 가능한지 확인해라.
_____ 경기장 내의 스태프가 리그전 동안 팀들이 한 시간 동안 빙판에서의 저녁 연습이 가능한지를 자각하고 있는지 확인해라. (연습을 담당하는 주심에게 닿을 수 있는 긴급 연락망이 충분히 확보되었는지를 확인하라는 것이다) 또한 만약 호텔이 걸어서 도착할 만한 위치에 있지 않은 경우 팀과 심판을 위한 교통수단이 마련되어 있어야 한다. 가능하다면 지역 의료 서비스 차원에서 지원받는 것이 좋다.
_____ 경기장 내에서 물이 원활하게 공급되는지 확인해라.

심판 대기실
_____ 모든 심판들이 편안하게 지낼 수 있을 만큼 큰지 여부를 확인해라.
_____ 심판들의 옷을 모두 걸 수 있을 만큼 수납공간이 충분한지를 확인해라.
_____ 심판마다 2개의 적당한 크기의 테이블과 의자가 있는지 확인해라.
_____ 쓰레기통이 있는지 확인해라.
_____ 가능하다면 심판 개개인당 개인 소지품을 위한 개인 물품 보관함을 마련해라. (만약 심판이 자물쇠를 필요로 한다면 명시해놓아라)
_____ 심판들이 먹을 수 있는 따뜻하거나 시원한 다과를 준비해라.
_____ 대기실마다 최소한 두 개의 열쇠를 준비해라. (가급적이면 심판당 하나의 열쇠를 준비해라)
_____ 라디오와 이어폰, 배터리와 충전기가 있는지 확인해라.
_____ 심판들의 근무 일정이 정해졌고, 공고되었는지 확인해라.
_____ 부착된 대진표를 확인해라.
_____ 모든 문서(양식)의 충분한 복사본이 있는지 확인해라.
_____ 인터넷 연결 상황을 확인해라.

Volunteers/ Equipment

______ Arrange date, time, and location for volunteer training / meeting
______ If team drivers are being used, get contact information
______ Schedule for volunteers, drawn up by supervisors, copies to CU
______ Collection/return station for volunteer equipment
______ Stopwatches, clipboards for observers and timers
______ Pencils, erasers and sharpener for observers and timers
______ If used at the event, magnetic boards with 16 magnets (8x dark, 8x light) CU should have extra magnets
______ Blankets & insulation (Styrofoam or similar) for under chairs if required

Arena and Ice

______ Team name boards and scoreboard numbers sorted
______ Arena Clock – easily seen by all officials and players, official time for games
______ Carpet cleaning – ensure the ice or cleaning staff will vacuum on-ice carpet daily and between each session if possible
______ Chief Umpire table and chairs (2)
______ Coach and alternate bench - suitable positions behind each sheet, correct number of places for each team, dark and light positions marked (dark on the right)
______ Sufficient power points (electrical outlets) available for each team
______ All windows subject to sun/day light covered to minimise adverse affect on ice
______ Confirm home end, sheets marked A, B, C, etc. Timer positions marked with A, B, C, etc.
______ Check teams' changing rooms
______ Changing rooms for opposite gender coaches
______ Toilet access during games
______ All rooms clearly signed (e.g. Changing Rooms, Medical, Physiotherapist, Umpires, Doping, etc.)
______ Location to post Evening Practice booking sheets
______ Location of team mail boxes if provided
______ Check with Ice Technicians when on-ice pre-competition check can be done (this includes items such as the accuracy of the houses, installation of courtesy lines, photographers' areas if required)
______ Location, number and accuracy of measuring sticks
______ Determine FOP access and travel time for coaches for time-outs
______ Check location of volunteers' room/lounge, if one is available

Media

______ Check position of media bench
______ Liaise with Media Relations Officer to control numbers, proper dress, footwear and conduct
______ TV Schedule – copies to all teams and Umpires

Forms

______ Original Team Line-up
______ Game Team Line-up
______ Change of Team Line-up
______ Draw Shot Challenge
______ Last Stone Draw
______ On-Ice Official's Scorecard
______ Game Timing
______ Hog Line Violation (in CU Manual if required)
______ Violation Chart (in CU Manual if required)
______ Procedure for Evening Practice
______ Reservation Sheet for Evening Practice – 4 or 5 sheets OR Schedule for Reserved Evening Practice
______ Play-Off Game Information
______ Stone Selection
______ Seating Coach Bench
______ Team Playing Uniforms

자원봉사자 / 장비

_____ 자원봉사자 교육/회의의 날짜, 시간, 장소를 정해라.
_____ 팀 운전기사가 있다면, 연락처 정보를 얻어라.
_____ 감독관이 만든 자원봉사자 일정을 주심에게 복사해 주어라.
_____ 자원봉사자 장비 수거/반품 구역을 확인해라.
_____ 관측자와 타이머(시간 재는 사람)을 위한 스톱워치, 클립보드를 마련해라.
_____ 관측자와 타이머를 위한 연필, 지우개 그리고 연필깎이를 마련해라.
_____ 행사에서 사용된다면, 16개의 자석(어두운색 8개, 밝은색 8개)과 자석보드가 필요하다. 주심은 여분의 자석이 더 필요할 것이다.
_____ 필요한 경우 아래의 의자에 담요 & 단열재(스티로폼 또는 유사한 것)를 준비해라.

경기장과 빙판

_____ 각 팀명이 적힌 판과 분류된 점수 기록판 숫자
_____ 모든 관계자들과 선수에게 공식적인 경기 시간이 잘 보일 수 있는 경기장 시계
_____ 깔개 청소 - 빙판이나 빙판 위의 카펫을 청소 담당 직원들이 매일, 그리고 가능하다면 매 시즌 사이에 청소하도록 관리해라.
_____ 주심의 책상과 의자(2)
_____ 코치 및 후보 선수석 - 각 시트 뒤에 적당한 위치, 각 팀을 위한 알맞은 수의 공간, 어두운 쪽을 오른쪽으로 표시하여 어둡고 밝은 위치로 표시해야 한다.
_____ 각 팀이 이용 가능한 충분한 수의 전기 콘센트를 마련해야 한다.
_____ 얼음에 해로운 영향을 최소화시키기 위해 태양이나 빛의 영향을 줄 수 있는 창문을 최소화해야 한다.
_____ A, B, C로 표시되어 있는 홈 앤드, 시트 등을 확인한다. A, B, C로 표시되어 있는 타이머의 위치를 확인한다.
_____ 팀의 탈의실을 확인해야 한다.
_____ 반대 성(性)의 코치들을 위한 탈의실
_____ 시합 도중 갈 수 있는 화장실(의 위치)
_____ 모든 방들의 분명한 명칭(예를 들면 탈의실, 양호실, 물리치료실, 심판실, 도핑룸 등등)
_____ 저녁 연습 예약 시트를 게시하기 위한 위치
_____ (만약 제공된다면)팀 메일박스의 위치
_____ 얼음 기술자에게 언제 시합 전 점검이 가능한지 확인하기(이것은 하우스의 정확도, 커티시 라인의 설치, 사진가들의 위치와 같은 것들이 포함된다)
_____ 측정 막대기의 위치, 개수 그리고 정확도 확인
_____ 타임아웃에 대비하여 감독들의 경기장 접근과 이동 시간 확인
_____ 자원봉사자들의 대기실/휴게실이 있다면, 위치를 확인한다.

매체

_____ 언론석 위치 확인
_____ 언론 관계자의 수, 적절한 복장과 신발, 그리고 행동을 통제할 수 있도록 연락을 취하라.
_____ 텔레비전 일정표 - 모든 팀과 심판들에게 복사해주어야 한다.

형식

_____ 기존 팀 라인업
_____ 경기 팀 라인업
_____ 팀 라인업의 변화
_____ 드로우샷 도전
_____ 마지막 스톤 드로우(LSD)
_____ 빙판 위 심판의 점수판
_____ 경기 시간
_____ 호그 라인 위반(요구된다면, 주심 메뉴얼에 있다.)
_____ 위반 도표(요구된다면, 주심 메뉴얼에 있다.)
_____ 저녁 연습 절차
_____ 저녁 연습을 위한 시트 - 4, 5개의 시트 또는 예약된 저녁 연습 일정
_____ 결승전 정보
_____ 스톤 선택
_____ 코치석 위치
_____ 팀 경기 유니폼

6. ON-ICE PRE-COMPETITION CHECK

Micrometre Measuring Stick(s)

______ Assembled correctly
______ Check gauge slides smoothly and feet slide easily on ice
______ Check measures *without* adjustable feet will clear sideboards
______ Perform test measures using stones

Biter Stick(s) - Six foot measure

______ With 2, mark 'home' and 'away' (if using 2, ensure both same length)
______ Conduct measures using a stone and/or straight edge in 8 locations on every house, Home & Away

Digital Measures for LSD

______ Check and set to metric with gauge arrow pointing towards stone
______ Check how close to the pin a stone can be measured
______ Check the readings are identical on all measures (on one set stone)
______ Confirm that the minimum reading is .1cm
______ If two or more measures are used, mark each one with the letter of the sheet(s) on which they will be used
______ Cool measures on ice prior to the first pregame practice, and then store off-ice between draws

Block To assist in some visual measures

All measures placed on ice

Ice Measurements / Stones

______ Ensure centre holes have been drilled to correct depth, width and location
______ Check accuracy of circles and other FOP measurements
______ Check stones & handles with Chief Ice Technician (including spares)
______ Check all stones are on the correct sheets
______ Confirm procedures with Ice Technician for checking and changing/replacing hog line sensor handles during games

Scoreboards

______ Association boards in both colours (minimum 2 dark, 2 light)
______ Boards marked with A, B, C, D, corresponding to sheets
______ Boxes containing numbers (0-9), X, W, L, '/' and hammer indicators
______ If electronic boards, ensure all are functioning properly

Time Clocks (number of sheets plus one spare)

______ Clocks mounted and working
______ Clocks positioned so that players and coaches easily see them
______ A, B, C, D, marked on each clock and indicated on timers' bench
______ Check sight lines for operators

Chairs/Tables

______ Game Umpires, cloth chair at both ends, if possible
______ End ice observers, cloth chair at both ends
______ Suitable sized tables or large box behind each scoreboard for team drinks, etc. and storage of player's equipment (subject to available space)

Waste bins / Disposable Tissues

______ Two per sheet and bins emptied after each session

6. 빙판 위에서의 경기 전 확인 목록

마이크로미터 측정 막대기(들)

_____ 정확히 모여 있는지 여부
_____ 측정 기구, 피트 표시 면이 쉽게 미끄러지는지 점검해라.
_____ 사이드 보드를 깨끗하게 만들 조정 가능한 피트(치수)가 없는 방법을 확인하여라.
_____ 스톤을 이용한 시범 측정을 해보아라.

비터 스틱(들) -6피트 측정

_____ 2개로 '홈'과 '어웨이'를 표시해라. (2를 사용한다면, 두 개가 같은 길이인지 확인하여라.)
_____ 스톤 그리고/혹은 홈&어웨이의 모든 하우스 8개 위치의 직선의 가장자리를 사용하여 측정하라.

LSD 전자 측정

_____ 스톤을 가리키는 기구의 눈금을 미터법으로 점검하고 설정하라.
_____ 스톤을 향해 있는 핀이 얼마나 가까이까지 측정될 수 있는지 확인해라.
_____ 한 세트의 스톤에서, 측정을 할 때마다 동일한 측정이 나오는지 확인해라.
_____ 측정 최솟값이 1㎝로 읽히는지 확인해라.
_____ 만약 두 개 혹은 그 이상의 측정기가 사용된다면, 어떤 것이 사용될 것인지 종이에 각각 표시하라.
_____ 처음의 경기 전의 연습에 앞서, 빙판에서 측정기를 식히고, 드로우 사이에는 빙판 밖에 보관하라.

블록(block) 시야 확보에 도움을 주기 위한 것

빙판 위에 있는 모든 측정 도구

빙판 측정/ 스톤

_____ 중앙 구멍이 정확한 깊이, 너비, 위치에 뚫렸는지 확인해라.
_____ 다른 경기장 측정 기준과 하우스의 정확도를 확인해라.
_____ 대표 얼음 기술자에게 스톤과 손잡이를 확인시킬 것. (여분의 것들도 포함)
_____ 모든 스톤들이 제대로 된 시트에 표시되어 있는지 확인
_____ 빙판 기술자와 함께 경기 중에 호그 라인 센서 핸들을 점검하고 바꾸고/대체하는 절차를 확인해라.

점수판

_____ 공동 점수판을 두 가지 색깔로 표시해야 한다. (최소한 어두운색 2개, 밝은색 2개)
_____ 시트와 일치하는 A, B, C, D라고 표시되어 있는 판
_____ 숫자(0-9), X, W, L, '/', 망치 표시가 담긴 상자
_____ 전자판이라면, 모든 것이 제대로 작동하는지 확인해라.

시간 측정 시계(시트의 개수만큼과 하나의 여분)

_____ 시계가 설치되었고, 작동되는지 확인하라.
_____ 선수들과 감독들이 쉽게 볼 수 있도록 시계가 위치하여 있는지 확인하라.
_____ 각각의 시계에 A, B, C, D로 표시되어 있고, 타이머석을 지칭하는지 확인하라.
_____ 타이머의 시야를 확인해라.

의자/책상들

_____ 경기 심판의 의자는 가능하면 양쪽 끝에 천으로 된 의자로 배치한다.
_____ 끝에 위치한 얼음 감별사에게 양쪽 끝에 천으로 된 의자를 배치한다.
_____ 각 점수판 뒤에 팀 음료수 등과 선수의 장비(이용가능한 공간의 물체들) 보관을 위한 적절한 크기의 탁자 혹은 큰 상자

쓰레기통/ 일회용 휴지

_____ 시트당 2개를 두고 매회 휴지통을 비워야 한다.

7. UMPIRE EQUIPMENT

Last Stone Draw (LSD) Measures
Biter Sticks (6-foot measures)
Micrometer Measure
Radios, earpieces & adequate number of chargers and outlet-strips (special box inside the equipment box)
Wooden Blocks (to assist with visual observations)
Stopwatches
Clipboards
Pencils
Pencil sharpener
Eraser
Stapler & refills
Scissors
Tape dispenser & refills
Roll of black tape
Paper punch (European 2 hole and/or 4 hole)
Stationery equipment (paperclips, etc.)
Calculator (to do DSC calculations)
Magnetic Boards & spare magnets, extra red & yellow dots
Measuring tape (25m) – not metallic
Set of screwdrivers
Allen key & other tools (small kit)
Copy of the Chief Umpire Manual
WCF Rule Books
Small first-aid kit
Small sewing kit
Electrical adaptors kit
Multi-plug extension cord
Pocket Knife
Duct Tape
Micro-fibre cloths for stone cleaning – Wheelchair & Mixed Doubles events

7. 심판 장비

라스트 스톤 드로우(LSD) 측정기구
비터 스틱(6피트 측정용)
마이크로미터 측정기구
라디오, 수화기, 필요한 만큼의 충전기와 멀티탭(장비 상자 안의 특별한 상자)
나무 블록(시야 확보에 도움을 주기 위해)
스톱워치
클립보드
연필
연필 깎기
지우개
스테이플러와 리필심
가위
테이프 디스펜서와 리필 테이프
검정 테이프 묶음
펀치(유럽 기준 2개 그리고/혹은 4개의 구멍)
고정 물품(클립 등)
계산기(LSD 거리계산을 위해)
자석 보드, 여분의 자석, 여분의 빨강과 노랑 점
측정 테이프(25미터) - 금속 재질 아닌 것
드라이버 세트
앨런 볼트용 렌치와 다른 도구들(조그마한 연장통)
주심 매뉴얼 복사본
세계컬링연맹 규칙 책자
작은 비상약품 상자
작은 반짇고리
전기어댑터 상자
멀티 플러그 연장 코드
접칼
강력 접착테이프
스톤 닦기 전용 초미세 합성섬유 천 - 휠체어 & 혼합복식(믹스더블) 경기

8. TEAM MEETING AGENDA

1. Confirmation of the presence of the Competing Teams
2. Introduction and Welcoming Comments
3. Umpires / Officials in charge of the Competition
4. Ice Technicians
5. Results / Statisticians
6. Original Team Line-up Form
7. Game Team Line-up Form
8. Change of Team Line-up (Substitution) Form
9. Team Health Information Form
10. Anti-Doping Control
11. Team Information Boxes
12. Ice Access Footwear
13. Ice Access Uniforms
14. Rules
15. System of Play
16. The Draw / Schedule of Games
17. Games
18. Stones
19. Colour of Stones
20. Playing Uniforms
21. Game Timing
22. Last Stone Draw
23. Draw Shot Challenge
24. Team Ranking Procedure
25. Practice before Round Robin Games
26. Practice Control
27. Evening Practice for Round-Robin
28. Practice for Post Round Robin Games
29. Ice for Post Round Robin Games
30. Stone Selection Post Round Robin Games
31. Chief Umpire Meeting with Teams for Post Round Robin Games

8. 팀 회의 의제

1. 경쟁 팀의 참석 확인
2. 소개 및 환영사
3. 심판/대회 관계자(위원)
4. 빙판 기술자
5. 결과/통계
6. 원래 팀(경기 참석 예정팀) 라인업 양식
7. 경기 팀 라인업 양식
8. 팀 라인업 변경(교체) 양식
9. 팀 의료 정보 양식
10. 반도핑 검사
11. 팀 정보 상자
12. 빙판에 허가되는 신발
13. 빙판에 허가되는 복장
14. 규칙
15. 게임 방식
16. 추첨/경기 일정
17. 경기(들)
18. 스톤
19. 스톤의 색깔
20. 경기 유니폼
21. 경기 시간
22. 마지막 스톤 드로우(LSD)
23. 마지막 스톤 드로우(LSD) 평균 거리를 측정하는 계산법
24. 팀 순위 현황
25. 각 팀이 참가 팀 모두와의 경기 전의 연습
26. 연습 관리
27. 라운드 로빈 전의 오후 연습
28. 포스트 라운드 로빈 게임 연습
29. 포스트 라운드 로빈 게임을 위한 얼음 상태
30. 포스트 라운드 로빈 게임을 위한 스톤 선별
31. 포스트 라운드 로빈 게임을 위한 주심과 선수들과의 만남

32. Scoring
33. Measures
34. Improper Conduct
35. Ice Abuse
36. Hog Line Violations
37. Post Game Procedure
38. Position of Players
39. Coach Bench
40. Kit Bags / Clothing
41. Drinks
42. Tidiness
43. Mobile Telephones / Cameras
44. Smoking
45. Opening, Medal and Closing Ceremonies
46. Sportsmanship Award
47. Media
48. Television
49. Social Media
50. Decision Making
51. Etiquette
52. The Spirit of Curling
53. Questions
54. Wrap-up / Good Curling

32. 점수 매기는 법
33. 조치
34. 부적절한 행동
35. 빙판 남용
36. 호그 라인 위반
37. 경기 이후 절차
38. 선수들의 포지션
39. 코치석
40. 키트 백(Kit bags)/옷
41. 음료
42. 위생(청결)
43. 휴대 전화/카메라
44. 흡연
45. 개회식, 수료식, 폐회식
46. 운동가 정신에 대한 상(스포츠맨십 시상)
47. (언론)매체
48. 텔레비전
49. 사회 매체(소셜 미디어)
50. 결정 사항
51. 예의범절
52. 컬링 정신
53. 질문
54. 마무리/좋은 경기를 위한 선언(good curling)

9. TEAM MEETING DOCUMENT (SAMPLE)

WORLD CURLING FEDERATION

TEAM MEETING DOCUMENT

20__ ______________________ CHAMPIONSHIP

CITY, COUNTRY **DATE**

To ensure that all competing teams are properly informed about the Team Meeting, the Chief Umpire, together with the Organising Committee, provides the following document before the start of the Championship(s).

There will also be final instructions given during the Team Meeting. Teams are reminded about WCF (year) _________ Rules of Competition C2 (h) that states, "All players and their coach must attend the Team Meeting. Failure to do so, without approval of the Chief Umpire, will result in the forfeit of the last stone advantage for that team in its first game".

If, due to exceptional circumstances outside their control, a team or any of its members are going to be delayed they should notify the WCF Secretary General as soon as possible who will then advise the Chief Umpire. Contact details are: info@worldcurling.org or phone +44 1738 451 630.

9. 팀 회의 문서(양식)

모든 경쟁에 참여한 팀들이 팀 회의, 심판위원장, 조직위원회에 대해 제대로 알고 있도록 하기 위해서, 세계선수권대회를 시작하기 전에 다음과 같은 문서를 제공한다.

또한 최종 지침 역시 팀 회의에서 나올 것이다. 팀들은 세계컬링연맹의 경쟁 규칙 C2(h)를 명심해야 한다. "모든 선수와 코치는 팀미팅에 참석해야 한다. 심판위원장의 허가 없이 이를 지키지 않을 경우 첫 게임의 마지막 스톤 어드벤티지가 몰수된다."

만약 통제할 수 없는 예외적인 상황으로 팀이나 선수들의 참석이 지연될 경우, 심판위원장에게 조언할 세계컬링연맹 사무총장에게 가능한 한 빨리 통보하여야 한다. 자세한 사항은 다음 연락처에 문의하면 된다. info@worldcurling.org이나 전화 +44 1738 451 630.

Team Meeting

Location

Time, Day, Date

1. Confirmation of the presence of the Competing Associations

MEN and/or WOMEN

Association name (3 letter country identification e.g. ABC or abc)

2. Introduction and Welcoming Comments

Name	______________________	Position (President, etc.)
Name	______________________	Chairman Host Committee
Name	______________________	Director of Competitions / WCF TD

3. Umpires / Officials

Chief Umpire	Name	________________	Country________________
Deputy Chief Umpire(s)	Name	________________	Country________________
Game Umpires	Name	________________	Country________________
Chief Timer	Name	________________	Country________________

4. Ice Technicians

Chief Ice Technician	Name	________________	Country________________
Deputy Chief Ice Tech.	Name	________________	Country________________

5. Results / Statisticians

Chief Statistician	Name	________________	Country________________
Deputy Chief Statistician	Name	________________	Country________________

팀 미팅

장소

시간, 날짜

1. 연맹의 참여 확정

남자 그리고/또는 여자

연맹 이름(세 문자로 신분확인 예- ABC 또는 abc)

2. 소개와 환영 코멘트

이름 ______________ 포지션(예-President, etc.)

이름 ______________ 위원회 위원장

이름 ______________ 경기 관계자/세계컬링연맹 기술 관계자

3. 심판/ 임원

심판위원장 이름 ______________ 국적 ______________

부심판위원장 이름 ______________ 국적 ______________

경기 심판 이름 ______________ 국적 ______________

시간 계측장 이름 ______________ 국적 ______________

4. 아이스 기술자

최고 아이스 기술자 이름 ______________ 국적 ______________

부아이스 기술자 이름 ______________ 국적 ______________

5. 결과/ 통계자

통계위원장 이름 ______________ 국적 ______________

부통계위원장 이름 ______________ 국적 ______________

6. Original Team Line-Up Form

This form, along with the one detailing Playing Uniforms, will be distributed and should be completed and returned to the Results Team or Game Umpire at the end of the Meeting.

7. Game Line-Up Form (*Not required for WMDCC*)

It is assumed that the team playing will be the team listed on the Original Team Line-Up Form. If any changes, either bringing in the Alternate or change of order, a Game Line-Up Form must be submitted prior to the pre-game practice. Any team found not complying with this policy will be required to submit a Game Line-Up Form for all games.

8. Change of Team Line-Up Form *(Not required for WMDCC)*

A Change of Team Line-Up Form, (Substitute Form), copies of which will be distributed before your first game, must be completed and returned to either the Chief Umpire or Deputy Chief Umpire if a team wishes to make a change either after the pre-game practice or during a game. This form **must** be completed before the alternate will be allowed onto the Field of Play.

9. Team Health Information Form

The completed Health Information Form, which has been sent to all team members, should be placed in a sealed envelope marked with the Team identity and returned to the Chief Umpire at the Team Meeting. These forms will be treated in the strictest confidence. Should any player be under 18 years of age a parental / guardian consent form for Dope Testing must accompany the Health Information Form. Where appropriate any Therapeutic Use Exemption Forms ("TUE") should be carried by the athlete for inspection if the athlete is selected for a doping test.

10. Anti-Doping Control

Testing for prohibitive substances may take place by random selection. All players are advised they should carry photo ID with them. This may be required by Anti-Doping Control.

11. Team Information Boxes

All teams will have a tray for results / instructions / information / mail, or this might be distributed by e-mail. The site of the team information boxes will be advised at the Team Meeting. If information is to be distributed by e-mail, the addresses will be obtained at the Team Meeting.

12. Ice Access (Footwear)

At **all** times the footwear worn within the playing area by players, coaches and officials must be clean (i.e. not worn outside). The acceptable routes for entering and exiting the Field of Play will be identified at the Team Meeting.

13. Ice Access (Uniform)

All team members must wear identical uniforms when accessing the Field of Play for games or practice sessions.

Coaches / Officials / Translators must wear a proper team or Association uniform when accessing the Field of Play for games or practice sessions.

Failure to wear the appropriate clothing will result in access to the Field of Play being denied. Please note that jeans are not considered as appropriate clothing.

6. 원래 팀 라인업 양식

이 양식은 경기 유니폼의 세부사항과 함께 배포될 것이며, 회의의 마지막에 완성된 사항이 결과 팀이나 게임 심판에게 돌아가야 한다.

7. 게임 라인업 양식(세계혼성(4인믹스) 컬링선수권대회에는 필요하지 않음)

이것은 경기 참여 팀이 원래 팀 라인업 양식에 나와 있는 팀이 될 것이라고 가정한 것이다. 변경 사항, 대체 또는 순서의 변경이 있는 경우, 게임 라인업 양식은 경기 전 연습 전에 미리 제출해야 한다. 정책을 준수하지 않는 모든 팀은 모든 경기에 대한 게임 라인업 양식을 제출해야 한다.

8. 팀 라인업 양식의 변경(세계혼성(4인믹스) 컬링선수권대회에는 필요하지 않음)

팀 라인업 양식, 변경된 대체 양식의 사본이 첫 번째 경기를 하기 전에 배포된다. 만약 팀이 경기 전 연습이나 경기 중에 변경하고 싶은 것이 있다면, 이 양식은 심판위원장이나 부심판위원장에게 완성되어 돌아가야 한다. 이 양식은 대체되기 전에 완료해야 하며 경기장에서 허용될 것이다.

9. 팀 건강 정보 양식

모든 팀 선수들에게 보낸 완성된 건강 정보 양식은 팀의 신원을 확인할 수 있도록 표시하여 밀봉된 봉투에 넣어, 팀 회의에서 심판위원장에게 반환해야 한다. 이러한 양식은 엄격한 비밀로 취급된다. 18세 미만의 모든 선수들은 도핑 테스트를 위한 부모/보호자의 동의서가 건강 정보 양식과 함께 첨부해야 한다. 모든 치료 목적 사용 면책 양식('TUE')은 적절한 경우 선수가 도핑 테스트를 위해 선택된다면, 선수에 의해 수행되어야 한다.

10. 반도핑 컨트롤

금지 물질에 대한 테스트는 무작위 선택에 의해 일어날 수 있다. 모든 선수에게 자신의 사진이 부착된 신분증을 휴대할 것을 조언한다. 이것은 반도핑 컨트롤에 의해 요구될 수 있다.

11. 팀 정보 박스

모든 팀은 결과/설명/정보/메일 용지함을 가지게 될 것이고, 또는 이메일로 배포될 수도 있다. 팀 정보 박스의 장소는 팀 회의에서 알려줄 것이다. 정보가 이메일에 의해 배포될 경우, 주소는 팀 미팅에서 알 수 있을 것이다.

12. 아이스 장비(신발)

항상 선수, 코치 및 관계자들은 경기 구역 내에서 착용하는 신발이(즉, 외부 착용하지 않음) 깨끗해야 한다. 경기장에 들어가고 나오기 위해 허용되는 경로는 팀 회의에서 확인될 것이다.

13. 아이스 장비(유니폼)

모든 팀 선수들은 경기나 연습을 위해 경기장에 들어갈 때 구분이 가능한 유니폼을 착용해야 한다. 코치/관계자/통역사들은 경기나 연습을 위해 경기장에 들어갈 때 팀이나 연맹의 유니폼을 적절하게 입어야 한다. 적절한 옷을 착용하지 않으면 경기장에 출입할 수 없다. 청바지가 적절한 옷으로 간주되지 않는다는 것을 기억해야 한다.

14. Rules

The rules for this Championship are the current World Curling Federation Rules of Curling and Rules of Competition, (year) __________. Any variation from these rules will be indicated at the Team Meeting.

15. System of Play

The Championship(s) will be played in the following stages:

- the round robin games
- the tie-breaker games
- the Page System
- the semi-final game
- the Bronze medal game
- the Gold medal game

16. The Draw / Schedule of Games

A copy has been sent to all Associations. Any changes will be advised at the Team Meeting.

17. Games

___ ends are scheduled and a minimum of ______ ends must be completed in the round robin and tie-breaker games. A minimum of ______ ends must be completed in all play-off games.

18. Stones

The curling stones used at this Championship are those belonging to, and supplied by, the __________________. Any further details will be made available at the Team Meeting.

All games during the round robin and tie-breaker games will be played with the stones on the sheet allocated. Where stones can be used from other sheets will be announced at the post round robin team meeting.

19. Colour of Stones

The team listed first in the draw will play the stones with the dark coloured handles; the team listed second will play the stones with the light coloured handles.

20. Playing Uniforms

Dark coloured playing uniforms will be worn when playing the stones with dark coloured handles and light coloured playing uniforms will be worn when playing the stones with light coloured handles.
N.B. Under WCF Rules of Competition C3 (a) - **red** is considered to be a **dark** colour.

21. Game Timing

Time clocks will be used and team time-outs as covered under the World Curling Federation Rules of Competition (C7 – Page 29) will apply. Coaches will be advised at the Team Meeting where to enter the Field of Play and also where they can walk and stand.

Players are reminded to call team time-outs with one of the Game Umpires. Travel time will be permitted and the amount allowed will be advised at the Team Meeting.

14. 규칙

이 대회의 규칙은 현재 세계컬링연맹과 대회 규칙인 ____________이다. 이 규칙의 모든 변동 사항은 팀 회의에서 제시된다.

15. 경기 시스템

선수권대회 경기들은 다음과 같은 단계로 진행된다.:

- 라운드 로빈 게임
- 타이 브레이커 게임
- 페이지 시스템
- 준결승 경기
- 동메달 결정전
- 금메달 결정전

16. 경기 스케줄

사본은 모든 협회에 보내진다. 모든 변경 사항은 팀 회의에서 알려줄 것이다.

17. 경기

____________ 엔드들이 예약되고 최소 ____________ 엔드에 라운드 로빈과 타이 브레이커 게임을 완료해야 한다. 최소 ____________ 엔드에 모든 플레이오프 게임을 완료해야 한다.

18. 스톤

이 선수권대회에서 사용되는 컬링 스톤은 __________ 에 의해 공급된다. 세부 사항은 팀 회의에서 알게 될 것이다.

라운드 로빈과 타이 브레이커 게임 동안에는 할당된 시트에서 스톤과 함께 진행될 것이다. 다른 시트에서 사용될 수 있는 스톤들은 포스트 라운드 로빈 팀 회의에서 발표된다.

19. 스톤의 색깔

라운드 로빈에서 첫 번째를 뽑은 팀은 어두운 색깔 핸들의 스톤으로 경기하게 된다. 두 번째 팀은 밝은 색깔 핸들의 스톤으로 경기한다.

20. 경기 유니폼

어두운색 핸들의 스톤으로 경기할 때는 어두운색깔의 연주 유니폼을 착용하고, 밝은색 핸들의 스톤으로 경기할 때는 밝은색의 유니폼을 착용한다. 세계컬링연맹 규칙 C3(a)하의 N.B.에 따르면 빨간색은 어두운색으로 간주된다.

21. 경기 시간

타임 클록은 세계컬링연맹 규칙(C7. 페이지 29)에 따라 사용되고 팀이 타임아웃이 된다. 코치들은 팀 미팅에서 경기장에 출입하고 걷고 설 수 있는 곳에 대해 알게 될 것이다.

선수들은 타임아웃을 부르기 위해 경기 심판들 중 한 명과 상의해야 한다는 것을 명심해야 한다. 트레블 타임은 허용되며 허용된 양은 팀 미팅에서 알려줄 것이다.

Team Time-outs

Procedures for team time-outs are as follows:

- Only the players on the ice may call a team time-out.
- Team time-outs may be called by any on ice team player only when that team's game clock is running.
- Players signal a team time-out by using a "T" hand signal. The game clock is stopped during the travel time and restarts when the time-out begins.
- Only one person, who is sitting in the designated coaching area and a translator, if required, of the team that called the team time-out is allowed to meet with the team.
- The 60-second team time-out begins as soon as contact is made with the team.
- Where walkways are beside the sheet, that person must not stand on the playing ice surface.
- The team is notified when there are 10 seconds remaining in the team time-out.
- When the 60-second team time-out has expired, the person from the coach's bench must stop conferring with the team and leave the playing area immediately.

Technical Time-Out

A technical time-out may be called by a team to request a ruling, for an injury, or in other extenuating circumstances. Game clocks will be stopped during technical time-outs.
Procedures for technical time-outs are as follows:

- Only the players on the ice may call a technical time-out.
- Players signal a technical time-out by using an "X" signal with their arms.
- The team's game clock will be stopped on instruction by the Umpire to the Chief Timer.

In all games where an Umpire determines that a team is unnecessarily delaying a game, the Umpire will notify the skip of the offending team and, after the notification, if the next stone to be delivered has not reached the tee line at the delivering end within 45 seconds, the stone will be removed from play immediately.

OR:

Time clocks will **not** be used and team time-outs will **not** be permitted.

In all games where an Umpire determines that a team is unnecessarily delaying a game, the Umpire will notify the skip of the offending team and, after the notification, if the next stone to be delivered has not reached the tee line at the delivering end within 45 seconds, the stone will be removed from play immediately.

There will be a ________ minute break at the completion of the ________ end at which time teams are allowed to meet with a coach, the alternate player and one other team official / translator (maximum 7 people) within the Field of Play (FOP). Please be aware that other games may be in progress when entering, and leaving, the FOP.

Those entering the FOP are reminded that the correct uniform must be worn as described in Clause 12 and 13.

Where time adjustments are required, they will be made between ends except for the final end where adjustments will be made stone by stone.

22. Last Stone Draw (LSD) - to decide who has last stone in the first end

For round robin games, at the conclusion of the team's pre-game practice, any one player will deliver one stone to the tee at the home end with sweeping allowed. Any one of the five players on the team can deliver the stone. One team member will hold the brush in the house at the home end. Normal sweeping rules apply. Only four players can be on the ice surface during the LSD. The team with the lesser LSD distance will have the choice of delivering first or second stone in the first end. If neither team has a stone that finishes in the

팀 타임아웃

팀 타임아웃을 위한 절차는 다음과 같다 :

- 얼음 위에 있는 선수만이 팀 타임아웃을 요청할 수 있다.
- 팀 타임아웃은 팀의 타임 클록이 실행되는 경우에만 얼음 위에 있는 팀 플레이어에 의해 호출될 수 있다.
- 선수들은 'T'손 신호를 이용하여 팀 타임아웃을 요청한다. 게임 클록은 트레블 타임 동안에는 멈추고 타임아웃이 시작되면 다시 시작된다.
- 코치석에 있는 한 사람과 필요하다면 통역사와 함께 타임아웃을 요청한 팀과 만나는 것이 허용된다.
- 60초간의 타임아웃 시간은 이들이 이동하고 난 후나 선수들과 만나고 난 후부터 시작된다.
- 코치나 통역사가 있던 장소가 링크의 바깥쪽이라면 얼음판 위에 들어와서는 안 된다.
- 팀은 타임아웃 시간 종료 10초 전 통보를 받는다.
- 60초간의 타임아웃 시간이 종료되면 코치는 대화를 중단하고 즉시 그 자리를 떠나 벤치로 돌아가야 한다.

테크니컬 타임아웃

테크니컬 타임아웃은 부상이나 다른 어떤 정상참작이 되는 상황에서 팀에 의해 요청될 수 있다. 게임 시간 계측은 테크니컬 타임아웃 동안에 정지될 것이다.

테크니컬 타임아웃을 위한 절차는 다음과 같다 :

- 얼음 위에 있는 선수들만이 테크니컬 타임아웃을 요청할 수 있다.
- 선수들은 자신의 팔을 'X'신호로 만들어 테크니컬 타임아웃을 요청한다.
- 팀의 타임 클록은 최고 시간 계측자 심판의 지시에 의해 중지된다.

심판의 결정에 따른 모든 경기들에서 팀이 불필요하게 경기를 지연시키는 것으로 판단하면, 심판은 문제가 되는 팀의 스킵을 통지하고 통지한 후에 만약 다음 스톤이 엔드 내에서 티 라인에 45초 안에 도달하지 않은 경우, 스톤은 즉시 게임에서 제거될 것이다.

또는:

타임 클록은 사용되지 않으며 팀 타임아웃은 허용되지 않는다.

심판의 결정에 따른 모든 경기들에서 팀이 불필요하게 경기를 지연시키는 것으로 판단하면, 심판은 문제가 되는 팀의 스킵을 통지하고 통지한 후에 만약 다음 스톤이 엔드 내에서 티 라인에 45초 안에 도달하지 않은 경우, 스톤은 즉시 게임에서 제거될 것이다.

____________ 엔드 완료 시, ____________ 분의 휴식이 있을 것이다. 팀들은 경기장 내에서 코치와 대체 선수 그리고 다른 팀의 관계자나 통역사(최대 7명)를 만나는 것이 허용된다.

경기장에 들어오고 나올 때, 다른 게임이 진행될 수 있음을 유의하길 바란다.

경기장에 들어오는 사람들은 12.와 13.에 설명된 대로 올바른 유니폼을 착용해야 한다는 것을 명심해야 한다.

시간 조정이 필요한 경우, 그들은 마지막 엔드를 제외한 엔드들 사이에서 스톤을 사용해 조정이 이루어질 것이다.

22. 라스트 스톤 드로우(LSD) - 첫 번째 엔드에서 누가 마지막 스톤을 던질지 정하는 것

라운드 로빈 게임들을 위해서, 팀이 공식연습 종료 시에 라스트 스톤 드로우(LSD)가 행해진다. 한 선수가 홈엔드의 티를 향해 한 개의 스톤을 딜리버리하게 되며 스위핑이 허용된다. 팀에서 5명의 선수 중 하나는 스톤을 딜리버리할 수 있다. 한 팀 선수는 하우스에서 브러시를 가지고 홈엔드에 있을 것이다. 보통의 스위핑 룰이 적용된

house, or both teams record the same distance, a coin toss will decide which team has the choice of delivering the first or second stone in the first end. During the LSD the extra player / coach / team official within the FOP should take up a position behind the scoreboard (if space available) at the home end, or at the coaches' bench.

It is assumed that any team that wins the LSD will choose to deliver the second stone in the first end, if this is not the case for any game, the team must tell the Game Umpire before the start of its pre-game practice.

Teams are given a maximum of 60 seconds to deliver the LSD. If the stone has not reached the tee line at the delivering end within 60 seconds (observed by an Umpire) it will be recorded as 185.4 cm.

23. Draw Shot Challenge

The DSC is the average distance of the Last Stone Draws, which were played by a team during the round robin portion of the competition. The single least favourable LSD result is automatically eliminated before calculating this average distance.

OR:

Each team will be required to complete the Draw Shot Challenge (at a time selected by the Chief Umpire). A total of four team members will deliver one stone each to the tee to the home end with sweeping allowed. A team with only three players will have each player deliver one stone and the average distance is recorded for the fourth stone. All stones finishing in the house are measured and the cumulative distance from the tee recorded. Stones that do not finish in the house will be recorded as 185.4 cm. Stones that finish so close to the centre that a measurement cannot be made will be recorded as 0.0 cm. 5th players, coaches and any team officials must stand behind the scoreboard or in a position so as not to distract the delivering players during the Draw Shot Challenge.

24. Team Ranking Procedure

Teams will be ranked at the conclusion of the round robin in accordance with Rule C9.

25. Practice Before Round Robin Games

There will be a nine (9) minute practice followed by the Last Stone Draw for both teams before the round robin games with the first practice starting thirty (30) minutes before the game start time (See Clause 37).

For the round robin games the team that is named first in the schedule will have first pre-game practice, except for each team's first game where a coin toss will determine which team has first and second practice.

Teams should meet with their opposition for their first game before they leave the Team Meeting to do the coin toss and advise a Game Umpire which team is going to practice first.

For all pre-game practices only the 5 declared team players, the team coach, and a 2nd team official or translator, (maximum 7 people) may enter the playing area.

The team not practicing should stand behind the scoreboards whenever possible. Those entering the Field of Play area are reminded that the correct uniform must be worn as described in Clause 12 and 13.

다. 오직 네 명의 선수만이 LSD 동안 아이스 위에 있을 수 있다. 더 적은 LSD를 기록한 팀이 첫 엔드에서 첫 번째 또는 두 번째 스톤을 결정하게 된다. 만약 어느 팀도 하우스 내에 도달치 못했거나 기록이 같을 경우엔 동전 던지기로 첫 엔드 스톤 결정권을 갖게 한다. LSD 동안 경기장 내에서 다른 선수들/코치/팀 관계자는 점수 판 뒤(공간 사용 가능한 경우)에 위치한 홈 엔드 또는 코치들의 벤치에서 자리를 차지해야 한다.

LSD를 승리하는 팀은 첫 엔드에서 두 번째 스톤을 딜리버리하는 것으로 간주되고, 그 팀은 반드시 경기 전 연습을 시작하기 전에 심판에게 알려야 한다.

팀들에게는 LSD를 딜리버리하기 위해 최대 60초가 주어진다. 만약 스톤이 60초 내에(심판의 판단에 의해) 딜리버리하는 엔드 쪽의 티 라인에 도달하지 않은 경우, 그것은 185.4㎝로 기록될 것이다.

23. 드로우 샷 챌린지(Draw Shot Challenge)

DSC는 대회 중의 라운드 로빈 동안 팀이 경기한 LSD의 평균거리이다. 가장 나쁜 하나의 LSD 결과는 평균거리 계산 전에 자동 제외된다.

또는:

각 팀은 심판위원장이 선택한 시간에 의해서 DSC를 완료할 것이 요구된다. 전체 네 명의 선수들은 홈앤드의 티를 향해 한 개의 스톤을 딜리버리하게 되며 스위핑이 허용된다. 단 3명의 선수들만 각자 하나의 스톤을 딜리버리하고 평균거리는 네 번째 돌에 기록된다. 하우스에서 마무리된 모든 스톤들은 측정되고, 티라인에서의 누적거리가 기록된다. 스톤들이 하우스에 미치지 못하면 185.4㎝로 기록된다. 측정이 어려울 정도로 티에 너무 가까운 스톤들은 0.0㎝로 기록이 된다. 드로우 샷 챌린지를 하는 동안 딜리버리하는 선수들을 방해하지 않도록 다섯 번째 선수, 코치 및 팀 관계자는 점수판 뒤 또는 다른 위치에 서 있어야 한다.

24. 팀 랭킹 부여 절차

팀은 연맹규칙 C9에 따라 라운드 로빈의 결과로 기록될 것이다.

25. 라운드 로빈 게임 전 연습

30분간의 첫 번째 연습을 하는 라운드 로빈 게임 전의 두 팀에게 LSD에 따른 9분간의 연습시간이 주어질 것이다(C 37 참고).

라운드 로빈 방식에서의 시합 전 연습 일정은 첫 번째로 스케줄이 등록된 팀부터 진행되며, 동전 던지기로 첫 번째와 두 번째 연습을 결정한 각 팀의 첫 게임은 제외한다.

팀들은 첫 번째 상대팀을 팀미팅을 마치기 전에 만나서 코인토스를 하고 코인토스 결과에 따라 어느 팀이 첫 번째로 연습을 할지를 심판위원장에게 말해야 한다.

모든 연습게임에는 5명의 공식 선수와 팀 코치, 두 번째 팀 관계자 또는 통역사, (최대 7명)만이 경기장에 들어갈 수 있다. 연습이 없는 팀은 가능한 한 점수판 뒤에 서 있어야 한다. 경기장에 들어가는 사람들은 C12, 13에 설명된 내로 올바른 유니폼을 착용해야 함을 명심해야 한다.

26. Practice Control

An Umpire will control all practices. The following clear instructions will be given. Please wait for the appropriate announcement before beginning practice, or checking the stones.

- One minute to the start of first practice, sliders may be cooled but please no practice slides.
- First practice may begin.
- *After (eight) minutes* – one minute to the end of first practice.
- *After (nine) minutes* – practice is over, please prepare for your Last Stone Draw.
- Please deliver your Last Stone Draw.

(Down time of approx. thirty seconds to allow players to leave the ice after the Last Stone Draw is completed)

- Second practice teams your sliders may be cooled, but no practice slides. Please be aware of any stones that still need to be measured.
- Second practice may begin.
- *After (eight) minutes* – one minute to the end of second practice.
- *After (nine) minutes* – practice is now over, please prepare for your Last Stone Draw
- Please deliver your Last Stone Draw.
- Please assist the ice crew by returning all stones to the home end.

Following practice the ice will be cleaned, and if deemed necessary by the Chief / Deputy Chief Ice Technicians the slide paths will be re-pebbled.

Two further announcements will be made:

- Games will begin in one minute – practice slides may be taken.
- Games may begin; the ice is yours; good luck and good curling.

27. Evening Practice

There will be optional evening practices during the round robin portion of the Championship. An Umpire will be present to control the evening practices.

Pre-Allocated Evening Practice

Six sessions of 10 minutes are allotted for evening practice on each sheet. These sessions are reserved for the six teams who will play on that sheet in the next day's draw in the order they appear on the schedule. For example, on a Monday evening, the sessions for each sheet of ice would be reserved as follows:

Session 1 – Red stones on the Tuesday morning draw
Session 2 – Yellow stones on the Tuesday morning draw
Session 3 – Red stones on the Tuesday afternoon draw
Session 4 – Yellow stones on the Tuesday afternoon draw
Session 5 – Red stones on the Tuesday evening draw
Session 6 – Yellow stones on the Tuesday evening draw

Each team in the competition is given a copy of the schedule.

Teams are asked to let the Chief Umpire know if they are not going to use the session reserved for them, but there is no penalty for failing to do so. If the next team waiting for that sheet is ready, they can move forward into that slot.

Teams will only train on the sheets on which they will play the next day – if they have only one game the next day, they will have only one training session.

No team will be allowed to have extra training if any sessions are unused.

26. 연습 조정

심판은 모든 연습들을 조정한다. 다음의 제대로 된 매뉴얼이 주어질 것이다. 연습을 시작하기 전이나 스톤들을 체크하기 전에 적절한 설명이 나올 때까지 기다려야 한다.

- 첫 연습을 시작한 1분은 슬라이더들이 냉각될 것이지만 슬라이드에서 연습하면 안 된다.
- 첫 연습이 시작될 것이다.
- 8분 후 — 첫 연습 끝의 1분
- 9분 후 — 연습이 끝나고, LSD를 준비한다.
- LSD를 실시한다.

약 30초의 다운 타임간 LSD를 완료한 선수들이 아이스 위를 떠나게 한다.

- 두 번째 연습 팀들, 슬라이더들은 냉각될 것이고 슬라이드에서 연습할 수 없다. 아직 측정이 필요한 스톤이 있을 수 있다는 것에 유의해야 한다.
- 두 번째 연습이 시작될 것이다.
- 8분 후 — 두 번째 연습 끝의 1분
- 9분 후 — 연습이 끝나고, LSD를 준비한다.
- LSD를 딜리버리한다.
- 모든 스톤들을 홈 엔드로 반환하여 얼음 관리팀들을 돕는다.

연습 후 아이스 위는 모두 청소가 될 것이고, 최고/차장 아이스 기술자들이 필요하다고 인정하는 경우 슬라이드 경로는 다시 페블이 뿌려진다.

두 개의 추가 언급이 있을 것이다:

- 게임은 1분 후에 개시될 것이다. — 연습 슬라이드들이 준비될 것이다.
- 게임이 시작될 것이다; 빙판 위는 당신들의 것이다; 행운을 빌고 좋은 컬링이 되길 바란다.

27. 저녁 연습

챔피언십의 라운드 로빈 동안 추가적인 저녁 연습이 있을 것이다. 심판이 저녁 연습에 참석하여 컨트롤할 것이다.

저녁 연습 사전 할당

각 시트에 10분의 여섯 세션이 저녁 연습에 할당된다. 이 세션들은 다음 날의 추첨에 의해 일정에 나타나는 순서에 따라 해당 시트에서 경기할 여섯 팀을 위해 예약되어 있다. 예를 들어, 다음과 같이 월요일 저녁에, 아이스의 각 시트에 대한 세션이 예약될 것이다.

세션1 - 화요일 아침에는 빨간 스톤들
세션2 - 화요일 아침에는 노란 스톤들
세션3 - 화요일 오후에는 빨간 스톤들
세션4 - 화요일 오후에는 노란 스톤들
세션5 - 화요일 저녁에는 빨간 스톤들
세션6 - 화요일 저녁에는 노란 스톤들

각 팀은 시합 기간 동안 일정표를 복사하여 받게 된다.

팀은 그들이 예약한 세션을 사용하지 않을 경우 심판위원장에게 알려야 하지만, 그렇지 않을 경우에 대한 처벌은 없다. 그 시트를 기다리고 다음 팀이 준비되면, 그들은 그 슬롯에 전진할 수 있다.

팀들은 그들이 다음 날 경기하는 시트에서만 훈련할 것이다. - 그들은 다음 날 경기를 가지고 있다면, 그들은 하나의 훈련 세션만을 가진다.

어느 팀도 모든 세션이 사용되지 않는 경우 별도의 훈련을 가질 수 없다.

OR

Evening Practice where the teams have to sign-up for reservations

Start time: Approximately five minutes after the last game of the day, as soon as the Ice Technicians finish preparing the ice.

Practice length: Four sessions each of fifteen minutes.

Ice access: A maximum of seven persons will be allowed into the Field of Play; five players, one coach and one other team official / translator who all must be dressed according to the requirements of Clause 12 and 13. No person will be allowed to participate in more than two practice sessions on any evening.

Schedule: Posted in a location and at a time decided by the Chief Umpire. Teams will be informed of the location and time at the Team Meeting.

At ______ hrs: A team may reserve one session only on any sheet.

At ______ hrs: A team may reserve a second session. No team may practice on the same sheet twice on the same evening.

Penalty for failure to use a reserved practice session: Future practice reservations for that Association will be delayed until ______ hrs each day.

Closure: The daily schedule will close at _______ hrs.

28. Practice for Post Round Robin Games

Pre-game practice for all post round robin games will be 10 minutes for each team. For all qualified teams' practice sessions, times will be determined by the Chief Umpire / Deputy Chief Umpire and teams advised as soon as possible once any tie-breaker games are known.

29. Ice for Post Round Robin Games

Will be determined by the Chief Umpire / Deputy Chief Umpire.

30. Stone Selection Post Round Robin Games

The first stone in the first end of post round robin games is determined as set out in Rule C8 (c) and (e).

Additionally:

- The team with the last stone in the first end will practice first.
- When stones can be used from various sheets, the teams will advise the Chief Umpire in writing no later than 15 minutes before the start of their pre-game practice which specific stones they wish to use. Handles cannot be changed from stone to stone.

31. Chief Umpire Meeting with Teams for Post Round Robin Games

Any teams involved in tie-breaker games should meet with the Chief Umpire / Deputy Chief Umpire thirty minutes after the last round robin game in a location to be advised.

For all post round robin games the teams (a maximum of two persons per team) will meet with the Chief Umpire following the last round robin game when post round robin games will be discussed using the above criteria and also referring to Rule C9. Any team decision(s) must be made at that time, before leaving the meeting. Mobile phones or use of any other forms of electronic communication are not permitted once the meeting has begun.

또는

저녁 연습 참여 팀들은 예약을 해야 한다.

시작시간: 그날 마지막 경기 끝내고 약 5분 후 얼음 기술자는 가능한 한 빨리 빙판 준비를 완료한다.

경기시간: 15분마다 4개의 세션씩

경기장(빙판) 진입: 최대 7명이 경기장에 들어올 수 있다. 5명의 선수, 코치 1명, C12, 13의 요구사항에 따라 적합한 1명의 팀 관계자/통역사. 어떤 사람도 모든 저녁 연습에 두 개 이상의 연습 세션에 참여하는 게 허용되지 않는다.

일정: 심판위원장이 결정한 시간에 장소에 게시된다.

팀들은 팀 회의에서 장소와 시간에 대해 알게 될 것이다.

______________ 시간에: 팀은 모든 시트에 하나의 세션을 예약할 수 있다.

______________ 시간에: 팀은 두 번째 세션을 예약할 수 있다. 어떤 팀은 그날 저녁에 두 번 같은 시트에서 연습을 하지 않을 수 있다.

예약된 연습 세션을 사용하지 않아 발생한 문제에 대한 벌: 협회에 대한 앞으로의 연습 예약은 시간까지 지연된다.

종료: 하루 스케줄은 ____________ 에 종료된다.

28. 포스트 라운드 로빈 게임을 위한 연습

모든 포스트 라운드 로빈 게임을 위한 사전 연습은 각 팀에게 10분씩 주어진다. 자격을 갖춘 모든 팀들의 연습 세션, 시간은 심판위원장/부위원장에 의해 결정되고 타이 브레이커 게임은 가능한 한 빨리 팀들에 알려진다.

29. 포스트 라운드 로빈 게임 아이스

심판위원장/부위원장에 의해 결정

30. 포스트 라운드 로빈 게임 스톤 선택

포스트 라운드 로빈 게임의 첫 엔드에서의 첫 번째 스톤은 C8(c)과 (e)에 의해 결정된다.

추가적으로:

- 첫 엔드에서 마지막 스톤을 사용하는 팀이 처음으로 연습을 한다.
- 여러 시트들에서 스톤들이 사용될 수 있는데, 팀은 사전 연습 시작 15분 전에는 사용하고 싶은 스톤의 세부사항에 대해 심판위원장에게 알려야 한다.

31. 포스트 라운드 로빈 게임을 위한 심판위원장과 팀 미팅

어느 팀이든지 타이 브레이커 게임 동안에는 마지막 라운드 로빈 게임 후 공지한 장소에서 심판위원장/부위원장과 30분간 만나야 한다.

모든 포스트 라운드 로빈 게임(팀당 최대 두 명)에 참여하는 팀은 마지막 라운드 로빈게임 후 포스트 라운드 로빈 게임에서 위의 사항들의 사용에 대해 논의하고 C9에 대해 논의하기 위해 심판위원장을 만날 것이다.

모든 팀의 결정은 미팅을 떠나기 전에 그때 완성되어야 한다. 휴대폰 또는 다른 전자기기 등을 이용한 의사소통은 미팅이 시작된 후 허용되지 않는다. 포스트 라운드 로빈 미팅에 참석하지 않거나 결정이 준비되지 않은 경우 팀에서 결정될 게임 선택권들(라스트 스톤 어드밴티지, 스톤 색깔 등)은 박탈된다.

A team that does not attend a post round robin meeting, or is not prepared to make a decision, forfeits the game choices (last stone advantage, stone colour, etc.) to which the team is entitled.

32. Scoring

After the score has been agreed for an end please advise the Game Umpire of the colour that scored and the number of points. The score and total will then be marked on the scoreboard.

Only **one** score card will be used for each game and should be completed in full for that game. At the end of the game it is the responsibility of a player from each team to confirm the score by signing the scorecard.

33. Measures

Where a measure is required at the completion of an end players are asked to clear away all stones not involved in the measure and to move either to the hog line or behind the hack leaving the ice free for the Umpire. The persons in charge of the house at the completion of the end will be allowed to observe the measure provided there is no attempt to either interfere with, or influence, the Umpire.

Where a Free Guard Zone measure has to be made visually by an Umpire and provided that stone, or stones, remain untouched for the remainder of that end, no measure by instrument will be made as the visual decision will stand.

34. Improper Conduct

Improper conduct, foul or offensive language, equipment abuse, or wilful damage on the part of any team member is prohibited. Any violation may result in the ejection from that game of the offending person(s) by the Chief Umpire. If ejected the person(s) must leave the Field of Play and immediate areas, but may stay in the locker room or leave the building. An alternate player(s) may not be substituted into that game for the ejected player(s).

35. Ice Abuse

No player shall cause damage to the ice surface by means of equipment, hand prints, or body prints - Rule R10 (a). Procedures:

1st incident = 1st official on-ice warning, repair damage
2nd incident = 2nd official on-ice warning, repair damage
3rd incident = repair damage and remove player from the game

These warning are cumulative during the round robin and tie-break portion of the event, any subsequent warning after the 3rd warning means immediate removal during that game. The process begins again (3 warnings before removal) during the playoff portion of the event.

36. Hog Line Violations

Electronic handles will be in use to detect hog line violations. Teams are reminded that if the lights on the handle show flashing red after delivery it is the responsibility of the delivering team to remove the stone from play immediately. That team's time clock will continue to run until the stone crosses the back line.

No form of glove may be used when delivering these electronic handled stones. To prevent damage, the players must refrain from touching the handles with their feet or brushes when moving stones. Stones should not be tipped so that the handle rests on the ice surface.

Failure to activate the handle, or wearing any form of glove, when delivering a stone will result in the stone being considered a hog line violation and the stone will be removed from play.

32. 점수계산(스코어링)

한 엔드의 점수가 동의된 후에는 심판위원장에게 점수를 얻은 스톤의 색깔과 획득한 점수를 알려야 한다.

오직 한 개의 스코어 카드만이 각 게임에서 사용되며 그 경기를 위해서만 완성되어야 한다. 경기의 마지막에 각 팀의 선수가 스코어 카드에 사인을 하며 스코어에 대한 확인을 할 책임이 있다.

33. 방법

마지막 선수들이 완료했을 시 모든 스톤들은 치워지도록 요청되고, 호그 라인 또는 핵 뒤로 이동하라는 메시지가 심판에 의해 표시된다. 마지막 시도가 완료되었을 때 하우스에서 있는 사람들은 돌을 방해하려는 시도 또는 영향, 심판 등이 없었는지 관찰하도록 허용된다.

프리 가드 존 조치가 심판의 시각에 의해 만들어진 경우 또는 스톤을 제공하는 경우, 엔드에 남은 나머지 건드려지지 않은 스톤들은 놔두고, 시각에 의해 측정되었으면 기계에 의한 측정은 없다.

34. 부적절한 행동

부도덕한 행동, 자극적인 언어 사용, 장비 남용, 팀 멤버에 대한 고의적인 상해는 금지된다. 사람에 대한 위협과 자극 등 어떠한 폭력이든 심판될 것이다.

만약 퇴장당한 사람은 반드시 경기장을 떠나야 하며, 락커룸에 있거나 빌딩 내에 있을 수 있다. 대체 선수는 퇴장당한 선수 대신에 들어올 수 없다.

35. 아이스 훼손

선수는 장비나 손자국, 또는 신체 자국 등으로 아이스 표면을 손상하지 말아야 한다. - R10의 과정에 따라

첫 번째 사건 = 첫 번째 공식 경고, 상처 복구
두 번째 사건 = 두 번째 공식 경고, 상처 복구
세 번째 사건 = 상처 복구 그리고 선수 퇴장

이 경고들은 라운드 로빈과 타이 브레이크 동안에 축적되며, 어느 경고든지 세 번째 경고 후에는 그 즉시 그 경기에서 퇴장된다. 이 과정은 순위 결정전(플레이오프) 동안에 다시(퇴장 전 세 번 경고) 재개된다.

36. 호그 라인 위반

전자 핸들은 호그 라인을 측정하는 데 사용될 것이다. 각 팀들은 딜리버리한 후 핸들에 빨간불이 계속 들어올 경우, 딜리버리한 팀이 그 스톤을 즉각 치워야 한다는 책임이 있다는 것을 명심해야 한다.

팀의 타임클록은 스톤이 백 라인을 가로지를 때까지 계속될 것이다. 스톤을 딜리버리하는 동안에 딜리버리하는 손에는 장갑이나 벙어리장갑을 착용하지 말아야 한다. 손상을 방지하기 위해 선수들은 스톤이 움직일 때 발이나 브러시로 핸들을 만지는 것을 자제해야 한다. 스톤들의 핸들은 아이스 표면 위를 거치도록 만들 수 없다.

핸들을 움직이는 데 실패하거나 스톤을 딜리버리할 때 어느 형태의 장갑을 착용했다면 호그 라인을 넘지 못한 것으로 간주되며, 그 스톤은 경기장에서 제거된다.

1. 교대로 빨간색과 녹색 조명이 빠르게 깜박이는 것은 핸들이 제대로 설정되지 않았음을 나타낸다. 선수는 스톤을 전달하기 전에 핸들을 다시 설정해야 한다.

2. 빨간색과 초록색 조명이 천천히 깜박이는 것은 배터리가 부족하다는 것을 나타낸다. 딜리버리하는 선수는 심판에게 X자로 수신호를 보내야 한다. 선수는 딜리버리하기 전에 핸들을 교체하거나 심판이 호그 라인에

1. Alternating red and green lights flashing quickly indicate that the handle has not been properly set. The player must reset the handle before delivering the stone.

2. Alternating red and green lights flashing slowly indicate a low battery. The delivering player should call for an Umpire using the "X" signal. The player will then have the option of having the handle changed before the delivery or continuing with the delivery while an Umpire views the release at the hog line.

3. No lights indicate a faulty connection. The delivering player should call for an Umpire using the "X" signal. The player will have the option of having the handle changed before the delivery or continuing with the delivery while an Umpire views the release at the hog line.

4. If flashing red lights are believed to have come on before the stone had reached the hog line at the delivering end – the sweepers should pull the stone to the side of the sheet, get it across the back line as quickly as possible, and call for an Umpire using the "X" signal. The Umpire will call for an Ice Technician to test the handle. If the Ice Technician deems the handle to be properly functioning, the stone will be considered a hog line violation. If the handle is deemed to be faulty, the player will be allowed to redeliver. The time clock will not run during that delivery.

   Any stone that shows red lights must be stopped before it crosses the hog line at the playing end or it will be treated as a hog line violation.

37. Post-Game Procedure

To avoid interference with games still in progress, at the end of games alternate players, coaches and team officials are **not** allowed to enter the Field of Play but must wait for their team to exit the playing area.

38. Position of Players

During the process of delivery:

The player who is in charge of the house is positioned inside the hog line, and completely on the ice surface of the playing end of the team's sheet, while the team is in the process of delivery. If a stone is delivered when the proper player is not in this position, the delivered stone is removed from play, and any displaced stones are replaced to their original positions by the non-offending team.

The players of the non-delivering team should take stationary positions along the side lines between the courtesy lines.

The skip and / or the vice-skip of the non-delivering team may take stationary positions **behind** the back line at the playing end providing they are not interfering with the choice of place of the skip / vice skip of the delivering team.

The player who is to deliver next may take a stationary position to the side of the rink behind the hacks at the delivering end.

39. Coach Bench

Special seating has been arranged and will be advised at the Team Meeting. Power points (electrical outlets) for lap top computers will be provided.

There will be three positions for each team. Teams will be asked to name the persons who will occupy these positions. Only the named persons will be allowed onto the special seating area. This must be the alternate plus maximum 2 other team officials, one of whom is the translator (if required). If a properly accredited translator is assisting a team, access to the FOP and the Coach Bench will be allowed providing the translator is properly dressed and is listed as one of the people on the Coach Bench (i.e. – during a game, only the people from the Coach Bench can have access to the Field of Play.)

서 보고 있는 것을 선택할 수 있다.

3. 불빛이 나오지 않는 것은 연결이 제대로 되어있지 않음을 나타낸다. 딜리버리하는 선수는 심판에게 X자로 수신호를 보내야 한다. 선수는 딜리버리하기 전에 핸들을 교체하거나 심판이 호그 라인에서 보고 있는 것을 선택할 수 있다.

4. 만약 스톤이 딜리버리 엔드에서 호그 라인에 도착하기 전에 빨간불이 들어온다면 - 스위퍼들은 스톤을 시트의 사이드로 끌어내고 가능한 한 빨리 백 라인으로 가져간다. 그리고 X 수신호를 보내 심판을 부른다. 심판이 핸들을 테스트하는 아이스 기술자를 호출할 것이다. 얼음 기술자가 핸들이 제대로 작동한다고 간주하는 경우, 스톤은 호그 라인 위반으로 간주된다. 핸들이 고장 난 것으로 간주되는 경우, 선수가 다시 딜리버리할 것을 허용한다. 타임 클록은 딜리버리하는 동안 실행되지 않는다.

경기 끝에 호그 라인을 교차하거나 호그 라인 위반으로 처리하기 전에 빨간 불빛을 내는 모든 스톤들은 멈춰야 한다.

37. 포스트 게임 과정

여전히 진행 중인 게임의 간섭을 피하기 위해 게임 끝의 대체 선수, 코치 및 팀 관계자는 경기장에 들어갈 수 없으며 팀이 경기장에서 나올 때까지 기다려야 한다.

38. 선수의 위치

딜리버리 과정 동안:

하우스의 책임자가 된 선수는 투구를 하는 동안 호그 라인 안이나 자신의 팀 시트의 경기진행 엔드(플레잉 엔드) 쪽 아이스 위에 위치할 수 있다. 만약 스톤이 적절한 선수가 포지션에 위치해 있지 않을 때 딜리버리되었다면, 딜리버리된 스톤은 경기에서 제거되고 공격하지 않은 팀의 스톤들은 원래 위치로 다시 위치시킨다.

딜리버리하지 않는 팀의 선수들은 커티시 라인들 사이의 사이드 라인을 따라 위치를 고정해야 한다.

스킵이나 바이스스킵은 플레이 엔드의 백 라인에 서 있을 수 있지만 투구하는 팀의 스킵이나 바이스 스킵을 방해해서는 안 되고, 다음에 투구해야 할 선수는 엔드 중에 링크의 사이드나 핵의 뒤에 있을 수 있다.

39. 코치석

팀 미팅에서 특별한 자리들은 조정이 되고 알려질 것이다. 랩톱 컴퓨터의 파워포인트 등이 제공될 것이다. 각 팀에는 세 가지 포지션이 있을 것이다.

이 포지션을 차지한 사람에게 팀의 이름에 대한 질문을 받게 될 것이다. 오직 이름이 등록된 사람만이 특별한 자리에 앉을 수 있다. 필요한 경우 최대 두 명의 팀 관계자, 한 명의 통역사가 추가될 수 있다.

만약 적절한 공인 통역사가 팀을 지원하는 경우, 경기 중인 경기장에 접근하고 코치 벤치에 가는 것이 허락될 것이다. 단 적절히 옷을 입고 코치석에 이름을 올려야만 한다. (즉, 경기 동안 오직 코치 벤치에서 경기장에 접근할 수 있는 사람만이 가능하다)

코치 벤치 사람들과 아이스 위의 팀들 간의 의사소통(말 또는 다른 방법으로)은 허용되지 않는다. 또한 지정된 영역에 앉아 있지 않은 사람은 코치석에서 어떤 종류의 커뮤니케이션도 허락되지 않는다. 이 규칙의 위반은 심판위원장 또는 부심판위원장에 의해 그 게임의 경쟁 영역에서 배출된다.

팀 마스코트 또는 깃발을 내놓는 것은 허용되지 않으며, 코치 벤치는 항상 '깨끗'해야 한다. 팀의 환호와 고함은 허용되지 않는다.

Communication, verbal or otherwise, between persons on the Coach Bench and teams on the ice is not allowed and is considered unacceptable conduct. There shall also be no communication of any sort from the Coach Bench to anyone who is not sitting in that designated area. Violation of this rule could result in that person being ejected from the competition area for that game by the Chief Umpire or Deputy Chief Umpire.

Displaying a team mascot or flag is not allowed, and the Coach Bench must be "clean" at all times. Team cheers and yelling are not permitted.

When the team is delivering the dark coloured handled stones, coaches will sit on the right side (as you face the Field of Play) and when delivering the light coloured handled stones on the left side (as you face the Field of Play).

Alcohol in the playing area and on the Coach Bench is not allowed.

Access to the Coach Bench will only be allowed when your team is playing.

The proper dress code must be adhered to when occupying a position on the Coach Bench, or access will be denied. This means no blue jeans, proper footwear, and either the team uniform or the Association jacket. A warm jacket may be worn over the uniform, but must be removed before entering the Field of Play.

If a team wishes to change a person on the Coach Bench the CU or Deputy CU will consider the circumstances and their decision is final.

40. Kit Bags / Clothing

Arrangements of where to store kit bags and clothing will be advised at the Team Meeting. Clothing discarded during games should not be dropped directly behind or to the side of the ice. At the end of games all team and personal equipment must be removed from the Field of Play.

41. Drinks

These have been supplied by the Organising Committee and are for all players so please show your consideration by not taking them away from the Field of Play.

42. Tidiness

Please help to keep the Field of Play tidy by placing all your rubbish in the bins provided and at the end of the game by clearing away all rubbish.

43. Mobile Telephones

Please switch off mobile telephones before entering the Field of Play. Photos should not be taken by participants from inside the Field of Play.

44. Smoking

Smoking is prohibited in the venue.

45. Opening and Closing Ceremonies

Details of the Opening & Closing Ceremonies will be given at the Team Meeting. Teams are asked to wear their playing uniforms for the ceremonies. The WCF and the Host Committee reserve the right to refuse participation in the ceremonies to any player(s) not wearing their proper team uniform.

46. Sportsmanship Award

Ballots will be distributed at the conclusion of your last round robin game. Please return the ballots to the Chief Umpire before leaving the arena.

팀이 어두운 색깔의 스톤을 딜리버리할 때, 코치들은 오른쪽(경기장 정면에서)에 앉아 있고, 밝은 색깔의 스톤일 때는 왼쪽(경기장 정면에서 봤을 때)에 앉는다.

경기장과 코치 벤치에는 주류가 허용되지 않는다.

적절한 의상은 코치석에 있을 때 준수해야 하며, 접근은 거부된다. 이것은 청바지는 허락되지 않고, 적절한 신발 및 팀 유니폼 또는 협회 재킷 중 하나를 입을 것을 의미한다. 유니폼 위에 따뜻한 재킷을 입을 수 있으나 경기장에 들어가기 전에는 반드시 벗어야 한다.

만약 팀이 코치석의 사람을 바꾸길 원할 경우, 심판위원장이나 부심판위원장이 상황과 그들의 결정을 고려하여 결정할 것이다.

40. 키트 가방/의상

키트 가방과 의상을 보관하는 곳에 대한 약정은 팀 회의에서 알려줄 것이다. 의상은 게임 중에 직접 뒤나 아이스 측면에 둘 수 없다. 게임의 끝에 모든 팀들은 개인적인 장비들을 경기장에서 치워야 한다.

41. 음료

조직위원회에 의해 음료는 제공되며 모든 선수들은 경기장에 이것들을 버리지 않도록 주의해야 한다.

42. 단정, 정숙

모든 쓰레기는 게임이 끝난 후 멀리 설치되어 있는 쓰레기통에 버려야 하며, 경기의 정숙이 유지되도록 협조해야 한다.

43. 핸드폰

경기장에 들어갈 때는 반드시 핸드폰 전원을 꺼야 한다. 경기장에 들어간 참가자들은 사진을 찍어서는 안 된다.

44. 담배

담배는 금지된다.

45. 개막, 폐막식

개막식 및 폐막식의 세부 사항은 팀 회의에서 알려진다. 팀은 행사에서 자신의 경기 유니폼을 착용하라는 메시지를 받게 된다. 세계컬링연맹과 게스트 위원회는 선수(들)이 자신의 적절한 팀 유니폼을 입고 있지 않을 때에 행사 참여를 거부할 수 있는 권리를 보유한다.

46. 스포츠맨십 상

투표용지는 마지막 라운드 로빈 게임이 끝나면 배포된다. 경기장을 떠나기 전에 심판위원장에 투표용지를 전달하기를 바란다.

47. 미디어

컬링은 언론의 도움이 필요하다. 선수들과 코치들은 모든 합리적인 요구들에 협조하지만 어떤 문제가 있는 경우 심판위원장이나 부심판위원장에게 말하길 바란다.

47. Media

Curling requires media support. Players and coaches are requested to co-operate with all reasonable requests, but should you have any problems please refer to the Chief Umpire or Deputy Chief Umpire.

48. Television

This event will be televised. Details will be provided at the Team Meeting.

49. Social Media

General conversation on social media is acceptable but posts relating to race, faith, disability, sexual orientation or which are interpreted as inappropriate comments directed towards officials, athletes or coaches, risk punishment and possible exclusion from the competition. All athletes and coaches are responsible for content posted on their accounts regardless if third parties run them. Copying posts and re-tweeting inappropriate content also incurs such penalties. Social Media Guidelines are also available in the Resources section of the WCF website but if you have any questions about social media please speak to a Media Relations Officer.

50. Decision Making

It is hoped that all players and coaches will conduct themselves in a fair and sporting manner and that the Umpires do not have to get overly involved in games. If an Umpire is asked to make a ruling this will be done in complete fairness, and always according to the rules.

51. Etiquette

Etiquette is the backbone of curling and the following statement can be found in the World Curling Federation 'Rules of Curling and Rules of Competition' book.

THE SPIRIT OF CURLING

Curling is a game of skill and of tradition. A shot well executed is a delight to see and it is also a fine thing to observe the time-honoured traditions of curling being applied in the true spirit of the game. Curlers play to win, but never to humble their opponents. A true curler never attempts to distract opponents, nor to prevent them from playing their best, and would prefer to lose rather than to win unfairly.

Curlers never knowingly break a rule of the game, nor disrespect any of its traditions. Should they become aware that this has been done inadvertently, they will be the first to divulge the breach.

While the main object of the game of curling is to determine the relative skill of the players, the spirit of curling demands good sportsmanship, kindly feeling and honourable conduct.

This spirit should influence both the interpretation and the application of the rules of the game and also the conduct of all participants on and off the ice.

52. Questions?

Good luck and good curling

Name ____________________

Chief Umpire ____________________

Date ____________________

48. 텔레비전
이 이벤트는 TV로 중계될 것이다. 자세한 사항은 팀 미팅에서 공지될 것이다.

49. 대중매체
대중매체에 일반 대화는 허용하지만, 인종, 신념, 장애, 성적 취향 또는 다른 어떤 것에 관한 게시물은 관계자, 운동선수 또는 코치들에게 영향을 미쳐 처벌할 수 있으며 경기에서 가능한 한 배제되어야 하므로 부적절한 코멘트로 해석된다. 모든 선수와 코치 등 다른 사람이 이것들을 실행하는 경우에 다른 여부와 관계없이 자신의 계정에 게시된 콘텐츠에 대한 책임이 있다. 게시물을 복사하고 다시 트위터를 리트윗하여 부적절한 내용을 게시하는 것 또한 처벌한다. 대중매체 안내 양식은 세계컬링연맹 웹사이트의 자료 섹션에서도 사용할 수 있다. 대중매체에 대한 질문이 있는 경우 언론 관계 책임자에게 문의하길 바란다.

50. 의사 결정
모든 선수와 코치가 공정하고 스포츠 매너를 지켜 실시하고 있으므로, 심판이 게임에 지나치게 관여할 필요가 없다. 심판이 판결을 하도록 요청되는 경우, 이 규칙에 따라 항상 완벽하고 공정한 상황에서 수행될 것이다.

51. 매너
매너는 컬링의 중추이며, 다음과 같은 문장은 세계컬링연맹의 책인『컬링과 경쟁의 규칙』에서 찾을 수 있다.

컬링의 정신

컬링은 기술과 전통의 게임이다. 잘 던져진 샷은 보는이에게 기쁨을 주며 진정한 스포츠 정신이 배어 있는 컬링의 유구한 전통을 관전하는 것 또한 역시 좋은 것이다. 컬러들은 이기기 위해서 경기를 하지만 결코 상대편을 얕보지 않는다. 진정한 컬러는 상대편에게 혼란을 야기하거나 다른 컬러로 하여금 최선을 다하는 경기를 하지 못하도록 절대로 방해하지 않으며, 비열하게 이기기보다는 오히려 지는 편을 택한다.

컬러는 고의적으로 경기규칙을 어기거나 그 전통을 경시하지 않는다. 그러나 만약 어떤 컬러가 그렇게 의도와 달리 어긴 것을 알아차렸다면 그는 제일 먼저 그 위반을 폭로할 것이다.

컬링 게임의 주목적이 선수들의 상대적 기술을 판별하는 것이지만, 게임의 정신은 훌륭한 스포츠맨십, 온화한 감정과 존경할 만한 품행을 요구한다.

이 정신은 게임 규칙의 해석과 적용은 물론, 모든 참가자들의 경기장 내외에서의 품행에도 영향을 주는 것임에 틀림없다.

52. 질문
마무리/ 좋은 경기를 위한 선언(good curling)

이름 ______________________

심판위원장 ______________________

날짜 ______________________

10. POST ROUND ROBIN STONE SELECTION

A team which does not attend a post round robin meeting within the allotted time (explained in the TMD), or which is not prepared to make a decision, forfeits the game choices (last stone advantage, stone colour, etc.) to which the team is entitled.

1. Tie-Breakers / Relegation Games

- All tie-breaker games shall be played with the stones from the sheet assigned.
- Stone handles shall not be changed from one set of stones to another.
- The Chief Umpire will make all decisions with regard to sheet assignment.

2. Playoffs

- Stone handles shall not be changed from one set of stones to another.
- The choice of delivering first or second stone in the first end is awarded to the team with the better win/loss record during the round robin competition.
- If the teams are tied with an equal win/loss record, the team that won the round robin game between them will be given the choice of delivering first or second stone in the first end.
- The team delivering the first stone of the first end has the choice of stone handle colour, and the team shall declare its selection during the playoff meeting with the CU (within 10 minutes of being asked). Failure to comply shall result in that team's opponent being given the opportunity to select stone handle colour (within 5 minutes of being asked). Failure to do so will result in the Chief Umpire deciding team stone handle colours for that game.
- In the Bronze medal game (when using Page system), the choice of delivering first or second stone in the first end is given to the loser of the semi-final game.
- In the Gold medal game (when using the Page system), the choice of delivering first or second stone in the first end is given to the winner of the 1 v 2 game.

3. Stone selection when only 1 sheet is being used in the playoffs

- Teams may select any 8 game stones and one reserve stone of the same colour from any of the sheets that were used in round robin play.
- For Mixed Doubles the team must select 5 stones and one reserve stone from the stones approved for play on that day.
- Stones selected do not all have to come from the same sheet.
- The reserve stone may only be used if one of the 8 game stones is damaged and becomes unsuitable for play (confirmed by the Chief Ice Technician).
- Teams will advise the Chief Umpire in writing no later than 15 minutes before the start of their pre-game practice which specific stones they wish to use for the pregame practice and game.
- Teams may re-select stones for any subsequent playoff game.

4. Stone selection when 2 or more sheets are being used at the same time

Same as #3 except the Chief Umpire shall designate from which sheets stones may be selected.

5. Playoffs following play in separate groups

If teams are from different groups - the team with the lesser DSC has choice of either the first or second practice or the stone handle colour. The LSD will then determine which team has the choice of delivering the first or second stone in the first end - C8 (d).

If teams are from the same group – the team with the better win/loss record (or if tied the team that won the round robin game) has the choice of either the last stone in the first end or the stone handle colour – C8 (c) (i) & (ii).

10. 라운드 로빈 이후의 스톤 선택

할당된 시간 동안 라운드 로빈 이후 미팅에 참석하지 않거나 결정을 내릴 준비가 되지 못한 팀은 팀에게 부여된 게임선택권(마지막 스톤 어드밴티지, 스톤 색 등)을 박탈당한다.

1. 타이 브레이커/강등전

- 모든 타이 브레이커 경기는 시트에 배정된 스톤으로 경기한다.
- 스톤 손잡이는 다른 스톤의 세트와 바뀌어질 수 없다.
- 주심은 시트 배정에 따라 모든 결정을 내린다.

2. 플레이오프

- 스톤 손잡이는 다른 스톤의 세트와 바뀌어질 수 없다.
- 첫 번째 엔드에서 처음과 두 번째 스톤을 움직일 선택은 라운드 로빈 경쟁에서 더 좋은 승/패 기록을 가진 팀에게 돌아간다.
- 만일 두 팀이 승/패 기록이 같다면 두 팀 간의 라운드 로빈 게임에서 이긴 팀이 첫 번째 엔드에서 처음과 두 번째 스톤을 움직일 선택권을 갖는다.
- 첫 엔드에서 첫 번째 스톤을 움직이는 팀은 스톤 손잡이 색을 선택하게 된다. 그리고 그 팀은 주심과 만나는 플레이오프 동안의 선택을 선언하여야 한다. 이를 어길 시 팀을 상대하는 쪽이 색을 결정할 기회를 5분 동안 얻게 된다. 그것조차 이루어지지 않는다면 주심이 스톤 손잡이 색을 결정한다.
- 동메달 결정전에서, 첫 번째나 두 번째 스톤을 움직일 선택권은 준결승에서 진 팀에게 돌아간다.
- 금메달 결정전에서, 첫 번째나 두 번째 스톤을 움직일 선택은 라운드 로빈 1, 2위 결정전의 승자에게 돌아간다.

3. 플레이오프에서 오직 하나의 시트만 사용될 때의 스톤 고르기

- 팀들은 라운드 로빈 경기에 사용되는 시트로부터 8개의 경기 스톤과 같은 색의 예비 스톤 하나를 선택한다.
- 혼합복식(믹스더블)에서 팀은 5개의 스톤과 같은 색의 예비 스톤 한 개를 선택한다.
- 스톤 선택 시에 모든 스톤을 같은 시트에서 가져올 필요는 없다.
- 예비 스톤은 오직 8게임 스톤이 손상되어 경기를 할 수 없을 때 사용된다.
- 팀들은 주심에게 경기 전 연습 시작 15분 전까지 연습경기와 경기 중 사용할 스톤을 서면으로 알려야 한다.
- 팀들은 차후 어떤 플레이오프 경기에서 스톤을 다시 선택할 수 있다.

4. 2개 이상의 시트가 동시에 사용될 때 스톤 선택하기

- 주심이 선택할 시트를 지정하지 않는 경우에 한해 #3과 동일하다.

5. 나눠진 그룹에서 경기한 플레이오프

- 팀이 다른 그룹으로부터 왔다면, 낮은 DSC(LSD 거리)를 가진 팀이 처음, 두 번째 실행이나 스톤 손잡이 색을 선택한다. 그러고 나서 LSD로 어느 팀이 첫 엔드에서 첫 번째나 두 번째 스톤을 움직일지를 결정한다. 팀이 같은 그룹에서 왔다면 더 좋은 승/패 기록을 가진 팀이 첫 엔드 마지막 스톤이나 스톤 손잡이를 선택하게 된다.

11. HANDLING OF HEALTH INFORMATION FORMS

1. Each team member competing in a WCF Event is required to complete and submit a health information form.

2. Each individual form should be placed in a sealed envelope, marked "Health Information Form" with the person's name and the Association's name on the outside. Then these individual forms from that Association should be placed in a sealed envelope, marked "Health Information Form" with the person's name, the Association's name, the team's gender (if required) on the outside.

3. Health information forms will be collected by the Chief Umpire at the team meeting.

4. All health information forms remain sealed unless required.

5. All forms must be kept in a secure place.

6. The health information forms are to be available during each draw and given only to authorised medical or paramedical personnel when indicated by the situation with the consent of the athlete, if at all possible.

7. At the conclusion of the competition, the Chief Umpire is responsible for destroying all the health information forms.

8. Chief Umpires may wish to prepare their own envelopes for storage of the forms.

9. Chief Umpires should confirm in their Chief Umpire Report that all health forms were destroyed.

11. 건강 정보 양식 관리

1. 세계컬링연맹에 참가하는 각각의 팀 구성원은 건강정보양식을 채워 제출하여야 한다.
2. 각각의 개인 양식은 봉인된 봉투에 선수명과 협회 명이 회부에 써진 채 '건강 정보 양식'이라고 써진 곳에 놓여야 한다. 그러고 나서 이러한 협회의 개인 양식은 선수명과 협회 명, 성별이 외부에 써진 채 '건강 정보 양식'이라고 써진 곳에 봉투에 함께 봉인되어야 한다.
3. 건강 정보 양식은 팀 미팅 때 주심으로부터 수집된다.
4. 모든 건강 정보 양식은 필요할 경우가 아니라면 봉인된 채로 있어야 한다.
5. 모든 양식은 안전한 장소에 보관되어야 한다.
6. 건강 정보 양식은 뽑힐 수 있고 선수 동의하의 상황에서 가능하다면 권위 있는 의료진이나 준의료진에게만 줄 수 있다.
7. 시합이 끝나면 주심은 모든 건강 정보 양식을 파기할 책임을 진다.
8. 주심은 양식 보관을 위해서 그들이 소유한 봉투를 준비해도 된다.
9. 주심은 그들의 주심 보고서로 모든 건강 양식이 파기된 것을 확실히 하여야 한다.

12. CHIEF UMPIRE'S REPORT

This report should be sent to the WCF Director of Competitions within 30 days of the completion of the event.

Not all the topics need be covered and should be selected as necessary.

Heading -	The authority responsible for the Event
Event -	Title, place and dates
Officials -	Chief Umpire
	Deputy Chief Umpire(s)
	Game Umpire(s)
	Chief Timer
	Hog Line Supervisor(s)
	Chief Statistician
	Note any changes from original officials
Ice Technicians -	Chief Ice Technician
	Deputy Chief Ice Technician(s)
Competing Teams -	Listed
Results / Ranking -	Listed
Draw Shot Challenge Results -	Indicate if the DSC was used to rank the teams

Pre-Event communications with Organising Committee:

Travel Arrangements -	Indicate if there were problems
Accommodation -	Indicate if there were problems
Accreditation -	Availability on arrival
	Suitability for access to all areas in arena for work
	Suitability for wearing for identification
Umpires' Room -	Access
	Correctly furnished (tables, chairs, clothing space)
	Drinks facility
	Proximity to Field of Play
	Size
	Security
Arena -	Overview
	Lighting
	Carpet / Floor covering kept clean
	P.A. System with roving microphone
	Waste disposal

12. 주심 보고서

이 보고서는 대회경기 30일 내에 시합의 세계컬링연맹장에게 보내져야 한다. 모든 항목이 포함되거나 필수로 선택될 필요는 없다.

주최 -	대회 책임단체
대회 -	이름, 장소, 날짜
임원들 -	주심, 부주심, 경기심판, 시간 계측장, 호그 라인 감독, 통계장, 기존 임원들로부터의 변경된 점
얼음 기술자들 -	얼음(빙판) 기술장, 얼음(빙판) 부기술장
경쟁 팀 -	명단
결과/랭킹 -	명단
DSC(LSD 거리) 결과 -	DSC(LSD 거리)가 팀을 랭크하는 데 사용된다면 표기해야 한다.

위원회 구성을 위한 대회 이전의 상의 (내용)

출장 준비 -	문제가 있을 시 표기
숙소 -	문제가 있을 시 표기
승인 -	도착 가능 여부, 작업을 위한 아레나에서 접근 적합성, 신분 확인할 때의 적합성
심판실 -	접근, 올바른 가구 배치, 음료 시설, 경기장과 인접성, 크기, 안전성
경기장 -	개관, 조명, 카펫/바닥이 깔끔하게 덮여있는지, 무선 마이크를 포함한 장내방송설비, 폐기물 처리

Ice -	Note any discrepancies or problems found at the pre-Event checks. Any particular comments from the competing teams should be noted and become part of the report. Otherwise leave the report to the Ice Technicians.
Volunteers -	Numbers and quality of performance
	Size of room available
	Equipment
	Meeting
	Schedule
	Suitable collection point for work sheets
	Uniform
Team Meeting -	Venue suitability, set up properly
	Equipment available, e.g. – microphone
	Overall impression of the meeting
Game Timing -	Positioning and numbering of clocks
	If no problems, say so
	If problems, note them – if old clocks include serial number(s)
Anti-Doping Control -	Comments
Schedule of Games -	Comments
Measures -	Quality and number of measures that were available
Media -	Did Media follow the established code of practice?
Summary of Umpiring Activity -	Violations report, etc.
Hog Line -	Problems with 'eye-on-the-hog' handled stones
	Problems related to 'human' eye calling
Score Boards -	Positioning for 'line of sight'
	Last stone symbols, numbers, win/loss signs
Association Boards -	In dark & light colours for Associations / Teams
	Correct mounting for score boards
	Correct size for score boards
Radio Hand Sets -	Number of radios available
	Channel awareness, charging availability
	Ear pieces
Practice Sessions -	Pre-Event
	Pre-Game
	Evening Practice
	Additional Practice post round robin games
Safety -	Any accidents, injuries, or health problems

빙판 -	대회 전 검사에서 발견된 불일치 사항이나 문제를 표기. 경쟁 팀의 특정 의견을 언급하고 보고서의 일부를 만든다. 그렇지 않으면 얼음 기술자에 대한 보고서를 남긴다.
자원봉사자 -	참석 수와 자격, 방의 크기 조절 가능 여부, 장비, 미팅, 일정, 워크 시트의 수집 의견이 적절한지, 유니폼
팀 회의 -	장소 적합성, 제대로 지어졌는지, (마이크 등의) 장비 작동 여부, 회의의 전반적인 인상
경기 시간 측정 -	시계의 위치와 수, 문제없다면 그렇게 말해라, 문제가 있다면 문제를 말해라.
도핑방지장치 -	언급
경기일정 -	언급
측정 -	가능한 측정 기구의 상태와 수
매체 -	매체가 직업 규약을 준수하는지
심판활동 요약 -	폭력 보고서 등등.
호그 라인 -	다뤄지는 스톤의 호그 라인 감지 원리에 관한 문제, 육안으로 봤을 때의 문제
점수판 -	시선이 향하는 곳에 위치, 마지막 스톤 상징, 수, 승/패 사인
위원회 -	협회/팀의 어둡고 밝은색, 득점판의 올바른 설치, 득점판의 올바른 크기
무선 수신기 -	사용가능한 무선 수신기의 수, 채널 인식, 충전 가능 여부, 수화기
시합 부분 -	대회 이전, 경기 이전, 밤 경기, 추가 포스트 라운드 로빈 경기
안정성 -	어떠한 사고, 부상이나 건강상의 문제

Event Forms -	Have any forms been stored for one year, where?
	Who destroyed or shredded the Health forms?
Ice Access -	Entry to Field of Play
Dress code violations -	
Team Information Boxes -	Situation in proximity to changing rooms
Stones -	Stone History – who owns them, purchased from?
	Was a list of the stones and their pairing available?
	Any problems – list stones and numbers
Teams -	Conduct/cooperation - Opening & Closing Ceremonies
	Sportsmanship
	Conduct of players and coaches - comments positive or negative
	Coach / Alternate Player Bench
Sportsperson Awards -	List recipient(s)
Television -	Schedule, any problems
On-Ice Team -	General comments on the Umpires, Ice Crew, Time Clock Operators, etc. can be included. This document could have a wide distribution, therefore specific comments (positive or negative) on individual performances should be sent in a separate document directly to the Director of Competitions.
Overall Summary -	Problems and resolutions
Recommendations -	Important for the Director of Competitions

Date and Signature

대회 양식 -	1년 동안 보관된 어떠한 양식이 있는지, 있다면 어디에 있는지/누가 건강 양식을 파기하였는지 표기
얼음 접근 -	경기장 입장
복장 규정 위반	
팀 정보 박스 -	방을 바꿀 때의 접근성에서의 상황
스톤 -	스톤 정보 - 소유주, 구입처/스톤의 목록 존재 여부/사용 가능 여부/다른 문제점들(목록의 스톤과 그 숫자)
팀 -	지휘/협동 - 개막/폐막식, 스포츠맨십, 선수와 코치의 지휘 - 긍정적인가 부정적인가, 코치/교체 선수석
선수상 -	수령인 기록
텔레비전 -	일정, 문제 여부
얼음 위의 팀 -	심판, 얼음 관리 직원, 시간 운영자 등등에 대한 일반적인 의견이 포함될 수 있음. 이 문서는 널리 배포될 수 있음. 따라서 개인 행동의 특정한 코멘트(긍정적이거나 부정적)는 직접 대회 임원에게 분류되어 전송되어야 함.
전체 요약 -	문제와 해결
권고 -	대회임원에게 있어 중요함

날짜와 서명

13. GAME UMPIRES

DUTIES

Game Umpires are normally appointed by the OC and Organising Body (WCF) to assist the Chief Umpire in the running of the event both on and off the Field of Play.

All Game Umpires should wear the uniform for the competition only while working. They may also wear it to and from the accommodation, but if "off duty" and/or a "spectator" they should not be identifiable as Umpires.

PRE-COMPETITION

1. Be familiar with the Team Meeting Document (TMD) especially particular procedures for that event
2. Arrive in time to assist on "Preparation Day" prior to the team practice day
3. Undertake tasks as allocated from sections on "Chief Umpire's check list" and "On-Ice Pre-Competition Check"
4. Assist on the team practice day

DURING THE COMPETITION

Observe the following and undertake allocated duties given for each session that may include:

1. Run pre-game practice
2. Collect Game Line-up forms and give copies to the Results Team
3. Perform LSD measures
4. Introduce yourself to skips of your assigned game(s)
5. Concentrate on your assigned game(s) only
6. Assist teams - answer questions, provide information
7. Ensure fair play between teams
8. Be neutral and fair in decision making
9. Intervene only to make corrections or if a rule is broken
10. Perform measures
11. Avoid casual conversation with players, coaches, other Umpires, media personnel or spectators
12. Record any violations and inform the Chief Umpire (minor infractions can be dealt with at the end of the game)
13. Report any improper communication between players and coaches
14. Verify score before posting on the scoreboard

13. 경기 심판들

직무

- 경기 심판들은 경기장 안팎의 주심의 운영을 돕기 위하여 일반적으로 조직위원회와 운영위원회(세계컬링연맹)로부터 지명된다.

모든 경기 심판들은 오직 일할 때만 대회를 위한 유니폼을 입어야 한다. 그들은 또한 숙소를 오고갈 때도 입어야 한다. 그러나 만일 비번이거나 관중인 상태라면 그들은 심판으로 보여서는 안 된다.

<시합 이전>

1. 팀 회의 자료, 특히 그 대회의 특정한 절차와 친숙해져라.
2. 팀 연습 날 전에 연습(준비)을 돕기 위해 제시간에 도착해라.
3. 주심 체크 리스트와 얼음 위에서의 시합 전 확인 부분의 할당된 업무를 수행해라.
4. 팀 연습 날에 도움을 주어라.

<시합 중>

아래 내용을 숙지하고 포함될 수 있는 각각의 부분에서 할당된 직무를 수행해라.

1. 시합 이전에 할 것들을 준비해라.
2. 경기 라인업 양식을 수집하고 이긴 팀에게 복사본을 주어라.
3. LSD 측정을 실행해라.
4. 배정받은 경기의 스킵들에게 자신을 소개해라.
5. 배정받은 경기에만 집중해라.
6. 어시스트 팀 - 질문에 대한 대답을 하고 정보를 제공해준다.
7. 양 팀에게 공정하고 매너 있는 경기를 할 것을 숙지시켜라.
8. 결정을 할 때 중립적이고 공평해라.
9. 원칙이 깨졌다면 올바르게 하기 위해서만 개입해라.
10. 측정을 수행해라.
11. 선수, 코치, 다른 심판, 미디어나 관중들과 격식 없는 대화를 삼가라.
12. 어떠한 위반이든 기록하고 주심에게 알려라.
13. 선수와 코치 간 적절하지 않은 의사소통이 있다면 알려라.
14. 점수판에 기록하기 전에 점수를 확인해라.

15. Remember to change the totals
16. If no time clocks are in operation:
17. - Monitor breaks between ends (normally one minute)
18. - Monitor mid-game break (normally 5 minutes) and inform teams when one minute remains
19. Complete the scorecard
20. Obtain a signature from both teams on the scorecard
21. Finalise scoreboards (at both ends) including the X's if appropriate
22. Return all forms to the Chief Umpire

Note: *If an end ice observer is available, they may perform some of the above tasks.*

Additionally, attend meetings as required by the Chief Umpire and run any additional (evening/post-round robin) practice sessions as necessary.

If questioned by media about a situation or incident that may have occurred during a game, politely refuse to make a comment and inform them that the Chief Umpire will answer any questions they may have.

AFTER THE COMPETITION

1. Assist in getting teams (if required by OC) into the arena for the Closing Ceremony/Medal Presentation
2. Clear Umpire's room, plus pack equipment (e.g. numbers/score boxes)

15. 총점을 바꾸는 것을 기억하고 있어라.
16. 시합 시 타임 클락이 없다면:
17. 엔드 간 휴식을 측정해라(일반적으로 1분).
18. 게임 중간 휴식을 측정하고(일반적으로 5분), 1분이 남았을 때 팀들에게 알려라.
19. 스코어카드를 완성해라.
20. 스코어카드의 팀들에게 서명을 받아라.
21. X를 포함해서 스코어카드를 마무리 지어라.
22. 주심에게 모든 양식을 제출해라.

추가적으로, 주심 미팅에 참석하고 다른 추가적인 업무가 필요하면 해라. 경기 도중 상황이나 사건에 대한 미디어의 질문이 있다면 정중하게 거절하는 코멘트를 하고 주심이 대답을 해줄 것이라고 알려라.

<시합 후>

1. 팀을 이루어 경기장의 폐막식과 메달 수여식을 도와라.
2. 심판실과 장비들을 깨끗이 해라.

14. END-ICE OBSERVER

DUTIES

The primary duty is observation. The end-ice observer is there to be an extra set of eyes and acts as a liaison between players and the Game Umpire. End-ice observers are not decision makers.

CODE OF CONDUCT

- Be aware of shift times.
- Give a minimum of 3 hours notice if unable to work.
- Advise the Chief Timer of any duty change.
- Abstain from alcohol from 6 hours before duty.
- Concentrate on the game that has been allocated.
- Conform to dress code.
- Maintain confidentiality at all times.

BEFORE THE GAME

1. Check in with your supervisor at the time indicated by the Chief Umpire and collect your equipment – this will include clipboard, scorecard, pencil(s), magnetic board, and may also include a stopwatch, violation sheet, and team line-up form.

2. Check that the scorecard has been printed with the correct draw, date, sheet and team names.

3. Check that all 16 magnets are on the magnetic board.

4. Move into your position in the Field of Play at the time directed.

5. Dress warmly and in approved clothing – black pants, clean shoes.

DURING THE GAME

1. The Game Umpire will advise you who has the last stone in the first end. The LSFE symbol on the scoreboard should not be moved after each end (except in Mixed Doubles).

2. Note the actual game start time on the scorecard and fill in all required information.

3. Concentrate and watch only the game to which you are assigned. In case of a dispute over an incident on the ice, the on-ice Umpire will look to you for a report.

4. Place your magnetic stones on the board to reproduce the positions where they lie throughout the end. You may fractionally reposition the stones during the end if you think they are not quite accurate.

5. Make sure the players' equipment, clothing and bags are behind the scoreboards or stored away from the walking area.

6. Do not update your magnetic board immediately after the stones have come to rest – an infraction may have occurred which requires re-positioning of stones and if you have been super-efficient, the

14. 엔드 아이스 관찰자

직무

주된 업무는 관찰이다. 엔드 아이스 관찰자는 추가 관측을 위해서 그곳에 있으며, 선수와 경기 심판 사이의 연락을 담당하는 듯 행동한다. 엔드 아이스 관찰자는 결정자는 아니다.

행동강령

- 시간 이동을 숙지해라.
- 일할 수 없을 때 최소 3시간의 보고를 해라.
- 시간 계측자에게 직무 변경된 것이 있으면 알려라.
- 직무 이전의 6시간 전에는 술을 마시지 마라.
- 배정된 경기에 집중해라.
- 복장규정을 준수해라.
- 항상 자신감을 가져라.

경기 전

1. 당신의 감독관과 함께 주심이 지시해준 시각에 입장하고 당신의 장비를 점검해라.
   - 장비는 클립보드, 점수카드, 연필, 자석판, 스톱워치, 규정 위반 시트, 팀 라인업 양식을 포함한다.
2. 점수카드가 올바른 경기, 날짜, 시트, 팀 이름에 맞게 인쇄되었는지 체크해라.
3. 16개의 자석들이 자석판 위에 있는지 체크해라.
4. 시간이 되면 경기장의 당신의 자리로 이동해라.
5. 따뜻하게 입되, 인가된 옷을 입어라 - 검은 바지, 깨끗한 구두

경기 중

1. 심판은 당신에게 첫 엔드에서 누가 마지막 스톤을 가지는지 알려줄 것이다. 점수판 위 첫 번째 엔드의 마지막 스톤 상징은 혼합복식(믹스더블)을 제외하고 각각의 엔드가 끝나면 움직일 수 없다.
2. 점수판에 실제 경기 시작 시간을 작성하고 모든 필수 정보를 채워 넣는다.
3. 오직 당신이 배정된 경기만 집중하고 관찰해라. 얼음 위에서 일어난 사건에 관한 논란의 경우, 얼음 위의 심판은 당신에게 보고하기 위하여 찾을 것이다.
4. 엔드 동안 당신의 자석 돌을 판에 배치하라. 당신은 그들이 꽤 정확하지 않다고 생각될 때에 약간 조정할 수 있다.
5. 선수들의 장비, 옷, 그리고 가방을 스코어보드 뒤나 걷는 곳으로부터 떨어진 곳에 확실히 보관하도록 해라.
6. 스톤이 멈추고 난 직후에 자석판을 곧바로 업데이트하지 마라. 위반이 발생하여 스톤을 재배치할 일이 생길 수도 있고, 만일 당신이 재빠르게 자석을 바꿨다면 당신이 가지고 있는 기록의 장점이 사라질 수 있다. 갱신할 때의 올바른 시간은 다음 선수가 그의 스톤을 움직이기 바로 직전이다. 가장 무거운 운반일지라도 갱신하는 데 15초나 있다.

benefit of your recording has been lost. The correct time to update is just before/as the next player delivers his/her stone. Even with the heaviest take-out, you have 15 seconds to update your board.

7. Chart violations if required to do so. When play is coming towards you, chart every violation noted from the near hog line to the near backboard. When play is going away, all violations from the near backboard to the far hog line are recorded. If there is only one end-ice observer per sheet, he/she should be positioned at the playing end and record all violations for that sheet. Record any illegal coach communication.

8. Remain seated as much as possible, but once the stone has been delivered, you may move to more clearly view a critical shot. Make sure not to distract players on adjacent sheets.

9. Do not engage in casual conversation with the competitors, other officials, media personnel, spectators or coaches during the game.

10. If an incident occurs, do not intervene. Observe and wait to be consulted on the position of any stones prior to the shot that has just been played. If the players cannot solve the problem, call an Umpire. The only situation where you can intervene without being asked is if a stone touches a sideboard and finishes in play unnoticed by the teams.

11. If you need to leave the ice during a game, advise the Umpire and wait for a replacement before leaving your position.

12. Notify the Game Umpire if the teams request a measurement or ruling.

13. Mark up the score at both ends as soon as possible for both teams: 0-0, 1-0, 2-0, etc. and remember to adjust the totals at the end of the scoreboard. No matter how obvious, the score is not marked until verified by the players in charge of the house.

14. If time clocks are not available, at the completion of regular ends monitor the one-minute break and inform the teams when 10 seconds remain.

15. If time clocks are not available, at the completion of the end that defines the halfway point monitor the break and inform the teams when one minute remains.

AFTER THE GAME

1. Complete the scorecard. When a team concedes the game before the completion of an end, the score of the end is determined as per Rule R11 (h).

2. Note the time, record the final score and have a player from both teams verify the score and sign the score card.

3. If the game finishes early at the away end, have players leave the stones at that end so as not to disrupt other sheets by moving stones to the home end.

4. Return scorecards and charts to the appropriate Umpire.

5. Check that all 16 stones are still on the magnetic board.

6. Return all equipment to the storage area.

7. Never make comments to media or spectators about situations or incidents that may have occurred during a game.

7. 위반이 있다면 기록해라. 시합이 당신에게 배정된다면, 호그 라인 근처부터 백보드 근처까지 모든 위반사항을 기록해라. 시트당 엔드아이스 관찰자가 한 명밖에 없다면 그는 경기 엔드에 위치해야 하고 해당 시트에 모든 위반사항을 기록하여야 한다. 불법적인 코치 의사소통 또한 기록한다.
8. 최대한 앉은 채로 있어라. 그러나 일단 스톤이 움직였다면 당신은 더 명확하게 보기 위하여 움직여야 한다. 인접한 시트의 선수들에게 방해가 안 되도록 하는 것을 명심해야 한다.
9. 선수나 다른 임원들, 미디어, 관중들이나 코치들과 시합 도중 일상적인 대화를 나누지 마라.
10. 사건이 발생해도 개입하지 마라. 관찰하고 방금 벌어진 샷 전의 스톤 위치에 대한 정보요청을 기다려라. 만일 선수가 문제 해결을 할 수 없다면, 심판을 불러라. 요청 없이 당신이 개입할 수 있는 유일한 상황은 스톤이 사이드보드를 터치했을 때와 팀으로 알려지지 않은 경기를 끝낼 때밖에 없다.
11. 당신이 시합 도중 얼음을 떠나야 할 경우 심판에게 말하고 떠나기 전에 대체자를 기다려라.
12. 팀이 측정이나 판결을 요청하면 경기심판에게 알려라.
13. 양측에 대한 점수를 최대한 빨리 체크해라(0-0, 1-0, 2-0 등등). 기억하고 있다가 스코어보드 끝에 총합을 조정해라. 아무리 명확해도 하우스 담당 선수가 확인하기 전까지는 점수를 기입하지 않는다.
14. 시간기록계가 없다면, 시합의 정기적인 엔드에 1분 휴식을 알려주고, 10초가 남았을 때 팀에게 알려준다.
15. 시간기록계가 없다면, 시합 중간 휴식을 공지하고 1분 남았을 때 팀에게 알려준다.

경기 후

1. 점수판을 완성해라. 한 팀이 엔드 끝나기 전에 패배를 인정하면, 엔드의 점수는 R11규칙에 따라 결정된다.
2. 시간을 기록하고 최종점수를 기록하고, 양측 팀의 선수들에게 점수를 확인시키고 스코어카드에 서명을 받는다.
3. 만일 경기가 어웨이 엔드에서 일찍 끝나면, 해당 엔드의 선수들은 홈엔드로 이동했을 때 다른 시트에 방해되지 않게 하기 위해서 스톤을 남겨둔다.
4. 해당 심판에게 스코어카트와 차트를 제출한다.
5. 16개의 돌이 여전히 자석판 위에 있는지 체크한다.
6. 창고에 모든 장비를 갖다놓는다.
7. 시합 중에 있었던 상황이나 사건에 대하여 미디어나 관중들에게 일절 언급하지 않는다.

15. END-ICE OBSERVER – MIXED DOUBLES CURLING

DUTIES

The primary duty is observation. The end-ice observer is there to be an extra set of eyes and acts as a liaison between players and the Game Umpire. End-ice observers are not decision makers. They play an active role in sustaining the flow of play from one end to the next. The end-ice observer is required to act efficiently and accurately within the one-minute break at the completion of each end.

BEFORE THE GAME

1. Check in with your supervisor at the time indicated by the Chief Umpire and collect your equipment – this will include clipboard, scorecard, pencil(s), and may also include a stopwatch and violation sheet.
2. Check that the scorecard has been printed with the correct draw, date, sheet and team names.
3. Move into your position in the Field of Play at the time directed.
4. Dress warmly and in approved clothing – black pants, clean shoes suitable for ice access.

PLACEMENT OF STONES

1. Use the designated stones, one of each colour for each end of the ice, each marked with a black 'X'. If there is a rotation of the designated stones (to keep the wear on the running edges the same), the markings on the stones will have to be changed to match the rotation order.
2. Place the stones not being used together behind the hack and away from the game stones (providing there is sufficient space between the hack and back board. Placing stones behind a bumper is also an option).
3. The team that scores OR blanks an end will deliver the first stone in the next end UNLESS YOU ARE TOLD OTHERWISE BY THE TEAMS.
   - The team delivering first has the guard stone.
   - The team delivering second has the stone at the back of the tee centre.
4. The end-ice observer (or Game Umpire) at the other end will indicate which team (colour of stone) scored or blanked the previous end to enable you to set up stones for the next end as quickly as possible. They may use a signal of hand held high (team on top of scoreboard) or hand held low (team on bottom) to indicate which team (colour) has last stone.
5. Clean the running surface of the two positioned stones with a micro-fibre cloth before moving them forward to their locations. When ice conditions are very good (i.e. - clean and frost-free) the cleaning of positioned stones may be done pre-game and at the mid-game break. Take care in tipping stones to clean. Always clean stones near the backboard, never ahead of the hack area.
6. Umpires will inform the end-ice observers at the start of each game what the designated position is for the guard stone.

ORDER OF PLAYING STONES

1. The first player (which can change from end to end) on each team delivers the first and the last stone for their team.
2. The second player delivers the next three stones.

15. 혼합복식(믹스더블) 컬링에서의 엔드 아이스 관찰자

직무

주된 업무는 관찰이다. 엔드 아이스 관찰자는 추가 관측을 위해서 그곳에 있으며, 선수와 경기심판 사이의 연락을 담당하는 듯 행동한다. 엔드 아이스 관찰자는 결정자는 아니다. 그들은 경기에서 한 엔드에서 다음 엔드로 넘어갈 때 흐름을 유지하는 적극적인 역할을 한다. 엔드 아이스 관찰자는 효율적으로 행동해야 하며 각각의 엔드가 끝날 때 1분 휴식을 정확히 지켜야 한다.

경기 전

1. 당신의 감독관과 함께 주심이 지시해준 시각에 입장하고 당신의 장비를 점검해라.
   - 이것은 클립보드, 점수카드, 연필, 자석판, 스톱워치, 규정 위반 시트를 포함
2. 점수카드가 올바른 경기, 날짜, 시트, 팀 이름에 맞게 인쇄되었는지 체크해라.
3. 시간이 되면 경기장 당신의 자리로 이동해라.
4. 따뜻하게 입되, 인가된 옷을 입어라 - 얼음에 적합한 검은 바지, 깨끗한 구두

스톤의 위치

1. 지정된 스톤을 사용해라, 각각의 엔드에 각각의 색깔로, 각각의 스톤은 검은색 X로 표기된다. 지정된 스톤에 로테이션이 있다면 로테이션 순서에 매치되게 변경시켜서 스톤을 마킹한다.
2. 사용되지 않는 스톤을 한데 모아 판 뒤에 두어라 그리고 경기 스톤과 떨어뜨려 놓아라.
3. 엔드에서 점수를 따거나 따지 못한 팀은 다음 엔드에서 첫 번째 스톤을 움직일 것이다. 당신이 아니라도 팀으로라도.
   - 처음으로 움직이는 팀은 가드 스톤이 있다
   - 두 번째로 움직일 때는 티 센터의 뒤에 스톤이 있다.
4. 다른 엔드에서 엔드 아이스 관찰자나 심판은 어느 팀이 점수를 얻고 얻지 못하였는지에 대하여 말할 것이다. 다음 엔드에서 스톤을 최대한 빨리 설치하기 위해서. 그들은 수신호를 높거나 낮게 하여 어떤 팀이 마지막 스톤이 남았는지를 알린다.
5. 두 개의 위치한 스톤의 표면을 그들의 위치가 앞으로 움직이기 전에 초미세 합성섬유로 깨끗이 해라. 얼음 상태가 매우 좋다면 위치한 스톤을 깨끗이 하는 것은 경기 전과 경기 중반 휴식에서 끝난다. 끝에 위치한 스톤을 깨끗하게 해라. 백보드 근처의 스톤을 항상 깨끗하게 하고 판 구역 앞에 위치시키기 않도록 한다.
6. 심판은 엔드 아이스 관찰자에게 어떤 지정된 위치가 가드스톤인지 경기 시작할 때 알려준다.

시합 시 순서

1. 각 팀에서의 첫 번째 선수는 그들의 팀에서 첫 번째와 마지막 스톤을 담당한다.
2. 두 번째 선수는 다음 3개의 스톤을 담당한다.

3. Keep a chart to make sure that the first player does NOT deliver the first two stones. After the end is completed, your sheet may look like this:

RED	M F F F M
YELLOW	F M M M F

4. If a team is about to throw in the wrong order, tell the Umpire who will stop the player.

DURING THE GAME

The system of end-ice observers may vary from event to event, depending on the number of volunteers available, the type of club or arena, the number of Game Umpires and the number of ice sheets in play.

Each end-ice observer may be working one end of two sheets, or moving from end to end on one sheet. An end-ice observer may also be assigned to update scoreboards on several sheets, as well as assisting with positioning stones for other end-ice observers when possible to ensure the stones are placed in time (one-minute break between ends).

1. The end-ice observers should be at the home end backboard with the scorecard at the completion of each team's practice session The Game Umpires will record the LSD measurements. The Umpire will advise who has the last stone in the first end.
2. Note the actual game start time on the scorecard and fill in all required information.
3. Concentrate and watch only the game to which you are assigned. In case of a dispute over an incident on the ice, the Game Umpire will look to you for a report.
4. Make sure the players' equipment, clothing and bags are behind the scoreboards or stored away from the walking area.
5. Chart violations if required to do so. When play is coming towards you, chart every violation noted from the near hog line to the near backboard. When play is going away, all violations from the near backboard to the far hog line are recorded. If there is only one end-ice observer per sheet, they should be positioned at the playing end and record all violations for that sheet. Record any illegal coach communication. Game Umpires may make notations on the violation sheet.
6. Remain seated as much as possible, but once the stone has been delivered you may move to more clearly view a critical shot. Make sure not to distract players on adjacent sheets.
7. Do not engage in casual conversation with the competitors, other officials, spectators or coaches during the game.
8. If an incident occurs, do not intervene. Observe and wait to be consulted on the position of any stones prior to the shot that has just been delivered. If the players cannot solve the problem, call an Umpire. The only situation where you can intervene is when a stone touches a sideboard and finishes in play unnoticed by the teams.
9. If you need to leave the ice during a game, advise the Umpire and wait for a replacement before leaving your position.
10. Notify the Game Umpire if the teams request a measurement or ruling.
11. Place the "Hammer" marker in the end to be played for the team who has last stone in that end.
12. Mark up the score at both ends as soon as possible for both teams: 0-0, 1-0, 2-0, etc. and remember to adjust the totals at the end of the scoreboard. No matter how obvious, the score is not marked until verified by the players in charge of the house.

3. 첫 번째 선수가 첫 두 스톤을 담당하지 않도록 표를 유지하도록 한다. 엔드가 끝나면, 시트는 다음과 같을 것이다.

RED	M F F F M
YELLOW	F M M M F

4. 만약 팀에서 잘못된 순서로 던지면 심판에게 선수를 중단시키도록 말해라.

경기 중

엔드 아이스 관찰자의 시스템은 대회마다 다양하다. 자원봉사자들의 숫자, 경기장 유형, 경기심판의 수, 시합에서의 시트 수 등에 따라 달라진다.

각각의 엔드 아이스 관찰자는 두 시트의 한 엔드에서 일하거나 한 엔드에서 다른 엔드로 이동한다. 그들은 스코어보드 업데이트로 배정되고 시간 내에 스톤을 위치시키기 위해서 스톤 위치시키는 것을 돕는다.

1. 엔드 아이스 관찰자는 각각의 팀의 연습이 끝나면 스코어카드를 들고 홈엔드 백보드에 있어야 한다. 심판은 LSD 측정법으로 기록할 것이다. 심판은 누가 첫 엔드에서 마지막 스톤을 가지고 있는지 알려줄 것이다.
2. 점수판에 실제 경기 시작 시간을 작성하고 모든 필수 정보를 채워 넣는다.
3. 오직 당신이 배정된 경기만 집중하고 관찰해라. 얼음 위에서 사건에 관한 논란의 경우에 얼음 위의 심판은 당신을 보고하기 위하여 찾을 것이다.
4. 선수들의 장비, 옷, 그리고 가방을 스코어보드 뒤나 걷는 곳으로부터 떨어진 곳에 보관하는 것을 확실하게 해라.
5. 위반이 있다면 기록해라. 시합이 당신에게 배정된다면, 호그 라인 근처부터 백보드 근처까지 모든 위반사항을 기록해라. 시트당 엔드 아이스 관찰자가 한 명밖에 없다면 그는 경기 엔드에 위치해야 하고 해당 시트에 모든 위반사항을 기록하여야 한다. 불법적인 코치 의사소통 또한 기록한다.
6. 최대한 앉은 채로 있어라. 그러나 일단 스톤이 움직였다면 당신은 더 명확하게 보기 위하여 움직여야 한다. 인접한 시트의 선수들에게 방해가 안 되도록 하는 것을 명심해야 한다.
7. 선수나 다른 임원들, 미디어, 관중들이나 코치들에게 시합 도중 일상적인 대화를 나누지 마라.
8. 사건이 발생해도 개입하지 마라. 관찰하고 방금 벌어진 샷 전의 스톤 위치에 대한 정보요청을 기다려라. 만일 선수가 문제해결을 할 수 없다면, 심판을 불러라. 요청 없이 당신이 개입할 수 있는 유일한 상황은 스톤이 사이드보드를 터치했을 때와 팀으로 알려지지 않은 경기를 끝낼 때밖에 없다.
9. 당신이 시합 도중 얼음을 떠나야 할 경우 심판에게 말하고 떠나기 전에 대체자를 기다려라.
10. 측정이나 판결을 팀이 요청하면 경기심판에게 알려라.
11. 해당 엔드에 마지막 스톤을 가지고 있었던 팀의 엔드에 해머 마크 표시를 해라.
12. 양측에 대한 점수를 최대한 빨리 체크해라(0-0, 1-0, 2-0 등등). 기억하고 있다가 스코어보드 끝에 총합을 조정해라. 아무리 명확해도 하우스 담당 선수가 확인하기 전까지는 점수를 기입하지 않는다.

13. If time clocks are not available, at the completion of regular ends monitor the one-minute break and inform the teams when 10 seconds remain.

14. If time clocks are not available, at the completion of the end that defines the halfway point monitor the break and inform the teams when one minute remains.

AFTER THE GAME

1. Complete the scorecard. When a team concedes the game before the completion of an end, the score of the end is determined as per Rule R11 (h).

2. Note the time, record the final score and have a player from both teams verify the score and sign the scorecard.

3. If the game finishes early at the away end, have players leave the stones at that end so as not to disrupt other sheets by moving stones to the home end.

4. Return scorecards and charts to the appropriate Umpire.

5. Return all equipment to the storage area.

6. Never make comments to media or spectators about situations or incidents that may have occurred during a game.

13. 시간기록계가 없다면, 시합의 정기적인 엔드에 1분 휴식을 알려주고 10초가 남았을 때 팀에게 알려준다.
14. 시간기록계가 없다면, 시합 중간 휴식을 공지하고 1분 남았을 때 팀에게 알려준다.

경기 후

1. 점수판을 완성해라. 한 팀이 엔드 끝나기 전에 패배를 인정하면, 엔드의 점수는 R11규칙에 따라 결정된다.
2. 시간을 기록하고 최종점수를 기록하고, 양측 팀의 선수들에게 점수를 확인시키고 스코어카드에 서명을 받는다.
3. 만일 경기가 어웨이 엔드에서 일찍 끝나면, 해당 엔드의 선수들은 홈엔드로 이동할 때 다른 시트에 방해되지 않게 하기 위해서 스톤을 남겨둔다.
4. 해당 심판에게 스코어카트와 차트를 제출한다.
5. 창고에 모든 장비를 갖다놓는다.
6. 시합 중에 있었던 상황이나 사건에 대하여 미디어나 관중들에게 일절 언급하지 않는다.

16. ICE PLAYER ASSISTANT (IPA) - WHEELCHAIR CURLING

Each sheet should have two IPAs per game, one at the delivery end and one at the playing end. Their role is an integral part of wheelchair curling and essential to the running of a game.

Before the game

- Introduce yourself as an IPA to both teams.
- Check with each team for their stone delivery order. List handle number in order on the Stone Delivery card.

IPA - Delivery end

- Arrange the stones so that the # 8 stone (or the last one to be delivered) is just touching the tee line and the other stones are in a straight line in the direction of the hog line. Handles should be pointing straight up the ice. The stones of the team delivering first should be closer to the centre. This may mean changing the position of stones for the first end after the pre-game practice depending on which team has last stone advantage in the first end of the game.
- The players will indicate to the IPA where they would like the stone placed for their delivery. A micro-fibre cloth, not the hand, should be used to clean the running surface of all stones, and the ice area where the stone is cleaned, unless otherwise directed by the team. Once a player has been given his/her stone, the IPA should stand still and out of the vision of the delivering player, well behind that player near the side line (see ice chart).
- It is important to have the first stone cleaned and in position to avoid delays.
- After the last stone of an end has been delivered, the IPA at the delivery end should proceed along the side of the sheet to the other end to assist in getting the stones lined up in delivery order for the next end of play.

IPA - Playing end

- Stand to the side of the sheet (out of the delivering player's sight line), near the corner where the out-of-play stones will be collected.
- Assist players in clearing any stones that are not in the Field of Play (stones that have not crossed the hog line, or have touched a side line or cleared the back line).
- Place out-of-play stones in two rows parallel to the side boards and with the handles pointing straight up the ice (keep them in the delivery order if possible).
- If a take-out shot is being played, move forward in anticipation of stones possibly going towards an adjacent sheet.
- After the score for the end has been agreed between the vice-skips and it has been communicated to the Game Umpire, both IPAs can move the stones up to the delivery position on the right side of the sheet for the next end.
- Arrange the stones in correct order for the next end, but one IPA should follow the first stone back to the other end.
- The IPA can arrange any remaining stones after the 1st stone is delivered.
- If a measure is required, don't move any stones. Call an Umpire who will oversee the situation and who will then enlist your help as required. Communication problems have occurred in the past and the wrong stones have been removed. However, players (at their team's risk) are free to move stones themselves before a measure.
- Offer assistance only when requested.
- If asked to comment on any situation regarding play/position of the stones, make it clear that is not your role and such comments should be directed towards the end-ice observer or Game Umpire. But if an Umpire or end-ice observer is not present and the players ask if a stone has touched the side boards, and you have observed it, then you may comment.
- If you see anything, which the players "miss" (e.g. stone touched by a wheel), it is not your duty to bring it to their attention, but you can tell the Game Umpire.

16. 빙상 선수 보조자(빙상 선수 보조자) - 휠체어 컬링

각각의 시트에는 한 게임당 두 명의 빙상 선수 보조자가 있어야 하는데, 한 명은 딜리버리 엔드에 다른 한 명은 플레잉 엔드에 있어야 한다. 그들은 휠체어 컬링에서 필수적인 부분을 차지하고 게임 진행에 있어서 없어서는 안 될 역할을 한다.

게임 시작 전에

- 양 팀에 당신이 빙상 선수 보조자임을 소개한다.
- 각각의 팀과 그들의 스톤 딜리버리 순서를 확인한다. 스톤 딜리버리 카드에 핸들 숫자를 순서대로 기입한다.

빙상 선수 보조자-딜리버리 엔드

- 스톤 번호 8번(혹은 가장 나중에 딜리버리될 스톤을)이 티 라인에 맞닿고, 다른 스톤들이 호그 라인의 방향으로 일렬로 있도록 스톤을 정렬한다. 핸들은 빙판 바로 위로 향하게 해야 한다. 팀에서 가장 먼저 딜리버리될 스톤은 중앙에 더 가까워야 한다. 이것은 어떤 팀이 게임의 첫 번째 엔드에서 마지막 스톤에 대한 어드벤티지를 얻을 것인지에 따라 프리 게임에서 연습이 끝난 후 첫 번째 엔드에서 스톤의 위치가 바뀔 수도 있음을 의미한다.
- 선수들은 그들의 딜리버리 위치에서 스톤을 어디에 위치하고 싶은지 빙상 선수 보조자에게 나타낼 것이다. 손이 아닌 미세섬유 직물이 스톤의 활주 표면과 팀에 의해 다르게 지시되지 않는 한, 스톤의 활주 표면과 스톤이 정돈된 얼음 표면은 손이 아닌 미세 섬유 직물에 의해서 닦아질 것이다. 일단 선수가 자신의 스톤을 건네주었다면, 빙상 선수 보조자는 가만히 서있어야 하고 선수 곁에 사이드 라인(아이스 차트 참고) 뒤에 서서 딜리버리하는 선수의 시야에서 사라져야 한다.
- 첫 번째 스톤이 정돈되고 제 위치에 있는 것은 경기를 지연하는 것을 피하기 위해 매우 중요하다.
- 한 엔드의 마지막 스톤이 딜리버리된 후에, 딜리버리 엔드에 있는 빙상 선수 보조자는 시트의 가장자리를 따라서 다른 엔드로 다음 엔드에서 스톤이 딜리버리 순서에 따라 정렬되도록 도움을 주기 위해 나아가야 한다.

빙상 선수 보조자-플레잉 엔드

- 인플레이 중이 아닌 스톤들이 수거될 모퉁이 근처인 시트의 측면(딜리버링 하는 선수의 시야 바깥)에 선다.
- 선수가 경기 중 필드 안에 있지 않은 스톤을 치우는 것을 도와준다. (호그 라인을 지나지 않은 스톤들이나 사이드 라인을 건드렸거나 혹은 백 라인을 통과한 스톤들)
- 인플레이 중이 아닌 스톤들을 측면 보드들과 평행이 되도록 두 줄로 위치시키고 핸들이 얼음 바로 위로 가도록 위치시킨다. (가능하다면 그것들을 딜리버리 순서에 맞게 둔다)
- 만약에 테이크아웃 샷이 경기되었다면, 스톤들이 인접한 시트를 향해 갈 것을 예상하고 앞으로 움직인다.
- 바이스들 간에 엔드의 점수가 합의되고 이것이 게임 심판과 이야기된 후에, 두 빙상 선수 보조자는 다음 엔드를 위해 딜리버리 위치인 시트의 오른쪽 측면으로 스톤들을 옮길 수 있다.
- 다음 엔드를 위해 스톤들을 알맞은 순서로 위치시킨다, 하지만 한 명의 빙상 선수 보조자는 첫 번째 스톤을 다른 엔드까지 따라가야 한다.
- 빙상 선수 보조자는 첫 번째 스톤이 딜리버리된 후 남아 있는 아무 스톤들을 정렬할 수 있다.
- 만약에 측정이 필요하다면, 아무 스톤도 움직이지 않아야 한다. 이 상황을 보고 있는 심판을 부를 경우 그 심판이 당신의 도움이 필요하다면 당신을 부를 것이다. 과거에는 소통이 문제가 되어 잘못된 스톤이 치워지기도 했다. 그러나 지고 있는 팀의 선수들은 측정이 행해지기 전에 자신들이 스톤을 움직일 수 있다.
- 요구되었을 때에만 조력자의 도움을 받을 수 있다.
- 만약에 스톤들의 경기, 위치에 관한 상황에 대하여 발언하라는 요청을 받는다면, 이것이 당신의 역할이 아니고 이러한 발언권은 엔드-빙상 관찰자 혹은 게임 심판에게 있음을 명확히 밝힌다. 그러니 만약 심판이나 엔드-빙상 관찰자가 자리에 없고 선수들이 보드의 측면을 스톤이 건드리지 않았냐고 묻고, 그것을 당신이 관찰했다면 그때는 당신이 발언할 수 있다.
- 만약에 당신이 선수를 '놓친'(예를 들어 바퀴에 의해 스톤이 건드려진 경우) 것을 본다면, 이것으로 선수들의 주의를 기울이게 하는 것은 당신의 의무가 아니지만, 당신은 경기 심판에게 말해줄 수 있다.

17. HAND-OUT: ICE PLAYER ASSISTANT (IPA)

- Change shoes after arriving at the arena; wear clean shoes for on-ice duties (curling shoes or gym shoes)
- Dress warmly in clothes that allow free movement; wear gloves
- Have a micro-fibre cloth to clean stones
- Before the game but after the practice introduce yourself to the teams – check what order they will throw the stones. Do they have a left-handed player?
- Record throwing order on stone order card

Duties of the IPA: Delivering End

- Line up the stones in two neat rows in the correct playing order for each team.
- Team delivering first - place their stones closest to the centre at the side of the sheet.
- Clean the stone at the side of the sheet, making sure not to bruise the ice with the striking edge of the stone. Use your foot to brace the stone when turning it over.
- Clean the stone with a micro-fibre cloth unless directed otherwise by a team.
- Slide the stone to the area from which the player will deliver and place it near the front of the player's front wheel. If you have picked up some debris after the stone is cleaned take it back to side and re-clean it.
- Move back to the side of the sheet behind the player, making sure you are quiet and still when he/she is getting ready to deliver.
- In placing a stone for a left-handed delivery, ask where they want their stone placed, i.e. beside the wheelchair, or in front of the wheelchair.
- Move to the playing end after the last stone is delivered, and help to sort stones at the completion of the end. Follow the first delivered stone back to your assigned end.

If a team delivers from in front of the house:

Stones are lined up from the tee line forward, with all handles pointing straight up the ice. The last stone to be delivered in the end is touching the tee line, with all other stones in order of delivery.

If a team delivers from inside the house:

Stones are lined up from the back line forward, with all handles pointing straight up the ice. The last stone to be delivered is touching the back line, with all other stones in order of delivery.

Duties of the IPA: - Playing End

- Help players remove hogged stones from play when asked.
- Catch any stones that cross the backline and assist with stones out of play to clear the backline when asked by the delivering team.
- Organise stones in corner- two neat parallel lines with handles pointing straight up the ice.
- Only after the score is decided and the go ahead is given to clear the house can the stones be moved from the back to the delivery position.

17. 유인물: 빙상 선수 보조자(빙상 선수 보조자)

- 기장에 도착 후 신발을 갈아 신는다; 얼음 위에서의 책임을 위해 깨끗한 신발을 신어야 한다. (컬링 신발 또는 체육관 신발)
- 자유롭게 움직이는 것이 가능하고 따뜻하게 옷을 입는다. 장갑을 낀다.
- 스톤을 닦기 위한 미세 섬유 직물을 지닌다.
- 경기 전, 연습 후에 당신을 팀에게 소개한다. - 그들이 어떤 순서로 스톤을 던질지, 왼손잡이 선수가 있는지를 파악한다.
- 스톤 순서 카드에 던지는 순서를 기록한다.

빙상 선수 보조자가 해야 할 일: 딜리버리 엔드

- 스톤을 각각 팀에 정확한 경기 순서에 맞게 두 줄로 깔끔하게 정렬한다.
- 팀 딜리버링 첫 번째 - 그들의 스톤을 시트 측면의 중앙에 가깝게 둔다.
- 시트의 가장자리에서 스톤을 깨끗이 하고, 스톤 엣지로 얼음이 훼손되지 않게 한다.
- 팀에서 다른 방법을 지시하지 않는 한, 스톤을 미세 섬유 직물로 닦는다.
- 스톤을 선수들이 딜리버리할 부분에 미끄러트리고 선수 앞바퀴의 앞부분 근처에 위치시킨다. 만약 당신이 스톤을 닦은 후에 부스러기를 주웠다면 이것을 다시 가장자리로 가지고 가서 다시 청소를 한다.
- 선수 뒤쪽인 시트의 가장자리 부분으로 이동해서, 선수들이 딜리버리 준비를 할 때 조용하고 가만히 있도록 한다.
- 왼손잡이 선수의 딜리버리를 위해 스톤을 위치시킬 때, 그들의 스톤이 어디에 위치되기를 원하는지(ex. 휠체어의 옆 또는 휠체어의 앞) 물어본다.
- 마지막 스톤이 딜리버리된 후 플레잉 엔드로 이동하고, 엔드의 마지막에 스톤을 추려내는 것을 도와준다. 처음 딜리버리된 스톤을 당신이 배정된 엔드로 옮긴다.

만약 팀이 하우스의 앞에서 딜리버리를 한다면:

스톤은 모든 핸들이 빙상 바로 위를 향하도록 하여 백 라인 앞쪽에 정렬되어 있다. 엔드에서 가장 마지막으로 딜리버리되어야 할 스톤과 딜리버리 순서에 따른 다른 스톤들이 백 라인에 닿아 있다.

만약 팀이 하우스 안에서 딜리버리를 한다면:

스톤은 모든 핸들이 빙상 바로 위를 향하도록 하여 백 라인 앞쪽에 정렬되어 있다. 엔드에서 가장 마지막으로 딜리버리되어야 할 스톤과 딜리버리 순서에 따른 다른 스톤들은 백 라인에 닿아 있다.

빙상 선수 보조자가 해야 할 일 - 플레잉 엔드

- 선수들이 요청한다면 경기에서의 양 끝에 처진 스톤들을 치우는 것을 도와준다.
- 백 라인을 통과하는 스톤은 모두 잡아야 하며, 딜리버리하는 팀에서의 요청이 있을 시 인플레이 중이 아닌 스톤이 백 라인이 통과하게 하는 것을 도와준다.
- 스톤들을 모퉁이에 정리한다. - 핸들이 얼음 바로 위를 향하게 하여 두 줄의 깔끔한 평행선으로 정렬시킨다.
- 점수가 정해졌거나 하우스를 정리하라는 지시가 주어졌을 때에만, 스톤은 딜리버리 위치 뒤로부터 움직여질 수 있다.

Timing: 8 end games, game time 68 minutes per team, extra end 10 minutes per team.

Pre-game practice is 10 min. for each team followed by 1 min. for their team's Last Stone Draw (LSD - to determine last stone in the first end). Sometimes it will be necessary to change the position of Yellow and Red to match the team delivering the first stone of the game.

The last stone advantage is decided after the 2nd practice by comparing the LSD measures.

Each team has a one-minute time-out during the game and one additional time-out in each extra end. The team makes this call with a "T" hand signal to the Game Umpire. IPAs can help to get the attention of the Game Umpire. The clock will be stopped for the travel time of the coach to the team. During the time-out the team clock continues to run. The Umpire will control the time-out, which starts when the coach reaches the team.

IPAs must have the first stone of the game ready when the official announces the games may begin. The game clocks are started when the delivering team's stone reaches the hog line.

Break between ends - 1 minute. The break will start when the end is completed and the score has been decided and the teams clear the stones from the house.

With 2 IPAs on each sheet: at the completion of an end both work together to move the stones to the delivery order in preparation for the next end. One IPA returns to the playing end to remove stones and assist the players.

The most important job is to make sure the **1st stone of each end is ready for the team, and they are not waiting for you to clean and place the stone.** The team who scored in the last end delivers the first stone in the next end. You can continue to sort stones after placing the first stone, but make sure after the start of play you do not distract the delivering player. Line up the stones so that the team that is delivering the 1st stone of the end has its stones closest to the centre line. The team delivering last stone of the end has its stones closest to the sideboard (delivery order cards match the line-up colour order).

Mid-game break – after 5 min. the delivering team's clock will start.
IPAs must have the first stone in the delivery position after the ice has been cleaned and prior to the end of the 5 min. break.

IPAs have an opportunity for a short break after the 4th end, but must watch the clock so they will be in position when the team is ready to deliver.

End of an end – it is the teams' responsibility to remove the stones in the house area, but the IPAs will assist. When clearing stones from the house they should be moved to the side just in front of the tee-line.

If teams leave the house area without helping the IPAs, the IPAs should start by placing the stones from the back out of play area to the delivery position, and stones can be left in the house until teams assist the IPA.

Make sure the 1st stone of the end is cleaned, ready and in position even if stones are still in the house waiting for removal. When the break time expires the delivering team's clock will start.

DO NOT MOVE ANY STONES IN THE HOUSE IF A MEASURE HAS BEEN REQUESTED!

타이밍: 8엔드의 경기, 경기 시간은 각 팀 간 68분, 추가 엔드는 각 팀당 10분

사전 연습 경기는 10분이고 뒤이어 각 팀의 마지막 스톤 드로우(LSD-첫 엔드에서 마지막 스톤을 결정하는 것)는 각 팀당 1분이다. 때때로 노란색 스톤과 빨간색 스톤의 위치를 바꾸는 것은 경기에서 팀의 첫 번째로 딜리버리할 스톤을 일치시키기 위해 필수적일 것이다.

마지막 스톤 어드벤티지는 두 번째 연습 경기가 끝난 뒤 LSD의 측정 결과로 결정한다.

각 팀은 경기 중에 1분의 타임아웃이 있고 추가로 각 추가 엔드에서 타임아웃이 있다. 팀은 이 콜을 'T' 모양의 손 신호로 경기 심판에게 만들어 보낸다. 빙상 선수 보조자들은 경기 심판의 주의를 끌도록 도와줄 수 있다. 코치가 팀에게 가 있는 동안 시계는 멈추어 있는다. 타임아웃 동안에 팀 시계는 계속해서 간다. 심판이 타임아웃을 관리하며, 이 타임아웃은 코치가 팀에세 다가가는 순간 시작된다.

빙상 선수 보조자들은 공식적으로 경기가 시작된다는 방송이 있은 다음, 즉 후 경기의 첫 번째 스톤을 가지고 있다가, 딜리버리 팀의 스톤이 호그 라인에 도달하면 경기 시계가 작동하기 시작한다.

엔드 사이의 휴식 - 1분. 엔드가 끝나고 점수가 결정되고 팀이 하우스에서 스톤을 정리한 뒤 휴식이 시작된다.

각 시트에 두 명의 빙상 선수 보조자와 함께: 엔드가 끝난 뒤 두 사람은 다음 엔드 준비를 위한 스톤을 딜리버리 오더로 움직이기 위해 함께 움직인다. 한 명의 빙상 선수 보조자는 스톤을 치우고 선수들을 돕기 위해 플레잉 엔드로 돌아온다.

각 엔드 팀의 첫 번째 스톤이 준비되도록 하는 것이 가장 중요한 임무이며, 그들은 당신들이 스톤을 정리하고 위치시키는 것을 기다려 주지 않는다. 마지막 엔드에서 점수를 낸 팀이 다음 엔드에서 첫 번째 스톤을 딜리버리한다. 당신은 첫 번째 스톤을 위치시킨 후 스톤을 추려내는 것을 계속해서 할 수 있지만, 경기가 시작된 후 당신이 딜리버리하는 선수를 방해하지 않도록 주의한다. 엔드에서의 첫 번째 스톤을 딜리버리하는 팀의 스톤이 중앙선과 가장 가깝도록 스톤을 정렬한다. 엔드의 마지막 스톤을 딜리버리하는 팀은 사이드 보드에 가장 가깝도록 스톤을 둔다. (딜리버리 순서 카드는 정렬 색깔 순서와 일치한다)

중간 경기 휴식 - 5분 후, 딜리버리하는 팀의 시계가 작동될 것이다.

빙상 선수 보조자들은 얼음이 정빙이 되고 5분 휴식 시간이 끝나기 전에 첫 번째 스톤을 딜리버리 위치에 두어야 한다.

빙상 선수 보조자들은 4번째 엔드 후에 휴식을 가질 기회가 있지만 팀이 딜리버리 할 준비가 되어 있도록 시계를 확인해야만 한다.

엔드의 끝 - 하우스 영역에서 스톤을 치우는 것은 팀의 의무이지만 빙상 선수 보조자들이 도와줄 것이다. 하우스로부터 스톤을 치울 때 그 스톤들은 티 라인의 바로 앞인 측면으로 옮겨져야 한다.

만약 선수들이 빙상 선수 보조자들을 도와주지 않은 채 하우스를 떠난다면, 빙상 선수 보조자들은 스톤을 뒤의 인플레이 중이 아닌 스톤 영역에서 딜리버리 위치로 옮기게 되면, 스톤들은 팀이 빙상 선수 보조자를 도와줄 때까지 하우스 안에 남아있게 된다.

엔드의 첫 번째 스톤이 정리되었는지, 만약 스톤들이 옮겨지기 위해 하우스 안에 아직 기다리고 있더라도 준비시키고 제 위치에 놓였는지 확인한다. 휴식 시간이 끝나면 딜리버리하는 팀의 시계는 작동될 것이다.

측정이 요구되었다면 하우스에서 어느 스톤들도 이동시키지 않는다.

Out-of-play stones are placed in two neat parallel rows, handles pointing straight up the ice.

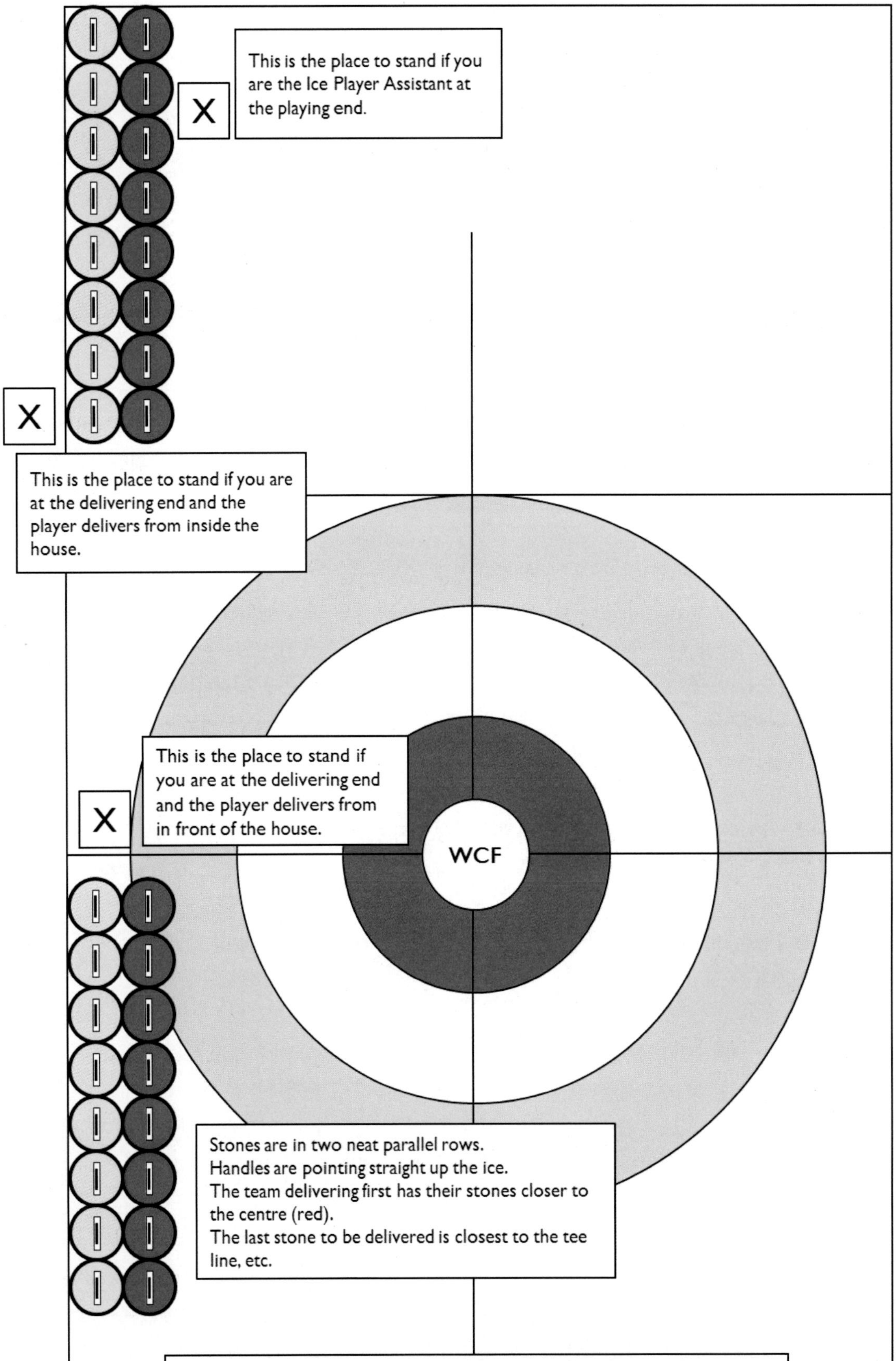
X
This is the place to stand if you are the Ice Player Assistant at the playing end.
X
This is the place to stand if you are at the delivering end and the player delivers from inside the house.
X
This is the place to stand if you are at the delivering end and the player delivers from in front of the house.
WCF
Stones are in two neat parallel rows.
Handles are pointing straight up the ice.
The team delivering first has their stones closer to the centre (red).
The last stone to be delivered is closest to the tee line, etc.

Ice Player Assistant and stone delivery order set up

인플레이 중이 아닌 스톤들은 깔끔하게 두 줄로 정렬되고, 핸들은 얼음 바로 위를 향해 놓여진다.

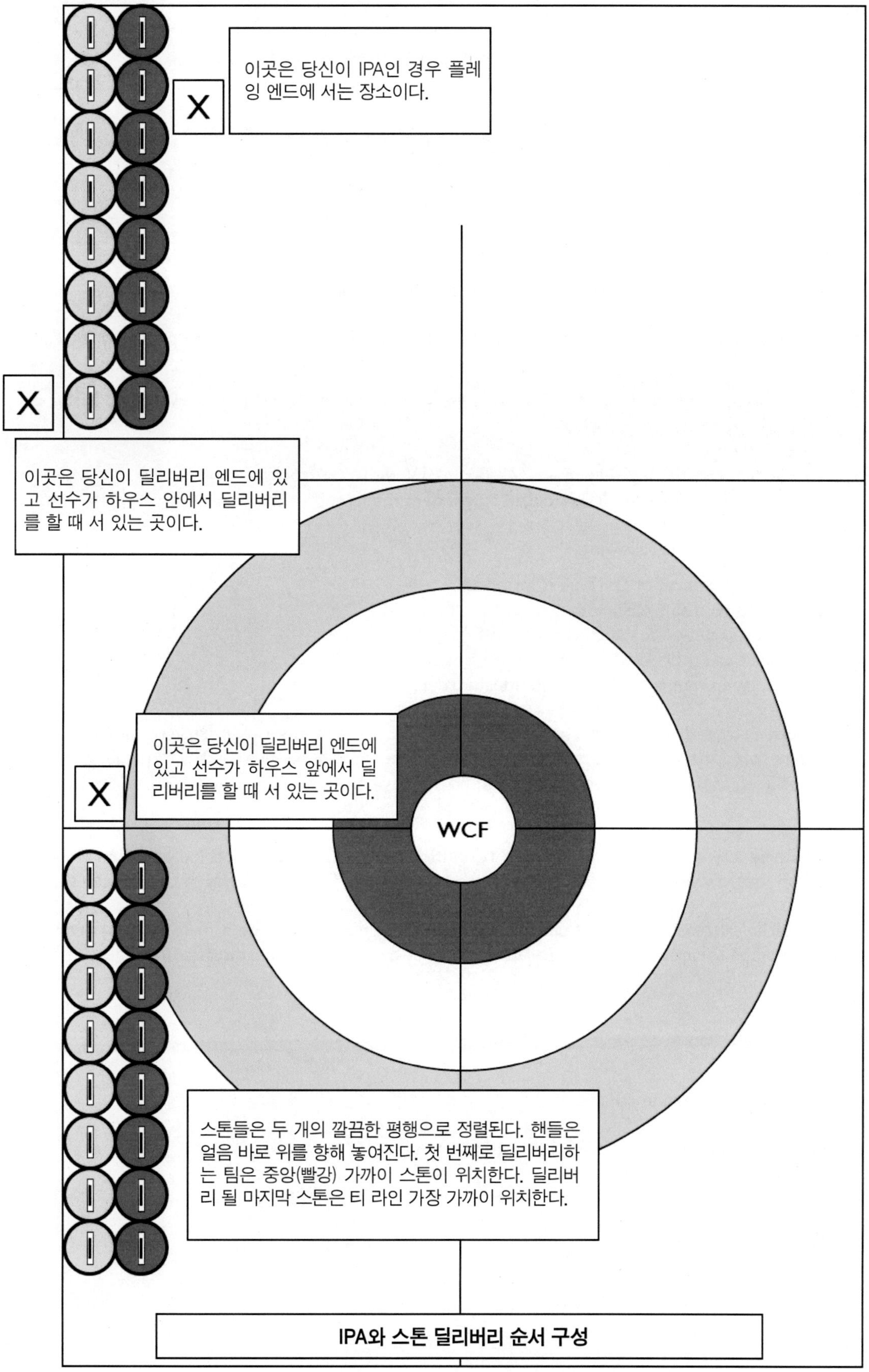

X
이곳은 당신이 IPA인 경우 플레잉 엔드에 서는 장소이다.
X
이곳은 당신이 딜리버리 엔드에 있고 선수가 하우스 안에서 딜리버리를 할 때 서 있는 곳이다.
X
이곳은 당신이 딜리버리 엔드에 있고 선수가 하우스 앞에서 딜리버리를 할 때 서 있는 곳이다.
WCF
스톤들은 두 개의 깔끔한 평행으로 정렬된다. 핸들은 얼음 바로 위를 향해 놓여진다. 첫 번째로 딜리버리하는 팀은 중앙(빨강) 가까이 스톤이 위치한다. 딜리버리 될 마지막 스톤은 티 라인 가장 가까이 위치한다.

IPA와 스톤 딜리버리 순서 구성

18. CHIEF TIMER

RESPONSIBILITIES

In an event where a Chief Timer (CT) is appointed, the CT is answerable to the Chief Umpire (CU) and takes instructions from the CU and the Game Umpires (GU's). The CT shall follow the Official's Code of Conduct.

The CT is responsible for ensuring all equipment for game timing is in place, and that a rota of volunteer timers, appointed by the Organising Committee (OC) will time all games correctly.

EQUIPMENT

The CT should be familiar with all aspects of the operation of the equipment being used.

If the *CurlTime* computer based program is being used, the following equipment should be provided for each sheet of ice:

- 1 x **Laptop** computer – with 2Gb RAM, running Windows XP (SP3), Windows Vista, or Windows 7; with a VGA socket
- 1 x USB Mouse
- 1 x Flat Screen **Display** (Minimum 32" -80cm) TV with VGA socket
- 1 x High Quality Shielded **VGA cable** to connect the laptop to the display (max length 40m)

Laptop Check each laptop for the following:

- Most recent version of *CurlTime* is installed
- Connected to mains electricity
- Any wireless network switch is set to 'off'
- The touch-pad is disabled and the mouse is working
- The display output is set for an additional screen.

If the laptop has been provided by the OC (rather than the WCF), then any other background operation which could interfere with the uninterrupted running of *CurlTime* should be switched off, including: auto-update pop-ups, scheduled virus scans, screen savers and power-saving. An extra laptop should be available as a spare.

Display This should be a wide screen display with a resolution of at least 1024 x 768 for optimum viewing. The display should be securely sited where players, coaches and Umpires from both ends of the ice, can see it.

VGA Cable For technical reasons, this should not exceed 40m. There should be a male (all pin) fitting at either end, and it should be securely fitted to both laptop and display. It must be best quality shielded.

LAYOUT

In the diagram below, the ideal layout is ***Position 1***.

The following cables would be required: 2 x 25m; 2 x 20m; 1 x 6m

If ***Position 2*** has to be used, then the cables required would be: 2 x 40m; 3 x 30m

18. 시간 계측 담당자

의무들

시간 계측 담당자가 지정된 경기에서, 시간 계측 담당자는 주심에게 책임이 있고 주심과 경기 심판에게 지시 사항을 듣는다. 시간 계측 담당심판은 행동의 공식적인 코드를 따라야 한다.

시간 계측 담당심판은 경기 타이밍의 모든 장비가 제자리에 있는지 확인을 할 책임이 있으며, 타이머 지원자 당번은 조직 위원에 의해 지정되어 모든 경기의 시간을 정확히 재게 될 것이다.

장비

시간 계측 담당심판은 경기에 사용되는 장비 작동의 모든 양상과 익숙해야 한다.

만약 Curltime 컴퓨터에 기초한 프로그램이 사용된다면, 다음 장비는 각각의 아이스 시트에 공급되어야 한다:

- 1 X노트북 컴퓨터: 2GB RAM, 작동되는 Windows XP(SP3), Windows Vista 혹은 Windows7; VGA 소켓과 함께
- 1 X USB마우스
- 1 X 평면 화면 디스플레이(최소 32"-80츠) TV와 VGA 소켓
- 1 X 노트북 전시를 위해 선택하기 위한 고품질로 보호된 VGA 유선(최대 40㎝)

노트북에서 다음 사항들을 확인해야 한다:

- 가장 최근 버전의 Curltime이 설치되어 있는지
- 주요 전기에 연결되었는지
- 다른 무선 네트워크가 'off' 되어 있는지
- 터치패드가 쓸 수 없게 되어있고 마우스가 작동하는지
- 디스플레이 결과가 추가 화면에 설정되어 있는지

만약 노트북이 조직위원회(세계컬링연맹보다는)에 의해서 공급받게 된다면, Curltime 작동에 방해될 수 있는 바탕의 다른 프로그램 작동은 꺼져있어야 하며 다음도 역시 꺼져있어야 한다: 자동 갱신 팝업, 일정이 잡힌 바이러스 조사, 스크린 세이버 그리고 파워 세이빙. 추가의 노트북은 여분으로 사용 가능할 수 있다.

디스플레이(화면)는 최소 1024×768의 최적의 해상도로 된 넓은 스크린이어야 한다. 디스플레이는 얼음의 양쪽 엔드의 선수들, 코치들 그리고 심판들이 볼 수 있도록 확실하게 설치되어야 한다.

VGA케이블은 유선 기술적인 이유로, 40m를 넘어서는 안 된다. 거기에는 양쪽 엔드 끝에 핀이 있어야 하고 이것은 양쪽 노트북과 디스플레이에 확실하게 들어맞아야 한다. 이것은 가장 좋은 품질로 감싸져 있어야 한다.

배치

밑의 그림에서, 가장 이상적인 배치는 Positon 1이다.

다음의 유선의 필요 사항은: 2×25m; 2×20m; 1×6m이다.

만약 Position2가 사용된다면 필요한 유선의 길이는: 2×40m; 3×30m이다.

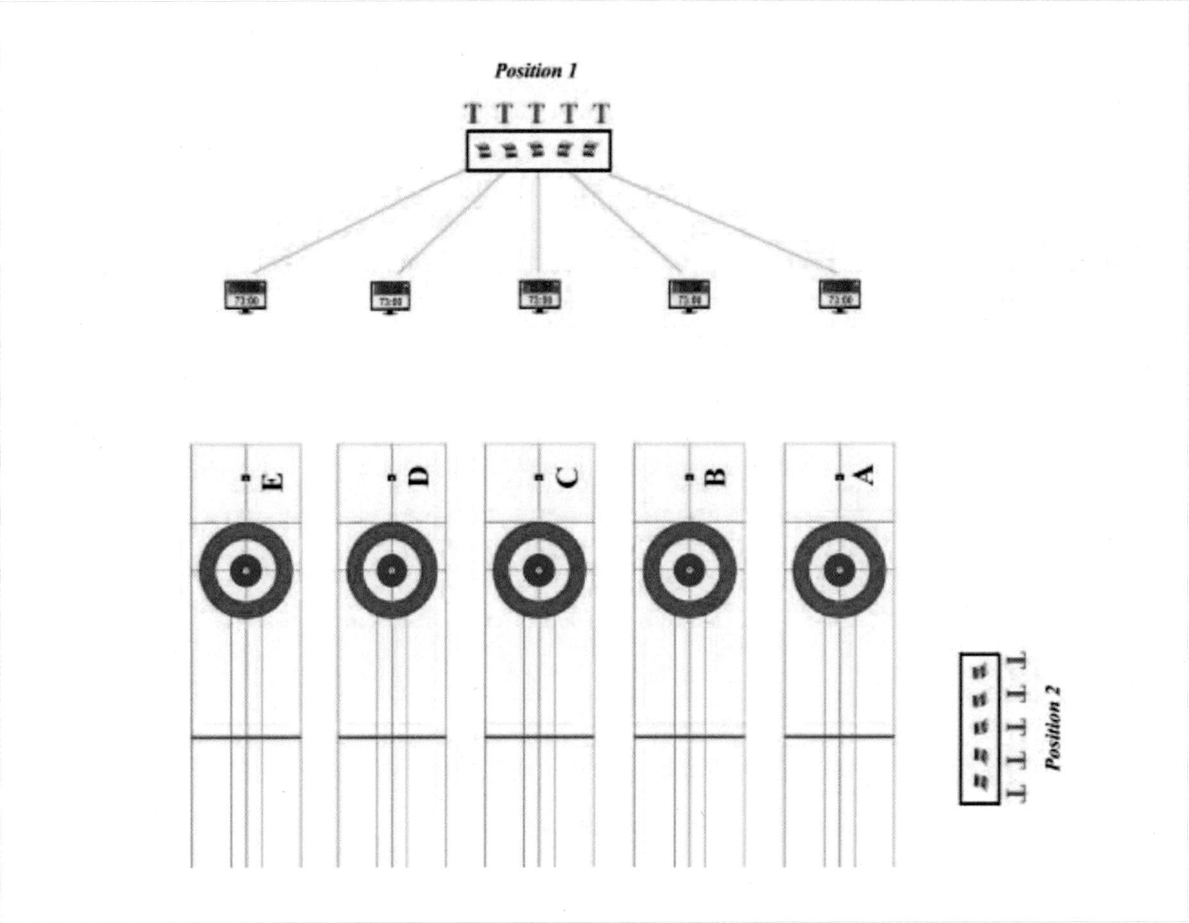

Where a CT is used, only the CT will have a radio, so all timers should sit together.

Each timing station should be labelled 'A', 'B', 'C', 'D' to correspond with the sheets being timed.

The area round the timing bench should be checked for safety hazards, especially if the bench is situated on a temporary structure.

The CT should ensure each timer is provided with a chair, clipboard, pencil and stopwatch. The CT should have two stopwatches, a notebook and pencil.

There should be easy access to rubbish disposal, toilet and hot-drink facilities, and changing facilities should be available.

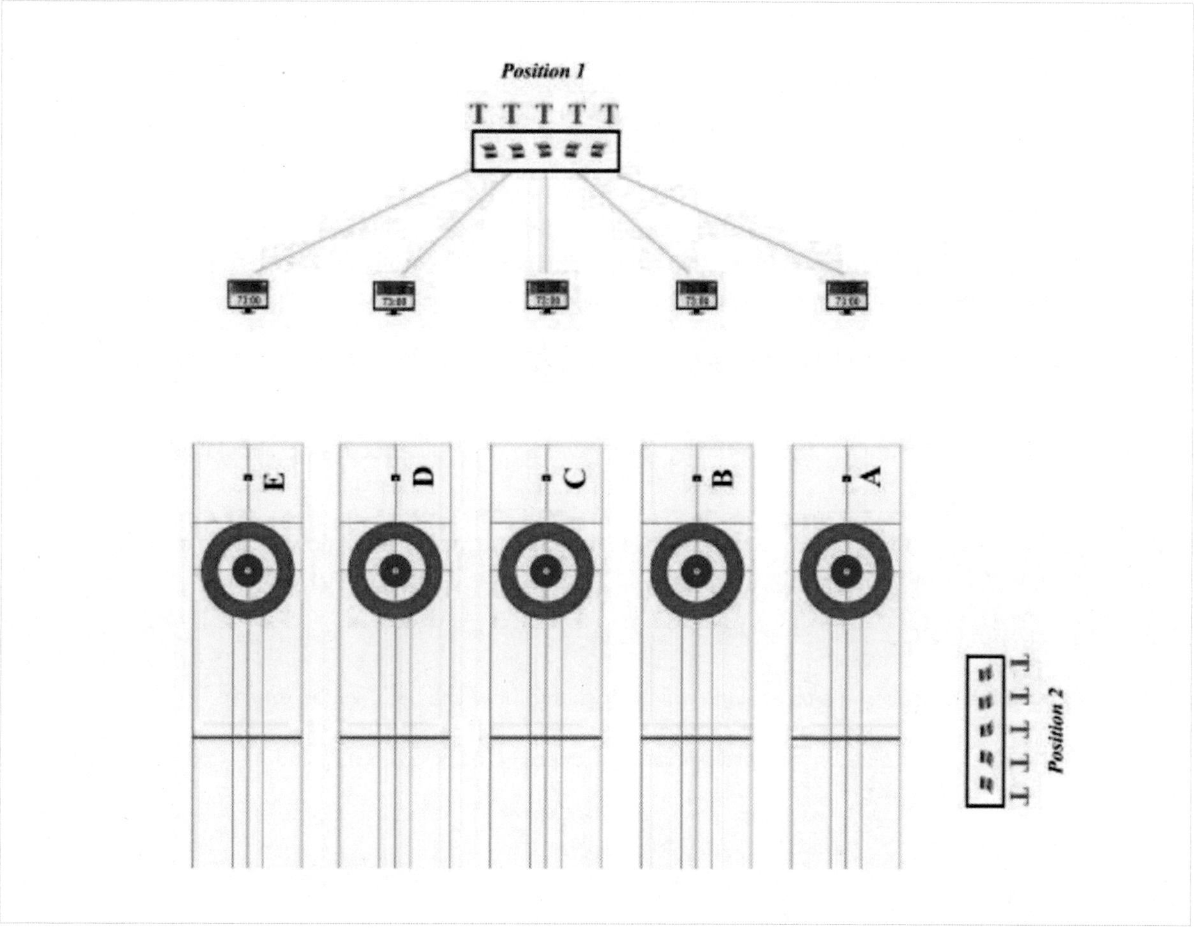

시간 계측 담당심판이 사용되는 곳에 모든 타이머들이 함께 있을 수 있도록 오직 시간 계측 담당심판만 라디오를 갖게 될 것이다.

각각의 시간 계측 위치는 시간이 계측되고 있는 시트와 일치하게 'A', 'B', 'C', 'D' 로 표시될 것이다.

타이밍 벤치 주변의 영역은 안전 위험을 대비해 살펴져야 하는데, 특히 벤치가 간이구조물에 위치해 있는 경우 그렇다.

시간 계측 담당심판은 각각의 타이머가 의자, 클립보드, 연필 그리고 스톱워치와 함께 공급되어 있는지 확인해야 한다. 시간 계측 담당심판은 두 개의 스톱워치, 공책 그리고 연필을 갖고 있어야 한다.

쓰레기통, 화장실 그리고 따뜻한 음료를 마실 수 있는 곳과 가까워야 하며 탈의실이 이용 가능해야 한다.

PRE-COMPETITION

The installation and running of all timing equipment should be checked.

A pre-competition meeting should be arranged with the volunteer timers, and a note of their experience made during introductions. The rules and principles of timing should be reviewed, and an opportunity given for practice with the equipment.

The CT will make up a rota of timers from the draw. This can be done as Team A and Team B. There should be a spare timer on standby for each draw. Volunteers are assigned to Team A or Team B.

If no deputy CT has been appointed to the event, then a suitably experienced volunteer timer may be allocated to this task.

The CT should establish from the CU if game-timing forms will be available, but if not, should be ready to prepare them.

Timers should be reminded of their dress code and code of behaviour, and must know whom to contact if they are unable to appear for duty.

The CT should check with the CU on:

- How the pre-game practices are to be run (which clock and how the LSD will be timed)
- If the CT is to be responsible for the pre-game radio check (Check CU, GU's and Ice Crew – usually after the start of 2nd practice)

BEFORE THE GAME

The CT should arrive 1 hour before the game to switch on the equipment and check the *CurlTime* parameters for the event.

The timers should report 40 minutes before the game starts. Any absences with 35 minutes to start should be reported to the CU and the OC.

Supervise the timing of the pre-game practices – begins 30mins before the start.

Carry out a radio check (if required).

Check all timers have the correct game forms and compare with scoreboards.

DURING THE GAME

After the LSD, check all timers know who has the last stone in the first end and which colour starts.

Check all clocks are started properly.

Supervise all timers using spot-checks and anticipating any problems.

Ensure clocks are run correctly during any on-ice violations.

Ensure times are recorded after each end and that breaks are run properly.

사전대회

모든 타이밍 장비들의 설치와 작동은 점검되어야 한다.

사전대회의 미팅이 타이머 지원자와 소개 동안 생긴 그들의 경험 노트와 함께 이루어져야 한다.

시간 계측 담당심판은 경기로부터 시간 계측자의 당번표를 만들 것이다. 이것은 Team A와 Team B와 같이 지정될 수 있다. 모든 경기에는 대기하고 있는 여분의 타이머가 있어야 한다. 지원자들은 Team A나 Team B로 지정될 것이다.

만약 시간 계측 부심이 당일에 지정되어 있지 않았다면, 이 자리에 경험이 많은 지원자가 시간 계측자로 대신 배정될 수 있다.

시간 계측 담당심판은 만약 경기 타이밍 형태가 가능하다면 주심으로부터 제정되어야 하지만 그렇지 않다면 그것이 준비되어 있어야 한다.

타이머들은 자신들의 복장과 행동 수칙에 대해 숙지하고 있어야 하며, 당일 날 나타날 수 없다면 누구에게 연락을 취해야 하는지 알고 있어야 한다.

시간 계측 담당심판은 주심과 다음 사항을 확인해야 한다.

- 어떻게 사전 경기가 진행될 것인지(어떤 시계가 사용되는지, 어떻게 LSD가 측정될 것인지)
- 만약 사전 경기의 시간 계측 담당심판이 라디오에 책임이 있는 자라면 다음 사항을 체크해야 한다. (주심 체크, 경기 심판과 빙판 직원들 - 보통 두 번째 연습이 시작된 후)

경기 시작 전

시간 계측 담당심판은 장비를 바꾸고 Curltime 매개변수를 체크하기 위해서 경기 1시간 전에 도착해야 한다.

타이머는 경기 시작 40분 전에 보고해야 한다. 경기 시작 전 35분에 어떠한 결원이 있다면 주심과 운영 위원회에게 보고되어야 한다.

사전 경기 연습에서의 타이밍을 감시한다. - 경기 시작 30분 전에 시작한다.

필요한 경우에만 라디오를 점검한다.

모든 타이머들이 알맞은 경기 형태에 있는지 확인하고 점수판과 비교해야 한다.

경기 중

LSD 이후, 누가 첫 엔드의 후공을 가져갔는지와 스톤의 색깔을 확인한다.

모든 타이머들이 제대로 시작했는지 확인한다.

스팟 체크(무작위 검사)를 사용하고, 발생 가능한 문제들을 예측하는 모든 타이머들을 감독한다.

빙상 위에서의 위반 항목 중, 시계들이 제대로 가고 있는지 여부를 확실히 확인해야 한다.

각 엔드 후에 시간이 기록되었는지, 휴식이 제대로 진행되는지 확실히 해야 한다.

경기 심판이 주의할 수 있도록 중간 경기 끝나기 1분 10초 전에 타이머들이 알릴 수 있도록 해야 한다.

팀의 순서들과 기술적인 타임아웃이 제대로 작동되는지 확실히 하고, 모든 타임아웃은 기록되어야 한다.

어떠한 타이밍 오류나 오작동이 있으면 즉각적으로 경기 심판에게 알려야 한다.

시계에 어떠한 수정사항이 있는지 잘 살피고 기록해야 한다.

Ensure timers advise the CT 1min 10 sec. to end of mid-game break so that GU can be warned.

Ensure the procedures for team and technical time-outs are followed correctly, and that all time-outs are recorded.

Promptly advise the GU of any timing errors or malfunctions.

Supervise and record any adjustment of clocks.

Advise the CU when a team is running short of time – e.g. when at start of last end they have only 5 minutes left on their clock.

Advise CU when a team has 2 minutes left on their clock.

Supervise the creation of an Extra End and Break if required.

Collect and hand in completed timing forms.

AFTER THE GAME

Meet with the CU and GU's to deal with any timing issues.

Reset *CurlTime* for the next game, or close down and secure all equipment at the end of the day.

By the end of the round robin games, the Chief Timer should have prepared a rota of the timers required for any tie-breaker games, the play-off games, and the final.

팀의 시간이 부족한 경우 주심에게 알려야 한다. - ex. 그들의 시계상 마지막 엔드의 시작에서 시간이 5분밖에 남지 않은 경우

팀이 그의 시계상 시간이 2분밖에 남지 않은 경우 주심에게 알려야 한다.

필요한 경우 추가 엔드와 휴식이 생겼는지 잘 살펴보아야 한다.

작성된 시간 계측표를 수거하고 제출한다.

경기 후

시간 계측 문제를 다루기 위해 주심과 경기 심판과 함께 만남의 자리를 가진다.

다음 경기를 위해 Curltime을 리셋하거나, 마지막 날 모든 장비를 안전하게 하기 위해 잠궈 놓는다.

라운드 로빈 경기의 끝 무렵, 시간 계측 담당자는 타이 브레이커 경기, 플레이오프 경기 그리고 결승 경기에 필요한 타이머 순번을 준비해놓아야 한다.

19. CurlTime INSTRUCTIONS

Opening Screen

Game Pre-sets

There are four game pre-sets that will apply default WCF game settings for the type of game indicated. An option screen will appear containing all of the options outlined below. This is to allow any variation of the options from the defaults. When the options are satisfactory, click ***Save***. These settings are now saved to your computer, and for all subsequent games simply selecting ***Click to Continue*** will set the game with all of the options chosen.
Choosing the ***Default Settings*** button on this screen will reset everything back to WCF default settings, including changing the stone colours back to yellow and red.

Set Up Options

Set Time
Click on this menu selection to set the playing time. Set the time interval by clicking the up/down arrows on the side or by typing in the number of minutes to be played by each team.

Time-outs
Select the length of time-outs here. The default length is one minute. Change the number of time-outs by clicking on the time-out box located in the upper right hand corner of the main time clock screen.

Allow Travel Time for Coach
Check this box if you wish to allow travel time for coaches. The time-out clock will not start until the timer presses the ***Start*** button.

Don't Start Game Clock during Time-out
Check this box if you do not want the main game clock to count down while the time- out clock is running.

Warm up (Pre-game Practice)
Select the time the teams will get for their pre-game practice. Range is from one to 15 minutes.

Between Ends
Select the amount of time teams have between ends before game clocks are activated again. Select 1, 2 or 3 minutes **OR** 30, 60 or 90 seconds.

Mid-Game Break
Select the amount of time teams have at the completion of the end that defines the halfway point in a game. Range is 0 to 10 minutes.

Extra End
Select the amount of time teams have for an Extra End. Range is 0 to 15 minutes.

Shot Clock
This is a feature for the timer. To ensure that there is an accurate assessment of the length of time a team has taken to make a decision on what shot to play, a very small shot clock will appear in the lower right corner of the team's game clock. Timers may note any excessive length of time taken to make a decision. If you do not wish to have this displayed, simply unchecking the box will turn it off.

19. CurlTime 지시사항들

스크린 열기

경기 우선 설정
표시된 종류의 경기를 위한 세계컬링연맹 경기 설정 기본을 적용할 우선 설정은 네 경기가 있다. 선택사항 스크린이 아래 윤곽을 나타낸 선택사항들을 포함한 채 나타나게 될 것이다. 이것은 기본에서 선택사항의 변화를 가능하게 할 것이다. 선택사항이 만족스럽다면 저장을 누른다. 이러한 설정은 이제 당신의 컴퓨터에 저장이 되고, 계속 클릭함으로써 선택되는 이후의 모든 경기들은 선택된 사항들로 설정될 것이다. 화면에서 기본 설정 단추를 누르면 화면은 스톤 색깔을 노란색과 빨간색으로 바꾸는 것을 포함하여 세계컬링연맹 기본 설정으로 모든 것이 돌아가게 된다.

설정 옵션

설정 시간
경기 시간을 설정하기 위해 이 메뉴를 선택한다. 측면의 아래/위 화살표를 선택하거나 각 팀에 몇 분씩 경기를 할 것인지 숫자를 입력함으로써 시간 간격을 설정할 수 있다.

타임아웃
여기에서 타임아웃의 시간을 선택한다. 기본 시간은 1분이다. 화면에서 메인 시계의 오른쪽 모퉁이에 있는 타임아웃 박스를 선택하여 타임아웃의 숫자를 바꿀 수 있다.

코치에게 허락된 이동 시간
당신이 코치가 떠나있는 시간을 허용하기 위해 이 박스를 선택한다.
타임아웃 중에는 경기 시작 시계를 시작하지 않는다.
주 경기의 시계가 타임아웃 시계가 가는 동안 가지 않기를 원한다면 이 박스를 선택한다.

몸풀기(사전 경기 연습)
팀이 그들의 사전 경기 연습에 얻을 시간을 선택한다. 범위는 1분에서 15분 사이이다.

엔드 사이
경기 시계가 다시 가기 전에 엔드 사이에 팀이 갖게 될 시간의 양을 선택한다. 1, 2분 혹은 3분을 선택하거나 30, 60초 혹은 90초를 선택한다.

경기 중간 휴식
경기에서의 중간 점수를 정의하는 엔드의 끝에 팀이 갖게 될 시간(휴식 시간)의 양을 선택한다. 범위는 0분에서 10분이다.

추가 엔드
추가 엔드에 팀이 갖게 될 시간의 양을 선택한다. 범위는 0분에서 15분이다.

투구 제한 시간 측정(shot clock)
이것은 타이머의 기능이다. 경기에서 어떤 샷의 결정을 내릴지 팀이 결정을 내린 시간이 정확한지 측정을 확실히 하기 위해서, 매우 작은 투구 제한 시간 측정 시계가 팀의 경기 시계의 우측 하단 모서리에 나타나게 된다. 타이머들은 결정을 내리기 위해 사용한 시간이 초과되는 것을 기록할 수 있다. 만약 당신이 이것이 표시되지 않기를 원한다면, 단순히 상자를 체크하지 않음으로 이것은 꺼질 것이다.

Save
All the settings will be saved to your computer. In future, merely clicking the ***Click to Continue*** button on the opening screen will retrieve these settings and bring you to the main CurlTime screen.

Default Settings
If you were making changes and decided to go back to the default settings, just click this button and everything will be set back to the defaults for the competition you had selected.

Click to Continue
By selecting this, you will proceed to the main CurlTime screen. If you have chosen one of the presets, those settings will be applied. If you just click this button, the settings saved on your computer will be applied.

Main Screen

Entering Team Names
Enter the Association/Federation (or the Skip's name) of the teams so that they will appear on the game clock. The coloured circles on the right of the names indicate the colour stone the team is delivering.

Select Stone Colours
Click this button to open a screen that allows you to change the colour of stones depending on the venue. The default is RED for team 1 and YELLOW for team 2. Coloured curling stones next to the team names will indicate the colour stone for that team. These colours may be changed and saved so that they become the default colours.

Begin Game
Select the ***Begin Game*** button to open the timing clock window.

Warm Up (Pre-game Practice)
This activates the pre-game practice clock.

Exit
Exit from the program.

Game Clock

Start Buttons
Depending on which team delivers the first stone, press either the top ***Start*** button (it will say ***Start Red*** depending on the stone colour selection) or the bottom ***Start*** button. This will begin the game clock.

Switch Clocks
When the other team takes possession of the ice, press the ***SPACEBAR*** to switch clocks.
Whichever team has possession of the ice will have all of their buttons activated while the other team's buttons will be greyed out... this is normal so as to prevent accidentally clicking on the non-delivering team's buttons.

Time-outs
This option **MUST** be selected while the game clock is still running. It will automatically pause the time.
To start the time-out, click the ***Start*** button (or press S or Alt-S).
To stop the time-out, click the ***Stop*** button (or press Alt-T).
If the time-out was called for the wrong team, clicking on ***Switch*** will set the time-out for the other team. This option is made inactive once the time-out starts (press Alt-W).
To exit time-out and start the appropriate game clock, choose ***End*** (or press Alt-N).
To exit the time-out screen and restore the game clock to the state it was in before the time- out was called, choose ***Cancel***. This is useful if a time-out was activated in error (Alt-C).

저장

모든 설정은 당신의 컴퓨터에 저장될 것이다. 미래에, 단지 오프닝 화면에 있는 계속하기 위해 선택을 선택함으로 이러한 설정들을 복구할 것이고 당신을 CurlTime의 메인 화면으로 안내할 것이다.

초기 설정

만약 당신이 변화를 기록하는 도중에 초기 설정으로 돌아가고 싶다면, 이 버튼을 누르면 모든 것이 당신이 선택했던 경쟁의 초기 상태로 돌아갈 것이다.

계속(진행)하기 위한 선택

이것을 선택함으로써, 당신은 CurlTime의 메인 화면으로 돌아갈 것이다. 만약 당신이 미리 설정 중 하나를 선택했다면 이 설정이 적용될 것이다. 만약 이 버튼을 단지 누르기만 한다면, 당신 컴퓨터에 저장한 설정들이 적용될 것이다.

메인 화면

팀 이름 입력하기

경기 시계에 나타나도록 팀의 협회/연맹(혹은 스킵의 이름)을 입력한다.

스톤 색깔 선택

이 버튼을 눌러서 개최지의 상황에 따라서 스톤의 색깔 변경을 허락하도록 하는 화면을 연다. 초기 설정은 팀1은 빨간색이고, 팀2는 노란색이다. 팀 이름 옆에 색칠된 컬링 스톤들은 그 팀의 색깔을 나타낼 것이다. 이러한 색깔들은 그것들이 초기 설정 색깔로 변할 수 있도록 변경되거나 저장될 수 있다.

게임 시작하기

게임 시작하기 버튼을 눌러 타이밍 시계 창을 연다.

몸풀기(사전 경기 연습)

이것은 사전 경기 연습 시계를 활성화시킨다.

출구

프로그램에서 나간다.

경기 시계

시작 버튼

어떤 팀이 첫 번째 스톤을 딜리버리하느냐에 따라서, 위에 있는 시작 버튼 (이것은 스톤 색깔 선택에 따라서 빨간색으로 시작하기라고 표시될 것이다) 혹은 밑의 시작 버튼을 누른다. 이것은 경기 시계를 시작되게 할 것이다.

시계 바꾸기

다른 팀이 빙상에서의 소유권을 갖는다면 시계를 바꾸기 위해 스페이스 바를 누른다.

던질 차례를 갖고 있는 팀의 버튼은 다른 팀의 버튼이 회색이 되었을 때 활성화되게 될 것이다. 이것은 딜리버리하고 있지 않는 팀의 버튼을 실수로 클릭하는 것을 예방하기 위한 통상적인 것이다.

The small clock next to the ***End*** button is there to ensure travel time is accurately measured. The Game Umpire will normally time the travel time, but he/she may wish to radio the Chief Timer to ensure that his/her stopwatch is in sync with the travel time clock.
The small box in the upper right corner of each team's game clock will indicate how many time-outs that team have remaining. Once they have 0, the time-out timer will not activate again.

In the event that you mistakenly click on the *Time-out* button, it can be added back to the available time-outs by clicking on the Time-out box located in the upper right hand corner of the main time clock.

Stopping Time
If the time needs to be stopped for any reason, just press ***Stop Clock***. To activate the time again, press on the ***Start*** button of the corresponding team.

Between Ends
This activates a one-minute timer to time between ends. The main game clocks must be paused first. If the teams begin play before the one-minute has finished, you may activate the corresponding clock from within the timer by selecting the appropriate team. If the one-minute expires before play resumes, you must then start the clock of the team who is delivering first by clicking the corresponding button, or you can select ***Autostart*** when the timer is first activated. By doing so, the team you selected for ***Autostart*** will have their clock begin automatically when time expires.
The time remaining for each team is shown on this screen. On the edges of the display there are up and down arrows. The arrows on the right will adjust the seconds and those on the left will adjust the minutes if there was an error during the game.

Mid-Game Break
This activates a 5 minute timer while both teams take their break at the halfway point of the game. It works much the same as the ***Between Ends*** timer in the sense that the game clock can be re-started from within this timer if the teams decide to resume play before the 5 minutes have expired. If the time expires before play resumes, you must then start the clock of the team who is delivering first by clicking the corresponding button, or you can select ***Autostart*** when the timer is first activated.
The time remaining for each team is shown on this screen. On the edges of the display there are up and down arrows. The arrows on the right will adjust the seconds and those on the left will adjust the minutes if there was an error during the game.

Reset
This will bring you back to the main screen where you can enter the names/associations of the new teams that will be playing on the sheet. **Do not use this unless you intend to begin timing a new game.**

Adjust Time
Although most time corrections should be done between end or mid-game breaks, this screen will allow you to type in changes during a non-standard stoppage in play such as a technical time out, or at the end of a game, or during an extra end when there is no natural break.
Occasionally it may be necessary to add or subtract seconds to a team's game clock because the clock was started too early or too late. By clicking on this button, a window will open displaying the time the team has now, but it will also allow you to type in the adjusted time. When you click the ***Adjust Time*** button, the changes will be displayed on the main game clock.
The Link button is **NOT** automatically selected. When it is selected it will automatically subtract seconds from one team as you add them to the other. If you just want to add or subtract time from one team, remove the check from the box and only one team will be affected.

Extra End
If the game requires extra ends, choose this button. It will automatically reset the game clocks to the appropriate time for your competition and reset the time-outs to one per team.

타임아웃

이 버튼은 반드시 경기 시계가 아직 가고 있을 때 선택되어야 한다. 이것은 자동적으로 시계를 멈출 것이다.

타임아웃을 시작하기 위해, 시작 버튼을 누른다(혹은 S 또는 Alt-S를 누른다).

타임아웃을 멈추기 위해, 멈춤 버튼을 누른다(혹은 Alt-T를 누른다).

타임아웃을 선언한 팀이 잘못 설정되었다면, 변경을 클릭하여 다른 팀에 타임아웃을 설정하게 할 것이다. 이 선택권은 타임아웃이 시작되면 비활성화된다(Alt-W를 누른다).

타임아웃에서 벗어나고 적절한 경기 시계를 시작하려면, 끝내기를 선택한다(혹은 Alt-N을 누른다).

타임아웃 화면에서 벗어나고 그 상태에서 경기 시계를 타임아웃이 시작되기 전의 상태로 되돌리기를 원한다면 취소를 선택한다. 이것은 만약 타임아웃이 실수로 활성화된 경우 유용하다. (Alt-C)

종료 버튼 옆의 작은 시계는 (코치)이동 시간이 정확히 재어지는지 확실히 하기 위해 존재한다. 경기 심판이 (코치)이동 시간을 기본적으로 잴 것이지만, 그는 시간 계측 담당자에게 그의 스톱워치가 (코치)이동 시간 측정 시계와 함께 측정되고 있음을 확실히 하기 위해 무선 연락을 할 수 있다. 팀의 경기 시계의 우측 상단 모서리의 작은 상자는 팀의 타임아웃이 얼마나 있는지 나타낼 것이다. 한번 그들의 타이머가 0이 되면, 타임아웃 타이머는 다시 활성화되지 않을 것이다.

당신이 실수로 타임아웃 버튼을 눌렀을 경우, 주 시간 시계의 우측 상단 모서리에 위치한 타임아웃 상자를 클릭함으로써 이용 가능한 타임아웃에 더해질 수 있다.

시간 정지

만약 어떤 이유에서건 시간이 필요하다면, 시계 정지를 클릭한다. 다시 시간을 활성화시키려면, 일치하는 팀의 시작 버튼을 누른다.

엔드 사이

이것은 엔드 사이 시간에 1분 타이머를 활성화시킨다. 주 경기 시계는 처음에 멈추어야만 한다. 만약 팀이 1분이 끝나기 전에 팀이 경기를 시작한다면, 당신은 적절한 팀을 선택하여(선공 팀을 선택하여) 일치하는 시계를 활성화할 수 있다. 만약 경기가 시작되기 전에 1분이 종료된다면, 당신은 일치하는 버튼을 눌러서 처음으로 딜리버리하는 팀의 시계를 반드시 시작하도록 하거나 타이머가 처음 활성화되었을 때 자동시작을 선택할 수 있다. 이렇게 함으로써, 자동시작을 위해 당신이 선택한 팀은 시간이 종료되었을 때 자동적으로 다시 시작될 것이다.

각 팀의 남은 시간은 이 화면에 보인다. 화면의 가장자리에 위, 아래 화살표가 있습니다. 오른쪽의 화살표는 초를 조정할 것이고, 왼쪽에 있는 화살표는 만약 경기 중에 오류가 있었을 경우 조정을 하기 위해 존재한다.

경기 중간 휴식

두 팀이 경기의 중간 점수 때 휴식을 취하고 있을 때 5분 타이머를 활성화시킨다. 휴식 시간은 경기 시계가 만약 5분이 종료되기 전 팀이 경기를 재개하기로 결정한 경우, 이 타이머 안에서 다시 시작된다는 맥락에서 중간 엔드 타이머와 같게 작용한다. 만약 경기를 재개하기 전에 시간이 만료된다면, 당신은 일치하는 버튼을 눌러 처음으로 딜리버리하고 있는 팀의 시계를 반드시 시작하거나, 당신은 타이머가 처음으로 활성화되었을 때 자동시작을 선택할 수 있다.

각 팀에 남은 시간은 이 화면에 보인다. 화면의 가장자리에 위, 아래 화살표가 있다. 오른쪽의 화살표는 초를 조정하고 왼쪽에 있는 것은 만약 경기 중간에 오류가 있다면 분을 조정하기 위해 있다.

리셋

이것은 당신을 시트에서 경기하게 될 새로운 팀의 이름/협회를 입력할 수 있는 메인 화면으로 되돌려 줄 것이다. 새로운 경기의 시간 측정 시작을 의도하지 않는 한 이것을 사용하지 말아야 한다.

Keystrokes (helps facilitate "Thinking Time")

You may also control several features using the keyboard.

Main Screen
All keys with an underlined letter are activated using a combination of the underlined letter on the button and the ALT key (i.e. ALT-B will activate the ***Begin Game*** button). This is true on all screens where you see an underlined letter on the button.

Main Clock
Not ALL buttons have an underlined letter on this screen. By having Function keys operational, the timer can activate the main functions using only ONE button press.
Q – start/stop RED clock (TOP)
Z – start/stop YELLOW clock (BOTTOM)
F1 – open Between End break
F5 – open Mid-Game Break
T – open Time-out screen

Between Ends, Mid-Game Break
Q - Start RED clock (TOP)
Z - Start YELLOW Clock (BOTTOM)
Alt-A selects ***Autostart*** for the top clock
Alt-S selects ***Autostart*** for the bottom clock
C - Cancel

Time-outs
Pressing **S or Alt-S** will start the time-out.
Alt-T will stop the time-out.
Alt-W will switch the time-out to the other team. This is only used if the timer entered the time-out for the wrong team. Once the time-out has begun, this selection is no longer active.
Alt-N will end the time-out and start the appropriate game clock.
Alt-C will cancel the time-out and reset all values on the main clock to where they were before the time-out was called.

All other screens are controlled by the ALT + [letter] combinations.

시간 조정

비록 대부분의 시간 조정은 엔드 사이 혹은 중간 경기 휴식 때 행해져야 하지만, 이 화면은 기술적인 타임아웃, 혹은 게임 끝에서 혹은 자연적인 휴식이 없을 때의 추가 엔드 중과 같은 경기에서의 기본적이지 않은 중단에서의 변화를 입력하는 것을 가능하게 한다.

때때로 팀의 경기 시계에 몇 초를 더하거나 빼는 것이 필요할 수 있는데 이것은 왜냐하면 시계가 너무 빨리 혹은 너무 늦게 시작되었기 때문이다. 이 버튼을 클릭함으로써, 현재 팀의 시간을 보여주는 창이 열릴 것이지만, 수정된 시간을 입력하는 것 또한 가능하게 할 것이다. 만약 시간 조정 버튼을 누른다면, 주 경기 시계에 변경 사항이 나타날 것이다.

링크 버튼은 자동적으로 선택되지 않는다. 선택되었다면 이것은 다른 팀에 더하는 것처럼 한 팀의 초를 자동적으로 차감할 것이다. 만약 당신이 한 팀에서 시간을 더하거나 차감하고 싶다면, 상자에서 체크를 없애면 한 팀만 영향을 줄 것이다.

추가 엔드

만약 경기가 추가 엔드가 필요하다면 이 버튼을 선택한다. 이것은 자동적으로 당신의 경기와 타임아웃 리셋을 경기 시계를 알맞은 시간으로 각 팀당 하나씩 리셋하게 할 것이다.

키 스트로크('생각하는 시간'을 용이하게 하는 데 도움을 준다)

당신은 키보드를 사용해 다양한 기능을 조정할 수 있다.

메인 화면

밑줄 처진 글자가 있는 모든 키들은 버튼의 밑줄 된 글자들과의 결합과 ALT 키(예를 들어 ALT-B는 경기 시작 버튼을 활성화할 것이다)로 활성화될 것이다.

주 시계

모든 버튼이 이 화면에서 밑줄 친 글자를 지니고 있지는 않다. 단축키를 작동하게 함으로써, 타이머는 단지 하나의 버튼을 누름으로 주요 기능을 활성화하게 할 것이다.

Q - 빨간 시계를 시작한다/멈춘다(위)
Z - 노란 시계를 시작한다/멈춘다(아래)
F1 - 엔드 중간 휴식 열기
F5 - 경기 중간 휴식 열기
T - 타임아웃 화면 열기

엔드 사이, 경기 중간 휴식

Q - 빨간 시계를 시작한다(위).
Z - 노란 시계를 시작한다(아래).
Alt-A 위의 시계를 위해 자동 시작을 선택
Alt-S 밑에 시계를 위해 자동 시작을 선택
C - 취소

타임아웃

S를 누르거나 Alt-S를 누르면 타임아웃을 시작할 것이다.

Alt-T는 타임아웃을 멈출 것이다.

Alt-W는 타임아웃을 다른 팀으로 바꿀 것이다. 이것은 타이머가 잘못된 팀에 타임아웃으로 들어갔을 경우 사용된다. 타임아웃이 시작되면, 이 선택은 더 이상 유효하지 않다.

Alt-N은 타임아웃을 끝내고 알맞은 경기 시계를 시작할 것이다.

Alt-C는 타임아웃을 취소시키고 타임아웃이 시작하기 전으로 주 시계를 되돌리도록 할 것이다.

다른 모든 화면들도 ALT+[글자]의 조합으로 조정된다.

CurlTime - Equipment Set Up

The World Curling Federation has adopted *CurlTime* as its timing programme. This chapter explains how to set up a typical system to run this software.

At international events, the Organising Committee will usually have set up the equipment.

Connecting Laptop and TV Screen
Each TV screen will require a mains power supply, and there should be a mains power supply to the timing bench, from which each laptop computer is fed. Each TV is connected to a corresponding computer by VGA cable. The 15 pin plugs at the VGA cable ends are easily damaged, so care must be taken when routing the cable between the two devices and when plugging in the VGA cables to ensure the ellipse shaped plug and socket are correctly aligned, and none of the pins become damaged.
Cabling should be laid to avoid safety issues, and to be unobtrusive.
When the TV and the laptop are connected, they can be switched on.
Check that each laptop is connected to the correct corresponding display – no crossed wires!

Setting up laptop
The laptop has to be in a mode where it sends a copy of its screen to an auxiliary screen. The commonest way of setting this up is by means of a function key on the top row of the keyboard. Look for the key with two screen icons side by side (e.g. F5). Hold down the 'Fn' key and press the appropriate function key (say F5). Each key press will cause a different mode to appear – choose the one which shows an auxiliary screen.

Setting up TV
The TV has to be in a mode in which it displays the picture coming from the laptop. This is chosen from the set-up menu of the TV – usually under the heading of 'source'. From the list under 'source' choose 'PC' or 'Computer'.

The television should now display the desktop picture of the laptop.

Two further adjustments may have to be made for the perfect picture.

If the picture is not properly centred on the TV screen, go to the set-up menu on the TV and under 'picture' choose 'auto-adjust'. This will automatically centre the picture on the TV screen.

If the picture is not the shape to properly fill the screen, then the picture resolution has to be adjusted on the laptop. Right-click on the desktop – choose Screen Resolution – then choose 1280 x 720. The picture of the desktop should now fill the TV screen properly.

컬타임(CurlTime) - 장비 설치

세계컬링연맹은 시간 계측 프로그램으로 컬타임(CurlTime)을 채택했다. 이 장은 이 소프트웨어를 실행하기 위해 전형적인 시스템을 어떻게 설치하는지 설명한다.

국제 행사에서는 조직위원회(OS)가 보통 장비를 설치할 것이다.

휴대용 컴퓨터와 TV 스크린 연결

각각의 TV 스크린은 주 전원 공급 장치를 필요로 할 것이고, 각 휴대용 컴퓨터가 있는 시간 측정 벤치에 주 전원 공급 장치가 있어야 한다. 각 TV는 상응하는 컴퓨터에 VGA 케이블로 연결된다. VGA 케이블의 끝에 있는 15개의 핀 플러그들은 쉽게 손상되므로, 두 장치들 간의 케이블을 연결할 때 타원 모양의 플러그와 소켓을 완전하게 나란히 하는 과정에서 VGA 케이블에 연결할 때 조심해야 한다. 그러면 어떤 핀들도 손상되지 않을 것이다.

케이블류는 안전 문제를 피하고 소란스럽지 않기 위해 설비되어야 한다.

TV와 휴대용 컴퓨터가 연결될 때, 그 둘을 켤 수 있다.

각각의 휴대용 컴퓨터가 올바로 상응하는 디스플레이에 연결되었는지 점검해라 - 꼬인 전선이 있어서는 안 된다!

휴대용 컴퓨터 설치

휴대용 컴퓨터는 스크린(화면)의 복사본을 보조 스크린으로 전송하는 모드여야 한다. 이것을 설치할 때 가장 흔한 방법은 키보드 맨 윗줄에 있는 기능키를 사용하는 것이다. 두 개의 스크린 아이콘이 나란히 있는 키를 찾아라(예: F5). 'Fn' 키를 누른 상태로 적절한 기능키를 눌러라(예: F5). 각 키 입력은 서로 다른 모드가 나타나게 할 것이다. - 보조 스크린에 나타난 것을 선택해라.

TV 설치

TV는 휴대용 컴퓨터로부터 전송되는 그림을 나타내는 모드여야 한다. 이 모드는 TV의 설정 메뉴에서 선택할 수 있다. - 보통 'source' 항목 밑에 있다. 'source' 밑의 목록에서 'PC' 또는 'Computer'를 선택해라.

(선택)이후에 TV는 휴대용 컴퓨터의 데스크톱 그림을 나타내야 한다.

완벽한 그림을 위해 두 번의 추가 조절이 이루어져야 할 수 있다.

만약 그림이 TV 스크린의 가운데에 제대로 있지 않으면, TV의 설정 메뉴로 가서 '그림' 밑에 있는 '자동-조절'을 선택해라. 이것이 자동으로 그림을 TV 스크린의 중심에 오도록 할 것이다.

만약 그림이 스크린에 제대로 채워지지 않은 형태라면, 이미지 해상도는 휴대용 컴퓨터에서 조절되어야 한다.

데스크톱의 오른쪽 버튼을 클릭해라 - 스크린 해상도를 선택해라 - 그다음에 1280×720를 선택해라. 이제 데스크톱의 그림은 TV 스크린을 제대로 채웠을 것이다.

CurlTime – Installation & Running

If *CurlTime* is already installed on the laptops, it should be checked that it is the latest version, and that it is not date-expired. If there is any doubt, it should be un-installed using Windows Control Panel, then re-installed with the latest version, which the Chief Timer should carry on a memory stick. While it is possible to download *CurlTime* from the WCF website, Internet access is not always available throughout all venues. Much better to come prepared! Close all other applications during the installation process.

CurlTime will run well on laptops with which have been properly set up with Windows XP SP3, Vista or Windows 7.

Problems can occur on brand new laptops and on borrowed laptops.

Newly purchased laptops will have programme software (including Windows) anxious to update itself. With a new laptop, these updates should be completed before *CurlTime* is installed.

Borrowed laptops should be fine, providing certain precautions are taken. These are mainly to avoid any programmes running in the background, which may upset *CurlTime*. The control panel of any anti-viral software should be looked at, and any scheduled scans of the computer temporarily disabled until after the competition.

Wireless or Wi-Fi capabilities should be switched off on all laptops at all times. Some laptops have a small switch marked ((i)) situated on the edge of the keyboard. This can be set to 'off' and left for the duration of the competition. On other laptops, the control is a function key marked with a similar symbol. This is used with the Fn key to toggle a temporary icon on the screen 'on' or 'off'. It may have to be reset each time the computer is re-booted.
The important thing is to have laptops isolated from any Internet access, so that no programme will attempt to look for updates and downloads whilst *CurlTime* is running.

On the Control Panel, under Power Options, set the display to dim after 5 minutes if running on battery. This is a reminder to ensure the laptop is running on mains while in use. When on mains, the display should be set to 'not switch off', and the computer set to 'never go to sleep'.

Also on the Control Panel, under Personalisation, any screen-saver should be turned off for the duration of the competition.

Finally, on all laptops the touch-pad should be disabled, and a corded USB mouse used instead. The touch-pad is usually switched off with a function key marked with an icon representing a hand touching a square. A disabled touch-pad prevents accidental activation of any of the buttons on the *CurlTime* screen.

컬타임(CurlTime) - 설치 & 작동

만약 컬타임(CurlTime)이 이미 휴대용 컴퓨터에 설치되어 있다면, 최신 버전인지, 유효기간이 지나지 않았는지 확인해야 한다. 만약 의심이 든다면, 시간 계측 담당심판이 메모리 스틱 안에 가지고 다녀야 하는 윈도우 콘트롤 패널(Windows Control Panel)을 사용하여 삭제하고 최신 버전으로 재설치를 해야 한다. 세계컬링연맹 홈페이지에서 컬타임(CurlTime)을 다운로드할 수 있다면, 모든 장소에서 인터넷 접속이 항상 가능하지 않을 수도 있으므로, 준비가 되어 오는 것이 훨씬 좋다! 설치가 진행되는 동안 다른 모든 응용프로그램을 닫아라.

컬타임(CurlTime)은 Windows XP SP3, Vista 또는 Windows 7에서 올바르게 설치된 휴대용 컴퓨터에서 잘 작동할 것이다.

새 휴대용 컴퓨터와 빌린 휴대용 컴퓨터에서 문제가 발생할 수도 있다.

최근에 구입한 휴대용 컴퓨터는 자동 업데이트되는 프로그램 소프트웨어(Windows를 포함하여)가 담겨있을 것이다. 새 휴대용 컴퓨터와 함께, 이런 업데이트들은 컬타임(CurlTime)이 설치되기 전에 끝나야 한다.

빌린 휴대용 컴퓨터는 특정 예방조치가 취해진다면 괜찮다. 예방조치는 주로 컬타임(CurlTime)에 혼란을 가져올 수 있는, 백그라운드에서 작동되는 모든 프로그램들을 피하는 것이다. 모든 항바이러스 소프트웨어의 원격 제어를 주의 깊게 봐야 하며, 대회가 끝날 때까지 모든 컴퓨터의 예정된 스캔들을 일시적으로 중지해야 한다.

모든 휴대용 컴퓨터에서 무선 또는 와이파이가 가능한 것들은 항상 꺼져있어야 한다. 몇몇 휴대용 컴퓨터들은 키보드 가장자리에 위치한 ((i))가 표시된 작은 스위치가 있다. 이것은 '끔'으로 설정될 수 있고, 대회가 계속되는 동안 남겨질 수 있다. 다른 휴대용 컴퓨터에서 컨트롤은 비슷한 상징으로 표시된 기능키이다. 이것은 스크린 '켬' 또는 '끔'의 임시 아이콘을 켰다 껐다 하기 위해서 Fn키와 함께 사용된다. 이것은 컴퓨터가 부팅을 다시 할 때마다 리셋해야 할 수 있다.
중요한 점은 휴대용 컴퓨터를 모든 인터넷 접속으로부터 차단시켜야 하는 것이다. 그러면 컬타임(CurlTime)이 작동되는 동안 어떤 프로그램도 업데이트와 다운로드를 시도하지 않을 것이다.

제어판의 전원 옵션에서, 만약 배터리를 다 써간다면 5분 뒤에 화면 밝기를 어둡게 해라. 이것은 휴대용 컴퓨터를 사용할 때 메인 화면에 작동하는 것을 보장하기 위한 것이다. 메인 화면에 있을 때, 디스플레이는 '끄지 마시오'라고 설정되어 있어야 하며, 컴퓨터는 '잠을 자지 않음'으로 설정되어 있어야 한다.

또한 제어판의 개인 설정에서, 대회가 진행되는 동안 모든 화면 보호 프로그램은 꺼져있어야 한다.

마지막으로, 모든 휴대용 컴퓨터는 접촉 패드의 사용이 불가능하고, 대신 유선 USB 마우스가 사용되어야 한다. 접촉 패드는 보통 정사각형을 접촉하고 손을 상징하는 아이콘이 표시된 기능키로 전원이 꺼진다. 사용이 불가능한 접촉 패드는 컬타임(CurlTime) 스크린에 있는 모든 버튼의 우연한 활성화를 방지한다.

20. TIME CLOCK OPERATOR

DUTIES

The Time Clock Operator is responsible for operating the time clock on an assigned sheet. The operator must be thoroughly familiar with the equipment, as well as the rules governing the use of time clocks. This requires good concentration, with no interruptions during the game.

CODE OF CONDUCT

- Be aware of shift times.
- Give a minimum of 3 hours notice if unable to work.
- Advise the Chief Timer of any duty change.
- Abstain from alcohol from 6 hours before duty.
- Concentrate on the game that has been allocated.
- Conform to dress code.
- Maintain confidentiality at all times.

PRE COMPETITION

1. Instruction in all procedures, including pre-game practice and LSD, and an opportunity to practise with the clocks should be given prior to the start of the competition.

2. The timer should be familiar with the duty roster, timing forms, use of a stopwatch, dress and behaviour codes.

BEFORE THE GAME

1. Check in with the Chief Timer a minimum of 40 minutes before the game. The timer should be in position 10 minutes before the start of the game.

2. Confirm that the game clocks are set for the correct amount of game time for each team.

PROCEDURES (For Mixed Doubles and Wheelchair curling see sections 25 and 26)

1. An announcement will be given to indicate when the games may begin. Time will start when the first stone of the game reaches the tee line at the delivering end.

2. The clock will run for the delivering team until:

   - **all** stones have come to rest or crossed the back-line, **and**
   - any stones that are displaced due to violations by the delivering team, and require repositioning, are returned to their original positions, **and**
   - the playing area has been relinquished to the other team (the person in charge of house moves behind back line, sweepers and deliverer move to the sides).

20. 시간 기록계 오퍼레이터

업무

시간 기록계 오퍼레이터는 배정된 시트에 있는 시계를 작동하는 데 책임이 있다. 오퍼레이터는 시계의 사용을 관리하는 규칙뿐만 아니라, 장비도 철저히 알아야 한다. 이것은 경기 중에 방해가 없는 상태에서 상당한 집중을 요구한다.

행동강령

- 변속시간을 알아야 한다.
- 작동이 불가능하면 최소 3시간 전에 예고해야 한다.
- 최고 기록자에게 모든 업무 변경을 알려야 한다.
- 업무 시간 전에 술을 삼가야 한다.
- 할당된 경기에 집중해야 한다.
- 복장 규정을 따라야 한다.
- 항상 비밀을 유지해야 한다.

경기 전

1. 경기 전 연습과 LSD(라스트 스톤 드로우)를 포함하여, 모든 절차의 설명과 시계를 가지고 연습할 기회는 경기 시작 전에 미리 주어져야 한다.
2. 기록자는 근무 당번표, 타이밍 형식, 스톱워치의 사용, 복장과 행동 규칙을 알아야 한다.

경기 시작

1. 경기 시작 최소 40분 전에 시간 계측장과 함께 와야 한다. 계측자는 경기가 시작하기 10분 전에 자기 위치에 있어야 한다.
2. 경기 시계가 각 팀에게 정확한 양의 경기 시간으로 설정되어있는지 확인해야 한다.

절차(혼합복식(믹스더블)과 휠체어 컬링은 세션 25와 26을 보아라)

1. 경기가 언제 시작하는지에 대한 안내가 나올 것이다. 첫 번째 스톤이 딜리버링 엔드에 있는 티 라인에 도달하면 기록은 시작될 것이다.
2. 시계는 딜리버리하는 팀에게 작동할 것이다.
   - 모든 스톤이 휴식하거나 백 라인을 넘을 때까지
   - 딜리버리하는 팀의 방해로 인해 옮겨지거나, 모든 스톤이 원래 위치로 돌아올 때까지
   - 플레이 구역을 다른 팀에게 내주었을 때까지(하우스를 담당하는 사람이 백 라인 뒤로 움직이고, 스위퍼와 딜리버리하는 사람이 양쪽으로 움직인다)

One clock or the other is running until the end is over, UNLESS:

- A team calls a team time-out by signalling the "T" sign. A team may only call a time-out whilst its clock is running. The timer should immediately initiate the team time-out procedure.

- A team will request a technical time-out by making the "X" sign. (See Section 22. Procedures for Time-outs).

3. When the last stone of an end has been completed, the game clock is stopped and will remain stopped until the score is determined, including the time taken for any measurements.

4. As soon as the score for the end is agreed, the break time is started. (See section 23. Timing between ends).

5. When a team is running low on time: (See section 21. Procedure When a Team is Running Low on Time).

6. When an extra end is required, each team receives 9 minutes of playing time plus one team time-out, regardless of time remaining after the regular scheduled ends. This applies to all extra ends.

7. Errors or malfunctions must be reported to the Chief Timer immediately. Any timing adjustments must only be made under the direct supervision of the Chief Timer.

8. VIOLATIONS and SPECIAL SITUATIONS

If a team commits a rule violation in the playing of a stone, then that team's game clock continues to run until the violation is resolved.

Such violations include:

Hogged Stone. A stone fails to clear the Hog Line at the playing end. The clock must run until it is taken behind the Back Line.

Free Guard Zone (FGZ) Violation. A team removes an opposition stone from play from within the FGZ Area before the fifth stone of the end. Its clock must continue to run until the stone is satisfactorily replaced, and its stone is put behind the Back Line.

Wrong Colour Played. If a team plays the wrong colour of stone, its clock should continue to run until the stone is satisfactorily replaced by the correct stone.

Hog Line Violation. Where a player, during delivery, has not released the stone before reaching the delivery-end Hog Line, the stone should be immediately removed from play by his team. That team's clock will run until the stone is behind the Back Line. If it is not immediately removed and strikes another stone, it is removed from play and displaced stones are returned to their original positions by the non-offending team, during which time the offending team's clock will continue to run.

Touched Stones. Where a team has accidentally touched a stone, its clock will continue to run until all stones have been replaced to the satisfaction of the non–offending team.

Stone Delivered Too Soon. This may happen when a team is trying to save time. A team may deliver a stone only when its game clock is scheduled to be running. Any violation results in the stone being redelivered after any displaced stones have been returned to their original positions. The offending team's game clock runs during the replacement of stones and the redelivery.

아래의 조건을 제외하고, 엔드가 끝날 때까지 시계가 작동한다:

- 팀이 'T' 사인 신호를 보냄으로써 팀 타임아웃을 요청한다. 팀은 시계가 작동하는 동한 오직 한 번의 타임아웃을 요청할 수 있다. 기록자는 팀 타임아웃 절차를 즉시 시작해야 한다.
- 팀은 'X' 사인을 만듦으로써 기술적인 타임아웃을 요청할 수 있다. (세션 22-타임아웃을 위한 절차-를 보아라.)

3. 엔드의 마지막 스톤이 완료되면 경기 시간은 멈추고, 모든 측정을 위한 시간을 포함하여 점수가 결정될 때까지 시간 정지를 유지할 것이다.
4. 엔드 점수가 합의되면, 휴식 시간이 시작된다. (세션 23-엔드 사이의 시간 계측-을 보아라)
5. 팀이 시간이 부족하면: (세션 21-팀이 시간이 부족할 때의 절차-을 보아라)
6. 추가 엔드가 요청되면, 기본적으로 예정된 엔드 이후에 남는 시간과 상관없이, 각 팀은 9분의 경기 시간과 한 팀의 타임아웃을 받는다. 이것은 모든 추가 엔드에 적용된다.
7. 오류나 고장은 즉시 시간 계측장에게 알려야 한다. 모든 시간 계측 수정은 오직 최고 기록자의 직접적인 감독하에 이루어져야 한다.
8. 위반과 특수 상황

만약 팀이 스톤으로 경기할 때 규칙을 위반한다면, 그 팀의 경기 시간은 위반이 해결될 때까지 시간이 간다.

그러한 위반은 아래의 내용을 포함한다. :

호그된 스톤. 스톤이 경기 엔드에서 호그 라인을 넘지 못하면, 스톤이 백 라인 뒤까지 올 때까지 시간이 간다.

프리가드 존 침해. 5번째 스톤의 엔드 전에 프리가드 존 내에서 상대편의 스톤을 치우는 것을 말한다. 시계는 스톤이 충분히 다시 놓아질 때까지 계속되어야 하고, 이 스톤은 백 라인 뒤에 놓여 있어야 한다.

잘못된 스톤 색깔로 경기하기. 만약 팀이 잘못된 색의 스톤으로 경기를 하면, 그 시계는 스톤이 올바른 스톤으로 충분히 다시 놓일 때까지 계속되어야 한다.

호그 라인 침해. 딜리버리 중에 선수가 딜리버리 엔드 호그 라인에 도달하기 전에 스톤을 놓지 않았다면, 스톤은 바로 그 팀으로부터 제거되어야 한다. 그 팀의 시계는 스톤이 백 라인 뒤에 올 때까지 계속 간다. 만약 스톤이 바로 제거되지 않고 다른 스톤을 맞추는 경우에는, 스톤은 경기로부터 제거되고 자리를 벗어난 스톤들은 위반하지 않은 팀에 의해 그들의 원래 자리로 돌아온다. 그 시간에 위반한 팀의 시계는 계속 간다.

터치된 스톤. 팀이 실수로 스톤을 터치했을 때, 시계는 모든 스톤이 위반하지 않은 팀이 만족하는 제자리에 올 때까지 계속 간다.

너무 일찍 딜리버리된 스톤. 팀이 시간을 아끼려고 할 때 일어난다. 팀은 경기 시계가 작동할 때만 스톤을 딜리버리해야 한다. 잘못 위치된 스톤 이후에 다시 딜리버리된 스톤 때문에 발생한 모든 위반된 스톤들은 원래 자리로 돌아온다. 위반한 팀의 경기 시간은 스톤의 교체와 딜리버리 중에 계속 흘러간다.

Wrong Hack. A stone delivered from the wrong hack must be removed from play, and any displaced stones returned to their original positions by the non-offending team. The offending team's game clock continues to run.

No Skip/Vice-skip. A team must have the player in charge of the house positioned inside the hog line and on the ice surface at the playing end of the sheet while the team is delivering. If not, the team's game clock will run until the Game Umpire removes any offending stone.

Throw Through. If the last stone of an end is not to count, but is to be 'thrown through', then that team's clock will run until the stone is behind the back line.

Redelivered Stone. Following a problem with an electronic handle, an Umpire may direct that a player re-deliver a stone without the game clock running.

Replaying an end. An Umpire can direct that an end be replayed. For example, where a stone or stones have been upset by an external force, and agreement cannot be reached as to their replacement.
On receiving this information, the Chief Timer should start a between ends break and reset the clocks to the values at the end of the previous end. When the adjustment is complete, this should be confirmed to the Umpire.

21. PROCEDURE WHEN A TEAM IS LOW ON TIME

The Chief Umpire must be advised when:

- A team has 5 minutes on its clock with still an end to play.
- A team has 2 minutes on its clock with stone(s) left to play.

The procedure is then for the Chief Umpire to ask a Game Umpire to stand in line at the delivery end tee line with a stop watch at the ready.

As the game clock counts down, the Umpire starts his stop watch exactly as the game clock reaches a memorable point (e.g. 30 seconds). The Umpire then watches the stone being delivered and stops his watch exactly as the stone reaches the delivery end tee line.

If the watch reads less than the time interval chosen (e.g. less than 30 seconds) the stone was played in time.

If the watch reads more than the time interval chosen, the stone was played out of time and the Chief Umpire is advised by radio immediately.

Throughout the game, Timers should be encouraged to note on their time sheets where teams use up time – for example - starting late after breaks, or having long discussions about a shot.

잘못된 핵. 잘못된 핵으로부터 딜리버리된 스톤은 경기로부터 제거되어야 하고, 잘못 위치한 스톤은 그들의 원래 자리로 위반하지 않은 팀에 의해 돌아가야 한다. 위반한 팀의 경기 시간은 계속 흘러간다.

스킵/바이스 스킵의 부재. 팀이 딜리버리를 실시할 때 플레잉 엔드에 호그 라인 안과 얼음 표면 위에 위치한 하우스를 책임지는 선수가 있어야 한다. 만약 없다면, 팀의 경기 시간은 심판이 모든 위반된 스톤을 제거할 때까지 계속 흘러간다.

통과된 투구. 만약 엔드의 마지막 스톤이 세어지지 않고 '통과되는 투구'가 된다면, 그 팀의 시간은 스톤이 백 라인 뒤에 정지할 때까지 흘러간다.

다시 딜리버리된 스톤. 전자 핸들의 문제로 인한 것은 경기 시간이 흘러가지 않는 상태로 선수가 스톤을 다시 딜리버리할 수 있게 심판이 지시할 수 있다.

엔드 재경기. 심판은 엔드가 다시 경기하도록 지시할 수 있다. 예를 들어, 스톤이 외부 힘에 의해 교란될 경우, 교체에 대한 합의가 이루어지지 않을 수 있다. 이 정보를 받을 때, 시간 계측장은 엔드 사이의 휴식시간에 시작해야 하고 시계를 이전의 엔드의 마지막으로 다시 맞춰야 한다. 조정이 끝나면, 심판에게 확인시켜야 한다.

21. 팀이 시간이 모자랄 때의 절차

최고 심판은 아래의 내용을 알려야 한다.

- 팀이 아직 엔드에 있는데 5분 남았을 때
- 팀이 한 개 또는 여러 개의 스톤이 남았는데 2분 남았을 때

주심은 준비절차로 초시계를 가지고 딜리버리 엔드의 티 라인에 서있으라고 경기 심판에게 요청해야 한다.

경기 시계가 초읽기를 할 때, 심판은 그의 초시계를 기억할 만한 시점에 도달했을 때(예를 들어 30초) 정확히 시작해야 한다. 심판은 스톤이 딜리버리되는 것을 보고 그의 초시계를 정확히 스톤이 딜리버리 엔드 티 라인에 도달할 때 멈추어야 한다.

만약 초시계가 선택된 시간 간격보다 적게 읽힌다면(예를 들어 30초보다 적게), 스톤은 정확한 시간에 경기된 것이다.

만약 초시계가 선택된 시간 간격보다 많게 읽힌다면, 스톤은 시간을 넘어서 경기된 것이고 최고 심판은 무선으로 즉시 권고해야 한다.

경기 중에, 시간 계측자는 팀이 다 쓴 시간이 있는 타임 시트에 적어야 한다. - 예를 들어 - 휴식 이후에 늦게 시작하거나, 샷에 대한 긴 논의를 할 때.

22. PROCEDURES FOR TIME-OUTS

When a team calls a time-out

1. A team uses the "T" hand signal, directed towards the timer or game Umpire. The game clock is stopped to allow travel time for the coach. (The coach travel time is set by the Chief Umpire and advised at the Team Meeting.) The Game Umpire and Chief Timer confirm that a time-out has been called and the Umpire times the travel time for the coach.

2. When the coach makes contact with the team, or when the coach travel time has expired, the Umpire will signal the timer that the 60-second time-out starts by raising a hand above the head. If the time clock has the capability to show the 60-second time-out, it will be started together with the game clock, and the Umpire will lower the hand. Otherwise, the game clock is restarted and the Umpire controls the coach time-out on a stopwatch. If the coach makes no attempt to join the team, the Umpire will end the time-out procedure and ask for the team's game clock to be re-started.

3. If walkways are provided the coach must stand on the walkway, either beside or behind the sheet. The Umpire ensures that the other team is not blocking the coach's view.

4. If there are no walkways, the coach may walk up the dividing line of the sheet, but may only stand between the hog lines or behind the sheet. The coach should be instructed to remain on the dividing line and not to step into the centre of the sheet. Specifics on where the coach may stand should be given at the Team Meeting.

5. When 10 seconds remain in the time-out, the Umpire raises a hand in the air and notifies the team and coach of the time remaining.

6. When the time-out expires, the Umpire ensures that the coach ends all discussion with the team and leaves the Field of Play promptly.

7. The time-out is recorded on the game timing form and on the scorecard.

When a team requests a technical time-out for a ruling, injury or other circumstance

1. If a team wants a technical time out, it uses the "X" hand signal directed towards the game Umpire or timer, who will stop the team's game clock.

2. If the reason is considered valid (e.g. – FGZ measure) by the Umpire, then it is considered a technical time-out. The game clock is restarted at a point indicated by the Umpire (e.g. - when the subsequent stone reaches the tee line at the delivering end, or for wheelchair curling when the subsequent stone reaches the hog line).

3. If the reason is considered not valid (e.g. – stopping the game because a player wants to return to the locker room to pick-up forgotten equipment, etc.), the game clock is re-started immediately and the amount of time the clock was stopped (determined by the Umpire) shall be deducted from that team's clock at the conclusion of the end. Last end adjustments will made immediately.

4. Coaches and players must be notified of the decision.

22. 타임아웃을 위한 절차

팀이 타임아웃을 외칠 때,

1. 팀은 기록자나 경기 심판을 향하여 'T' 손 모양을 사용한다. 경기 시계는 코치의 이동 시간을 허용하기 위해 멈춘다. (경기 시계는 최고 심판에 의해 설정되며 팀 미팅에서 권고된다) 경기 심판과 시간 계측장은 타임아웃이 요청되는 것을 확인하고 심판은 코치의 이동 시간을 측정한다.

2. 코치가 팀과 접촉할 때, 또는 코치의 이동 시간이 만료됐을 때, 심판은 손을 머리 위로 듦으로써 60초 타임아웃이 시작되었다고 타이머 신호를 보낼 것이다. 만약 시계가 60초 타임아웃을 보여줄 수 있다면, 경기 시계와 함께 시작될 것이고, 심판은 손을 내릴 것이다. 그렇지 않으면, 경기 시계는 다시 시작되고 심판은 코치의 타임아웃을 초시계로 측정할 것이다. 만약 코치가 팀에 접촉하지 않는다면, 심판은 타임아웃 절차를 끝내고 팀의 경기 시계를 다시 시작하도록 요청할 것이다.

3. 만약 통로가 제공된다면 코치는 통로에 서있어야 한다, 옆 또는 시트 뒤에서. 심판은 다른 팀이 코치의 시선을 막지 않아야 한다.

4. 만약 통로가 없다면, 코치는 시트를 나누는 선으로 갈 수 있지만 호그 라인 사이 또는 시트 뒤에만 서있을 수 있다. 코치는 나뉜 라인에 있고, 시트의 중간에 오지 못하도록 지시되어야 한다. 팀 미팅에서 코치가 어디에 서있어야 하는지에 대한 세부사항을 줘야 한다.

5. 타임아웃에서 10초가 남았을 때, 심판은 허공에 손을 들어서 팀과 코치에게 남은 시간을 알려야 한다.

6. 타임아웃이 만료되면, 심판은 코치가 팀과의 모든 논의를 끝내고 경기장을 지체 없이 떠나도록 해야 한다.

7. 타임아웃은 경기 타이밍 용지와 득점표에 기록된다.

팀이 규칙, 부상 또는 다른 사항을 위한 기술적인 타임아웃을 요청할 때

1. 만약 팀이 기술적인 타임아웃을 원할 때, 팀의 경기 시계를 멈출 수 있는 경기 심판이나 기록자를 향해 "X" 손 모양을 사용한다.

2. 만약 이유가 심판에 의해 타당하다고 생각되면 (예를 들어 - 프리 가드 존 측정), 기술적인 타임아웃으로 고려된다. 경기 시계는 심판에 의해 표시된 지점에서 다시 시작된다. (예를 들어 - 그다음의 스톤이 딜리버링 엔드의 티 라인에 도달했을 때, 아니면 휠체어 컬링에서 그다음 스톤이 호그 라인에 도달했을 때).

3. 만약 이유가 타당하다고 생각되지 않는다면 (예를 들어 - 선수가 가져오는 것을 잊어버린 물품을 가지러 선수가 라커로 돌아가기 위해 경기를 멈추는 것 등), 경기 시계는 즉시 다시 시작되고 멈췄던 동안의 시간만큼 마지막 엔드에 팀의 시계에서 감해질 수 있다(심판에 의해 결정된다). 마지막 엔드는 즉시 조정된다.

4. 코치와 선수들은 결정을 통지받아야 한다.

23. TIMING BETWEEN ENDS

1. The length of the breaks will normally be:
   (i) 1 minute at the completion of each end, except as noted in (ii).
   (ii) 5 minutes at the completion of the end that defines the halfway point in the game.

2. When the score for an end has been determined, timing of the break will start. If a measurement is required the break begins at the completion of the measurement.

3. When ten (10) seconds of the break remain, the Umpire for that sheet will raise an arm and the teams may begin play. When the ten (10) seconds have elapsed (the Umpire's arm will be brought down), or when the delivering team's first stone of the end reaches the tee line (hog line for wheelchair curling) at the delivering end, the delivering team's clock will start, whichever occurs first.

4. If necessitated by television/media obligations/commitments the break times may be changed. This information will be obtained from the official broadcasters and the teams will be informed as soon as possible, usually at the Team Meeting. When one or more games are being televised and the break times are altered for those games, the altered times will be applied to all games. Where a game is being televised, the between end and mid-game break times may be subject to the control of an Umpire directed by the TV controller. If so, a team is not penalised where the break time exceeds the allotted time, and its clock is started on its stone reaching the delivery end tee line.

5. For the break that defines the halfway point of the game the teams will be notified when one minute remains in the break. The Umpire will only notify teams that are at the sheet, and will not go looking for teams. When teams cannot begin play because the ice-crew has not finished preparing the ice after the mid-game break, the timer should await instructions from the game Umpire, or start the clock when the first stone reaches the delivery end tee line.

23. 엔드 중간의 시간 측정

1. 휴식 시간의 길이는 보통:
   (i) 각 엔드가 완료된 후 1분, (ii)에 명시된 것을 제외한다.
   (ii) 경기의 절반이 지난 지점에서 각 엔드가 완료된 후 5분

2. 엔드의 점수가 결정되면, 휴식 시간이 시작된다. 만약 측정이 요구되면 측정이 완료되고 휴식이 시작된다.

3. 휴식시간의 10초가 남았을 때, 그 시트의 심판은 팔을 들고 팀들은 경기를 시작한다. 10분이 지났을 때 (심판의 팔은 내려올 것이다), 또는 딜리버링 엔드에서 팀의 첫 번째 스톤이 티 라인을 도달했을 때 (휠체어 컬링은 호그 라인), 딜리버리하는 팀의 시계는 무엇이 먼저 발생하든 시작한다.

4. 만약 텔레비전/매체, 의무/투입이 필요하다면 휴식 시간이 변경될 수 있다. 이 정보는 공식 방송 사업자에 의해 얻어지고 팀들은 주로 팀 미팅에서 가능한 바로 통지받는다. 하나 이상의 경기가 방송되고 휴식 시간이 그 경기들로 인해 변경된다면, 변경된 시간은 모든 경기에 적용된다. 경기가 방송되는 곳에서는 사이 엔드와 경기 중간 휴식 시간이 텔레비전 관리자에 의해 지휘되는 심판의 통제를 받을 수 있다. 만약 그렇다면, 팀은 휴식 시간이 할당된 시간을 넘어설 때 처벌받지 않고, 이 시계가 스톤이 딜리버리 엔드 티 라인에 도달할 때 시작된다.

4. 경기의 중간 지점에 규정된 휴식 시간에는 휴식 시간이 1분 남았을 때 통지받는다. 심판은 시트에 있는 팀들에게 알려야 할 뿐, 팀들을 찾아다니지 않는다. 빙판 전담팀이 경기 중간의 휴식 이후에 빙판을 준비하지 못해서 팀들이 경기를 시작할 수 없다면, 기록자는 경기 심판의 지시를 기다리거나 첫 번째 스톤이 딜리버리 엔드 티 라인에 도달할 때 시간 재는 것을 시작해야 한다.

24. TIME CLOCK ADJUSTMENTS

1. If a time clock malfunction or error has been recognised, the time to be given back should be noted and the necessary adjustments to the clock made during the next break between ends. If the malfunction occurs during the last scheduled end, or an extra end, a technical time-out will be called and the necessary adjustments to the time clock will be made immediately. Time will only be added where required, but never taken away due to a timing error.

2. Time should be adjusted as follows: The time on the clock before adjustment is recorded. The agreed time adjustment is applied and the new time recorded alongside the previous figure. The game clock is then set to this time.

3. The Chief Umpire/Deputy Chief Umpire will notify the coaches of the occurrence and of the action taken. The Game Umpire will notify the skips of the occurrence and of the action taken.

4. If there are repeated occurrences of time clock malfunction, the time clocks for that sheet will be shut down. If subsequent play on that sheet seems to be excessively slow, stopwatch timing may be used. Both coaches and both skips will be notified.

5. If a player is allowed to redeliver a stone, the Game Umpire decides if the time required is to be deducted from the game time for that team.

6. If an end is to be replayed, the game clocks are reset to the time recorded at the completion of the previous end.

7. When a team delays the start of a game, the playing time allotted to each team is reduced by 7 minutes (8 minutes in wheelchair curling, 6 minutes in mixed doubles curling) for each end that was considered completed.

8. When extra ends are required, the game clocks are reset and each team receives 9 minutes of playing time for each extra end (10 minutes in wheelchair curling, 8 minutes in mixed doubles curling).

24. 시간 조정

1. 만약 시계의 오작동 또는 오류가 인식되면, 돌려질 시간은 언급되어야 하고, 필요한 시계의 조정은 엔드 사이의 다음 휴식시간에 이루어진다. 만약 오작동이 마지막 엔드 또는 추가 엔드에 발생한다면, 기술적인 타임아웃이 요청되고 시계의 필요한 조정은 즉시 이루어진다. 시간은 필요한 곳에만 추가되고, 시간 계측 오류로 인해 없어지지 않는다.

2. 시간은 다음에 따라서 조정되어야 한다.: 조정 이전의 시간은 기록된다. 합의된 시간 조정은 적용되고 새로운 시간은 이전의 숫자 옆에 기록된다. 경기 시계는 이 시간으로 맞춰진다.

3. 주심/부심은 코치에게 문제 발생과 취해진 조치를 알릴 것이다. 경기 심판은 문제 발생과 취해진 조치를 스킵에게 알릴 것이다.

4. 만약 시계 오작동이 반복적으로 발생한다면, 그 시트의 시계를 정지시킬 것이다. 만약 그 시트의 다음 경기가 지나치게 느리다면, 초시계가 사용될 수 있고, 양 코치들과 양 스킵들은 통지받는다.

5. 만약 선수들이 스톤을 다시 딜리버리하도록 허락받으면, 경기 심판은 요구된 시간이 그 팀을 위한 경기 시간으로부터 감해지는지 결정해야 한다.

6. 만약 엔드가 다시 경기된다면, 경기 시계는 이전 엔드의 마지막에 기록된 시간으로 다시 맞춰진다.

7. 팀이 경기 시작 시간을 지연한다면, 각 팀에게 할당된 경기 시간이 끝난 것으로 판명된 각 엔드에서 7분(휠체어 컬링은 8분, 혼합복식(믹스더블) 컬링은 6분) 줄어든다.

8. 추가 엔드가 요청되면, 경기 시계는 다시 맞춰지고 각 팀은 9분의 추가 엔드 경기 시간을 받는다(휠체어 컬링은 10분, 혼합복식(믹스더블) 경기는 8분).

25. TIMING - MIXED DOUBLES CURLING

See also Timing related Sections: 20 – 24

1. All games are 8 ends; a minimum of 6 ends must be played.

2. Each team receives 46 minutes of playing time, and one 60-second time-out. When a player signals a time-out, the time clock will be stopped for the coach travel time (determined by the Chief Umpire). The clock restarts and the time-out begins when the coach reaches the team, or the travel time has expired. (see Section 22)

3. If a team delays the start of the game, playing time allotted to each team is reduced by 6 minutes for each end considered completed.

4. For each extra end each team receives 8 minutes of playing time and one 60-second time-out. (see Section 22)

5. The game, and the delivering team's clock, starts when the first stone of the game reaches the tee line at the delivering end.

6. The delivering team's clock continues to run until:
   - all stones have come to rest or have crossed the back line, and
   - any stones that are displaced due to violations by the delivering team, and require repositioning, are returned to their original positions, and
   - the playing area has been relinquished to the other team, and the person in charge of the house has moved behind the back line

7. A team delivers stones only when its game clock is running or scheduled to be running. Any violation results in the stone being redelivered after any displaced stones have been returned to their original positions. The offending team's clock runs during replacement of stones and redelivery.

8. If stones need to be repositioned due to a violation caused by the non-delivering team, that team's game clock will be started.

9. If stones need to be repositioned due to a violation caused by an external force both clocks are stopped.

10. Both clocks stop when final stone of the end, and all stones it affects, have come to rest or have crossed the back line. When both teams have agreed on the score, or a measurement is completed, there is a break:
    - 1 minute after each end, except
    - 5 minutes at the completion of the 4th end

11. Game clocks are stopped any time an Umpire intervenes (i.e. – a team requests a ruling, accidents, injury, faulty or broken equipment, etc.).

12. If an end is to be replayed, game clocks are reset to the time recorded at completion of the previous end.

13. If the positioned stones have not been placed by the end-ice observer, and the end-ice observer has not returned to the back board before the 1 minute break has elapsed, the game clock should remain stopped and only started when the first stone of the delivering team reaches the nearer tee line. This pause will allow the delivering team time to set up for their first shot of the end. The clock would start if the team delays delivery unnecessarily. Timers shall relay any concerns about delays to the Chief Timer. It may be advisable to disable the auto start feature in CurlTime for the one-minute break.

14. Each team must complete its part of a game in the time given. If a stone reaches the tee line at the delivering end before time expires, the stone is considered delivered in time.

25. 시간 측정 - 혼합복식(믹스더블) 컬링

시간 재기와 관련된 부분도 보기: 세션 20~24

1. 모든 경기는 8엔드이다. ; 최소 6엔드 경기는 해야 한다.
2. 각 팀은 경기 시간 46분과 한 번의 60초 타임아웃을 받는다. 선수가 타임아웃 신호를 보내면, (주심의 결정에 의해) 코치 이동 시간을 위해 시계를 멈춘다. 시계는 다시 시작하고 코치가 팀에 도달하거나 이동시간이 만료됐을 때 타임아웃이 시작된다. (세션 22를 보아라)
3. 만약 팀이 경기 시작을 지연한다면, 각 팀에게 할당된 경기 시간은 완료되었다고 판단된 각 엔드의 6분씩 줄어든다.
4. 각 추가 엔드에 각 팀은 8분의 경기시간과 한 번의 60초 타임아웃을 받는다. (세션 22를 보아라)
5. 경기와 딜리버리하는 팀의 시계는 경기의 첫 번째 스톤이 딜리버링 엔드의 티 라인에 도달할 때 시작한다.
6. 딜리버링 팀의 시간은 계속 흘러간다. :

- 모든 스톤이 정지해 있거나 백 라인을 넘었을 때
- 딜리버링 팀의 위반 때문에 움직이고, 위치를 다시 바꿔야 하는 모든 스톤은 그들을 원래 자리로 돌아올 때
- 경기 하는 곳이 다른 팀에게 내주고, 하우스를 책임지는 사람이 백 라인 뒤로 움직일 때

7. 경기 시계가 가고 있거나 가려고 할 때만 팀은 스톤을 딜리버리할 수 있다. 모든 반칙은 어떤 잘못 위치한 스톤이 원래 자리로 돌아온 후에 다시 딜리버리된 스톤 때문이다. 위반한 팀의 시계는 스톤의 교체와 다시 딜리버리하는 동안에 시간이 간다.
8. 만약 스톤을 딜리버리하지 않는 팀에 의한 반칙 때문에 재배치해야 한다면, 그 팀의 시계가 시작될 것이다.
9. 만약 외부 힘에 의한 반칙 때문에 스톤이 재배치되어야 한다면 두 시계 모두 멈춘다.
10. 엔드의 마지막 스톤과 그것이 영향을 미치는 모든 스톤이 정지해 있거나 백 라인을 넘었을 때 두 시계 모두 멈춘다. 두 팀이 점수에 합의를 하거나, 측정이 완료되면, 휴식이 주어진다:
    - 각 엔드 이후의 1분
    - 4번째 엔드가 끝나고 5분을 제외한다.
11. 경기 시계는 심판이 개입하면 언제든지 멈춘다. (예를 들어 - 팀이 규칙, 사고, 부상, 잘못 또는 장비 고장 등)
12. 만약 엔드가 다시 경기되어야 한다면, 경기 시계는 이전 엔드에 기록된 시간이 리셋된다.
13. 만약 배치된 스톤이 엔드의 빙판 관찰자에 의해 위치되지 않고, 엔드의 빙판 관찰자가 1분의 쉬는 시간이 지나기 전에 백 보드로 돌아오지 않는다면, 경기 시계는 멈춰있어야 하고, 딜리버링 팀의 첫 번째 스톤이 가까운 티 라인에 도달할 때만 시작할 수 있다. 정지는 딜리버링 팀의 시간이 그들의 엔드의 첫 번째 시도로 설정되는 것을 허락한다. 시계는 팀이 딜리버리를 불필요하게 지연할 때 시작할 수 있다. 기록자는 주심에게 지연에 관한 어떠한 우려도 전달할 수 있다. 1분의 쉬는 시간을 위해 컬타임(CurlTime)에 자동 시작을 못 하도록 권할 수 있다.
14. 각 팀은 주어진 시간 안에 각 파트의 경기를 끝내야 한다. 만약 스톤이 시간이 만료되기 전 딜리버링 엔드에 티 라인에 도달하면, 스톤은 제시간에 딜리버리된 것으로 판단된다.

26. TIMING - WHEELCHAIR CURLING (See also Sections: 20 - 24 & 27)

1. All games are 8 ends; a minimum of 6 ends must be played.

2. Each team receives 68 minutes of playing time. One 60-second time-out per team is allowed per game. When a player signals a time-out, the time clock will be stopped for the coach travel time (determined by the Chief Umpire). The clock restarts and the time-out begins when the coach reaches the team, or the travel time has expired. (see Section 22)

3. If a team delays the start of the game, playing time allotted to each team is reduced by 8 minutes for each end considered completed.

4. Each team receives 10 minutes of playing time and one 60-second time-out for each extra end. (see Section 22)

5. The game, and the delivering team's clock, starts when the first stone of the game reaches the hog line at the delivering end.

6. The delivering team's clock continues to run until:
   - all stones have come to rest or have crossed the back line, and
   - stones that are displaced due to violations by the delivering team, and require repositioning, are returned to their original positions, and
   - the playing area (including delivery area) has been relinquished to the other team, and the person in charge of the house has moved behind the back line.
     (If the team who is next to deliver moves into position at the delivering end to get ready to play its shot, and it does not interfere with the delivering team, the clock is not switched until the delivering team moves behind the backline.)

7. A team delivers stones only when its game clock is running or scheduled to be running. Any violation results in the stone being redelivered after any displaced stones have been returned to their original positions. The offending team's clock runs during replacement of stones and redelivery.

8. If stones need to be repositioned due to a violation caused by the non-delivering team, that team's game clock will be started.

9. If stones need to be repositioned due to a violation caused by an external force both clocks are stopped.

10. Both clocks stop when final stone of the end, and all stones it affects, have come to rest or have crossed the back line. When both teams have agreed on the score, or a measurement is completed, there is a break:
    - 1 minute after each end, except
    - 5 minutes at the completion of the 4th end

11. Game clocks are stopped any time an Umpire intervenes (e.g. – a team requests a ruling, accidents, injury, faulty or broken equipment, etc.).

12. If an end is to be replayed, the game clocks are reset to the time recorded at completion of the previous end.

13. Each team must complete its part of a game in the time given. If a stone reaches the hog line at the delivering end before time expires, the stone is considered delivered in time.

26. 시간 측정 - 휠체어 컬링(세션 20-24 & 27도 보아라)

1. 모든 경기는 8엔드이다. ; 최소 6엔드 경기는 해야 한다.

2. 각 팀은 경기 시간 68분을 받는다. 팀당 한 번의 60초 타임아웃이 한 경기당 허용된다. 선수가 타임아웃 신호를 보내면, (주심의 결정에 의해) 코치 이동 시간을 위해 시계를 멈춘다. 시계는 다시 시작하고 코치가 팀에 도달하거나 이동시간이 만료됐을 때 타임아웃이 시작된다. (세션 22를 보아라)

3. 만약 팀이 경기의 시작을 지연한다면, 각 팀에게 할당된 경기 시간은 완료되었다고 판단된 각 엔드의 8분씩 줄어든다.

4. 각 팀은 각 추가 엔드에 10분의 경기 시간과 한 번의 60초 타임아웃을 받는다. (세션 22를 보아라)

5. 경기와 딜리버링 팀의 시계는 경기의 첫 번째 스톤이 딜리버링 엔드의 티 라인에 도달할 때 시작한다.

6. 딜리버링 팀의 시간은 계속 흘러간다. :
- 모든 스톤이 정지해 있거나 백 라인을 넘었을 때,
- 딜리버링 팀의 위반 때문에 움직이고, 위치를 다시 바꿔야 하는 스톤이 그들을 원래 자리로 돌아올 때
- 경기 하는 곳(딜리버링 구역을 포함해서)을 다른 팀에게 내주고, 하우스를 책임지는 사람이 백 라인 뒤로 움직일 때 (다음이 딜리버리하는 팀이 딜리버리 엔드에 위치한다면, 그리고 딜리버링 팀을 간섭하지 않는다면, 시간은 딜리버링 팀이 백 라인 뒤로 움직일 때까지 바뀌지 않는다)

7. 경기 시계가 가고 있거나 가려고 할 때만 팀은 스톤을 딜리버리할 수 있다. 모든 반칙은 어떤 잘못 위치한 스톤이 원래 자리로 돌아온 후에 다시 딜리버리된 스톤 때문이다. 위반한 팀의 시간은 스톤의 교체와 다시 딜리버리하는 동안에 흘러간다.

8. 만약 스톤을 딜리버리하지 않는 팀에 의한 반칙 때문에 재배치해야 한다면, 그 팀의 시계가 시작될 것이다.

9. 만약 외부 힘에 의한 반칙 때문에 스톤이 재배치되어야 한다면 두 시계 모두 멈춘다.

10. 엔드의 마지막 스톤과 그것이 영향을 미치는 모든 스톤이 정지해 있거나 백 라인을 넘었을 때 두 시계 모두 멈춘다. 두 팀이 점수에 합의를 하거나, 측정이 완료되면, 휴식이 있다. :
    - 각 엔드 이후의 1분.
    - 4번 째 엔드가 끝나고 5분을 제외한다.

11. 경기 시계는 심판이 개입하면 언제든지 멈춘다. (예를 들어 - 팀이 규칙, 사고, 부상, 잘못 또는 장비 고장 등)

12. 만약 엔드가 다시 경기되어야 한다면, 경기 시계는 이전 엔드에 기록된 시간이 리셋된다.

13. 각 팀은 주어진 시간 안에 각 파트의 경기를 끝내야 한다. 만약 스톤이 시간이 만료되기 전에 딜리버링 엔드의 티 라인에 도달하면, 스톤은 제시간에 딜리버리된 것으로 판단된다.

27. WHEELCHAIR CURLING - TIMING RELATED SCENARIOS

Abbreviations

- CU – Chief Umpire
- GU – Game Umpire
- CT – Chief Timer
- IPA – Ice Player Assistant

1. FGZ infractions – the time clock runs for the delivering team until stones are replaced. GU will advise if necessary.

2. Hogged stone – time runs until the stone is taken past the back line. The players can deal with a hogged stone themselves, or an IPA and/or a GU can assist. In the event that the IPA or the GU is delayed in assisting, the GU will advise the CT if any time adjustments are required.

3. The clock is stopped for GU to make a visual ruling at the hog line and the back line – GU will advise CT.

4. In the event that the 1st stone of the end is hogged and the IPA has not reached the playing end, the GU may go out to remove the stone. It will be a judgement call if the situation is one where the GU or IPA is delayed, and team has called for help. GU will advise the CT as required.

5. Hog line Violation – The delivering team's time clock continues to run until the stone is over the back line. If any stones need to be replaced the clock continues to run for the offending team. If the delivery stick stays with stone and the stone reaches the near hog line it is considered a hog line violation – time as usual. The GU will advise CT if any adjustments are required.

6. Miscue during the delivery process:

   - Case 1: the delivered stone reaches the near hog line.
     It is a hogged stone and the players and/or IPA(s) have to get it past the back line. Clocks continue to run, so note that prompt action is required. GU will advise CT.
   - Case 2: the delivered stone does not reach the near hog line.
     If the delivering player stops the stone prior to the stone reaching the hog line, the stone can be redelivered, and the clock continues to run. The IPA may help retrieve.
     If the delivery stick is broken the GU will advise the CT.

7. Intentional throw through – Timed normally, clock switches when stone crosses the back line. The GU will advise CT if necessary.

8. Team doesn't want to deliver last stone of the end (e.g. stone is just pushed over the near hog line for fear of doing harm) - Stone must be delivered. Clock continues to run until stone crosses the back line at the playing end. GU will advise CT if necessary – If stone is just pushed over hog line the timer should alert the CT if this takes place.

9. Variable delivery position – timing may be affected when a team uses a variable delivery position e.g. – a team delivers from near the hack line sometimes.

   A player would normally take up his/her position and then the stone would be placed in front of the chair. If they wish to change position after the initial set up it will be on their time. The stone should be given to players wherever they set-up.

   The team that delivers the next stone should be allowed to get into position while a stone is going down the ice. This might block the view of the players delivering from near the hack, so the

27. 휠체어 컬링 - 시간 측정과 관련된 양식

축약

- CU - Chief Umpire(주심)
- GU - Game Umpire(경기 심판)
- CT - Chief Timer(시간 계측장)
- IPA - Ice Player Assistant(경기 선수 보조자)

1. 프리 가드 존 위반 - 스톤이 대체될 때까지 딜리버링 팀의 시간이 흘러간다. 필요하면 경기 심판이 조언해 줄 것이다.

2. 호그된 스톤 - 스톤이 백 라인을 넘을 때까지 시간이 흘러간다. 선수들은 스스로 호그된 스톤을 다룰 수 있어야 하며, 또는 빙상 선수 보조자나 경기 심판이 도울 수 있다. 빙상 선수 보조자나 경기 심판이 돕는 것에 있어 시간이 지연된다면, 경기 심판은 조정이 요구되는 언제든 시간 계측 담당자에게 권고할 수 있다.

3. 시계는 호그 라인과 백 라인에 시각적 규칙을 만들도록 경기 심판이 멈출 수 있다. - 경기 심판이 시간 계측 담당자에게 권고할 것이다.

4. 엔드의 첫 번째 스톤이 호그되고 빙상 선수 보조자가 경기 엔드에 도달하지 못한다면, 경기 심판은 스톤을 치우기 위해 나갈 수 있다. 만약 경기 심판이나 빙상 선수 보조자가 지연되고, 팀이 도움을 요청하는 상황이라면 개인적인 판단에 따른 결정이 될 것이다. 경기 심판은 요구에 따라 시간 계측 담당자에게 권고할 것이다.

5. 호그 라인 위반 - 딜리버리하는 팀의 시간은 스톤이 백 라인을 넘을 때까지 흘러간다. 만약 어떤 스톤이 재배치돼야 한다면 시간은 위반한 팀을 위해 흘러간다. 만약 딜리버리 스틱이 스톤과 있고, 가까운 호그 라인에 스톤이 도달한다면 호그 라인 반칙으로 판단된다. - 시간은 보통(정해진 규정)과 같다. 경기 심판은 만약 조정이 요구될 때 시간 계측 담당자에게 권고할 것이다.

6. 딜리버리 과정에서의 실책
   - 경우 1: 딜리버리된 스톤이 가까운 호그 라인에 도달한다.

     이것은 호그된 스톤이며 선수 또는 빙상 선수 보조자는 백 라인을 넘도록 해야 한다. 시간은 계속 흘러가므로, 신속한 행동이 요구되는 것을 명심해라. 경기 심판은 시간 계측 담당자에게 권고할 것이다.
   - 경우 2: 딜리버리된 스톤이 근처의 호그 라인에 도달하지 않는다.

     만약 딜리버리하는 선수가 스톤을 호그 라인에 도달하기 전에 멈춘다면, 스톤은 다시 딜리버리될 수 있고, 시간은 계속 흘러간다. 빙상 선수 보조자가 수습하는 것을 도와줄 수 있다. 만약 딜리버리 스틱이 부러졌다면 경기 심판은 시간 계측 담당자에게 권고할 것이다.

7. 의도적으로 통과된 투구 - 일반적으로 시간이 맞춰지는 시계는 스톤이 백 라인을 넘었을 때 바꾼다. 경기 심판은 필요하다면 시간 계측 담당자에게 권고할 것이다.

8. 팀은 엔드의 마지막 스톤을 딜리버리하지 않기를 원한다. (예를 들어, 해를 끼칠 것 같은 두려움으로 인해 호그 라인 근처로 스톤을 그저 밀어버린다) 시계는 스톤이 경기 엔드에서 백 라인을 넘어설 때까지 시간이 간다. 경기 심판은 필요하다면 시간 계측 담당자에게 권고할 것이다 - 만약 스톤이 호그 라인에 그저 밀어진다면 기록자는 이때 시간 계측 담당자에게 알려야 한다.

9. 가변적인 딜리버리 포지션 - 시간 재기는 팀이 가변적인 딜리버리 포지션을 사용할 때 영향이 미칠 수 있다. 예를 들어 - 팀이 가끔 핵 라인 근처로부터 딜리버리할 때.

   선수는 일반적으로 자신의 포지션을 선택하고 스톤을 의자 앞에 둔다. 만약 최초로 설정한 이유에 포지션을 바꾸고 싶다면 그들의 시간이 소비될 것이다. 그들이 어디에 설정하든 스톤은 선수들에게 주어진다.

delivering team will have to move to a position where they can see, hopefully the teams will cooperate and not interfere with the player preparing for the next delivery. This should make it easier for the IPAs to get the stone to the players in a timely fashion, no matter where they set-up.

10. Extra time is used when a team requests changes in the playing order of stones – Timers are not sure if it is an IPA mistake or a player request to get a different stone.

    Time should continue to run for that team unless the GU advises the CT that the clock should stop. If the mistake was inadvertently made by the IPA the time can be adjusted if so directed by the GU. A card system with the stone playing order will be used by the IPA. Changes will be dealt with by the GU between ends.

11. Stones deflecting – when to stop the clock if GU or IPA is delayed.

    GU and IPA can assist in removing dead stones. The GU can call a technical time-out if the situation warrants. Always use common sense if things are really confused and/or altered. GU will advise CT.

12. Delivering team player's movement after delivery:

    - Case 1: Players vacate the delivery area before their stone stops at the playing end. Opposition moves in to their delivery position even before their clock starts – timer continues to time the delivered stone until the stone comes to rest and the delivering team skip has moved behind the back line.
    - Case 2: Players stay in the delivery position until the stone stops in play or crosses the back line. The timer will not switch to next team until the delivering team moves to the back line and out of the way of the next team.
    - Case 3: A player proceeds down the ice after delivery of his/her shots. The player should proceed down the side of the sheet. If he/she proceeds down the middle, time will run. The player may have to wait at far hog line if other team is ready to deliver – the delivering team must not be distracted.
    - When a player follows a shot down the sheet and the stone has come to rest, that person should stop and check to see if the delivering team is ready to deliver prior to entering the playing end. If the next player is ready to deliver and is waiting for him to stop moving the time clock of the player who is moving should continue running.

    The delivering team has to relinquish the playing area before its clock will stop.

13. If the ice crew is delayed, or requested to perform extra work during the 4th end break, the GU will advise when to start the clock for that sheet where the delay has occurred.

14. The IPA actions of placing, cleaning, ordering, moving, or catching deflections may affect timing.

    A team should not be penalised when an IPA's actions are delayed for any reason. Examples include placing the wrong colour or number of stone in front of the player or not being ready with the first stone of the end or removing dead stones. Timers shall relay any concerns about delays to the Chief Timer.

    If a player drops a delivery stick during delivery preparation, an IPA can assist if requested. Time continues for the delivering team.

다음 스톤을 딜리버리하는 팀은 스톤이 얼음을 따라가는 동안 포지션을 취할 수 있다. 이것이 근처 핵으로부터 딜리버리하는 선수의 시선을 막을 수 있어서, 딜리버리하는 팀은 그들이 볼 수 있는 포지션을 취해야 하고, 바라건대 팀들은 협동해야 할 것이며 다음 딜리버리를 준비하는 선수를 방해해서는 안 될 것이다. 이것은 그들이 어디에 설정하든, 시기에 적절한 방법으로 빙상 선수 보조자들이 선수들에게 스톤을 갖다 주기 쉬울 것이다.

10. 팀이 스톤 순서의 변화를 요구할 때 추가 시간이 사용된다. - 기록자들은 빙상 선수 보조자의 실수인지 다른 스톤을 원하는 선수의 요구인지 정확히 알 수 없다.
    경기 심판이 시간 계측 담당자에게 시계를 멈추라고 권고하지 않는 이상 시간은 계속 흘러간다. 만약 실수가 빙상 선수 보조자의 부주의로 일어났다면 경기 심판의 감독하에 시간은 조정될 수 있다. 스톤 순서의 카드 시스템은 빙상 선수 보조자에 의해 사용될 것이다. 변화는 엔드 사이에 경기 심판에 의해 이루어질 것이다.
11. 스톤의 편향 - 경기 심판이나 빙상 선수 보조자가 지연될 때 언제 시계를 멈출지.
    경기 심판과 빙상 선수 보조자는 아웃된 스톤을 치우는 것을 도울 수 있다. 경기 심판은, 만약 상황이 정당하다면 기술적인 타임아웃을 외칠 수 있다. 만약 일들이 헷갈리거나 변경된다면 언제나 상식을 이용해라. 경기 심판이 시간 계측 담당자에게 권고할 것이다.

12. 딜리버리 이후 선수의 움직임을 전달하는 것:
    - 경우 1: 선수들은 그들의 스톤이 플레잉 엔드에서 멈추기 전에 딜리버리 구역을 비운다. 반대 측은 심지어 시계가 시작하기 전에 그들의 딜리버리 포지션을 취한다. - 기록자는 스톤이 정지해 있고, 딜리버리하는 팀의 스킵이 백 라인 뒤로 움직이기 전까지 딜리버리 스톤의 시간을 측정한다.
    - 경우 2: 선수들이 스톤이 멈추거나 백 라인을 지날 때까지 딜리버리 포지션을 유지한다. 기록자는 딜리버리하는 팀이 백 라인으로 움직이고 다음 팀을 위해 비킬 때까지 다음 팀으로 전환하지 않을 것이다.
    - 경우 3: 선수가 그의 딜리버리 이후에 아이스로 진행한다. 선수는 시트의 사이드로 진행해야 한다. 만약 그가 가운데로 진행한다면, 시간이 다 될 것이다. 선수는 다른 팀이 딜리버할 준비가 될 때 먼 호그 라인에서 기다려야 할 것이다 - 딜리버링 팀은 교란되면 안 된다.
    - 선수가 시트를 따라 샷을 날리고 스톤이 정지해 있을 때, 그 선수는 멈춰서 딜리버링 팀이 플레잉 엔드에 들어서기 전에 딜리버리할 준비가 됐는지 확인해야 한다. 만약 다음 선수가 딜리버리할 준비가 됐고, 움직이고 있는 선수의 시계를 멈추게 하도록 기다리고 있다면 계속 작동되어야 한다.

    딜리버리하는 팀은 시계가 멈추기 전에 플레잉 구역을 내어 주어야 한다.

13. 만약 얼음 전담팀이 지연되거나 4번째 엔드의 쉬는 시간 동안 추가적인 일을 하도록 요청받는다면, 경기 심판은 지연이 발생한 그 시트에서 시계가 언제 시작해야 할지를 권고할 것이다.
14. 빙상 선수 보조자의 놓기, 정리하기, 배열하기, 움직이기, 또는 편향 잡기 행동들은 시간에 영향을 줄 수 있다.
    팀은 어떠한 이유로 빙상 선수 보조자의 행동이 지연될 때 처벌받으면 안 된다. 예를 들어 선수 앞에 잘못된 색깔이나 숫자의 스톤을 놓거나 엔드의 첫 번째 스톤이 준비가 되지 않았거나 아웃된 스톤을 처리할 때. 기록자는 최고 기록자에게 지연과 관련된 모든 우려를 전달해야 한다.
    만약 선수가 딜리버리를 준비 동안 딜리버리 스틱을 떨어뜨린다면, 빙상 선수 보조자는 요청에 따라 도움을 줄 수 있다. 이때 딜리버리하는 팀의 시간은 계속 흘러간다.

28. HAND-OUT: TIMING - WHEELCHAIR CURLING

Abbreviations

CU – Chief Umpire	IPA – Ice Player Assistant
DCU – Deputy Chief Umpire	LSD – last stone draw
GU – Game Umpire	LSFE – last stone first end
CT – Chief Timer	TO – time-out

TIME CLOCK OPERATOR DUTIES:
Timers are responsible for operating the time clock on the sheet to which they are assigned. This requires careful and continuous observation of the game and a good working knowledge of wheelchair curling and the time clocks that are being used. Timers must be able to concentrate and cannot be interrupted during a game. If the CU modifies any of the following information or procedures, timers will be updated accordingly.

PRE-GAME:

1. Check in with the CT 30 minutes before draw time, any updated instructions on the timing procedures and clocks will be given. The timer should be in position on the timers' bench 15 minutes before the start of the game.

2. The CT will ensure that the game clocks are set for the correct amount of game time and between end breaks for each sheet of ice.

3. Note: A timer assigned to time the pre-game practice will have to report to the CT at the bench 40 minutes before draw time. If possible, the time clock on sheet C - "Charlie" will be used to display the 10-minute pre-game practice for both teams. 1st practice is 30 min. prior to game time, 2nd practice follows approximately 15 min. prior to game time.

4. All timers should have at least one functioning stopwatch with batteries that are fresh for the current season. The CT should have at least two functioning stopwatches.

DURING THE GAME:
Be sure to start the proper clock – know which colour delivers first stone of the end at the start of the game and which team delivers first after the break between each end. Direct any questions or concerns to the CT.

1. START OF GAME PROCEDURES:
- There will be an announcement "one minute to game time" by the Umpire in charge of the practice session. The game, and the delivering team's clock, starts when
- The first stone of the game reaches the hog line at the delivering end.
- **Manual start for Wheelchair events.**

2. The timer will record on the Official Time Sheet the time remaining for the following:
- At the conclusion of each end.
- At the conclusion of the 8th end (or last end played).
- In the event that an extra end is played be certain that the time left at the conclusion of the 8th end is recorded before the extra end procedure is entered.
- The time remaining at the conclusion of each extra end is also recorded.

3. Team time-outs are recorded on the time sheet for the appropriate colour and in the correct end.

4. The timer should notify the CT who will notify the CU whenever a team is in danger of running out of time (i.e. – less than 4 minutes to play the last end, down to the last 60 seconds, etc.).

5. At the conclusion of the game the timer will verify with the CT that the time sheet has been completed and then sign his/her time sheet.

28. 핸드아웃: 휠체어 컬링 타임 계측

약어:

CU - 주심
DCU - 주심 대리자
GU - 경기 심판
CT - 시간 계측장
IPA - 얼음 위 선수 보조자
LSD - 라스트 스톤 드로우
LSFE - 첫 번째 엔드의 마지막 스톤
TO - 타임아웃

타임 키퍼의 의무들: 타이머는 그들이 배정된 시트에 시간 시계를 작동시켜야 하는 책임이 있다. 타임 키퍼는 경기에 대한 신중하고 지속적인 관찰과 휠체어 컬링과 사용되는 시계에 대한 작동 지식을 알고 있어야 한다. 타이머는 경기 중에 집중할 수 있어야 하고 경기 중에 방해받을 수 없다. 주심이 다음 정보와 절차 중 하나를 변경하는 경우 타이머는 이에 따라야 한다.

경기 전:

1) 시간 계측장은 경기 시간 30분 전에 타이밍 절차 및 시계에 어떤 업데이트 된 명령을 확인한다. 타이머는 경기를 시작하기 15분 전부터 타이머 벤치의 위치에 있어야 한다.
2) 시간 계측장은 경기 시간의 정확한 측정을 위해 얼음 각 시트의 종료 휴식 사이에 설정을 확인한다.
3) 참고: 경기 전 연습은 경기 시간 40분 전에 벤치에서 시간 계측장에 보고하여야 한다. (가능하면 C시트의 타임 클록 - 'C') 두 팀에게 10분의 경기 전 연습을 표시하는 데 사용된다. 첫 번째 연습은 30분이다. 경기 전 두 번째 연습은 약 15분이다.
4) 모든 타이머는 현재 시즌 새 배터리를 갖는 적어도 하나의 기능 스톱워치를 가지고 있어야 한다. 시간 계측장은 적어도 두 가지 기능 스톱워치를 가지고 있어야 한다.

경기 중:

적절한 시계로 시작하도록 해라. - 딜리버리를 하는 선수가 경기의 시작 엔드의 첫 번째 스톤을 어떤 색을 투구하였는지와, 각 엔드 사이의 쉬는 시간 이후에 어떤 팀이 먼저 딜리버리를 하는지 알고 있어라. 시간 계측장에게 직접 질문과 건의사항을 말하여라.

1. 경기를 시작하는 과정:
    - 발표 연습 세션을 담당하는 심판에 의해 "1분 뒤 경기가 시작할 것이다."라고 전해진다. 경기 및 제공 팀의 시계는 이때부터 시작한다.
    - 경기의 첫 돌은 딜리버리 엔드의 호그 라인에 도달한다.
    - 휠체어 이벤트 매뉴얼 시작
2. 타이머는 아래의 지시에 따라 공식적인 기록을 남겨야 한다.
    - 각 엔드 종료 시
    - 8번째 엔드(혹은 마지막 경기 엔드) 종료 시
    - 8번째 엔드의 종료 전에 시간이 남아있는, 엑스트라 엔드 경기가 확실시된 경기에서는 엑스트라 엔드 절차가 등록되기 이전에 기록된다.
    - 각 엑스트라 엔드의 종료 전의 남은 시간 또한 기록된다.
3. 팀 타임아웃은 적절한 색상의 타임 시트에 올바르게 마지막으로 기록된다.
4. 타이머는 팀이 시간이 부족한 상황에 처해 있다면 언제든지 주심에게 보고할 시간을 계측장에게 반드시 알려야 한다. (예 - 마지막 엔드 경기의 4분 이하가 남아 있는 상태에서, 60초가 지속되기까지 등)
5. 경기가 끝날 때 타이머가 타임 시트를 마무리한 시간 계측장에게 확인하고 그/그녀는 타임 시트에 서명한다.

TIMING OVERVIEW:

- All games are 8 ends; a minimum of 6 ends must be played.
- **68 minutes** of playing time for each team, with **one 60-second time-out** for each team for an 8 end game. 10 minutes for each extra end required, with one 60-second time-out per team in each extra end.

The delivering team's clock continues to run until:

- all moving stones have come to rest in play or have crossed the back line, and
- stones that are displaced due to violations by the delivering team and require repositioning are returned to their original positions, and
- the playing area has been relinquished to the other team, and the person in charge of the house has moved behind the back line. (If the team who delivers next moves into position to get ready to play their next shot, away from the delivering team, and they do not interfere with the delivering team, the clock is not switched until the delivering team moves behind the back-line.)

A team delivers stones only when its game clock is running. Any violation results in the stone being redelivered after any displaced stones have been returned to their original positions. The offending team's clock runs during replacement of stones and redelivery.

If stones need to be repositioned due to a violation caused by the non-delivering team, its game clock will be started.

If stones need to be repositioned due to a violation caused by an external force both clocks are stopped.

Both clocks stop when final stone of the end, and all stones it affects, have come to rest or have crossed the back line. Between end break occurs when both teams have agreed on the score or a measurement is completed.

Wheelchair teams are responsible for clearing the stones from the house and can ask the IPAs for assistance. If teams do not assist with the clearing of stones the IPAs can leave the stones in the house and start to arrange the delivery order of the stones by getting the 1st stone of the end ready and in position. The CT should be made aware of this situation and advise the timer when to start the between end time.

- 1 minute after each end, except
- 5 minutes at the completion of the 4th end

- Game clocks are stopped any time an Umpire intervenes, and for a technical time-out (i.e. – a team request for a ruling, injury, accidents, broken equipment, etc.).
- If an end is to be replayed, game clocks are reset to the time recorded at completion of the previous end.
- Each team must complete its part of a game in the time given. If a stone reaches the hog line at the delivering end before time expires, the stone is considered delivered in time.

PROCEDURES FOR TIME-OUT- Press the time-out button when signalled by the team using the T hand signal. Coaches cannot call or signal the players on ice to call a time-out. Announce to the CT the sheet letter and the colour of the stone handle. E.g. "Time-out, Alpha , Red."
Or the CT will advise "Time-out Alpha, (Bravo, Charlie, Delta, or Echo)".

The one-minute will be in front of the time display, and both clocks will be stopped.
The travel time for the coach to reach their team is controlled by the Game Umpire who will raise an arm when the travel time expires, or when the coach reaches the team. That is the signal to start the one-minute time-out. The time clock for the team calling the time-out continues to count down.
At the completion of the one-minute time-out, the GU tells the coach the TO is over.

시간 측정 개요(안내)

- 모든 경기는 8엔드이며, 최소 6엔드가 진행되어야 한다.
- 8엔드 경기에서 각 팀에 60초 정도의 시간제한과, 각 팀을 위한 68분의 경기 시간이 주어진다. 추가 엔드에는 각 팀에 60초 시간제한과 함께 각 추가 엔드의 10분이 요구된다.

딜리버리하는 팀의 시간은 계속 흘러간다. ~까지 :

- 모든 움직이는 스톤이 멈췄을 때 또는 백 라인을 넘어섰을 때,
- 투구한 팀의 위반에 의해 놓이거나 조정이 요구되는 스톤은 원래 위치로 돌아가고,
- 플레이 영역은 다른 팀에게로 포기되고, 하우스를 담당하던 사람은 백 라인으로 이동한다. (만약 다음 투구자의 팀이 다음 샷을 준비하기 위해 위치로 움직인다면, 투구 팀으로 떨어져서, 투구 팀을 방해해서는 안 되며, 투구 팀이 백 라인 뒤로 이동할 때까지 시계는 전환되지 않는다)
- 스톤은 경기 시간이 계측되고 있을 때 투구된 것만 유효로 한다. 어떤 위반이라도 생기면 이동된 스톤이나 재투구된 스톤은 원래 자리로 돌아가야 한다. 상대팀의 시계는 재투구하는 동안 계속 측정된다.

만약 투구하지 않는 팀의 위반 때문에 스톤이 재배치되어야 한다면, 경기 시계의 작동이 시작될 것이다.
만약 외력의 위반 때문에 스톤이 재배치되어야 한다면, 두 시계는 멈춘다.

양측 시간 계측은 엔드의 마지막 스톤이 모든 스톤에 영향을 미친 후 또는 백 라인을 넘어선 후 정지된다. 휴식시간 사이에, 두 팀이 점수에 동의했을 때, 또는 측정이 완료된다.

휠체어 팀은 하우스에서 스톤을 제거할 책임이 있고, 얼음 위 선수 보조자에게 도움을 요청할 수 있다. 만약 팀이 돌을 제거할 수 없을 경우, 얼음 선수 보조자는 하우스에 스톤을 두고 위치에 준비된 첫 번째 스톤의 딜리버리 순서의 정렬을 시작할 수 있다.
시작과 종료 시간 사이에 시간 계측장은 이 상황을 인식하고 타이머에게 조언한다.

- 각 엔드 후 1분
- 4번째 엔드 종료 시 5분

- 경기 시간은 심판이 개입하거나, 테크니컬 타임아웃 동안 멈춘다.(즉- 결정에 대한 재의 요청, 부상, 사고, 장비 고장 등)
- 엔드가 다시 플레이되어야 되는 경우, 경기 시간은 이전 엔드 완료의 타임 기록으로 리셋된다.
- 각 팀은 주어진 시간에 경기의 일부를 완료해야 한다. 만약 스톤이 시간이 만료되기 전에 딜리버리 엔드에 있는 호그 라인에 도달할 경우, 그 스톤은 제시간에 도달한 것으로 여겨진다.

타임아웃을 위한 절차: 팀에서 손으로 T신호를 만들어 신호를 보낼 때 타임아웃 버튼을 눌러라. 코치는 타임아웃을 요청하기 위해 얼음 위에 있는 선수를 부르거나 신호할 수 없다. 시간 계측장에게 시트 문자와 스톤 핸들의 색깔을 알려라. 예를 들어, "시간제한, A, 레드." 또는 시간 계측장은 "시간제한, A(B, C, D 또는 E)"를 알려 줄 것이다. 1분 동안 화면에 표시될 것이고, 그리고 두 시계는 멈출 것이다. 코치가 자기 팀에 도달하는 소요 시간은 이동 시간이 만료되거나, 코치가 팀에 도착할 때 경기 심판이 팔을 올려서 통제된다. 즉, 1분 시간제한을 시작하는 신호이다. 타임아웃을 요청하는 팀의 시간 시계의 카운트다운은 계속된다. 1분의 타임아웃 시간이 완료되면, 경기 심판은 코치에게 타임아웃이 끝났다고 말해준다.

TECHNICAL TIME-OUTS: STOP CLOCK – by pressing the stop button. These time-outs are called for rulings, injury, or in any other extenuating circumstances.

The GU notifies the CT by radio, the CT then relays info to the timer. **Technical time-out, Alpha (Bravo…) and ensures the time clock is stopped promptly.** Restart clock when Umpire or CT signals to start the clock.

The timer and CT ensure that the time-out is recorded correctly on the official time sheet.

If the reason for calling the time-is not considered valid by the GU, then the time-out will be charged against the team that called the time-out. Coaches and players will be notified of that decision.

TIME CLOCK ADJUSTMENTS:

1. If a time clock malfunction or error has been recognized, the time to be given back should be noted and the necessary adjustments to the clock made between ends, except during the final end when timing adjustments must be made stone by stone. Time will only be added where required, but never taken away.
2. If the malfunction occurs during the last scheduled end or during an extra end, a technical time-out will be called and the necessary adjustments to the time clock will be made immediately with the CT.
3. If a player is allowed to redeliver a stone, the GU decides if the time required is to be deducted from the game time for that team.
4. If an end is to be replayed, the game clocks are reset to the time recorded at the completion of the previous end.

PRE-GAME INFORMATION:

Time of day clock may be used for the start of the pre-game practice.
One timing display (sheet C – 10 minutes per team) is used for the pre-game practice.

- GU announcement at 1 minute to the start of the first practice, "*teams may cool their wheels and access the ice*" (coaches are allowed to move their stones to the delivery area)
- GU announcement, "*1st Practice may begin*". Start the clock.
- After 9 minutes, "*one minute remaining in 1st practice*"
- After 10 minutes, "*Practice is over, please prepare to deliver your LSD*"
- "*Deliver your Last Stone Draw*". Start the one minute.

The GU who is recording the LSDs will record the results of all 5 sheets. The same procedure is followed for the 2nd practice. After the 2nd practice is completed and the LSDs recorded, the CU or DCU assigns the LSFE.
If neither team has a stone that finishes in the house, or both teams record the same distance, a coin toss is used to decide which team has the choice of delivering the first or second stone in the first end.

- The GU in charge of the practice makes the announcement "one minute until game time". In the event that any delay is required, the GU or CU will advise the CT.
- There follows one more announcement, "*Games may begin, good luck and good curling.*"
- Be prepared to start the correct game clock when stone reaches the hog line.
- For post round robin games the pre-game practice is 10 min. per team – Team stone colour and LSFE is predetermined.

Game Notes

Manual start the clock with the correct colour at the start of the game for the delivering team, after time-outs, breaks between ends (1-3 and 5-7), 4th end break, and any extra end breaks. (Manual start procedure and aborting auto start will be discussed at the pre-event timers meeting if clocks are set to auto start).

All time adjustments will be done in liaison with the CU or GU – corrections may be necessary if timers have miscues or GU's advise CT of situations encountered during play requiring adjustments.

테크니컬 타임아웃: 시간 정지 - 정지 버튼을 누름으로써 이 타임아웃은 판정, 부상, 또는 다른 정상 참작을 위한 것으로 불린다. 경기 심판은 무선으로 시간 계측장에게 통지하고, 시간 계측장은 그런 다음 정보를 타이머에게 알려준다. 테크니컬 타임아웃, A(B…) 그리고 계측 시계는 즉시 멈춘다. 심판 또는 시간 계측장이 시작하라는 신호를 줄 때 다시 시작된다. 타이머와 시간 계측장은 시간제한이 공식 타임 시트에 정확하게 기록되어 있는지 확인한다. 만약 타임을 요청하는 이유가 경기 심판에 의해 유효한 것으로 간주되지 않으면, 타임아웃은 타임아웃을 요청한 팀에게 부과될 것이다. 코치와 선수는 그 결정을 통보받는다.

시계 조정:

1. 계측 시계가 고장이나 오류를 인식한 경우, 뒤에 주어진 시간은 기록되어야 하고, 필요한 시계 조정은 엔드 사이에 한다. 다만 마지막 엔드 동안의 타이밍 조정은 스톤과 스톤 사이에 이루어져야 한다. 시간은 필요한 경우에만 추가할 수 있지, 결코 사라지지 않는다.
2. 오작동이 마지막 예정된 엔드에 발생하거나 추가 엔드에 발생한 경우, 테크니컬 타임아웃이 요청될 수 있고, 시간 시계의 필요한 조정이 시간 계측장에 의해 즉시 만들어진다.
3. 선수가 스톤을 다시 딜리버리하는 것이 허용될 경우, 경기 심판은 그 팀을 위한 경기 시간으로부터 요구되는 시간을 공제할지 여부를 결정한다.
4. 엔드가 다시 플레이 되어야 하는 경우, 경기 시간은 이전 엔드의 완료 시 시간 기록으로 리셋된다.

경기 이전의 정보: 당일 시계의 시간은 경기 전 연습의 시작에 사용될 수 있다. 하나의 시간 측정 화면(시트 C - 팀당 10분)은 경기 전 연습에 사용된다.

- 첫 연습의 시작 1분 전에 경기 심판의 알림 "팀은 휠을 냉각하고, 얼음에 접근 할 수 있다."(코치는 스톤을 딜리버리 지역으로 이동시키는 것이 허용된다)
- 경기 심판의 알림 "첫 번째 연습을 시작합니다." 계측을 시작한다.
- 9분 후, "첫 번째 연습이 1분 남았습니다."
- 10분 후, "연습 경기가 끝났고, LSD를 딜리버리할 준비를 하십시오."
- "LSD를 딜리버리하십시오."라고 발언하며 1분을 시작한다.

LSD를 기록하는 경기 심판은 5시트의 결과를 기록할 것이다. 동일한 절차는 2번째 연습에도 이어진다. 2번째 연습이 완료되고, LSD가 기록된 후, 주심 또는 주심 대리자는 첫 번째 엔드의 마지막 스톤 순서를 배정한다.

어느 팀도 하우스에 스톤을 투구하지 못하거나, 두 팀의 스톤이 같은 거리로 기록된 경우, 동전 던지기는 첫 엔드에서 어느 팀이 첫 번째 또는 두 번째 스톤을 딜리버리할 것인지 결정하는 데 사용된다.

- 연습 담당 경기 심판은 "경기 시간까지 1분 남았습니다."라고 말한다. 지연이 요구되는 경우에는 경기 심판 또는 주심은 시간 계측장에게 조언한다.
- 알릴 것이 하나 더 있다. "행운을 빕니다. 좋은 경기하십시오."
- 호그 라인에 스톤이 도착할 때 정확한 경기 시계를 시작하는 것을 준비해라.
- 포스트 리그전의 경기 전 연습은 팀당 10분이다. - 팀의 스톤 색깔과 선후공은 미리 결정된다.

경기 노트

딜리버리하는 팀의 경기 시작부터 수동 시작 시계와 정확한 컬러는 타임아웃 후, 엔드(1~3 및 5~7) 사이, 4엔드 휴식, 그리고 추가 엔드 휴식에 중단된다(수동 시작 절차와 자동 시작의 중단은 시계가 자동 시작으로 설정되어 있으면 사전 이벤트 타이머 회의에서 논의될 것이다). 모든 시간 조정은 주심 또는 경기 심판과의 연락하에서 행해질 것이다. - 타이머의 실수 또는 경기 진행 동안 요구되는 조정이 충돌하는 상황에서 경기 심판이 주심에게의 통보가 필요할 경우 수정이 필요할 수 있다.

조정이 이루어지는 경우, 양 코치는 주심/주심 대리자에 의해 통지되고, 경기 심판은 스킵에게 통지한다.

중간 경기 휴식 5분 전에, 팀은 경기 심판에게 1분 전 알림을 받을 수 있고, 팀에게 남아있는 10초에는 딜리버리를 할 수 있다. 타이머는 시계가 '0'에 도달할 때나 스톤이 호그 라인에 도달할 때 팀의 시계를 시작할 준비를 해야 한다. 그렇지 않으면 경기 심판은 그 시트의 시계를 멈출 것을 요청해야 한다.

When an adjustment is made, both coaches are notified by the CU/DCU, and the GU notifies both Skips.

The mid-game break is 5 minutes, teams will be given a one min. warning by GU, and with 10 seconds remaining the team can commence delivery. Timer should be prepared to start the team's clock when the clock reaches "0" or when the stone reaches the hog line, unless the game Umpire requests to hold the clock for that sheet.

SPECIFIC SCENARIOS (timing related):

FGZ infractions – time runs for the delivering team until stones are replaced. GU will advise if necessary assistance is needed and the clock can be stopped.

Hogged stone – time runs until the stone is taken past the back line. The players can deal with a hogged stone themselves, or an IPA can assist. In the event that the IPA or the GU is delayed in their actions, the GU will advise the CT if any time adjustments are required.
The clock is stopped for GU to make a visual ruling at the hog line – GU will advise CT.

Hog line Violation – time continues for the delivering team. Its time clock continues to run, until the stone comes to rest or it crosses the back line. The GU will identify the delivered stone as a hog-line violation. Any displaced stones are returned to their original positions and the delivered stone must be moved over the back line.

Miscue during the delivery process:
Case 1: **stone goes over near hog line** - It is a hogged stone, and the players and/or GU and IPA(s) have to get it past the back line. Clocks will be stopped for assistance for the teams to remove the hogged stone past the back line.

Case 2: **stone not over hog line at the delivering end -** The delivering player stops the delivered stone prior to the stone reaching the delivery end hog line. The stone can be redelivered; clock continues to run. The IPA may help retrieve. If the delivery stick is broken the GU will advise the CT.

Variable delivery position – timing may be affected when a team uses a variable delivery position e.g. – a team delivers from near the hack line. Players would normally take up their position and then the stone would be placed in front of the chair. If they wish to change after this it will be in their time. The team that delivers the next stone should be allowed to get into position while a stone is going down the ice. This might block the view of the players delivering from near the hack, so the delivering team will have to move to a position where they can see; hopefully the teams will cooperate and not interfere with the player preparing for the next delivery. This should make it easier for the IPAs to get the stone to the players in a timely fashion, no matter where they set up.

Extra time used when a team changes order of throwing stone – Timers are not sure if it is a mistake or a request to get a different stone because the wrong stone was set out by IPA. Time should continue to run for that team unless the GU advises the CT that the clock should stop. If the mistake was made by the IPA the time can be adjusted if so directed by the GU.

A system of cards with the order of stones will be used by the IPA. Changes to the throwing order will be dealt with by the CU/GU between ends.

Stones deflecting – when to go to dead time if Game Umpire or IPA is delayed. GU and IPA can assist in removing dead stones. The GU can call a technical time-out if things are really confused and/or altered. GU will advise CT.

특정 상황(시간 계측 관련):

프리 가드 존 위반 - 스톤이 교체될 때까지 딜리버리하는 팀의 시간은 흐른다.
도움이 필요할 경우 경기 심판이 조언할 수 있고, 시계는 정지할 수 있다.

호그 된 스톤 - 스톤이 이전 백 라인으로 가게 될 때까지 시간은 계속 흐른다. 선수는 호그된 스톤을 처리할 수 있고, 얼음 위 선수 보조자 또한 지원할 수 있다. 얼음 위 선수 보조자 또는 경기 심판의 조치가 지연되는 경우에 시간 조정이 필요하면 경기 심판은 시간 계측장에게 조언할 수 있다.
경기 심판이 호그 라인에서 시각적인 판단을 하는 동안 시계는 정지된다. - 경기 심판은 주심에게 조언할 수 있다.

호그 라인 위반 - 시간은 팀이 딜리버리하는 동안 계속된다. 스톤이 멈추거나, 백 라인을 통과할 때까지 시계는 계속 작동된다. 경기 심판은 딜리버리된 스톤을 호그 라인 위반으로 식별할 수 있다. 어떤 대체된 스톤은 원래 위치로 돌아가고, 딜리버리 된 스톤은 백 라인으로 이동해야 한다.

딜리버리 과정 동안의 실수:

case 1: **스톤이 호그 라인 근처를 넘은 경우** - 그것은 호그된 스톤이고, 선수/경기 심판 및 얼음 위 선수 보조자는 이전 백 라인에서 스톤을 얻을 수 있다. 시계는 이전 백 라인으로 호그된 스톤을 팀이 제거하기 위해 멈출 것이다.
case 2: **스톤이 딜리버리 엔드 끝에서 호그 라인을 넘지 않은 경우** - 딜리버리하는 선수는 딜리버리된 돌을 딜리버리 엔드 호그 라인에 도달하고 있는 스톤에 앞서 딜리버리된 돌을 멈춘다. 스톤은 다시 딜리버리될 수 있고, 시간은 계속 흐른다. 얼음 위 선수 보조자는 그 과정에서 도움이 될 수 있다. 딜리버리 스틱이 부러진 경우 경기 심판은 시간 계측장에게 알려 줄 것이다.

가변적인 딜리버리 위치 - 팀이 가변적인 딜리버리 위치를 사용할 때 타이밍에 영향을 미칠 수 있다. 예를 들어 - 팀은 핵라인 근처에서 딜리버리한다.
선수들은 일반적으로 자신의 위치를 차지하고, 그리고 스톤은 의자의 앞에 배치된다. 만약 그들이 후에 변경하고자 한다면, 그 팀의 시간이 흘러갈 것이다. 다음 스톤을 딜리버리하는 팀은 스톤이 진행되는 동안 위치로 가는 것이 허용된다. 이것은 핵 근처로부터 딜리버리하는 선수의 시야를 막을 수 있으므로, 딜리버리하는 팀은 그들이 볼 수 있는 위치로 이동해야만 할 것이다. ; 팀은 협력할 것이고 선수가 다음 딜리버리를 준비하는 데 방해하지 않을 것이다.

팀이 스톤을 던지는 순서를 변경할 때 추가 시간의 사용 - 시간 계측자(타임 키퍼)는 실수인지 또는 잘못된 스톤이 얼음 위 선수 보조자에 의해 준비되어있어 다른 스톤을 얻기 위한 요청인지 확신할 수 없다. 경기 심판이 시간 계측장에게 시계를 중지하라고 하지 않는다면 시간은 계속 흐를 것이다. 얼음 위 선수 보조자에 의한 실수가 발생한다면 시간은 조정될 수 있다. 스톤의 순서와 카드 시스템이 얼음 위 선수 보조자에 의해 사용될 것이다. 던지는 순서 변경은 엔드 사이에 주심/경기 심판에 의해 처리된다.

스톤 편향 - 심판 또는 얼음 위 선수 보조자는 지연된다. 경기 심판과 얼음 위 선수 보조자는 죽은 스톤을 제거하는 걸 도울 수 있다. 경기 심판은 혼란스럽거나 변경되었다면 테크니컬 타임아웃을 요청할 수 있다. 경기 심판은 시간 계측장에게 알릴 것이다.

Delivering team players movement after delivery:

Case I – players vacate delivery area before their stone stops at playing end.

Opposition may move in to delivery position even before their clock starts. The clock runs for the delivering team until the stone comes to rest and the delivering team Skip has moved behind the back line.

Case 2 - players stay in the delivery position until their stone stops in play or crosses the back line.

Timer will not switch to next team until the delivering team moves to the back line and out of the way of the next team.

Case 3 – Skip proceeds down the ice between his/her shots.

Skip must proceed down the side of the sheet. If he/she goes down centre, time will run for that team. Skip may be caught at far hog if next team is ready to deliver but must not distract the delivering team. If the skip follows a shot down the sheet and the stone has come to rest that person should stop and check to see if the delivering team is ready to deliver prior to his/her entry into the playing end. If the next player is ready to deliver and is waiting for him to stop moving, the offending team will have its time continue to run. The delivering team has to relinquish the playing area before its clock will stop.

Case 4 – ice not ready after mid-game break.

If the ice crew is delayed during the mid-game break, the GU will advise if the auto start is to be aborted and will direct the CT when to start the clock. Start the clock when delivered stone reaches the hog line.

Ice Player Assistant (IPA) – their actions placing, cleaning, ordering, moving, catching deflections may affect timing. - A team should not be penalised or time should not be taken away from a team if an IPA is delayed in his/her actions for any reason. Timers shall relay any concerns about delays to the CT.

At the conclusion of an end the IPA will get the first stone of the next end cleaned and in position for the delivering team. Once this is done the delivering team's time will start when the between end time reaches "0" or the stone reaches the near hog line.

Once a stone is delivered, the team who will deliver next can get its stone cleaned and in position.

Stone placement for teams when delivering long and short (varying shot to shot) - Players usually take up their delivery position and then the stone is placed in front of the chair. Stone should be delivered to the players wherever they set up. They are allowed to do this while the previous stone is going down the ice.

If a player drops a delivery stick during delivery preparation, an IPA can assist if requested. Time continues for the delivering team.

딜리버리하는 팀 선수들의 딜리버리 후 움직임:

Case 1 - 선수들은 플레이하는 엔드에서 스톤이 멈추기 전 딜리버리 지역을 떠난다. 반대편 측은 자신의 시계가 시작되기 전에 딜리버리 위치로 움직일 것이다. 스톤이 멈추고 딜리버리 팀 스킵이 백 라인 뒤로 움직일 때까지 시계는 계속 갈 것이다.

Case 2 - 플레이에서 스톤이 멈추거나 백 라인 뒤로 넘어갈 때까지 선수는 딜리버리 위치에 머무른다. 딜리버리 팀이 백 라인으로 움직이고 다음 팀에 방해가 되지 않을 때까지 타이머는 다음 팀으로 바꾸지 않을 것이다.

Case 3 - 스킵은 그/그녀의 샷 사이에서 얼음 아래로 진행한다. 그/그녀가 중심으로 넘어지면 시간을 그 팀을 위해 흐를 것이다. 다음 팀이 딜리버리할 준비가 되어있으면 스킵은 멀리 떨어진 호그에서 발견될지 모른다. 그러나 딜러버리 팀을 방해해서는 안 된다. 스킵이 샷을 시트 아래에서 따르고 그 스톤이 멈추면 사람은 멈춰서 딜리버리 팀이 플레이하는 엔드에 그/그녀의 엔트리 이전에 앞서 딜리버리할 준비가 되어 있는지 아닌지를 체크해 보아야 한다. 다음 선수가 딜리버리할 준비가 되어 있고 그가 움직임을 멈추고 기다리고 있다면 문제가 되는 팀은 시간이 계속 흐를 것이다. 딜리버리 팀은 시계가 멈추기 전에 플레이하는 지역을 떠나야 한다.

Case 4 - 얼음은 중반 경기 휴식 후 준비되지 않은 경우. 만약 얼음 전담팀이 중반 경기 휴식 동안 지연된다면, 경기 심판은 자동 시작이 중지되었는지를 알려줄 것이고 시간 계측장에게 계측을 시작하라고 지시할 것이다. 딜리버리된 스톤이 호그 라인에 도착할 때 계측을 시작한다.

얼음 위 선수 보조자(약어: IPA) - 그들의 배치, 클리닝, 움직임 굴절의 캐치는 시간 계측에 영향을 준다. - 얼음 위 선수 보조자가 어떤 이유로 그들의 행동에 의해 지연될 경우 팀은 처벌되지 않거나 시간은 뺏기지 않는다. 타이머는 경기 지연에 대한 우려를 시간 계측장에게 표명한다.

한 엔드의 결과에 따라 얼음 위 선수 보조자는 다음 엔드의 첫 번째 스톤과 딜리버리 팀에 대한 위치를 알 수 있다. 한 엔드가 끝나면, 딜리버리하는 팀의 시간은 엔드 시간이 0에 도달하거나 스톤이 호그 라인 근처에 도달하는 사이에 있을 때 시작할 것이다.

일단 스톤이 딜리버리되면, 다음 딜리버리하는 팀의 선수는 그 위치에 놓음으로써 이전의 스톤을 테이크아웃할 수 있다.

딜리버리가 길거나 짧을 때 팀을 위한 스톤의 배치 - 선수는 정해진 딜리버리 위치에 자리하고, 스톤이 의자 앞에 위치된다. 스톤은 선수가 세워지는 어디든지 전달될 것이다. 이전 스톤이 얼음으로 나아가는 동안에 이러한 과정이 허용된다.

선수가 딜리버리 준비하는 동안 스틱이 떨어지면 요청이 있는 경우, 얼음 위 선수 보조자는 지원할 수 있다. 딜리버리 팀의 시간은 계속 간다.

29. HAND-OUT: TIMERS

TIMERS SHOULD KNOW HOW TO DO THE FOLLOWING:

1. Run Red time clock & switch to Yellow using the space bar.
2. Change from one team to the other when all stones have come to rest, or cross the back line, & the delivering team relinquishes the playing surface.
3. Between end break - one minute. Count the stones to determine if Red or Yellow still has a stone to deliver. Know how to start the break on the clock. Don't be too quick to start the break ... the break should not be started until the teams agree on the score of that end.
4. What to do if there is a delay in clearing the stones between ends, or a measure is requested.
5. How to abort the countdown if the team delivers early.
6. Which team has last stone in each end? The team that scores will deliver first in the next end.
7. Mid-game break - set time on clock ... know when to start it, and how to start.
8. Which team delivers first after the mid-game break? When the time count is 00:00 start the clock for the delivering team even if they are not ready.
9. If the ice technician has not completed cleaning the ice the Chief Timer (CT) will tell you to hold the clock ... wait until given the instruction from the CT before starting the clock.
10. Teams must not deliver early after the mid-game break - with 10 seconds remaining is acceptable. Know how to abort the countdown and start the delivering team's clock.
11. With the red clock running a team signals a time-out with the "T" hand signal. Announce "time-out alpha, red". Press the time-out button. Watch for the Umpire's signal to start the one minute time-out (raised arm - when the coach reaches the team, or the travel time expires).
12. If the wrong time clock is running for the delivering team, call the Chief Timer and record the amount of time owed and which colour receives the corrected time. E.g. Red owed 6 seconds, 4th end, 3rd stone.

29. 핸드 아웃: 타이머들(시간 계측자들)

타이머는 다음 작업을 수행하는 방법을 알고 있어야 한다. :

1. 빨간 시계를 실행 및 스페이스 바를 사용하여 노란색 시계로 전환한다.
2. 모든 스톤이 정지했거나, 백 라인을 넘은 경우 또는 딜리버리 팀이 양도했을 때 한 팀에서 다른 팀으로 바꿔라.
3. 엔드 휴식 사이 - 1분. 빨강, 노란색이 딜리버리할 스톤을 가지고 있는지를 확인하기 위해서 스톤을 세어라. 시계를 휴식시간 동안 멈추는 방법을 알아라. 휴식을 너무 빨리 시작하지 마라. 팀들이 엔드의 점수에 동의할 때까지 휴식이 시작되어서는 안 된다.
4. 엔드 사이에 스톤을 치우는 데 지연되거나, 측정이 필요할 때의 역할을 알고 있어야 한다.
5. 팀이 일찍 딜리버리할 경우 카운트다운을 중지하는 방법
6. 각 엔드에서 어떤 팀이 후공인지를 알아야 한다. 점수 낸 팀이 다음 엔드에서 첫 번째로 딜리버리할 것이다.
7. 중간 경기 휴식: 언제 어떻게 시작할지를 시계에 적용하여라.
8. 중간 경기 휴식 후에 어느 팀이 먼저 딜리버리할 것인가? 시간 카운터가 00:00이면 그들이 준비하지 않았더라도 딜리버리 팀을 위해 시계를 시작해라.
9. 빙판 기술자의 얼음 점검이 완료되지 않았다면 시간 계측장은 당신에게 시계를 멈추라고 말할 것이다. 시계를 시작하기 전 시간 계측장로부터 지시를 받기 전까지 기다려라.
10. 팀은 중간 경기 휴식 후 일찍 딜리버리하지 말아야 한다. 10초 남기고 허용된다. 카운트다운을 중지하는 방법을 알아라. 그리고 딜리버리 팀의 시계를 시작해라.
11. 빨간 시계가 작동하는 팀은 'T' 핸드 신호로 타임아웃 신호를 보낸다. "타임아웃, A, 레드."라고 알려라. 타임아웃 버튼을 눌러라. 1분 시간제한을 시작하는 심판의 신호에 대해 살펴보아라. (올려진 팔- 코치가 팀에 도착할 때, 이동 시간이 만료되었을 때)
12. 잘못된 시간 시계가 딜리버리하는 팀에 작동하고 있다면, 시간 계측장을 불러서 잘못된 시간을 기록해라. (예를 들어 - 빨간 팀이 6초 빚지고 있음, 4번째 엔드 3번째 스톤 차례)

30. HOG LINE OBSERVER

DUTIES

The hog line observer is solely responsible for observing whether the release of each stone is in accordance with the rules, and calling any infractions that occur. This requires intense concentration, good judgment, and a quick response. The hog line observer must be certain in his/her own mind that a violation has occurred. The decisions of the hog line observer are very sensitive and must be made by someone who will not be intimidated. When possible, calls should be confirmed by another hog line observer sitting directly across from the one who initiated the call. The observer should be placed on or slightly outside the hog line and concentrate the vision directly on the line and not on the deliverer. The hog line observer is in radio contact with the Game Umpires and Chief Umpire and reports any infraction of the delivery rules, including stones which have been delivered and retouched. The rules state that the stone must be clearly released before the front of the stone reaches the hog line.

PROCEDURES

1. Hog line Warning
   The first hog line warning is given at the pre-event Team Meeting, so any on-ice offence will be penalized.
   The correct call by the hog line observer is:
   "HOG LINE ...BRAVO ... RED"
   The acknowledgement by the hog line supervisor of the radio transmission is:
   "CONFIRMED / DENIED – BRAVO – RED"

2. The Game Umpire will move quickly to the designated sheet while noting stone positions. The violation will be announced to the offending skip who must remove the stone from play. The Game Umpire will oversee the removal of the stone and the replacement of any displaced stones.

3. At high-level competitions, a hog line call may need verification before it is official. A hog line supervisor may be assigned the responsibility of supervising hog line calls and verifying the call made by the hog line observer. The Game Umpire will then supervise the removal of the stone and the replacement of any moved stones.

RECORDING

All hog line violations are to be recorded by the hog line observer and by the end-ice observer on the record sheets provided.

NOTE

If there is a dispute regarding a hog line call, the Chief Umpire will make the final ruling based on discussion with the observer(s) making the call. Television or other recorded evidence is NOT admissible.

30. 호그 라인 관찰자

의무

호그 라인 관찰자는 딜리버리된 각 스톤이 규정에 맞는지를 관찰할 책임이 있고, 발생하는 위반을 발견할 책임이 있다. 강인한 집중과 신속한 대응이 필요하다. 호그 라인 관찰자는 위반이 발생하면 확신해야 한다. 호그 라인 관찰자의 결정은 매우 민감하고 외부에 의해 협박받지 않는 사람에 의해야 한다. 가능하면 호출자로부터 가로질러 앉아있는 다른 호그 라인 관찰자에 의해 확인되도록 해라. 관찰자는 호그 라인 약간 밖에 위치하고 딜리버리하는 사람을 관찰하는 게 아닌 라인에서 시야에 집중해라. 호그 라인 관찰자는 경기 심판 및 최고 심판을 무선으로 접촉하고 어느 스톤이 딜리버리되었고 다시 터치되었는지를 포함해 딜리버리 룰의 위반을 보고해라. 호그 라인에 도달하기 전에 스톤을 명확히 놓아야 된다고 규칙을 말해라.

절차

1. 첫 호그 라인 경고는 경기 이전 팀 미팅에서 주어지므로, 얼음 위에서 위법적인 행위는 처벌된다. 호그 라인 관찰자에 의한 올바른 호출은 다음과 같다. "호그 라인… B… 빨간 팀." 무선 전송의 호그 라인 관리자에 의한 인정은 "확인/거부 - B - 빨간팀"으로 이루어진다.
2. 경기 심판은 스톤의 위치를 확인하면서 지정된 시트를 신속하게 이동해야 할 것이다. 위반은 플레이로부터 스톤을 제거해야만 하는 스킵에게서 알려진다. 경기 심판은 스톤의 제거 및 위치된 스톤의 교체를 감독할 것이다.
3. 높은 수준의 대회에서, 호그 라인 호출은 공식적으로 되기 전 검증이 필요할지도 모른다. 호그 라인 감독자는 호그 라인 호출을 감독하는 책임을 부여받고 호그 라인 관찰자에 의한 호출을 확인한다. 경기 심판은 스톤의 제거와 이동된 스톤의 교체를 감독한다.

기록

모든 호그 라인 위반은 모든 호그 라인 관찰자와 엔드 아이스 관찰자에 의해 제동되는 기록 시트에 기록되어야 한다.

참조

호그 라인 호출과 관련하여 분쟁이 있을 경우, 주심은 호출을 하는 관찰자들과 논의에 기초하여 최종 판정을 할 것이다. 텔레비전 또는 다른 기록된 증거는 인정되지 않는다.

31. EYE ON THE HOG – HOG LINE VIOLATION DETECTION SYSTEM

1. GENERAL

Eye on the Hog is a system that provides impartial hog-line judging for the sport of curling. It uses innovative technology to detect a magnetic strip frozen into the ice at the hog line and a bare hand touching the handle. Circuitry in the handle turns on green lights after a valid release or flashes red lights if a violation has occurred.

2. OPERATION

Eye on the Hog electronics activate and the red LEDs flash when the stone is tilted to an angle of 70 degrees, with a bare hand touching the coated handle grip. When the stone is returned to the playing position and the grip is released, the green LEDs flash quickly for ten seconds and then slowly for two minutes. If the grip is not touched, the electronics will turn off after the slow flashing stops. If the grip is touched, the LEDs turn off to prevent distracting the curler during delivery. When the grip is released before the hog line, the green LEDs flash until the centre of the stone crosses the centre of the hog-line magnet; then, the green LEDs turn on for five seconds to indicate a valid delivery. If the grip is not released before the centre of the stone crosses the centre of the hog-line magnet, a violation is indicated for twenty-five seconds by flashing red LEDs. The touch sensor remains on for a short interval after the hog line is crossed. If the grip is touched in this interval, indication will switch from valid to violation. Alternating red and green LEDs indicates a low battery.

3. VERIFICATION TESTS

Handle operation should be verified before a competition.

<u>MOUNTED-HANDLE TEST</u> (USING HOG-LINE MAGNET)

With a bare hand touching the grip, tilt the stone on its striking surface to activate the electronics. The red LEDs should flash momentarily.

Return the stone to its running surface and release the grip. The green LEDs should flash rapidly.

Touch the grip with one finger. The LEDs should turn off.

Without touching the grip, push the stone over the hog-line magnet at a normal curling speed. The green LEDs should turn on for five seconds.

After the green LEDs turn off, wait two seconds and then reactivate the electronics. With a bare hand touching the grip, push the stone over the hog line magnet at a normal curling speed. The red LEDs should flash for twenty-five seconds.

31. EYE ON THE HOG – 호그 라인 위반 검출 시스템

1. 소개

호그 라인 위반 검출 시스템은 컬링 스포츠에서 호그 라인의 공정한 판단을 제공하는 시스템이다. 이것은 호그 라인에서 아이스로 냉동자기 띠와 핸들을 만지는 맨손을 감지하는 혁신적인 기술을 사용한다. 핸들에 있는 회로는 유효한 딜리버리 후에는 녹색 조명을 켜거나 위반이 발생할 땐 빨간 불빛을 깜빡인다.

2. 조작

호그 전자 장치 버튼을 활성화시키고 스톤이 70도 각도로 기울여지고 코팅된 핸들 그립을 맨손으로 만질 때 빨간색 LED가 깜빡인다. 스톤이 플레이 위치로 되돌아가고 그립을 놓으면, 그린 LED는 10초 동안 신속하게 깜빡이고 그런 다음 2분 동안 천천히 깜빡인다. 그립을 터치하면, 운반 동안에 경기자를 방해하는 것을 막기 위해 LED는 꺼진다. 호그 라인 전에 그립을 놓았을 때 스톤의 중심이 호그 라인 마그넷을 통과할 때까지 녹색 LED가 들어온다. 다음, 녹색 LED는 유효한 딜리버리를 나타내기 위해 5초 동안 점등된다. 스톤의 중심이 호그 라인 마그넷의 중심을 넘기 전에 그립이 놓이지 않은 경우, 빨간 LED가 25초 동안 위반을 나타내기 위해 켜진다. 호그 라인이 교차된 후 터치 센서는 짧은 간격 동안 유지된다. 이 간격 동안 그립이 터치되면, 유효에서 위반으로 표시가 전환된다. 빨강과 녹색 LED가 번갈아 나오는 경우 배터리 부족을 나타낸다.

3. 검증 테스트

핸들 조작은 경쟁하기 전에 확인해야 한다.

장착형 핸들 TEST(HOG-LINE의 자석을 사용)

맨손으로 그립을 터치하고, 전자를 활성화하기 위해서 스톤의 표면을 기울여라. 빨간 LED가 잠깐 들어온다.

스톤을 달리는 표면에 돌려 그립을 놓는다. 녹색 LED는 빠르게 비출 것이다.

한 손가락으로 그립을 터치해라. LED가 꺼질 것이다.

그립을 건드리지 않고, 보통 컬링 속도로 호그 라인 마그넷 위에 스톤을 밀어 넣어라. 녹색 LED는 5초 동안 켜질 것이다.

녹색 LED가 꺼진 후, 2초를 기다린 후 전자를 재활성해라. 그립을 맨손으로 만지고, 보통 컬링 속도로 호그 라인 마그넷 위에 스톤을 밀어 넣어라. 빨강 LED가 25초 동안 켜질 것이다.

4. CURLER'S INSTRUCTIONS

Curlers should be familiar with the following guidelines to ensure proper operation of the system. Prior to delivering a stone, the handle electronics must be activated by tilting the stone with a bare hand touching the grip. After it is activated, if the grip is not touched for two minutes the electronics will turn off and will have to be reactivated. To verify that the system is working, release the activated handle grip and observe that the green LEDs flash. Touch the grip and observe that the green LEDs turn off. The touch sensor in the handle was designed to detect a bare hand, therefore a glove or mitt must not be worn on the delivery hand during the delivery of a stone. Flashing red LEDs indicate a hog-line violation. Solid green LEDs indicate a valid release. Alternating red and green LEDs indicate a low battery. Inform the officials.

CAUTION: Brushes and shoes can damage the coated handle grip and the LEDs. Do not push on the handle with brushes or shoes.

CAUTION: Do not invert the stone on the ice with the grip contacting the ice. The grip coating can be damaged.

CAUTION: If a handle becomes loose, do not attempt to tighten it by rotating the handle. This can damage the battery carrier. Have an official or ice technician properly torque the mounting screw.

5. HISTORY

The concept for an electronic hog line violation detection system came from Professor Eric Salt at the University of Saskatchewan. He offered the concept as a fourth-year design project for a group of electrical engineering students. The original design team included Professor Eric Salt and students; Jarret Adam, Jason Smith, Johanna Koch, and Kevin Ackerman. Startco staff had some early involvement as Eric approached his long-time friend Joe Dudiak of Startco to mentor the students. The U of S design had a permanent magnet at the bottom of the stone and a magnetic field sensing strip imbedded in the ice cable connected to a display. The initial in-ice sensing strip was assembled in the Startco facility in the winter of 1999/2000.

After the students graduated, Startco was approached to finish the design and to take the product to market. Although the design was extensively modified, Startco pays royalties to the U of S and the students for sharing concepts and contacts. After over a year of research and development Startco released the Eye on the Hog system.

4. 선수 지침

선수는 시스템의 적절한 작동을 보장하기 위해 가이드라인을 잘 알고 있어야 한다. 스톤을 딜리버리하기 전, 전자 핸들은 그립을 만진 맨손으로 스톤을 기울여서 활성화되어야 한다. 활성화된 후, 그립이 2분 동안 접촉하지 않은 경우 전자는 꺼지고 다시 활성화되어야 한다. 시스템이 작동하는지 확인하려면, 활성화된 핸들 그립을 해제하고 녹색 LED가 켜지는지 확인해라. 그립을 터치하고 녹색 LED가 꺼지는지 관찰해라. 핸들에 터치 센서는 맨손을 감지하도록 설계되어 있어서 장갑 또는 미트를 스톤의 딜리버리 중 딜리버리 손에 착용하지 말아야 한다. 빨강 LED가 들어오는 것은 호그 라인 위반을 지시한다. 녹색 LED는 올바른 딜리버리를 했다는 것을 나타낸다. 빨간색과 녹색 LED가 깜빡이는 것은 배터리 부족을 나타낸다. 관리자에게 알려라.

주의: 브러시 및 신발은 코팅된 핸들 그립과 LED에 손상을 줄 수 있다. 핸들을 브러시와 신발로 밀지 말아라.

주의: 아이스 위의 스톤을 아이스에 접촉하는 그립과 뒤집지 말아라. 그립 코팅이 손상될 수 있다.

주의: 핸들이 느슨해지면, 핸들을 회전하여 조이려고 시도하지 마라. 이 행동은 배터리 캐리어를 손상시킬 수도 있다. 관리자나 얼음 기술자가 나사를 장착하는 토크를 가지고 있다.

5. 역사

호그 라인 위반 탐지 시스템에 대한 개념은 서스캐처원 대학에서 에릭 솔트 교수로부터 도입되었다. 그는 전기 공학 학생들의 그룹에 대한 4년의 설계 프로젝트를 제안했다. 원래의 디자인 팀은 에릭 솔트 교수와 학생들을 포함했다; 레트 아담, 제이슨 스미스, 요한나 코흐, 케빈 에커. Startco의 조 Dudiak에게 학생들의 멘토로서 접근한 에릭으로부터 Startco 스탭은 일부 초기 참여했다. 서스캐처원 대학의 디자인은 스톤의 아래에 영구적인 마그넷을 가지고 있고 마그네틱 필드 센서링 스트립은 디스플레이에 연결된 아이스 케이블에 박혀있다. 초기 아이스 센서링 스트립은 1999/2000년 겨울 Startco 시설에서 조립되었다.

학생들이 졸업한 이후, Startco는 디자인을 완료하고 시장에 제품을 내놓기 위해 접근했다. 비록 설계가 광범위하게 수정되었지만, Startco는 서스캐처원 대학과 학생들에게 개념 및 접촉 공유를 위한 로열티를 지불한다. 조사와 개발 수년 후에 Startco는 '호그 시스템의 눈(호그 라인 위반 탐지 시스템)'을 발표했다.

32. EYE ON THE HOG MALFUNCTION PROCEDURES

This information should be included in the Team Meeting Document so that players are aware of the following procedures:

13. Alternating red and green lights flashing quickly indicate that the handle has not been properly set. The player must reset the handle before delivering the stone.

14. Alternating red and green lights flashing slowly indicate a low battery. The delivering player should call for an Umpire using the "X" signal. The player will then have the option of having the handle changed before the delivery or continuing with the delivery while an Umpire views the release at the hog line.

15. No lights indicate a faulty connection. The delivering player should call for an Umpire using the "X" signal. The player will have the option of having the handle changed before the delivery or continuing with the delivery while an Umpire views the release at the hog line.

16. If flashing red lights are believed to have come on before the stone had reached the hog line at the delivering end – the sweepers should pull the stone to the side of the sheet, get it across the back line as quickly as possible, and call for an Umpire using the "X" signal. The Umpire will call for an Ice Technician to test the handle. If the Ice Technician deems the handle to be properly functioning, the stone will be considered a hog line violation. If the handle is deemed to be faulty, the player will be allowed to redeliver. The time clock will not run during that delivery.

    Any stone that shows red lights must be stopped before it crosses the hog line at the playing end or it will be treated as a hog line violation.

32. 호그 라인 위반 탐지 시스템 오작동 시 대처 방안

플레이어가 다음의 절차를 인식하도록 이러한 정보는 팀 회의 문서에 포함되어야 한다 :

13. 빨강과 녹색 불빛의 빠르게 깜빡이는 것은 핸들이 제대로 설정되지 않았음을 나타낸다. 선수는 스톤을 딜리버리하기 전에 핸들을 다시 설정해야 한다.

14. 빨강과 녹색 불빛이 천천히 깜빡이는 것은 배터리 부족을 나타낸다. 딜리버리하는 선수는 'X' 신호를 사용하여 심판을 호출해야 한다. 그리고 선수는 심판이 호그 라인에서 딜리버리 과정을 지켜보거나, 딜리버리하기 전이나 딜리버리 도중 핸들을 바꿀 수 있는 옵션을 가질 수 있다.

15. 빛이 없음은 결함 있는 연결을 나타낸다. 딜리버리하는 선수는 'X'신호를 사용하여 심판을 호출해야 한다. 선수는 심판이 호그 라인에서 딜리버리 과정을 지켜보거나, 딜리버리하기 전이나 딜리버리 도중 핸들을 바꿀 수 있는 옵션을 가질 수 있다.

16. 만약 스톤이 딜리버리 엔드에 있는 호그 라인에 도착하기 전에 빨간빛이 들어온다면, 스위퍼는 스톤을 시트 사이드로 당길 수 있고, 가능한 한 빨리 백 라인 뒤로 가로질러 둘 수 있고 'X'신호를 사용하여 심판을 호출할 수 있다. 심판은 핸들을 테스트하기 위해서 아이스 테크니션을 호출할 것이다. 테크니션이 제대로 작동한다고 판단한 경우, 스톤은 호그 라인 위반으로 간주된다. 핸들이 고장난 것으로 여겨질 경우, 선수는 다시 딜리버리하는 것이 허용된다. 타임 시간은 딜리버리하는 동안 작동되지 않는다.

빨간빛을 보여주는 스톤은 플레이 엔드에 호그 라인을 교차하기 전에 정지해야만 한다. 그렇지 않으면 호그 라인 위반으로 여겨질 것이다.

33. CHIEF STATISTICIAN

DUTIES

1. Appointed by the WCF in cooperation with the Organizing Committee (OC).
2. Provides a comprehensive results service to all teams, media, Umpires, OC, and WCF (Director of Competitions or Event Technical Delegate).
3. Responsible for training and overseeing the volunteer scorers.
4. Liaises between the Results Team and the Chief Umpire to ensure smooth running of the event.

PRE-COMPETITION

1. Ensure that a training session is provided for volunteer scorers. (Ideally a session would be done well before the event to provide practice time.) Assist in developing a work schedule.
2. Liaise with appropriate committees or facility staff to ensure that the volunteer scorers and Chief Statistician's work stations, computers and printers will be set up appropriately.
3. Determine if the Results Team or the Chief Umpire is going to provide the relevant forms to the Chief Statistician:
    - Original team line-up forms
    - Change of line-up forms
    - Game line-up forms
    - Game Timing forms
    - On-ice scorecards
    - Last stone draw (LSD) results
4. At the Team Meeting, identify the procedures for:
    - Distributing relevant forms and their return
    - Distributing results to the teams – paper or electronic format (e.g. Email addresses)
5. Establish requirements on updating scoreboards during games.
6. Establish requirements for ensuring availability of end of game times from the Timers.

DURING THE COMPETITION

1. Maintain communication/radio contact with the Chief Umpire/Game Umpires during games, to receive the following information:
    - Change of line-up
    - Confirmation of score at completion of the end and the game
    - Confirmation of an incident occurring on the ice, e.g. burnt stone, hog line violation, etc.
2. Confirm time for submission of game line-up forms by teams.
3. Monitor the computer program to ensure data is being entered correctly and that results are being uploaded to online scoring and statistics websites and media outlets appropriately.
4. Return on-ice scorecards and timing forms to the results office.
5. Submit scores and standings to the Chief Umpire after each draw.
6. Submit results to all teams, media, OC, and WCF Director of Competitions and/or Event Technical Delegate (TD).
7. Update the Draw Shot Challenge (DSC) results.
8. At the conclusion of the round robin, complete the standings and team rankings including the DSC. Depending on level of service offered, advise the Chief Umpire on best sheets to use for tie-breaker games and all play-off games once the relevant teams are known.

POST COMPETITION

Submit a complete set of results to teams, media, Umpires, OC, and WCF (Director of Competitions and/or TD).

33. 대표 통계 전문가

의무

1. 조직위원회(OC)와 협력하여 세계컬링연맹에 의해 임명.
2. 모든 팀, 미디어, 심판, 조직위원회, 그리고 세계컬링연맹에 대한 포괄적인 결과 서비스를 제공(경기 관리자 또는 경기 기술위원 대표).
3. 자원봉사 기록원을 훈련하고 감독할 책임이 있다.
4. 경기의 원활한 운영을 보장하기 위해 우승팀과 주심 사이에 연락을 취함.

경기 이전

1. 자원봉사 기록원을 위해 훈련 세션이 제공하는지 확인해라(이상적인 세션은 이벤트 전에 연습 시간을 제공하기 위해 잘 될 것이다). 근무 일정 향상에 도움이 된다.
2. 자원 봉사 기록원과 최고 통계 전문가의 작업실, 컴퓨터 그리고 프린터가 적절히 설정될 수 있는지 확인하기 위해 위원회 또는 시설 직원과 적절한 연락을 취해라.
3. 우승팀 또는 주심이 관련 양식을 대표 통계 전문가에게 제공할지를 결정해라.
    - 기존 팀 라인업 형태
    - 라인업 형태의 변경
    - 경기 라인업 형태
    - 경기 시간 측정 양식
    - 빙판 위에서 사용되는 스코어카드
    - 마지막 스톤 드로우(LSD) 결과
4. 팀 회의에서 절차에 대한 확인 :
    - 관련 양식 및 그들의 보고서를 배포
    - 팀에 결과를 배포 - 종이 또는 전자 형식 (예: 이메일 주소)
5. 경기 중 스코어 보드 업데이트에 대한 요구 사항을 설정.
6. 타이머에서 경기 시간의 끝의 가용성을 보장하기 위한 요구 사항을 설정.

경기 중

1. 경기 동안 다음과 같은 정보를 받기 위해 주심/경기 심판과 통신/무선 접촉을 유지:
    - 라인업 변경
    - 엔드와 경기의 완성에서 점수 확인
    - 아이스 위에서 발생하는 사건의 확인, 예 - 죽은 스톤, 호그 라인 위반 등.
2. 팀 경기 라인업 형태의 제출 시간을 확인.
3. 데이터가 올바르게 입력되고 결과가 온라인 스코어링, 통계 웹사이트, 언론 매체에 적절하게 업로드되고 있는지를 확인하기 위해 컴퓨터 프로그램을 모니터링해라.
4. 온 아이스 스코어카드와 타이밍 형태를 결과 사무실에 돌려주어라.
5. 각 경기 이후 점수와 순위를 주심에게 제출.
6. 모든 팀, 미디어, 조직위원회, 세계컬링연맹 파견 책임자 그리고 경기 기술위원 대표(TD)에게 결과를 제출.
7. 드로우 샷 챌린지(LSD 거리) 결과 갱신.
8. 라운드 로빈의 결과, 순위와 DSC를 포함한 팀 순위가 정해지면, 제공되는 서비스의 단계에 따라 관련 팀이 알려지면 타이 브레이크 경기와 모든 플레이오프 경기를 위해 시트를 사용하기 위해 적합한 시트에 있는 최고 심판에게 조언해라.

경기 발표

팀, 매체, 심판, 조직위원회 그리고 세계컬링연맹(대회 책임자 및 경기 기술위원 대표)에게 종료된 경기 결과를 제출.

34. STATISTICS SYTEM

OBJECTIVES OF THE STATISTICS SYSTEM

1. To create interest in the game for fans and players

2. To assist the media in their coverage of curling

3. To make curling and any particular event more attractive to sponsors

4. To provide additional information for coaches and players

GENERAL PRINCIPLES

1. Ideally, each scorer should be assigned to the same sheet of ice for the total duration of the event. This provides consistency in scoring and has each team evaluated by the same scorer the same number of games.

2. The scorer should apply the system generously so that the curlers are given the benefit of the doubt in all situations.

3. Shots should be evaluated according to what was called. Scorers must not consider the strategy employed by a team or whether there might have been a better call in their opinion.

4. Consideration should not be given to the scorer's opinion as to why a shot was missed. Whether or not the skip gave the wrong broom placement or the sweepers made a mistake should not be a factor.

SYSTEM OF SCORING

The method used is a four-point system. A shot executed correctly is given the maximum of four points.

A complete miss is given zero points. Partially successful shots are scored between zero and four. In a 10 end game the maximum score for a player is 80 points. Where a game is conceded before all stones have been delivered, a player's possible maximum points is reduced by four for each stone not delivered. When one or more extra ends have been played, a player's possible maximum points are increased by four points for each stone delivered.

A stone deliberately thrown through the house is not counted as a delivered stone. The paper score sheet (or computer score screen) is marked with an "X" as the type of shot thrown, and the player's maximum points are reduced by four each time this occurs.

34. 통계 시스템

통계 시스템의 목적

1. 팬과 선수에게 경기에 대한 관심을 높이기 위해
2. 컬링에서 매체를 돕기 위해
3. 컬링과 특정 경기를 후원사에게 더 매력적으로 만들기 위해
4. 추가 정보를 코치와 선수에게 제공하기 위해

기본 원칙

1. 이상적으로, 각각의 기록원은 이벤트의 총 지속 시간 동안 동일한 시트에 배정되어야 한다. 이것은 채점의 일관성을 제공하고 각 팀은 같은 기록원에 의해 같은 수의 경기를 평가받는다.
2. 기록원은 선수가 모든 상황에서 의심의 혜택을 받도록 기록원은 관대한 시스템을 적용해야 한다.
3. 샷은 어떤 호출이 있었는지에 따라 평가되어야 한다. 기록원은 팀에 의해 고용된 전략이나 그들의 의견에 더 나은 호출이 있었는지에 대해서 고려하지 않아야 한다.
4. 샷이 누락된 이유에 대해서 기록원의 의견이 고려되지 않아야 한다. 스킵이 잘못된 빗자루 위치를 주었다거나 스위퍼가 실수를 했는지 아닌지가 요소가 되지 않아야 한다.

채점 시스템

사용된 방법은 4점 시스템이다. 정확하게 실행되는 샷은 최대 4점이 주어진다.

완전한 실수는 0점을 받는다. 부분적으로 성공적인 샷은 0점과 4점 사이에서 부여된다. 10엔드 경기에서, 선수의 최대 점수는 80점이다. 모든 스톤이 딜리버리되기 전에 경기가 종료되는 경우, 선수의 가능한 최대 점수는 각각의 스톤이 딜리버리되지 않은 것에 의해 4점씩 감소된다. 하나 또는 그 이상의 추가 엔드가 플레이 되었을 때, 선수의 최대 가능 점수는 각각의 스톤이 딜리버리되는 것에 따라 4점씩 증가한다.

의도적으로 하우스를 통해 던져진 돌은 딜리버리된 돌로 간주되지 않는다. 종이 점수 시트(또는 컴퓨터 점수화면)은 이러한 형태의 샷이 던져지면 'X'로 표시되고, 선수의 최대 점수는 이것이 발생할 때마다 4점씩 감소된다.

35. MEASURING PROCEDURES

All measuring devices should be kept cool.

The persons in charge of the house are allowed to observe any measurement provided there is no attempt to either interfere with, or influence, the Umpire.

Inform the CU that a measure is requested and maintain radio contact during the measure.

Last Stone Draw (LSD): at the conclusion of the team's pre-game practice one player will deliver one stone to the tee. The Umpire will measure any stone that finishes in the house. Stones that do not finish in the house are recorded as 185.4 cm. A stone so close to the tee that it cannot be measured is recorded as 0.0 cm. Where a measure can be inserted, but the tape does not record a measurement, the stone is deemed to be measurable and the distance is recorded as half the first distance the tape records (i.e. if the first distance on the tape is 0.1 cm., the measure would be recorded as 0.05 cm.)

Free Guard Zone (FGZ):

- The block shall be used to decide whether a stone is within the FGZ-area at the hog line, or at the tee line beside the house.
- The biter stick shall be used to decide if a stone is touching the house. Do not move the stone and indicate by hand signal if in FGZ or not. If not possible because of other stones in the house the measure should be done visually. After a visual decision that stone shall not be measured again unless moved.

Measures in the house:

- Pick up the measuring device with the pointed end in your right hand (helps ensure measures are done in a clockwise direction, which is the preferred direction).
- If possible, enter the house at the 6 o'clock position after cooling your shoes.
- Ask the teams to clear the house of stones not involved in the measurement, and for which shot you are measuring.
- First put the feet of the measuring instrument on the ice and then the point into the centre hole.
- Measures can be done in a clockwise or counter clockwise direction, but maintain that direction throughout the entire measure.
- Identify the best stone by pointing at it and stating clearly that this is the shot stone. The observers should be given enough time to agree/question the decision. After that, whenever possible move the non-counting stone(s) away from the tee. However, if those stone(s) are on the opposite side of the house, the last stone to be measured can be moved in or out, depending on the result of the measure.
- After measuring, remove the point first.
- If stones are lying so close to the tee that an instrument cannot be used, there shall be a visual measure. If the Umpire cannot make a decision, or if a team asks for a second opinion, the Chief Umpire can be called to make a final decision.
- At the conclusion of an end, to determine if a stone is in the house or not, the biter stick shall be used. Assuming the stone is not to be measured against any other stone, then move it in if counting and out when it is not.
- For a three stone measure always measure the odd colour stone first.
- Based on the results of the measure, confirm with both teams what was scored.

Other measures: To measure if a stone is in play at the back line, hog line or at the side line (if no dividers), the block should be used. If the stone is exactly at the centre line in the back of the house and no stones are in the way, the biter stick shall be used.

35. 측정 절차

모든 측정 장치들은 차갑게 유지되어야 한다.
하우스에 위치한 사람들은 심판들에게 간섭하거나 영향을 주지 않도록 감시되어야 한다.
주심에게 측정 동안에는 무선 연락이 유지되고 요청된다는 것을 알려라.

라스트 스톤 드로우(LSD): 팀의 경기 전 연습이 종료되기 전, 한 선수는 티(하우스 중심의 원)로 스톤을 딜리버리한다. 심판은 하우스에 도착한 스톤을 측정한다. 하우스에 도착하지 못한 스톤들은 185.4㎝로 기록된다. 티에 상당히 가까운 스톤은 0.0㎝로 기록된다. 측정이 입력될 수 있지만, 테이프에 기록이 안 됐을 때, 스톤은 측정 가능하게 간주되고 거리는 테이프가 기록한 첫 번째 거리의 절반으로 기록된다. (즉 테이프의 첫 번째 거리가 0.1㎝라면, 측정은 0.05㎝로 기록된다)

프리 가드 존(FGZ):

- 블럭은 스톤이 호그 라인에 있는 프리 가드 존 구역 이내인지, 아니면 하우스 옆의 티 라인 쪽인지를 결정하는 데에 쓰일 수 있다.
- 비터 스틱은 스톤이 하우스에 접촉했는지를 결정하는 데에 쓰일 수 있다. 스톤을 움직이지 말고 수신호로 프리 가드 존 구역 안인지 아닌지를 알려라. 만약에 하우스에 있는 다른 스톤들로 인해 가능하지 않다면, 측정은 시각적으로 행해져야 한다. 스톤은 움직이지 않았다면 시각적 결정 이후에 다시 측정되면 안 된다.

하우스 안에서의 측정들:

- 측정 기구들을 오른손 끝으로 집어라(측정이 선호되는 방향인 시계 방향으로 되도록 해라).
- 가능하다면 너의 신발을 차갑게 한 후에 6시 방향으로 하우스로 들어가라.
- 팀들에게 측정에 하우스가 스톤들로 구성되지 않았음을 확실히 하고, 어떤 스톤을 측정하는지를 확인시켜라.
- 측정들은 시계 방향이나 반시계 방향으로 이루어질 수 있지만, 측정 내내 한 방향으로 유지해라.
- 하우스에 가장 근접한 스톤을 확인하고, 그것이 샷 스톤이라는 것을 확실히 측정해라. 관찰자들은 결정에 동의하거나 질문할 충분한 시간이 주어져야 한다. 그 후에, 티로부터 세지 않는 스톤(들)을 언제든지 움직일 수 있다. 하지만 만약에 그 스톤(들)이 하우스의 반대 측에 있다면, 마지막 측정되는 스톤은 측정의 결과에 따라 안으로 놓을지, 밖으로 놓을지 측정되어야 한다.
- 측정 후에 하우스의 스톤들을 제거해라.
- 스톤들이 기구들이 측정할 수 없을 정도로 티에 가깝게 놓여있다면, 시각적 측정이 이루어져야 한다. 만약 심판이 결정하지 못하거나 팀이 제2의 견해를 요청한다면, 심판장은 마지막 결정을 위해 소환될 수 있다.
- 최종 측정으로, 스톤이 하우스 안에 있는지 아닌지를 측정하기 위해 비터 스틱이 사용되어야 한다. 다른 스톤들에 기대어 스톤이 측정될 수 없다면, 셀 때는 안에 놓고 아니라면 밖에 놓아라.
- 세 스톤의 측정을 위해서 항상 특이한 색깔의 스톤을 먼저 측정해라.
- 측정의 결론들에 기초하여, 두 팀에게 점수를 확인시켜라.

다른 측정들: 만약 스톤이 백 라인, 호그 라인 또는 사이드 라인(나누는 것이 없다면)의 경기장 내에 있는가를 측정하려면, 블럭이 사용되어야 한다. 만약 스톤이 하우스 뒤에 있는 중앙선에 정확히 있고, 길을 막는 스톤들이 없다면, 비터 스틱이 사용되어야 한다.

4개의 스톤 측정

4 Stone measure

Choose one pair of stones of the same colour and use the one that is furthest away to compare against the other pair of stones. If necessary, measure between your selected pair to determine the one that is furthest from the tee.

Comparing that stone against each of the other pair will eliminate at least one stone – either one or both of the other stones, or the one that you've selected. The problem is then reduced to either a three or two stone measure, and is straightforward to decide.

Sample:
Let's call the two red stones R1 and R2, and the two yellow stones Y1 and Y2. You've found that R2 is the further away of the reds. R2 is then measured against Y1 and Y2. If R2 beats both, then it's a two count to Red. If R2 beats Y2 but not Y1, then it's a Y1 vs R1 measure. If R2 is beaten by both Y1 and Y2, then it's a R1 vs Y1 and Y2 measure.

5 Stone measure

Compare the 2-stones of the same colour and determine which is furthest away and set the gauge on that stone. Compare that stone with each of the 3-stones of the other colour. Any stone that is better has to remain untouched so it can be later measured against the better of the 2-stones. Any stone that is worse can be removed. If all three stones are worse, the 2-stones colour scores 2 points. If any of the 3-stones are better they are then be measured against the better 2-stone colour after the worse 2-stone colour has been removed.

Sample:
R1 and R2 against Y1, Y2 and Y3. After measuring, R2 is determined to be worse than R1, so the gauge is set on R2. R2 is compared to Y1 (Y1 is worse so it can be removed), then R2 is compared to Y2 (Y2 is better, so it remains untouched); then R2 is compared to Y3 (Y3 is worse so it can be removed); then remove R2 since it is worse than Y2; then do a normal measure against R1 and Y2.

4개의 스톤 측정

색이 같은 한 쌍의 스톤을 골라라, 그리고 다른 쌍과 비교했을 때 티에서 더 멀리간 것을 사용하여라. 만약 필요하다면, 어떤 것이 티에서 더 먼지를 결정하기 위해 당신이 고른 쌍의 사이를 측정하여라.

스톤을 비교해서 최소 한 개의 스톤을 제거해라 - 한 개나 두 개 모두, 또는 당신이 선택했던 스톤을. 세 개나 두 개의 스톤을 측정하는 것으로 결정이 쉬워진다.

예시:

빨간 스톤 두 개를 R1과 R2라 하자, 그리고 노란 스톤을 Y1, Y2라 하자. R2가 빨간 스톤 중에 더 멀다. 그러면 R2를 Y1, Y2와 비교하여라. 만약에 R2가 모두를 이긴다면, 레드 팀이 2점이다. 만약 R2가 Y2는 이겼지만 Y1는 이기지 못했다면, Y1과 R1을 측정하여야 한다. 만약 R2가 Y1, Y2 모두에게 졌다면, R1 대 Y1, Y2의 측정이 된다.

5개의 스톤 측정

같은 색의 두 개의 스톤 중 무엇이 더 먼지 비교하고, 더 멀리 간 스톤을 기준으로 삼아라. 그 스톤을 다른 색의 3개의 스톤과 비교하여라. 나중에 2개의 스톤에 대항하여 측정될 수도 있기에, 어떤 스톤이라도 안 건드리는 것이 좋다. 만약 세 개의 스톤이 모두 더 미치지 못했다면, 2개의 스톤이 2점을 얻는다. 만약 3개의 스톤 중 그들보다 더 나은 게 있다면, 더 나은 2개의 스톤은 더 못한 2개의 스톤이 제거된 후에 측정되어야 한다.

예시:

R1과 R2가 Y1, Y2, Y3와 대항한다. 측정 후에, R2가 R1보다 못하다고 측정되었다면, 기준은 R2로 설정된다. R2는 Y1과 비교되고(Y1이 더 못해서 제거될 수 있다) , R2는 Y2와 비교된다(Y2가 버튼에 더 가까워서, 건드려지지 않은 채로 남겨둔다). ; 그리고 R2는 Y3와 비교된다(Y3는 버튼에 더 멀어서 제거될 수 있다). ; R2는 Y2보다 못하기 때문에, 제거한다. ; 그런 후에 R1과 Y2를 측정한다.

36. LAST STONE DRAW (LSD)

The Last Stone Draw (LSD) is used to determine which team will have the choice of delivering first or second stone in the first end.

1. The LSD will take place at the conclusion of each team's pre-game practice (one minute will be given to deliver the LSD).
2. Teams will be informed at the Team Meeting that the Umpires will assume that every team that wins the LSD will want the last stone in the first end. If there is any time that a team does not want the last stone if they win the LSD, then they must inform the Umpire before the start of their practice.
3. Opposing teams must remain behind the scoreboard during their opponent's pre-game practice. If that is not feasible, then the opposition should stand as far behind the sheet as possible, so as not to distract or intimidate the other team.
4. One player from the team will deliver one stone to the tee at the home end. The person delivering the stone can be any one of the five players on the team. One team member will hold the brush in the house at the home end. Normal sweeping rules apply. Only four players can be on the ice surface during the LSD. The other team members must stand as far away from the ice surface as possible and must not give any instructions.
5. This process will be repeated during the second pre-game practice and the winner of the LSD determined.
6. Stones finishing in the house are measured.
7. Stones finishing so close to the tee that they cannot be measured are recorded as 0.0 cm.
8. Stones that do not finish in the house are recorded as 185.4 cm.
9. If a member of the delivering team touches a moving stone or causes it to be touched, the stone will be removed and recorded as 185.4 cm.
10. If a member of the non-delivering team or an external force (does not include debris that is on the ice) touches a moving stone or causes it to be touched, the stone will be redelivered.
11. If a member of the delivering team moves a stationary stone, or causes it to be moved before the Umpire completes the measurement, the stone will be removed and recorded as 185.4 cm.
12. If a team does not play the LSD stone (e.g. – late arrival) it is recorded as 185.4 cm.
13. If a member of the non-delivering team or an external force moves a stationary stone or causes it to be moved before the Umpire completes the measurement, the stone is replaced to its original position by the delivering team.
14. If a player fails to activate the handle prior to delivery of a stone, or there is a hog line violation, the stone will be removed and recorded as 185.4 cm.
15. If neither team has a stone that finishes in the house, or both teams record the same distance, a coin toss will decide which team has the choice of delivering the first or second stone in the first end.
16. Last stone advantage in the first end will be marked with an asterisk or hammer sign in the space allocated for this on the scoreboard. It remains in this position for the entire game and is not shifted from end to end, except for Mixed Doubles where the sign is moved each end to the team having last stone in that end.

36. 라스트 스톤 드로우(LSD)

LSD는 첫 드로우를 어떤 팀이 먼저 또는 두 번째로 시도할지를 결정할 때 쓰인다.

1. LSD는 각 팀의 경기 전의 연습 마지막에 이루어진다. (LSD를 위한 스톤을 옮기는 데에는 1분이 주어진다)
2. 팀들은 팀 미팅에서 심판진들이 LSD를 이긴 모든 팀이 첫 시도 때 마지막 스톤을 원한다고 예측함을 알릴 것이다. 만약 LSD를 이긴 팀이 마지막 스톤을 원하지 않는다면, 그들은 심판진들에게 연습의 시작 전에 알려야 한다.
3. 팀들은 상대 팀의 시합 전의 연습 동안에 점수판 뒤에 있어야 한다. 만약 이것이 가능하지 않다면, 다른 팀을 방해하거나 위협하지 않도록 시합장에서 최대한 멀리 떨어져 있어야 한다.
4. 팀의 한 선수가 한 스톤을 홈 엔드 끝에 있는 티로 투구할 것이다. 투구하는 사람은 팀에서 다섯 명의 선수들 중 아무나 가능하다. 한 선수 멤버가 홈 끝에 있는 하우스에서 브러시를 지니고 있을 것이다. 일반적으로 무차별적인 규칙들이 적용된다. 네 선수들만이 LSD 동안 얼음 면에 올라갈 수 있다. 다른 팀 멤버들은 얼음면으로부터 최대한 멀리 떨어져 있어야 하고 지시를 줘서는 안 된다.
5. 이 과정은 두 번째 시합 전 연습에서도 반복되고 LSD의 승자가 결정된다.
6. 하우스에서 멈춘 스톤들은 측정된다.
7. 티에 너무 가깝게 멈춰서 측정을 할 수 없는 스톤들은 0.0㎝로 기록된다.
8. 하우스 안에 도착하지 못한 스톤들은 185.4㎝로 기록된다.
9. 이동시키는 팀의 일원이 움직이는 스톤을 건드리거나 건드려지게 야기했다면, 스톤은 제거되고 185.4㎝로 기록된다.

9. 투구하지 않는 팀의 일원이나 외압(얼음 위의 파편은 포함하지 않는다)이 움직이는 스톤을 건드리거나 건드려지게 야기했다면, 스톤은 다시 투구된다.

11. 투구하는 팀의 일원이 심판이 측정을 마치기 전에 정지된 스톤을 움직이거나, 움직여지게 야기한다면 스톤은 제거되고 185.4㎝로 기록된다.
12. 만약 팀이 LSD 스톤을 하지 않았다면 (예를 들어 늦은 도착) 185.4㎝로 기록된다.
13. 투구하지 않는 팀의 일원이나 외압이 심판이 측정을 마치기 전에 정지된 스톤을 움직였거나 움직이게 야기했다면, 스톤은 투구하는 팀에 의해서 원래의 자리로 다시 놓인다.
14. 만약 선수가 투구 이전에 핸들을 이용하는 데에 실패했다면, 또는 호그 라인 방해가 있었다면, 스톤은 제거되고 185.4㎝로 기록된다.
15. 만약 어떤 팀도 하우스 안에 스톤을 도착 못 시켰다면, 또는 두 팀 다 같은 거리를 기록했다면, 동전 던지기가 첫 시도 때 어떤 팀이 첫 또는 두 번째 스톤을 투구할지를 결정한다.
16. 첫 시도 마지막에서 마지막 스톤 이점은 점수판에 지정된 공간에 별이나 망치 표시로 표시된다. 이것은 표시가 각 끝에서 마지막에 마지막 스톤을 가진 팀에게로 이동되는 혼합복식(믹스더블) 경기를 제외하고는 모든 경기 동안 이 위치에 유지되고 끝에서 끝으로 이동되지 않는다.

LSD announcements

The LSD is done at the end of the pre-game practice.

- With one minute remaining in practice (i.e. 8 minutes) "one minute to the end of practice"
- At the end of practice (i.e. 9 minutes) "Practice is over, prepare for the LSD"
- Delay of approx. 30 seconds (controlled by an Umpire for all sheets) "Please deliver your LSD"
- Teams will be given a maximum of 60 seconds to deliver the LSD. If the stone has not reached the tee line at the delivering end within 60 seconds (observed by an Umpire) it will be recorded as 185.4 cm.

LSD procedures

Although many play-off positions are determined without using the LSD rankings, it is still important to try and reduce the possibility of errors. In order to try and make the measures on Last Stone Draws as accurate as possible, the following is recommended:

1. Where more than one measure is being used, the tapes should be clearly marked for a specific sheet and used only on that sheet during the course of the round robin. As the teams rotate through the sheets, hopefully this would balance out any differences in the measures. If the difference is too great on one measuring tape, it should not be used.

2. All tapes to be used are set to metric with the arrow pointing towards the stone to be measured.

3. As it requires two people to conduct the measures in the eight foot and twelve foot, it is recommended that where possible the Umpires work in pairs. In a competition using four sheets the Umpires assigned to Sheets A and B would conduct the LSD measures on those sheets and the Umpires assigned to Sheets C and D would conduct the measures on those sheets. The two measures should be clearly marked "A-B" and "C-D".

4. The Umpires should make sure that the measure will register 0.1 cm and that the measure is reset to 0.0 before each measure.

5. If the measure is loose in the centre hole, it should be held firmly to the side of the hole nearest the stone to be measured.

6. The person for each team who holds the broom for the Last Stone Draw may view the measure.

7. The Umpires should be aware of the distance from the centre to each line marking the circles of the house so that they know the range within which the measure of the stone should fall (i.e. 182.9 cm for the 12 foot; 121.9 cm for the eight foot; 60.96 cm for the four foot; minimum of 15.24 cm for the inner circle).

8. The tape should be pulled out at as consistent a speed as possible for each measure and the end of the tape should contact the stone to be measured in the centre of the striking band so that the end of the tape is flush with the stone's surface.

9. The reading should be locked in once the measure is taken and both Umpires should view and confirm the reading.

LSD 발표

LSD는 시합 전의 연습에 끝에서 완료된다.

- 시합 1분을 남겨놓고(즉 8분) "시합의 끝까지 1분."
- 시합의 끝에서(즉 9분) "연습은 끝났고 LSD를 준비해라."
- 대략 30초의 지연(모든 시트를 담당하는 심판에 의해 통제) "당신의 LSD를 이동시켜라."
- 팀들은 LSD를 이동시키는 데에 최대 60초가 주어진다. 만약 60초 이내에 이동의 끝이 티 라인에 도착하지 못했다면(심판에 의해 관찰), 185.4㎝로 기록된다.

LSD 절차

비록 많은 결승 경기들이 LSD 순위들을 사용하지 않은 채 결정되지만, 시도해보고 오류의 가능성을 줄이는 것은 여전히 중요하다. LSD를 최대한 정확하게 측정들을 시도하고 결정하기 위해서, 아래 사항들이 추천된다. :

1. 하나 이상의 측정이 이용되는 곳에서, 테이프들은 특정 시트를 위해 확실히 기록되고 라운드 로빈 경기 동안에만 그 시트에만 사용된다. 시트들 동안 팀이 교대할 때, 이것은 측정들에 있는 어떠한 차이들을 균형 잡아 줄 것이다. 만약 차이가 한 측정 테이프에서 그렇게 크지 않다면, 이것은 사용되어서는 안 된다.
2. 사용될 모든 테이프들은 측정되어야 할 돌을 향하여 있는 화살표와 함께 미터법으로 설치된다.
3. 8피트와 12피트로 측정들을 하는 데에 두 사람이 필요해서 심판들이 짝으로 일하는 것이 추천된다. 네 시트를 이용하는 경쟁에서 시트 A와 B를 맡은 심판들이 그 시트들에서 LSD 측정들을 하고 시트 C와 D를 맡은 심판들이 이 시트들에서 측정들을 한다. 두 측정들은 'A-B'와 'C-D'로 명확하게 표시되어야 한다.
4. 심판들은 측정이 0.1㎝를 기록하고 매 측정 전에 0.0으로 재설정되게 확실히 해야 한다.
5. 만약 중심 홀에서 측정이 미진하다면, 측정될 스톤에서 가장 가까운 홀 쪽에서 이루어져야 한다.
6. LSD를 위한 브룸을 가진 각 팀의 사람은 측정을 본다.
7. 심판들은 그들이 스톤의 측정이 틀리는 범위를 알기 위해서 중심으로부터 하우스의 원들을 나타내는 각 선까지의 거리를 인식하고 있어야 한다(즉 12피트에는 182.9㎝; 8피트에는 121.9㎝; 4피트에는 60.96㎝; 내부 원에는 최소 15.24㎝).
8. 테이프는 최대한 등속도로 뽑혀야 하고 테이프의 끝이 스톤의 표면과 가지런하기 위해 테이프의 끝은 처진 선의 중심에서 측정될 스톤에 접촉해야 한다.
9. 해석은 측정이 이루어지는 동시에 분명히 밝혀지고 두 심판들은 보고 해석을 확인해야 한다.

37. DRAW SHOT CHALLENGE (DSC)

The Draw Shot Challenge (DSC) is used at competitions that use the Last Stone Draw (LSD) during the round robin portion of the competition.

The DSC is used to establish ranking in situations where teams are involved in unsolvable ties.

The DSC is the average distance of the Last Stone Draws that were played by a team during the round robin portion of a competition. The single least favourable LSD result is automatically eliminated before calculating this average distance.

The team with the lesser DSC receives the higher ranking.

If the DSCs are equal, then the team with the best non-equal LSD receives the higher ranking. In case all LSDs are equal, the team whose Association is ranked higher in the WCF World Rankings is ranked higher.

The distance recorded by an Umpire for any LSD can be disclosed whenever asked, and it can be publicly displayed (e.g. - on the Sportboards at the Olympics).

A chart will be maintained which records all the teams' LSDs.

The DSC calculation (average of the LSDs with the single least favourable LSD result eliminated) only needs to be done at the end of the round robin and can be made public at that time.

37. 드로우 샷 챌린지(DSC)

DSC는 시합의 리그전 동안에 LSD를 사용하는 시합들에서 사용된다.

DSC는 팀들이 해결할 수 없는 동점 상황에 있을 때 순위를 정하기 위해 이용된다.

DSC는 시합의 리그전 동안에 팀에 의해 행해진 LSD의 평균 거리이다. 하나의 가장 작은 유리한 LSD 결과는 자동적으로 평균 거리 계산 전에 지워진다.

더 적은 DSC를 가진 팀이 더 높은 순위를 갖는다.

만약 DSC가 같다면, 최고의 차별적인 LSD를 지닌 팀이 더 높은 순위를 갖는다. 모든 LSD가 같은 상황에서, 세계컬링연맹 세계 순위에서 더 높은 순위를 가진 국가의 팀이 더 높은 순위를 갖는다.

어떤 LSD에 대해 심판에 의해 기록된 거리는 요청된다면 발표될 수 있고, 공표될 수도 있다(예를 들어 올림픽의 운동게시판에).

차트는 모든 팀의 LSD를 기록한 채로 유지된다.

DSC 계산(하나의 가장 작은 유리한 LSD 기록을 제거한 LSD들의 평균)은 오직 리그전 마지막에 완성될 필요가 있고 그 당시에 공적으로 저장될 수 있다.

38. ACCESS TO FIELD OF PLAY (FOP)

1. Access to the Field of Play is allowed in the following circumstances:

- An Umpire is present inside the FOP
- Practice sessions – training day, pre-game and evening practice, playoff practices
- Team time-outs (restricted to one person, plus a translator if required, designated by the team i.e. - coach, alternate player, or national coach)
- In case of injury - medical personnel and coach, plus translator if required, will be allowed into FOP

Note: There will be **no access** to FOP at the conclusion of the games - coaches and alternate players may meet with their teams outside the boards so as not to interrupt other games in progress.

2. A maximum of 7 people from each Association are allowed inside the FOP for practice sessions: 5 team members, coach, and national coach or other team official/translator.

3. All (players/coaches/officials/translator) must wear proper uniforms when accessing FOP - this includes footwear that has not been worn outside. Players must be in identical uniforms for games and practice sessions as per Rule C3 (a). Coaches and other team officials may wear either a team uniform or an Association uniform.

Note: Jeans are not considered appropriate clothing.

4. Where accreditation is issued, all players/coaches/officials must have appropriate accreditation for access to FOP. If a player leaves to use the restrooms during a game, he/she does not have to take accreditation with him/her, provided he/she does not have to clear any security check-points.

5. Specific entrances at home or away end for access during team time-outs will be indicated by the Chief Umpire at the Team Meeting and will be included in the team document (if possible). Where possible, access will occur at the home end in a location that will not impact other games or media activities occurring inside the FOP.

6. Media access to FOP will be restricted to those with appropriate accreditation (armbands, etc.) and will be regulated by the WCF Media Relations Officer, in cooperation with the umpiring staff. Disruption of games should not occur.

7. The Chief Ice Technician will regulate Ice crew access. Ice crews should be aware that other games may be in progress and they should walk behind the scoreboards where possible.

8. Any team member ejected from a game by an Umpire is denied access to the FOP and the Coach Bench for the duration of the suspension.

38. 경기장 접근(입장, FOP)

1. 경기장에 접근하기 위해서는 다음 상황들이 요구된다. :
   - 심판진이 경기장 안에 있는다.
   - 연습 구역 - 훈련일, 연습 경기, 저녁 연습, 플레이오프 연습
   - 팀 타임(한 사람으로 제한된다, 필요 시 통역사까지. 즉 코치, 교체선수 또는 국제 코치)
   - 부상인 경우 - 의료 요원과 코치, 그리고 필요 시 통역사가 경기장 안에 들어가는 것이 허락된다.

   추신: 경기의 마지막에 경기장 안에 접근해서는 안 된다. 코치와 교체선수는 경기장 밖에서 자신들의 팀을 만나야 한다. 진행 중인 경기를 방해해서는 안 된다.

2. 한 팀에서 7명만이 연습을 위해 경기장에 들어가는 것이 허용된다.: 5명의 팀 멤버, 코치, 국제 코치나 팀의 다른 통역사나, 직원.

3. 경기장에 입장 시 모두(선수, 코치, 관계자, 통역사)는 반드시 자신의 유니폼을 입고 있어야 한다. - 이것은 실내용 신발을 포함한다. 선수들은 규칙 C3 (a)에 따라 경기와 연습 동안 자신의 유니폼을 반드시 착용하여야 한다. 코치와 다른 팀의 직원들은 연맹의 유니폼이나 팀 유니폼을 입어야 한다.

   추신: 청바지는 적당한 옷으로 분류되지 않는다.

4. 확인증이 중요한 곳에서는, 경기장에 접근하기 위해 모든 선수/코치/직원들은 적절한 확인증을 가지고 있어야 한다.

5. 타임-아웃 시간 동안의 홈 엔드로의 특정한 입장이나 퇴장은 팀 미팅에서 주심에게 지시되어야 하고, 팀 문서에 포함되어야 한다(가능한 한). 입장은 되도록 경기장 안의 다른 경기이나 매체 활동에 지장을 주지 않는 홈 엔드에서 해야 한다.

6. 미디어의 경기장 접근은 적절한 확인증(팔에 차는 확인증 등)에 한해 제한되고, 세계컬링연맹 언론 관계자와 심판에 의해 통제된다. 경기에 혼란을 야기해서는 안 된다.

7. 빙판 전담팀의 접근을 기술위원장이 규제한다. 빙판 전담팀은 다른 경기가 진행되고 있을 수 있다는 점을 인지하고, 가능한 한 스코어보드 뒤로 걸어야 한다.

8. 심판에 의해 퇴장된 팀 멤버는 퇴장된 동안 경기장과 코치석에 접근할 수 없다.

39. COACH BENCH

1. The Original Team Line-Up Form will be distributed at the Team Meeting, and teams must indicate on this form which person(s) will occupy the Coach Bench. For WCCs this must be the alternate plus a maximum 2 other team officials, one of whom is the translator (if required). For WMDCCs this is only the coach and translator (if required).

2. Only those person(s) may take a position on the Coach Bench.

3. Access to the Coach Bench will only be allowed when their team is playing.

4. Accreditation must be worn at all times. Only a nominated person showing the proper accreditation will be allowed access to the Coach Bench.

5. Any person occupying a position on the Coach Bench who is not listed on the form will be asked to leave immediately. Any team member ejected from a game by an Umpire is denied access to the Coach Bench and Field of Play (FOP) for the duration of the suspension.

6. The proper dress code must be adhered to when occupying a position on the Coach Bench, or access will be denied. This means no blue jeans, proper footwear, and either the team uniform or the Association jacket. A warm jacket may be worn over the uniform, but must be removed before entering the FOP.

7. Persons occupying a position on the Coach Bench should remain seated as much as possible except when leaving the Coach Bench or proceeding to the FOP.

8. When a team time-out is called, the person with Coach Bench privileges who goes to the FOP must have been sitting on the Coach Bench when the time-out was called.

9. Verbal, visual, written, electronic or other communication between persons on the Coach Bench and teams on the ice is not allowed and is considered unacceptable conduct. There shall also be no communication of any sort from the Coach Bench to anyone who is not sitting in that designated area. Violation of this rule could result in that person being ejected by the Chief Umpire, or Deputy Chief Umpire, from the competition area for that game.

10. Displaying a team mascot or flag is not allowed and the Coach Bench must be 'clean' at all times (please remove rubbish at the end of the game). Team cheers and yelling are not permitted.

11. Alcohol in the playing area and on the Coach Bench is not allowed.

12. When the team is delivering the stones with dark coloured handles, coaches will sit on the right side (as you face the Field of Play) and when delivering the stones with the light coloured handles on the left side (as you face the Field of Play).

13. If a team wishes to change a person on the Coach Bench the CU or Deputy CU will consider the circumstances and their decision is final.

14. If a properly accredited translator is assisting a team, access to the FOP and the Coach Bench will be allowed providing the translator is properly dressed and is listed as one of the people on the Coach Bench (i.e. – during a game, only the people from the Coach Bench can have access to the FOP).

39. 코치석

1. 팀의 라인업은 팀 미팅에서 정해지고, 팀은 어떤 사람이 코치석에 있을지 지정하여야 한다. 세계 컬링 선수권에서는 무조건 대안적으로 추가 최대 2명의 다른 팀 공식 멤버가 있어야 하며, 둘 중 하나는 (필요 시) 통역사이다. 세계 혼합복식(믹스더블) 컬링 선수권대회에서 이것은 코치와 (필요 시) 통역사만을 말한다.

2. 오직 그 사람들만이 코치석에 있을 수 있다.

3. 코치석으로의 접근은 그들의 팀이 경기 중일 때만 허용된다.

4. 확인증은 항상 가지고 있어야 한다. 적절한 확인증을 보여주는 지정된 사람만이 코치석으로 들어갈 수 있다.

5. 리스트에 올라있지 않은 사람이 코치석에 있다면 떠나라는 요청을 받을 수 있다. 팀 멤버 중 심판에 의해 퇴장된 사람은 경기 중에 코치석이나 경기장에 접근이 제한된다.

6. 적절한 복장은 코치석에 있을 때 중요하다, 이를 지키지 않으면 접근이 거부될 수 있다. 이것은 청바지를 입지 않는 것, 적절한 신발, 그리고 팀 유니폼을 입거나 연맹 재킷을 착용하는 것을 말한다. 따듯한 재킷은 팀 전체가 입을 수 있지만, 경기장 입장 전에 벗어야 한다.

7. 코치석에 있는 사람은 경기장으로 가거나 코치석을 떠날 때를 제외하고는 가능한 한 앉아있어야 한다.

8. 타임아웃이 불리면, 경기장에 가는 코치석에 가는 특권이 있는 사람은 코치석에 앉아있어야 한다.

9. 코치석과 빙판 위의 팀 사이에서 말로 행하는, 시각적으로 행하는, 글로 적힌, 전자적이거나 또 다른 커뮤니케이션은 제한되며, 받아들일 수 없는 행동으로 여겨진다. 코치석의 그 어떤 사람과 지정된 지역이 아닌 곳에 앉아있는 사람 사이의 커뮤니케이션은 있어서는 안 된다. 이 규정의 불이행은 경기장에 있는 주심이나 부심에 의한 퇴장을 초래할 수 있다.

10. 팀 마스코트나 깃발을 전시하는 것은 코치석에서는 금지되며, 항상 '깨끗'해야 한다. (경기가 끝난 후에는 쓰레기를 치워라) 팀 응원이나 소리 지르는 것은 허용되지 않는다.

11. 경기장이나 코치석은 주류 반입이 금지된다.

12. 진한 색의 손잡이가 있는 스톤을 투구할 때, 코치는 오른편에 앉아야 하고(경기장을 바라보았을 때), 그리고 더 밝은색의 손잡이가 있는 스톤을 투구할 때 코치는 왼편에 있어야 한다. (경기장을 바라보았을 때)

13. 만약 팀이 코치석의 인원을 교체하고 싶다면, 주심이나 부심이 상황을 고려할 것이며 그들의 결정이 최종이다.

14. 만일 정당히 선임된 통역사가 팀을 도와주고 있다면, 적절한 옷을 입고 있을 때에 경기장과 코치석의 출입이 허락되며 코치석의 일원으로 명단에 오른다. (경기 중에, 코치석의 그만이 경기장에 출입할 수 있다)

40. RULE CLARIFICATION – Late start

IF TEAMS DO NOT COMMENCE PLAY AT THE DESIGNATED TIME

	Team # 1	Team # 2	Both teams
Ready to start on schedule.	Yes	Yes	Use Last Stone Draw (LSD) or coin toss (the event's rule) to determine last stone. Score 0 – 0.
0:00 – 0:59 seconds late for the start of the game.	If only team # 1, no penalty. Use LSD or coin toss (the event's rule) to determine last stone. Score 0 – 0.	If only team # 2, no penalty. Use LSD or coin toss (the event's rule) to determine last stone. Score 0 – 0.	If both teams, no penalty. Use LSD or coin toss (the event's rule) to determine last stone. Score 0 – 0.
1:00 – 15:00 minutes late for the start of the game.	If team # 1 is late then team # 2 has last stone advantage, one end is considered completed, and the score is 0 – 1.	If team # 2 is late then team # 1 has last stone advantage, one end is considered completed, and the score is 1 – 0.	If both teams are late then one end is considered completed, use LSD or coin toss (the event's rule) to determine last stone and the score is 0 – 0.
15:01 – 30:00 minutes late for the start of the game.	If team # 1 is late then team # 2 has last stone advantage, two ends are considered completed, and the score is 0 – 2.	If team # 2 is late then team # 1 has last stone advantage, two ends are considered completed, and the score is 2 – 0.	If both teams are late then two ends are considered completed, use LSD or coin toss (the event's rule) to determine last stone and the score is 0 – 0.
30:01 minutes (or more) late for the start of the game.	If team # 1 is late then it forfeits the game and team # 2 is declared the winner. Final score is recorded with a W and L.	If team # 2 is late then it forfeits the game and team # 1 is declared the winner. Final score is recorded with a W and L.	If both teams are late then the game is considered over and both teams take a loss. If one team 'must' advance in the draw, then the DSC would decide, if no DSC done, then a coin toss will decide.
If one team is 1:00 – 15:00 minutes late and the other team is 15:01 – 30:00 minutes late: two ends will be considered played, the team that was 1:00 – 15:00 minutes late receives last stone advantage and 1 point.			

40. 규칙 명확화 – 늦은 시작

만약 팀이 정해진 시간에 경기를 시작하지 않는 경우

	팀 # 1	팀 # 2	양 팀
예정대로 시작할 준비가 되었는가	예	예	순서를 정하기 위해 LSD를 이용하거나 동전 던지기를 한다. 스코어 0-0
경기 시작에 0:00~0:59 초의 지각	팀 # 1만 지각 시, 페널티는 없다. 순서를 정하기 위해 LSD를 이용하거나 동전 던지기를 한다. 스코어 0-0	팀 # 2만 지각 시, 페널티는 없다. 순서를 정하기 위해 LSD를 이용하거나 동전 던지기를 한다. 스코어 0-0	만약 양 팀 모두 지각 시, 페널티는 없다. 순서를 정하기 위해 LSD를 이용하거나 동전 던지기를 한다. 스코어 0-0
경기 시작에 1:00~15:00 분의 지각	만약 팀 # 1이 지각했다면 팀 # 2가 마지막 스톤의 이점을 가진다, 한 세트가 끝났다고 간주하여, 스코어는 0 - 1	만약 팀 # 2가 지각했다면 팀 # 1이 마지막 스톤의 이점을 가진다, 한 세트가 끝났다고 간주하여, 스코어는 1 - 0	만약 두 팀 모두 한 세트보다 늦었다면, 순서를 정하기 위해 LSD를 이용하거나 동전 던지기를 한다. 스코어 0-0
경기 시작에 15:01~30:00 분의 지각	만약 팀 # 1이 지각했다면 팀 # 2가 마지막 스톤의 이점을 가진다, 두 세트가 끝났다고 간주하여, 스코어는 0 - 2	만약 팀 # 2가 지각했다면 팀 # 1이 마지막 스톤의 이점을 가진다, 두 세트가 끝났다고 간주하여, 스코어는 2 - 0	만약 두 팀 모두 두 세트보다 늦었다면, 순서를 정하기 위해 LSD를 이용하거나 동전 던지기를 한다. 스코어 0-0
경기 시작에 30:01분 이상의 지각	만약 팀 # 1이 몰수경기가 될 정도로 늦는다면 팀 # 2가 이긴 것으로 선포된다. 최종 스코어는 승과 패로 나뉜다.	만약 팀 # 2가 몰수경기가 될 정도로 늦는다면 팀 # 1이 이긴 것으로 선포된다. 최종 스코어는 승과 패로 나뉜다.	만일 양 팀 다 경기가 끝났다고 고려될 시간보다 늦는다면 양 팀 다 진 것으로 간주된다. 만일 반드시 승자가 나와야 한다면, DSC가 결정할 것이며, DSC를 하지 못한다면, 동전 던지기로 결정할 것이다.
만약 한 팀이 1:00~15:00분 늦고 다른 한 팀이 15:01~30:00 분 늦었을 때 : 두 세트가 진행되었다고 간주하고, 1:00~15:00 분 늦은 팀이 마지막 스톤의 이점을 가지며 1포인트를 가진다.			

41. RULE CLARIFICATION – Hand or Body Prints

R10 (a) – Equipment

No player shall cause damage to the ice surface by means of equipment, hand prints or body prints.

1. The Umpire shall stop the time clocks and take action if a serious incident is observed, or if the opposition team requests a ruling.
2. The Umpire should determine if the touch is "incidental" or "avoidable."
3. If the incident was avoidable (e.g. – placing the hand or knee on the ice for an extended period after delivering a stone, placing a hand on the ice in the house while calling sweeping) it has to be determined, with the assistance of the Chief Ice Technician or Deputy Chief Ice Technician, if damage was done.
4. If no damage, no action taken. If damage has been done it should be repaired.

Procedures

- warning and procedure explanation at the team meeting
- 1st incident = 1st official on-ice warning, repair damage
- 2nd incident = 2nd official on-ice warning, repair damage
- 3rd incident = repair damage and remove player from the game

These warnings will be cumulative and are counted within two sections:

Section 1 – the round robin, including any tie-breaker games (remove player on the 3rd cumulative incident)

Section 2 – the play-off games of the event (remove player on the 3rd cumulative incident)

If a player is removed from one game, he/she can return for the next game(s) within that section of the event. If a further incident occurs, he/she is removed immediately from that game.

41. 규칙 명확화 - 손이나 몸 자국

R10 (a) - 장비

어떤 선수도 장비나 손, 몸으로써 표면에 손상을 입혀서는 안 된다.

1. 심판은 시계를 멈추고 행동을 취해야 한다. 만약 심각한 사고가 발생하거나 상대 팀이 판결을 원할 시에.
2. 심판은 접촉이 '사고'였는지 '불가피'했는지 정해야 한다.
3. 만약 그 사고가 불가피했다면 (예를 들어 - 투구를 하고 난 후에 손이나 무릎이 얼음 위에 있는 것, 스위핑을 지시하는 동안 하우스 안에 얼음 위에 손을 두는 것) 만약 손상이 있다면, 주얼음기술자와 부얼음기술자의 도움 아래 결정되어야 한다.
4. 만약 손상이 없다면, 아무 조치도 없다. 만약 손상이 있다면 수리되어야 한다.

과정들

- 팀 미팅에서의 경고와 과정 설명
- 첫 번째 사고 = 첫 번째 공식적인 빙상에서의 경고, 손상 수리
- 두 번째 사고 = 두 번째 공식적인 빙상에서의 경고, 손상 수리
- 세 번째 사고 = 손상을 수리하고 선수를 경기에서 제거

이 경고들은 누적되며 두 개의 섹션으로 나뉘어 센다. :

섹션 1 - 타이 브레이커 경기를 포함한 리그전 (3번째 경고에서 선수가 제외된다)
섹션 2 - 플레이오프 경기 (3번째 경고에서 선수가 제외된다)

만약 선수가 한 경기에서 제외된다면, 그 사람은 그 섹션의 다음 경기에 돌아올 수 있다.
만약 사고가 또 발생하면, 그 사람은 즉시 경기에서 제외된다.

42. TEAM PARTICIPATION IN CEREMONIES

1. Teams participating in the event will also participate in any Opening/Closing ceremonies that the host committee plans.
2. For these team recognitions the players will be in either their game uniforms, or dress clothes - depending on how and when the activities occur.
3. Blue jeans are not acceptable attire for these events.
4. Special Dress Code Rules may apply for Olympic and Paralympic Winter Games. If NOCs or NPCs require official medal ceremony clothing to be worn, this will take precedence.

Opening Ceremonies (7): The team coach and the national coach may march with the team during the Opening ceremonies. Order of line-up shall be: Skip, Third, Second, Lead, Alternate, Coach, National Coach.

Pre-game Introduction (6): Players, alternate and coach shall march out when their team is being honoured, otherwise it will just be the five players (this could be reduced to just the four players for a particular game, if there is no march-in ceremony and the teams which are not being honoured just assemble at the end of their sheet).

Closing Ceremonies (6): The coach will march with the team during the Closing ceremonies. Order of line-up shall be: Skip, Third, Second, Lead, Alternate and Coach.

Medal Ceremonies (6): Players and the team coach will stand on the medal podium. Order: Skip, Third, Second, Lead, Alternate, and Coach.

For Olympic and Paralympic Ceremonies only the players (5) will be on the podium and receive medals.

March in for banquets: Normally team and Coach (6). However, this may change depending on requests from the OCs.

43. SPORTSMANSHIP BALLOTS

Ballots will be distributed to the players immediately after their last round robin game and will be collected before teams leave the arena.

The Chief Umpire shall be the only person to tabulate the results.

42. 개막/폐막식의 팀 참여

1. 대회에서의 팀 참여는 주최 위원회가 계획한 개막식이나 폐막식에도 해당된다.
2. 이러한 팀 인식을 위해서 선수들은 그들의 경기복장이나 드레스를 입어야 한다. - 언제, 어떻게 활동들이 일어나는지에 따라서
3. 청바지는 이러한 행사에 허용되는 옷이 아니다.
4. 특별한 드레스 코드 규정들은 올림픽이나 동계 패럴림픽에 적용된다. 만약 국내 올림픽 위원회나 국내 패럴림픽 위원회가 공식적인 메달 시상식 의상을 입기를 권고한다면, 이것은 우선사항이 될 것이다.

개막식(7): 팀 코치와 국가의 코치는 개회식 동안 팀과 함께 다녀도 된다. 인원 구성은: 스킵, 써드, 세컨드, 리드, 교체 선수, 코치, 국가적 코치로 요구된다.

시합 전의 지시(6): 선수들, 교체 선수와 코치는 팀이 수여될 때 밖으로 나온다. 그렇지 않으면 단지 5명의 선수들뿐일 것이다. (이것은 특정 시합에서는 4명의 선수들로 줄 것이다, 만약에 행진이 식에 없고 받지 않고 있는 팀들이 단지 그들의 시트의 끝에 모여 있다면)

폐막식(6): 코치는 폐막식 동안에 팀과 함께 다닌다. 인원 구성은: 스킵, 써드, 세컨드, 리드, 교체선수와 코치로 요구된다.

메달 수여식(6): 선수들과 팀 코치는 메달 시상대에 올라갈 것이다. 스킵, 써드, 세컨드, 리드, 교체선수와 코치로 요구된다.

올림픽과 패럴림픽 식들을 위해서 오직 다섯 명의 선수들이 시상대에 올라가고 메달들을 받을 것이다.

연회를 위한 입장: 일반적으로 코치를 포함해 한 팀당 총 여섯 명이지만, 조직위원회의 요청에 따라 달라질 수 있다.

43. 스포츠맨십 투표 용지

투표용지들은 마지막 리그전의 경기 이후에 즉시 선수들에게 나누어지고 팀들이 경기장을 떠나기 전에 모을 것이다.

심판장은 결과를 표로 만들 유일한 사람이 될 것이다.

44. OPENING CEREMONIES – WCF EVENTS

Every ceremony should have as much local colour and ideas as possible. The ceremonies do not have to always be exactly the same. This document simply gives a suggested format:

1. Pre-announcement … please be seated, the Opening Ceremonies start in 5 minutes.

2. MC introduces him/herself and welcomes spectators to the Opening Ceremonies.

3. Recorded music or band starts, which signals the march-in of the dignitaries. If the event has a mascot, it may lead the procession:

   a) WCF President
   b) Any politicians (i.e. – mayor or government representative)
   c) Representative of the title sponsor
   d) President of the hosting curling Association
   e) President of the Organising Committee
   f) Others: (i) other WCF Executive Board members if participating
      (ii) vice chairs of the Organising Committee
      (iii) the person delivering first stone & sweepers

4. March-in of the event players (5), the team coach (1) and the National Coach (1), per team. A a junior curler, cadet, etc. may carry a placard with the team's Association name and the team's flag may be carried by the team driver, coach, etc.

5. Any special entertainment should be scheduled at this time so that the players can also observe.

6. Introduction of all the dignitaries and then the Welcome speeches:

   a) WCF President
   b) Any politicians (i.e. –mayor or government representative)
   c) Representative of the title sponsor
   d) President of the hosting curling Association
   e) President of the Organising Committee

7. March-in of the event trophy.

8. Raising of the WCF event banner.

9. Introduction of the people involved in the delivery of the ceremonial first stone. A competitor's pin should then be presented to the person delivering this stone.

10. Declaration that the event is open for play – WCF President.

11. Playing of the National Anthem.

12. MC announces the end of the Opening Ceremonies (any special announcement – 1st draw time, etc.).

13. Music starts and the march-out begins, lead by the dignitaries and then the players and coaches.

44. 개회식

모든 의식은 최대한 지역적 특색과 아이디어를 가지고 있어야 한다. 행사(식)들은 항상 같을 필요는 없다. 이 문서는 간단한 형식을 제시할 뿐이다 :

1. 선 공지 - 착석하시기 바랍니다. 개회식은 5분 후에 시작합니다.
2. MC는 자기소개를 한 후 개회식 관객들을 환영한다.
3. 녹음된 음악 혹은 밴드의 음악이 시작되며 이 음악에 맞춰 내빈들이 입장한다. 만약에 이 행사에 마스코트가 있다면 마스코트가 이 진행을 이끌 수 있다.
   a) 세계컬링연맹 회장
   b) 정치인들
   c) 메인 스폰서의 대표
   d) 행사를 주최하는 컬링협회 회장
   e) 운영 협회 회장
   f) 기타: 1) 다른 세계컬링연맹 임원진, 만약 참여한다면
   2) 운영 협회의 부회장
   3) 첫 번째 스톤과 스위퍼를 운반하는 사람
4. 팀당 행사 선수들의 입장. (5), 팀 코치 (I) 그리고 국가대표 코치 . (I) 주니어 컬링선수, 후배, 기타 등은 팀의 협회의 이름이 적힌 플래카드를 들 수 있고 팀의 깃발은 팀의 운전자나 코치 혹은 기타의 사람에 의해 운반될 수 있다.
5. 특별히 예정된 공연이 있다면 선수들도 관람할 수 있게 이때 진행한다.
6. 모든 내빈에 대한 소개와 환영의 말
   a) 세계컬링연맹 회장
   b) 정치인들
   c) 메인 스폰서의 대표
   d) 행사를 주최하는 컬링협회 회장
   e) 운영 협회 회장
7. 행사 트로피 입장
9. 세계컬링연맹 행사 배너 게양
10. 세계컬링연맹 회장에 의한 경기 개막 선언
11. 국가의 연주
12. MC가 개회식의 끝을 알림(어떤 특별한 선언 - 첫 번째 draw time 등)
13. 음악이 시작 후 퇴장이 내빈, 선수들과 코치들 순서로 진행됨

45. CLOSING CEREMONIES – WCF EVENTS

Every ceremony should have as much local colour and innovative ideas as possible. The ceremonies do not have to always be exactly the same. This document gives a suggestion that works well, as there is usually a tight schedule because of television coverage:

1. MC introduces him/herself and welcomes spectators to the Closing Ceremonies.

2. Recorded music or band starts, which signals the march-in of the dignitaries. If the event has a mascot, it may lead the procession:

    a) WCF President (has to end up near the MC podium)
    b) President of the Organising Committee
    c) Representative of the title sponsor
    d) Representative of the next Organising Committee
    e) Person presenting the Sportsmanship Award
    f) Persons (Association Representatives) presenting medals
    g) Others: (i) other WCF Executive Board members
    (ii) vice chairs of the Organising Committee
    (iii) Association Representatives of non-medal teams

3. March-in of the non-medal players and one coach per team, along with a placard with the team's Association name (carried by junior curler, cadet, etc.) and the team's flag (carried by the team driver, coach, etc.).

4. March-in of the Bronze medal team (5 players & 1 coach). Best if they walk the full length of the ice and then mount the podium. While walking, the Association is introduced as the Bronze medal team from ____________________, but not the individual players.

5. March-in of the Silver medal team (5 players & 1 coach). Best if they walk the full length of the ice and then mount the podium. While walking, the Association is introduced as the Silver medal team from ____________________, but not the individual players.

6. March-in of the Gold medal team (5 players & 1 coach). Best if they walk the full length of the ice and then mount the podium. While walking, the Association is introduced as the Gold medal team from ____________________, but not the individual players.

7. Introduce the WCF President for a congratulatory speech to the winners. WCF President and Sponsor Representative present the championship trophy. Allow 30 seconds for photographs and then play the National Anthem of the winning team.

8. Association Representative presents the medals to the Bronze medal winners in this order: Coach, 5th Player, Lead, Second, Third and Skip. Players are named as they receive their medals. Then they are presented with the keeper awards, then the flowers and/or other special gifts. Allow a short period for photographs.

9. Association Representative presents the medals to the Silver medal winners in this order: coach, 5th Player, Lead, Second, Third and Skip. Players are named as they receive their medals. Then they are presented with the keeper awards, then the flowers and/or other special gifts. Allow a short period for photographs.

10. Association Representative presents the medals to the Gold medal winners in this order: Coach, 5th Player, Lead, Second, Third and Skip. Players are introduced as they receive their medals. Then they are presented with their keeper awards (mini-stones), then the flowers and/or other special gifts. Allow a short period for photographs.

11. The title sponsor representative is asked to make a speech and present the Championship rings to the winners (only at WMCC and WWCC events).

45. 폐회식 - 세계컬링연맹 행사들

모든 행사(식)는 최대한 지역적 특색과 아이디어를 가지고 있어야 한다. 행사(식)들은 항상 같을 필요는 없다. 이 문서는 흔히 존재하는 TV 방송의 빽빽한 스케줄에 적합한 제안을 제시한다.

1. MC는 자기소개를 한 후 폐회식 관객들을 환영한다.
2. 녹음된 음악 혹은 밴드의 음악이 시작되며 이 음악에 맞춰 내빈들이 입장한다. 만약에 이 행사에 마스코트가 있다면 마스코트가 이 진행을 이끌 수 있다.
   a) 세계컬링연맹 회장(MC 진행석 근처까지)
   b) 운영 협회 회장
   c) 메인 스폰서의 대표
   d) 차기 대회 운영 협회 대표
   e) 스포츠맨십 시상자
   f) 메달 시상자들(협회 대표들)
   g) 기타: 1) 다른 세계컬링연맹 임원진
      2) 운영 협회의 부회장
      3) 메달을 획득하지 못한 팀들의 협회 대표들
3. 입상하지 못한 선수들과 한 팀당 한 코치가 팀의 협회의 이름이 적힌 플래카드와 함께 입장(주니어 컬링선수나 후배 등이 운반할 수 있다) 그리고 팀의 깃발(팀의 운전자나 코치 등이 운반할 수 있다)
4. 동메달 입상 팀의 입장(5명의 선수와 1명의 코치). 링크 전체를 걸은 후 포디움에 오르는 것을 추천. 걷는 동안 동메달 팀의 국가는 소개되지만, 개인 선수들은 아님
5. 은메달 입상 팀의 입장(5명의 선수와 1명의 코치). 링크 전체를 걸은 후 포디움에 오르는 것을 추천. 걷는 동안 은메달 팀의 국가는 소개되지만, 개인 선수들은 아님
6. 금메달 입상 팀의 입장(5명의 선수와 1명의 코치). 링크 전체를 걸은 후 포디움에 오르는 것을 추천. 걷는 동안 금메달 팀의 국가는 소개되지만, 개인 선수들은 아님
7. 세계컬링연맹 회장이 승리자들에게 축하 연설하기 위해 소개됨. 세계컬링연맹 회장과 스폰서 대표는 우승 트로피를 수여함. 30초의 포토타임과 우승팀의 국가연주
8. 협회 대표가 동메달 입상자들에게 아래와 같은 순서로 시상: 코치, 5번째 선수, 리드, 세컨드, 써드 그리고 스킵. 선수들은 그들이 메달을 받을 때 호명된다. 그리고 그들은 상을 받고 꽃과/혹은 특별한 선물을 받는다. 약간의 포토타임을 갖는다.
9. 협회 대표가 은메달 입상자들에게 아래와 같은 순서로 시상: 코치, 5번째 선수, 리드, 세컨드, 써드 그리고 스킵. 선수들은 그들이 메달을 받을 때 호명된다. 그리고 그들은 상을 받고 꽃과/혹은 특별한 선물을 받는다. 약간의 포토타임을 갖는다.
10. 협회 대표가 금메달 입상자들에게 아래와 같은 순서로 시상: 코치, 5번째 선수, 리드, 세컨드, 써드 그리고 스킵. 선수들은 그들이 메달을 받을 때 호명된다. 그리고 그들은 상을 받고 꽃과/혹은 특별한 선물을 받는다. 약간의 포토타임을 갖는다.

12. Presentation of the Sportsmanship Award. Allow a very short period for photographs.
13. The President of the Organising Committee is asked to make a speech.
14. The Championship Banner is lowered and handed over to the next Organising Committee representative.
15. The representative of the next Organising Committee is asked to make a speech.
16. The WCF President is asked for some final words and closes the event.
17. MC thanks the spectators and announces the end of the Closing Ceremonies.
18. Music starts and the march-out begins, led by the dignitaries and then the non-medal players and coaches. The medal winners usually remain on the ice for photographs.

Determined at each event:

- When to bring in the volunteers?
- A speech from the winning Skip?

11. 메인 스폰서 대표는 연설과 우승 반지들을 선수들에게 수여하기를 부탁받는다. (세계 남자 컬링선수권, 세계 여자 컬링선수권 행사에서만)

12. 스포츠맨십 상의 수여. 매우 짧은 기념사진 촬영을 허락하여라.

13. 조직 위원회의 대표자는 연설을 부탁받는다.

14. 선수권의 배너는 내려지고 다음 조직 위원회 대표자에게 전달된다.

15. 다음 조직 위원회 대표자는 연설을 부탁받는다.

16. 세계컬링연맹의 장은 몇 마디 마침의 말을 부탁받고, 식을 마친다.

17. MC는 관중에게 감사를 표하고 폐회식을 마친다.

18. 음악이 시작되고 고위 관리, 메달을 따지 못한 선수들과 코치들에 이어 퇴장이 시작된다. 메달을 딴 선수들은 보통 기념사진 촬영을 위해 빙상에 남는다.

각 행사에서 정해져야 할 것:

- 언제 자원봉사자들을 모집할지?
- 승자의 연설을 건너뛸지?

CLOSING CEREMONY - TELEVISED EVENT (SAMPLE)

WORLD MEN'S CURLING CHAMPIONSHIP
BASEL, SWITZERLAND

DRAFT – IF ____________ WINS

CLOSING CEREMONIES

The game ends and the MC will give television about 20 seconds to get the appropriate celebration shot and for the audience to applaud.

1. MC – (30 seconds after the last stone stopping) Ladies and Gentlemen, welcome to the Closing and Medal Presentation ceremony of the 20__ World _______Curling Championship.

When that announcement is given, lively music is started (not overly loud as there are TV interviews going on) and the march-in of the non-medal teams, as well as the VIP party, begins (**NOTE: this starts only 30 seconds after the last stone has been played**).

Rocky (mascot) leads the procession, but moves aside as soon as entering the Field of Play, so as not to slow down the pace of the march-in.

Teams (5 players and coach carrying the flag) come in the normal entrance on the Sheet D side, they head in the direction of the VIP tables, walk by Sheets D, C and B and then down the walkway between Sheets A & B. They will then line-up on the ice on Sheet B. (**NOTE: the walkway between B & C must be kept clear for television**).

The VIPs follow the players, but turn in the opposite direction (towards the coach bench) and pass Sheets D & C and line-up behind sheet B (beside the MC).

The Bronze medal team is at the end of the non- medal teams march-in, and they are stopped behind sheet C, where they wait for the TV to cue their walk (six abreast) down sheet C to the podium.

The Silver and Gold medal teams will also march down Sheet C, on the cue of the TV, and go onto the podium.

The Gold and Silver Skips were interviewed beside Sheet D, but must join their teams before their walk down Sheet C.

2. MC – (on cue) Please welcome the bronze medal winners, ________________.

폐막식 – 방송 안내(양식)

세계 남자 컬링 챔피언십
바젤, 스위스

DRAFT - IF ________________ WINS

이 게임이 끝나고 사회자는 텔레비전에서 20초 동안 축하 샷과 청중들의 박수를 받을 것이다.

1. MC - (마지막 돌이 멈추고 30초 뒤) 20__년 세계 ___컬링 챔피언십 클로징 세레모니와 메달 수여식에 참석해 주신 여러분을 환영합니다.

이 말이 끝나면 라이브 음악(TV인터뷰가 진행되기 때문에 너무 크지 않게)과 함께 메달을 획득하지 못한 팀과 VIP의 행렬이 시작된다.

파티가 시작된다(참고: 마지막 돌이 플레이된 30초 뒤 시작한다). Rocky(마스코트)가 행진을 리드하지만, 행진의 속도를 늦추지 않도록 필드에 들어서자마자 옆으로 이동한다.

5명의 선수와 코치가 깃발을 들고 D석의 입구로 들어온다. 그들은 VIP석을 향하고, D, C 그리고 B석을 지나 A, B좌석 사이의 길을 내려온다.
그리고 그들은 B석 아이스링크에 위치한다(B와 C 사이의 통로는 방영을 위해 비워두어야 한다).

VIP들은 반대방향으로 돌아(코치 벤치를 향하여) 선수들의 뒤를 따르고 D와 C석을 통과하여 B석 옆에 위치한다(MC 옆).

동메달 팀은 비시상자들 행진 끝에 위치하고, (6명 나란히) C석으로 걸어 내려가고 단상에 멈춘다.

은메달과 금메달 시상자들 또한 C석으로 행진하고, 촬영이 시작되면 시상대로 올라간다.

금메달과 은메달 수상팀들의 주장은 D석 옆에서 인터뷰를 하고 C석으로 가기 전 팀에 합류해야 한다.

2. MC - (큐 사인에 맞추어) 동메달 수상 팀을 환영해주십시오, ____________________________.

3. MC – (on cue) Please welcome the silver medal winners, __________________.

4. MC – (on cue) Please welcome the 20__ World _______ Curling Champions, ________________.

These three teams come down the ice one at a time and go directly onto the podium. **Music stops when Gold Medalists are on the podium.**

5. MC – Ladies and Gentlemen, please welcome Kate Caithness, President of the World Curling Federation, who will bring greetings and congratulations.(1-minute speech)

6. MC – I now call upon ____________, __Presdent__ of the ___________ Curling Association, to present the bronze medals to the team from _____________.

   Coach: ________________________
   Alternate: ______________________
   Lead: _________________________
   Second: _______________________
   Third: _________________________
   Skip: __________________________

7. MC – I now call upon _______________, __President__ of the _____________ Curling Association, to present the silver medals to the team from _____________.
   Coach: _________________________
   Alternate: ______________________
   Lead: __________________________
   Second: ________________________
   Third: __________________________
   Skip: ___________________________

8. MC – I now call upon _________________, __President__ of the __________ Curling Association, to present the gold medals to the team from ________________.

   Coach: _________________________
   Alternate: ______________________
   Lead: __________________________
   Second: ________________________
   Third: __________________________
   Skip: ___________________________

9. MC – Kate Caithness will now present the World Championship trophy to ___________________.

10. MC – Ladies and gentlemen would you please rise for the national anthem of ___________________.

(Television will leave the telecast at this point, other photographers might want some pictures, and ________Keith___________ will cue the MC when to continue)

11. MC – ____________________, ______________________, would you please present the Champions' rings to our winners.

12. MC – Would ____________________, _______________________, please present keeper awards to the bronze medal team from ___________________.

3. MC - (큐 사인에 맞추어) 은메달 수상 팀을 환영해주십시오, ______________________ .

4. MC - (큐 사인에 맞추어) 20____세계________컬링 챔피언 ____________를 환영해주십시오.

이 세 팀은 얼음판 위로 다 같이 걸어와 시상대로 올라간다. 금메달 팀이 시상대에 올라서면 음악이 멈춘다.

5. MC-신사숙녀 여러분 감사의 인사와 축하를 건네줄 세계 컬링의 회장인 케이트 케이스네스(Kate Caithness)를 환영해주십시오. (1분의 연설)

6. MC-XX컬링연맹 대표를 대신해, ________팀에 동메달을 수여합니다.

코치: ______________________

후보: ______________________

리드: ______________________

세컨드: ______________________

써드: ______________________

스킵: ______________________

7. MC-XX컬링연맹 대표를 대신해, XX팀에 은메달을 수여합니다.

코치: ______________________

후보: ______________________

리드: ______________________

세컨드: ______________________

써드: ______________________

스킵: ______________________

8. MC-XX컬링연맹 대표를 대신해, XX팀에 금메달을 수여합니다.

코치: ______________________

후보: ______________________

리드: ______________________

세컨드: ______________________

써드: ______________________

스킵: ______________________

9. MC - 케이트 케이스네스가 세계 챔피언십 트로피를 우승팀에게 수여하겠습니다.

10. MC-신사숙녀 여러분 XX의 국가 연주를 위해 자리에서 일어나주시기 바랍니다.

(방송은 이때 끝나고, 사진기자들은 사진을 찍을 것이다. 케이트가 계속해야 할 때 MC에게 큐 사인을 줄 것이다)

13. MC – Would ________________________, ________________________, please present keeper awards to the silver medalists from ____________________.

14. MC – Would ________________________, ___________________________, please present the keeper awards to the champions.

15. MC – May I ask ________________________, Chairman of the Organising Committee, to present a special gift from his Committee to the Champions.

16. MC – The __________ ____________ AWARD is voted on by the curlers and is presented to the player who best displays the ideals of sportsmanship and skill. I would call upon Chief Umpire, ________________________, to present the 201___ Collie Campbell Award. (CU comes forward, announces the winner)

17. MC – At the beginning of the week we mentioned that sharing the WORLD CHAMPIONSHIP BANNER has become a significant tradition. The banner has been passed on from committee to committee and was raised here at the ____________________ prior to the start of the competition.

    The BANNER will now be lowered and delivered to the World Curling Federation for safe keeping until the 20__ _____ World _________ Curling Championship in ____________, _________________.

    (Lowering of the banner) (**Appropriate music**)

    I would now like to call upon ______________________, ____________________ Curling Association, to say a few words on behalf of the 20__ Host Committee.

18. MC – Would KATE CAITHNESS please come to the podium one more time. (30-second speech – officially closing the event)

19. MC – Thank you Ladies and Gentlemen – it's been a great week of curling here in _______________________. THANKS for coming – have a safe trip home.

Music starts again. The non-medal teams depart by heading in the direction of the VIP area (same path as entry), the VIPs depart at the same time, the medal winners stay in the Field of Play for photos.

11. MC - ____________________ , ____________________, 당신은 우리의 수상자로 챔피언스 반지를 보여주시기 바랍니다.

12. MC - ____________________, ____________________, ____________________에서 동메달 팀 골키퍼 상을 보여주시겠습니까.

13. MC - ____________________, ____________________, ____________________에서 은메달에 골키퍼 상을 보여주시겠습니까.

14. MC - ____________________, ____________________, 챔피언 골키퍼 상을 보여주시겠습니까.

15. MC - 사회자는 ____________________, 조직위원회의 의장에게 챔피언스 위원회에서 특별한 선물을 요청할 수 있다.

16. MC ________________ ________________ AWARD는 대회에서 뛰어난 스포츠맨십과 기술을 보여준 선수에게 수여하는 상으로서 컬링 선수들에 의해 투표되었습니다. The 201_ 콜리 캠벨(Collie Campbell) 상을 수여해주실 심판장님을 모시겠습니다(심판장님은 앞으로 나와서 수상자를 발표한다).

17. MC - 이 주가 시작될 때 말씀드렸듯이, 세계챔피언십 배너는 굉장히 중요한 전통이 되었습니다. 배너는 위원회에서 위원회로 전해졌으며 이 대회가 시작할 때 경기장에 게재되었습니다. 배너는 내려져 다음 대회까지 안전하게 보관하기 위하여 세계컬링연맹에 전달되겠습니다.
(배너가 내려간다) (적절한 음악)
이번 대회 주최 측을 대표하여 XX컬링연맹을 불러 20XX년 대회를 대표하는 말을 들어보도록 하겠습니다.

18. 케이트 케이스네스는 한 번 더 시상대로 와주십시오(30초 연설 - 공식적 클로징 멘트).

19. MC - 여러분 감사합니다. 이곳 ~에서의 한 주는 정말 멋졌습니다. 와주셔서 감사합니다. 집까지 안전하게 돌아가시길 기원하겠습니다.

음악이 시작된다. 비시상자들과 VIP들은 동시에 VIP 자리의 방향으로 출발하고, 수상자들은 사진촬영을 위해 대기한다.

46. PROCEDURES FOR BLOOD and HEAD INJURIES

While the risk of one athlete infecting another with HIV/AIDS during a competition is close to non-existent, there is a greater risk that other blood-borne infectious diseases can be transmitted. For example, hepatitis B can be present in the blood as well as in other body fluids. Precautions for reducing the potential for transmission of these infectious agents are important.

If a player incurs an injury that causes bleeding, the Umpire must immediately stop the game and require the player to leave the playing area, and summon medical personnel for appropriate treatment. If the Umpire does not notice the bleeding the athlete should approach the Umpire and request a technical time-out (injury).

Blood on clothing

If the blood is minimal and has not saturated the player's clothing or is not dripping, the player may choose to continue to play without changing uniforms but the uniform should be treated with blood spill kit contents. If the blood has saturated the player's clothing or is dripping and the player chooses to continue to play, the player is required to replace the affected clothing for the remainder of the game and to cover the open wound with a bandage that will withstand the activity. It is understood that the new uniform may not match the team's uniform. However, the player must wear the correct uniform for all other draws. The uniform must be washed according to hygienic methods. If the player chooses not to continue, the game will continue in accordance with WCF Rules of Curling. If the player cannot change the uniform in a reasonable amount of time, the game will continue in accordance with WCF Rules of Curling. Delay of game should be minimized.

Blood on equipment

Use blood spill kit procedures or replace. Delay of game should be minimized.

Blood on ice

- Let it freeze.
- Use the hand-blade to scrape it off, if necessary hot-mop.
- Use blood spill kit procedures. If, after applying the bleach solution, you want to clean it with water, always use HOT water – but make sure it is the same "quality" the ice-crew uses. The best is to inform the ice-crew and let them do the ice. After the affected section of ice has been cleaned, the section of ice may be re-pebbled. Delay of game should be minimized.

Blood on the stones

- Wipe off any blood.
- If necessary clean with a quickly evaporating but NOT oily fluid (e.g. Acetone).

Disposal of the liquid with the blood must be treated for 30 minutes with bleach before pouring down a drain. For any cloths (paper or cloth) used in mopping up the blood, use a treatment of bleach for the cloth, and dispose in an approved box for the purpose of hazardous materials.

STANDARD OPERATING PROCEDURES FOR SMALL BLOOD SPILLS

These procedures can be used for cleaning up spills of blood and other body fluids. For larger spills that go beyond your ability to clean with the supplies on hand, contact the medical staff.

46. 혈액과 머리부상 대처

대회 중 한 선수가 다른 선수에게 HIV/ADIS(에이즈)를 전염할 위험은 거의 없지만, 혈액을 통해 전염성 있는 병을 전달할 수도 있다. 예를 들어 B형 간염은 혈액뿐만 아니라 타인의 체액으로 인해 전염될 수 있다. 이들 병원체의 전달 가능성을 감소시키기 위한 예방 조치가 중요하다. 플레이어가 출혈이 있는 부상을 당한 경우, 심판은 즉시 경기를 중지하고 플레이어에게 경기장을 떠나기를 권고해야 하며, 적절한 치료를 위해 의료 인력을 소환해야 한다. 만약 심판이 공지하지 않으면 출혈 선수는 심판에게 접근하여 테크니컬 타임아웃(부상)을 요청해야 한다.

옷에 피가 있을 때

만약 선수의 옷에 피가 많지 않거나 흐르지 않을 때, 선수는 유니폼 교환 없이 경기를 계속할 것인지 결정해야 한다. 만약 선수의 옷에 피가 많이 묻거나 흐르고 선수가 경기를 계속하길 원할 때, 다른 선수를 위해 옷을 갈아입어야 하며, 상처를 밴딩해야 한다. 교체한 유니폼이 팀의 유니폼과 일치하지 않을 수 있지만, 선수는 반드시 팀원들과 같은 유니폼을 입어야 한다. 유니폼은 반드시 위생 방법에 따라 세척되어야 한다. 만약 선수가 경기를 지속하는 것을 원하지 않을 땐, WCF 컬링 규정에 따라 게임이 지속되어야 한다. 선수가 적절한 시간에 유니폼을 갈아입지 못하는 경우, 경기는 WCF 컬링 규정에 따라 계속된다. 경기지연은 최소화해야 한다.

장비에 혈액이 있을 때

혈액 유출 키트를 사용하거나 교체해야 한다. 경기지연은 최소화해야 한다.

아이스링크에 혈액이 있을 때

- 그대로 얼게 놔두어라.
- 핸드블레이드를 이용해 긁어내거나 필요 시 뜨거운 걸레를 사용한다
- 혈액 유출 키트 절차. 표백제 도포 후 물로 세척하기 원하면, 뜨거운 물을 사용한다. 하지만 반드시 아이스링크와 같은 품질의 물을 사용하여야 한다. 가장 좋은 방법은 링크관리자에게 알린 후 그들이 제거하는 것이다. 아이스링크 세정 후 그 부분을 다시 사용할 수 있다. 경기지연은 최소화되어야 한다.

스톤의 피

- 피를 닦아 낸다
- 청소가 필요하면 빨리 증발하는 것을 이용하지만, 기름기 있는 액체는 피한다(ex: 아세톤).
- 혈액과 용액은 혈액이 마르기 전 30분 안에 처리되어야 한다. 피를 닦아내는 데 사용된 천이나 종이는 표백제를 사용하여 처리 후에 유해물질 용도로 승인된 박스에 폐기한다.

적은 혈액 유출에 대한 표준 운영 절차

이 절차는 혈액 및 기타 체액의 유출 청소에 사용할 수 있다. 많은 출혈로 처리하기 어려울 땐 의료진에게 문의한다.

STEP 1: PERSONAL PROTECTIVE EQUIPMENT (PPE)

Prior to beginning the clean-up, don a pair of rubber, latex, PVC or similar type gloves. For small blood spills no other PPE should be required. For larger spills where there is a possibility of contaminating your face or other parts of your body, contact the medical staff.

STEP 2: BLOOD SPILL KIT EQUIPMENT

The following items may be needed in handling the spill:

- 10% bleach solution
- gloves
- clear plastic bags
- biohazard labels
- leak-proof sharps containers (seek source from your medical personnel)
- brush & dustpan, or tongs or forceps for picking up sharp objects
- disinfectant wipes

STEP 3: BLOOD SPILL KIT PROCEDURES

Cover the spill area with freshly mixed 10% bleach and water solution. Allow solution to soak into the contaminated material. Work from the outside edges of the spill inward when applying the bleach solution.

All glass, needles, or other sharp objects that may puncture the skin must not be picked up by hand. Only mechanical means such as a brush and dustpan, tongs, or forceps are allowed. If you do not have such equipment available, contact medical staff for clean-up.

Wipe bleached area with paper towels or absorbent pads. It may be necessary to use a scrub brush to remove the material if it impacted a hard porous surface such as concrete. If non-porous surfaces such as a carpet have been contaminated an outside vendor may be needed to clean an area.

DISPOSAL

Place bleached material, gloves and other disposable materials into a labelled biohazard bag or container. Ensure lids are firmly sealed on all waste containers when spill clean-up is complete and contact medical staff for disposal.

STEP 4: DECONTAMINATE RE-USABLE EQUIPMENT

Decontaminate with the bleach solution all potentially contaminated re-usable tools or protective equipment used in the clean-up. This includes dustpans, brooms, forceps, buckets etc. Anything that cannot be effectively cleaned (bleach solution must be able to make contact with all surfaces) must be disposed as waste. After the contaminated area has been cleaned, use fresh water to remove bleach residue from all surfaces.

STEP 5: WASH YOUR HANDS

If hand-washing facilities are not available at the venue use disinfectant wipes and then wash your hands as soon as possible.

1단계: 개인 보호 장비(PPE)

손질에 앞서 고무, 라텍스, PVC 또는 유사한 유형의 장갑을 낀다. 적은 출혈에는 PPE 이외의 방법이 요구되지 않는다. 출혈이 많아 얼굴이나 신체 다른 부분에 오염의 가능성이 있을 때는 의료진에게 문의한다.

2단계: 혈액 유출 키트 장비

다음은 혈액 유출을 다룰 때 필요한 것들이다.

- 10% 표백제
- 장갑
- 깨끗한 비닐봉지
- biohazard(생물재해) 라벨
- 누수 방지 보관함
- 브러시, 쓰레받기 혹은 날카로운 것들을 집을 수 있는 집게
- 소독 티슈

3단계: 혈액 유출 키트 절차

신선하게 혼합된 10% 표백제 및 물로 용액 누출 지역을 커버한다. 오염된 물질을 키트에 적신다. 표백제를 사용할 때 안쪽에 피가 흘린 곳의 가장자리의 바깥에서 작업한다. 피부에 상처를 낼 수 있는 모든 유리제품, 바늘, 또는 날카로운 물건들은 손으로 만지지 않는다. 브러시나 쓰레받기 등의 수단만 허용된다. 만약에 그런 것들이 없다면 의료진에게 연락하여 치운다. 종이 타올 또는 흡수패드로 표백된 곳을 닦아낸다. 콘크리트 같은 딱딱한 다공질질의 표면이라면 스크럽 브러시 등이 필요할 것이다. 만약에 카펫 등의 다공질 표면이 아닌 곳에 오염이 되었다면 그곳을 닦아내기 위해 외부 업체가 필요할 것이다.

처리

생물학적 위험이라고 표기된 가방이나 용기에 표백 물질, 장갑 및 기타 일회용 물품을 놓는다. 모든 폐기물 용기의 뚜껑이 단단히 닫히고 밀봉되어 있는지 확인한다. 유출 청소가 완료되면 처리를 위해 의료진에게 문의하라.

4단계: 재사용 장비의 오염제거

표백제 용액으로 청소에 사용된 모든 잠재적 오염 가능성이 있는 재사용 가능한 도구나 보호 장비의 오염을 제거한다. 이는 쓰레받기, 빗자루, 집게 등을 포함한다. 효과적으로 (표백제가 모든 표면과 접촉할 수 있어야 한다) 제거할 수 없는 것은 폐기물로 처리해야 한다. 오염 지역을 청소한 후, 모든 표면에 신선한 물로 표백제 잔류물을 제거한다.

5단계: 손 씻기

손 세척 시설을 사용하지 못할 경우, 지정된 장소에서 소독제를 사용하여 닦아내고 가능한 한 빨리 손을 씻는다.

BIOHAZARD EXPOSURE

If you believe you were exposed (skin puncture or splash to eyes or mucous membranes) to biohazard material that had not been decontaminated with the bleach solution follow these recommended steps:

Skin exposure: Remove contaminated clothing and shoes and vigorously wash affected skin with plenty of soap and water.

Eye exposure: Wash eyes for at least 10 minutes with copious amounts of water, lifting the upper and lower eyelids occasionally.

Seek follow-up medical attention as needed.

HEAD INJURIES

Recently, awareness of the impact of head injuries during sport activities has increased. Concussions are defined as a blow to the head or a bump. A concussion is a mild traumatic brain injury. Concussions will affect people in four areas of function and the symptoms might not occur immediately.

1 - FOUR AREAS AFFECTED

1. Physical - this describes how a person may feel; headache, fatigue, nausea, vomiting, dizziness, etc.
2. Thinking - Poor memory and concentration, responds to questions more slowly, asks repetitive questions. Concussions can cause an altered state of awareness.
3. Emotions - A concussion can make a person more irritable and cause mood swings.
4. Sleep - Concussions frequently cause changes in sleeping patterns, which can increase fatigue.

2 - YOUR ROLE AS AN UMPIRE:

Should you notice any of the above symptoms, the official should notify the coach that a player is apparently injured and advise that the player should be examined by an appropriate health care professional. Injured athletes can exhibit many or just a few of the signs and/or symptoms of concussion. **However, if a player exhibits any signs or symptoms of concussion, the responsibility is simple: remove them from participation**. In an effort to cause no further injury, caution should be exercised when removing a player from the ice following a fall if the athlete is not able to stand on his/her own. Removal should occur with the assistance and supervision of medical personnel.

Apart from the procedure for handling of blood and head injuries, all Umpires should be alert to any player or coach who may show signs of illness or injury.

생물학적 위험 노출

만약에 당신이 생물학적 위험 물질에 노출(피부 상처 또는 눈이나 점막에 튐)되었다고 생각된다면 표백제 방법을 사용하지 말고 아래 절차를 따라야 한다.

피부 노출: 오염된 의복 및 신발을 벗어 다량의 물과 비누로 영향을 받은 피부를 적극적으로 씻어낸다.

눈 노출: 임시로 위/아래 눈꺼풀을 들어 올려, 풍부한 양의 물로 적어도 10분 동안 눈을 세척한다.

필요에 따라 의사의 후속 진료를 받는다.

머리 부상

최근 스포츠 활동 중 머리 부상의 영향에 대한 인식이 증가하고 있다. 뇌진탕은 머리에 갑자기 일어나거나 타격으로 정의된다. 뇌진탕은 가벼운 외상성 뇌 손상이다. 뇌진탕은 인간의 네 가지 영역 기능에 영향을 미칠 것이며, 증상은 즉시 발생하지 않을 수 있다.

1 - 네 가지 영역에 영향

1. 물리적 - 사람이 느낄 수 있는 것들을 말한다. 두통, 피로, 구토, 현기증 등
2. 사고 - 기억력과 집중력 저하, 느린 대답과 반복적인 요구
3. 감정 - 뇌진탕은 사람을 과민하고 기분의 변화가 많게 한다.
4. 수면 - 뇌진탕은 피로를 증가시키는 수면패턴의 변화를 야기한다.

2 - 심판으로서의 역할

위 상황의 한 가지라도 알아차리면, 코치에게 선수가 부상당하였음을 명백히 알려야 하고, 부상 선수가 의료 전문가에게 검사를 받아야 한다고 충고해야 한다. 운동선수는 많거나 몇 가지의 뇌진탕의 징후를 나타낼 수 있다. 그러나 만약 선수가 뇌진탕의 아무런 증상은 나타내지 않으면, 대응은 간단하다. 경기에서 제외하라. 선수가 스스로 일어나서 아이스링크를 벗어나지 못할 때, 부상을 더 입지 않게 주의해야 한다. 선수 퇴장은 의료진의 통제에 따라 이루어져야 한다.

혈액 처리 절차 및 머리 부상 이외에도 모든 심판진은 질병이나 부상의 흔적을 보일 수 있는 선수 또는 감독에 대해 알고 있어야 한다.

47. COMPETITOR'S GUIDE (SAMPLE)

WORLD WHEELCHAIR CURLING QUALIFICATION 2012
3-8 November 2012
KISAKALLIO SPORTS INSTITUTE, LOHJA, FINLAND

COMPETITOR'S GUIDE

Prepared by the Secretariat
Perth
September 2012

47. 참가자 안내서(샘플)

세계 휠체어 예선 경기 2012

2012년 11월 3일 - 8일

KISAKALLIO SPORTS INSTITUTE, LOHJA, FINLAND

참가자 안내서

총무과

Perth

2012년 9월

Competitor's Guide

Contents

WCF President's Message ······ 196
WCF Officers ······ 198
KEY CONTACTS, EVENT ORGANISATION ······ 200
VENUE ······ 202
DRAW SCHEDULE ······ 204
TEAM MEETING, FUNTIONS, MEDIA RELATIONS, ······ 208
PINS AND BADGES, MEDICAL SERVICES, CLASSIFICATION, RULES
DOPE TESTING, CRESTING ······ 210
CRESTING POLICY FOR WHEELCHAIRS ······ 212
Caps, Member Association/Country Name & Emblem,
Manufacturers Trademark
PASSPORTS, TRAVEL, INSURANCE, ACCOMMODATION, MEALS ······ 214
MEAL TIMES, LAUNDRY, LOCAL CURRENCY, ······ 216
POWER ADAPTERS, MAIL, COUNTRY DIALING CODES,
TIPPING, WEATHER
IMPORTANT INFORMATION ······ 218

참가자 안내서

목차

세계컬링경기연맹 위원장님 메시지 ……… 197
세계컬링경기연맹 책임자 ……… 199
주요 담당자, 행사주관자, 경기임원 ……… 201
경기장 ……… 203
경기 스케쥴 ……… 205
팀 미팅, 행사, 미디어 홍보, 핀과 배지, 의료 서비스, 분류, 규칙 ……… 209
도핑 테스트, 장식 ……… 211
휠체어 컬링을 위한 장식 정책, 모자, ……… 213
임원단체/국가 이름 및 상징, 제조업자 상징
여권, 찾아오는 길, 보험, 숙박, 식사 ……… 215
식사시간, 세탁, 지역 환율, 전기 어댑터, 우편물, 지역 국번, 팁 ……… 217
중요한 정보 ……… 219

On behalf of the World Curling Federation and our 49 Member Associations, I would like to congratulate you on earning the right to represent your country at the World Wheelchair Curling Qualification event in Lohja, Finland.

This will be an unforgettable experience and I have no doubt that each and every one of you will take something away from here, both as a person and as an athlete. You will learn from competing in this event, which will help you develop as a curler. It will also be an opportunity for you to build new friendships whilst also experiencing the warm and welcoming hospitality of Lohja and Finland.

There are many items with which you need to be concerned in planning to come to the event and after you arrive. The purpose of this guide is to assist you by providing information and answers to some basic questions you may have.

I would also like to draw your attention to "THE SPIRIT OF CURLING" on Page 1 of the WCF rule book, which exemplifies the code under which the game should be played. Wheelchair curling provides inspiring examples of this 'spirit' and I know that this event will yet again provide the perfect opportunity to showcase our sport and the principles that make it so special.

We hope you find the information provided herein useful and wish you the utmost success and enjoyment at this, the 2012 World Wheelchair Curling Qualification event.

Kate Caithness

Kate Caithness
President
World Curling Federation

세계컬링연맹과 우리의 49개의 회원국을 대신하여, 저는 여러분이 조국의 대표로서 핀란드 로하에서 열린 세계 휠체어 컬링 예선 대회(World Wheelchair Curling Qualification)에 참가할 자격을 얻으신 것에 대해 축하하고 싶습니다.

이것은 여러분에게 잊을 수 없는 경험이 될 것입니다. 그리고 저는 여러분 각자 선수로서, 그리고 참가자로서 모두 여기에서 무언가를 얻어갈 것이라고 믿어 의심치 않습니다. 저는 여러분이 컬링 선수로서 발전하는 데 이 대회가 큰 도움이 될 것이라고 생각합니다. 또한, 여러분이 경쟁에서 열렬한 환영 및 환대를 경험하고 새로운 우정을 구축하는 기회가 될 것입니다.

여러분이 행사에 참여하는 데 많이 걱정하고 신경 쓸 여러 항목들이 있습니다. 이 가이드북의 목적은 여러분이 가질 수 있는 몇 가지 기본적인 질문에 대한 정보와 답변을 제공하여 여러분을 행사에 참여하는 데 지원하는 것입니다.

또한 경기를 수월하게 진행하기 위하여 여러 예제들을 제시한 세계컬링연맹 규칙 책의 1 페이지의 '컬링의 정신'에 주목해주시기 바랍니다. 휠체어 컬링의 정신은 이번 이벤트를 통해 다시 한번 우리의 스포츠가 특별한 원칙을 제시할 수 있는 완벽한 기회를 제공할 것이라고 생각합니다.

저희는 당신이 2012 세계 휠체어 컬링 예선 대회에서 유용한 정보를 얻어 최상의 성공과 즐거움을 얻어갈 수 있기를 기원하겠습니다.

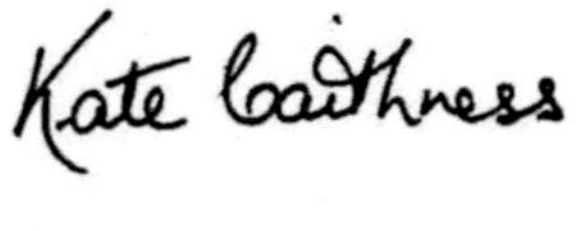

Kate Caithness
President
World Curling Federation

WCF Officers

President — kate.caithness@worldcurling.org
KATE CAITHNESS

Secretary General — colin.grahamslaw@worldcurling.org
COLIN GRAHAMSLAW

Director of Competitions & Development — keith.wendorf@worldcurling.org
KEITH WENDORF

Competitions & Development Officer — eeva.roethlisberger@worldcurling.org
EEVA RÖTHLISBERGER

Competitions & Development Officer — darrell.ell@worldcurling.org
DARRELL ELL

Competitions & Development Officer — scott.arnold@worldcurling.org
SCOTT ARNOLD

Competitions & Development Officer — allen.coliban@worldcurling.org
ALLEN COLIBAN

Media Relations Officer — media@worldcurling.org
JOANNA KELLY

Assistant Media Relations Officer — media@worldcurling.org
DANNY PARKER

WCF Secretariat
World Curling Federation
74 Tay Street
Perth PH2 8NP
U.K.
Tel. + 44 1738 451630
Email. info@worldcurling.org

세계컬링경기연맹 책임자

회장 KATE CAITHNESS	kate.caithness@worldcurling.org
사무총장 COLIN GRAHAMSLAW	colin.grahamslaw@worldcurling.org
대회 및 개발 이사 KEITH WENDORF	keith.wendorf@worldcurling.org
대회 및 개발 책임자 EEVA RÖOTHLISBERGER	eeva.roethlisberger@worldcurling.org
대회 및 개발 책임자 DARRELL ELL	darrell.ell@worldcurling.org
대회 및 개발 책임자 SCOTT ARNOLD	scott.arnold@worldcurling.org
대회 및 개발 책임자 ALLEN COLIBAN	allen.coliban@worldcurling.org
미디어 관계 책임자 JOANNA KELLY	media@worldcurling.org
보조 미디어 관계 책임자 DANNY PARKER	media@worldcurling.org

세계컬링경기연맹 사무국
World Curling Federation
74 Tay Street
Perth PH2 8NP
U.K.
Tel. + 44 1738 451630
Email. info@worldcurling.org

KEY CONTACTS

Director of Competitions & Development	Keith Wendorf
WCF Technical Delegate	Eeva Roethlisberger
Event Chairman	Lauri Ikävalko
Secretary General & Contact Person	Lauri Ikävalko

EVENT ORGANISATION

2012 World Wheelchair Curling Qualification

Main contact
Lauri Ikävalko lauri.ikavalko@kisakallio.fi +358445628549

Competition Assistant
Kimmo Fäldt kimmo.faldt@kisakallio.fi

Technical support
Jukka Pakarinen jukka.pakarinen@kisakallio.fi +358500482775

Restaurant services
Ukko-Pekka Louhivaara ukko-pekka.louhivaara@kisakallio.fi +358504088030

Competition Co-ordinator
Jari Moberg jari.moberg@kisakallio.fi +35845773l3980

Website for the event will be available from mid-September through www.kisakallio.fi.

COMPETITION OFFICIALS

Chief Umpire	Ian Addison (SCO)
Deputy Chief Umpire	Alan Stephen (SCO)
Game Umpire	Pirjo Hautanen (FIN)
Game Umpire	Erkki Lill (EST)
Game Umpire	Harri Lill (EST)
Chief Timer	Allen Coliban (WCF)
Chief Classifier	Young-Hee Lee (KOR)
Classifier	Marc Deperno (USA)
Chief Ice Technician	Scott Henderson (SCO)
Deputy Chief Ice Technician	Jørgen Larsen (DEN)

주요 담당자

대회 및 개발 이사	Keith Wendorf
WCF 기술 대표	Eeva Roethlisberger
경기 위원장	Lauri Ikäavalko
사무총장 & 담당자	Lauri Ikäavalko

행사주관자

2012 세계 휠체어 컬링 예선 대회

주요 담당자

Lauri Ikäavalko	lauri.ikavalko@kisakallio.fi	+358445628549

경기 보조

Kimmo Fäaldt	kimmo.faldt@kisakallio.fi	

기술 보조

Jukka Pakarinen	jukka.pakarinen@kisakallio.fi	+358500482775

음식점 서비스

Ukko-Pekka Louhivaara	ukko-pekka.louhivaara@kisakallio.fi	+358504088030

경기 조직위원회

Jari Moberg	jari.moberg@kisakallio.fi	+3584577313980

9월 중순 경기 홈페이지 www.kisakallio.fi를 이용할 수 있을 것이다.

경기임원

주심	Ian Addison (SCO)
부주심	Alan Stephen (SCO)
경기심판	Pirjo Hautanen (FIN)
경기심판	Erkki Lill (EST)
경기심판	Harri Lill (EST)
시간 계측 심판	Allen Coliban (WCF)
책임등급분류사	Young-Hee Lee (KOR)
분류사	Marc Deperno (USA)
주아이스기술자	Scott Henderson (SCO)
부아이스기술자	Jørgen Larsen (DEN)

VENUE

Kisakallio Sports Institute
Kisakalliontie 284, FI-08360
Lohja, Finland
Tel. +358 19 31 511
Fax +358 19 3151 290

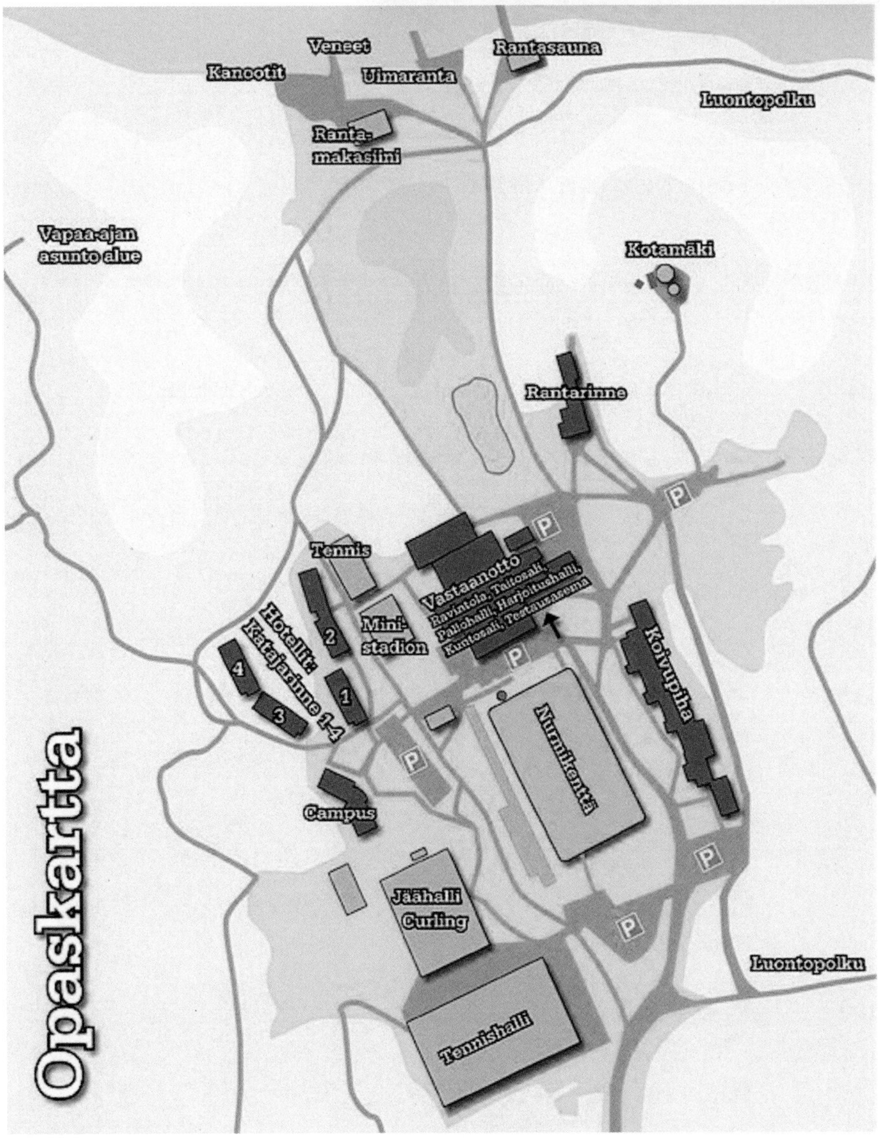

(Team Accommodation in Buildings 1-4)

경기장

키사칼리오 스포츠협회
키사칼리온티에, 284, FI-08360
로하, 핀란드
전화 +358 19 31 511
팩스 +358 19 3151 290

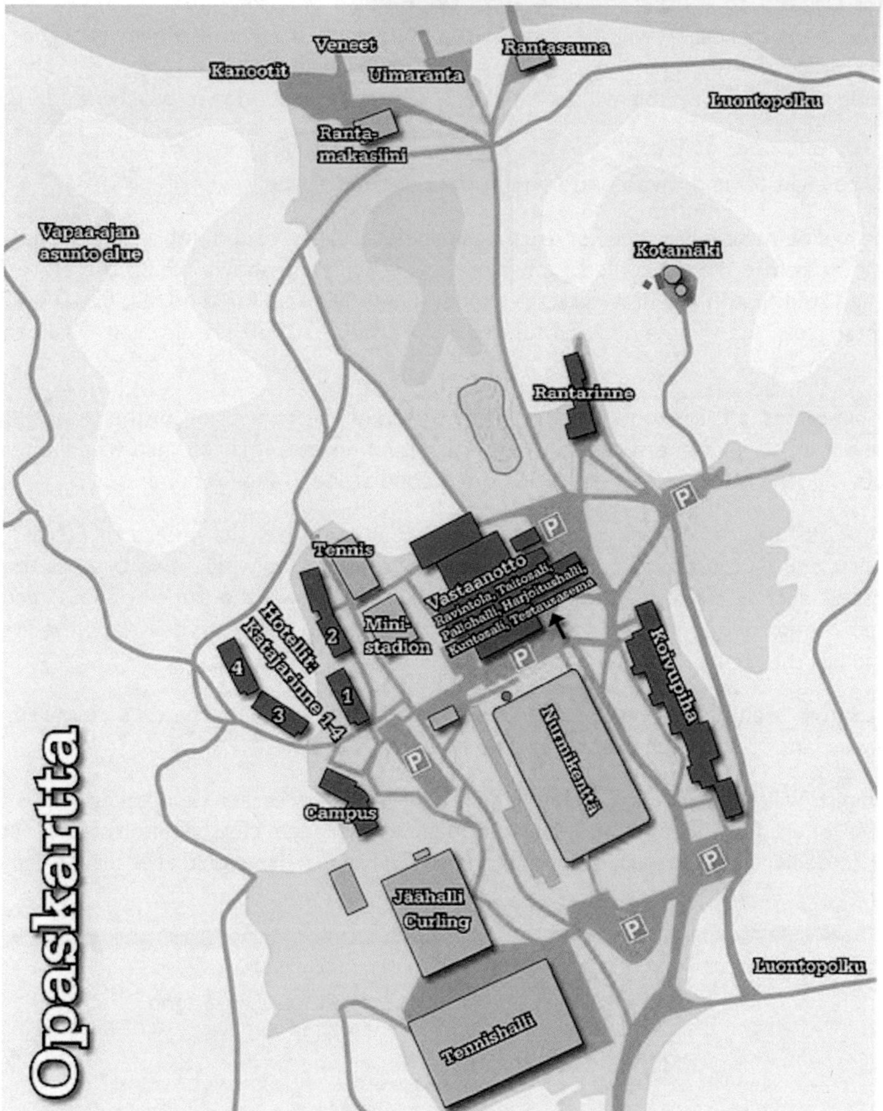

(빌딩 안의 팀 숙박시설 1-4)

DRAW SCHEDULE

WORLD WHEELCHAIR CURLING QUALIFICATION 2012
3-8 November 2012
KISAKALLIO SPORTS INSTITUTE, LOHJA, FINLAND

1. World Curling Federation (WCF) rules apply, unless otherwise indicated below, or stated during the official Team Meeting, which is scheduled between 10:30 – 11:00 in the Mirror Hall (main building) on Saturday, 03 November 2012.

2. The 11 teams will play a round robin series. At the end of the round robin there will be a ranking established for places 1 to 4 using the June 2011 WCF Rules of Competition (C9) -Team Ranking Procedure. The team ranked 1st will play against the team ranked 2nd, the winner qualifying for the 2013 WWhCC. Also the team ranked 3rd will play a game against the team ranked 4th. The loser of the 1 v 2 game will then play the winner of the 3 v 4 game, the winner qualifying for the 2013 WWhCC.

3. All games will be eight (8) ends, with extra end(s) to break tied games.

4. There will be a nine-minute practice for each team before every round robin game. The practice starts 30 minutes before the scheduled game time (i.e. – schedule shows 09:30, therefore 09:00 – 09:09 the team listed first in the draw practices; one minute allowed for the LSD; 09:10 – 09:19 the other team practices; one minute allowed for the LSD; 09:20 – 09:30 ice cleaning, 09:30 the game starts).

5. For round robin games, a Last Stone Draw (LSD) is played at the conclusion of the team's pre-game practice. One player delivers one stone to the tee at the home end. It is assumed that the team with the lesser LSD will take the choice of delivering the second stone in the first end.

6. In the tie-breakers, the team which won the round robin game has the choice of first or second stone in the first end. In the playoff games, the team with the better win/loss record has the choice of playing first or second stone in the first end, if both teams have the same win/loss record, the winner of their round robin game has that choice. In these games, the team delivering the first stone of the first end has the choice of stone handle colour.

7. First named team in each of the round robin games plays the stones with the dark coloured handles and should wear dark coloured upper playing garments.

8. The Chief Umpire will determine the schedule and ice for any necessary tie-breaker games as soon as the number of games required and the opponents have been clearly determined. The Chief Umpire will also decide additional training times and sheets, and the sheets for the playoff games.

<u>Teams:</u>

CZE – Czech Republic
DEN – Denmark
FIN – Finland
GER – Germany
ITA – Italy
JPN – Japan
LAT – Latvia
NOR – Norway
POL – Poland
SUI – Switzerland
TUR – Turkey

경기 스케줄

세계 휠체어 컬링 예선
2012, 11월 3-8
핀란드 LOHJA, KISAKALLIO 스포츠 단체

2012년 12월 3일 토요일 10:30~11:00에 Mirror Hall에서 스케줄 되어있었던 공식적인 팀 미팅 동안 드러났거나 말하였던 것을 제외하고, 세계컬링연맹은 규칙을 적용한다.

11팀은 라운드 로빈 경기를 할 것이다. 한 로빈 라운드의 마지막에는 2011년 7월 세계컬링연맹의 랭킹 규정에 따라서 1위부터 4위까지의 랭킹이 있을 것이다. 랭킹 1위에 오른 팀은 2위에 오른 팀과 경기를 한다, 그 승자는 2013년 세계 휠체어 컬링 선수권대회에 참가할 자격을 얻게 된다. 3위에 오른 팀 또한 4위에 오른 팀과 경기를 한다. 1위 vs 2위 경기의 패배자는 3위 vs 4위 경기의 승자와 경기를 한다, 그 승자는 2013년 세계 휠체어 컬링 선수권대회에 참가할 자격을 얻게 된다.

모든 경기는 8엔드이며, 무승부를 방지하기 위해 엑스트라 엔드를 실시한다.

모든 라운드 로빈 경기 시작 전에 9분간 아이스 체킹 시간이 주어진다. 아이스 체킹은 경기 시작 30분 전에 실시한다.(예시 - 경기 일정이 9:30분일 경우, 첫 번째 연습 팀은 09:00-09:09까지 연습한 후, 1분간 LSD를 실시한다. 두 번째 연습은 09:10-09:19까지 이루어지며 1분간 LSD를 실시한다. 09:20 - 09:30까지 아이스 클리닝 타임이고 경기는 9:30분에 시작하게 되는 것이다)

라운드 로빈 경기를 위해서 LSD는 경기 시작 전 연습을 종료한 팀이 투구한다. 한 선수가 티 라인을 향해 홈 엔드에서 투구한다. LSD 수치가 낮게 나오는 팀이 첫 엔드 후공을 선택할 수 있게 된다.

동률일 경우, 라운드 로빈 경기에서 이겼었던 팀이 선공이나 후공을 선택할 수 있게 된다. 플레이오프에서 승/패 기록이 더 좋은 팀이 첫 엔드의 선공이나 후공을 선택할 수 있고, 만약에 두 팀 다 같은 승/패 기록이라면, 라운드 로빈 경기에서 승리한 팀이 선택할 수 있다. 이러한 경우 그 팀은 선공의 스톤을 투구하기 위한 스톤의 핸들 색깔을 선택해야 한다.

각각의 라운드 로빈 경기에서 첫 번째 이름의 팀은 어두운 스톤 핸들 색상과 함께 어두운 상의를 입어야 한다.

주심은 필요한 경기가 끝나자마자 추가의 타이브레이크 경기와 상대가 확실히 결정되면 아이스 일정을 결정할 것이다. 또한, 주심은 플레이오프 경기를 위한 추가의 연습 시간과 시트를 결정해야 한다.

팀

CZE- 체코
DEN- 덴마크
FIN- 핀란드
GER- 독일
ITA- 이탈리아
JPN- 일본
LAT- 라트비아
NOR- 노르웨이
POL- 폴란드
SUI- 스위스
TUR- 터키

WORLD WHEELCHAIR CURLING QUALIFICATION 2012
3-8 November 2012 - KISAKALLIO SPORTS INSTITUTE, LOHJA, FINLAND

DRAW SCHEDULE

Day	Date	Time	Draw	Sheet A	Sheet B	Sheet C	Sheet D	Sheet E
Sat	3 Nov.	0900	Training	x	CZE	JPN	SUI	LAT
		1030	**TEAM MEETING** – Mirror Hall (main building)					
		1130	Training	x	FIN	TUR	DEN	NOR
		1300	Training	GER	x	ITA	x	POL
		1600	1	CZE – JPN	SUI – LAT	FIN – TUR	DEN – NOR	GER – ITA
		1930	**WELCOME RECEPTION** – Lobby Restaurant (main building)					
Sun	4 Nov.	0930	2	POL – FIN	GER – JPN	NOR – CZE	TUR – ITA	DEN – SUI
		1400	3	LAT – NOR	CZE – DEN	POL – SUI	GER – FIN	JPN – TUR
		1830	4	DEN – GER	NOR – TUR	ITA – LAT	SUI – JPN	CZE – POL
Mon	5 Nov.	1030	5	SUI – TUR	POL – ITA	DEN – JPN	LAT – CZE	NOR – FIN
		1630	6	JPN – ITA	FIN – SUI	GER – NOR	POL – TUR	LAT – DEN
Tue	6 Nov.	0930	7	FIN – CZE	JPN – NOR	LAT – POL	ITA – SUI	TUR – GER
		1400	8	NOR – SUI	LAT – GER	CZE – ITA	FIN – DEN	POL – JPN
		1830	9	ITA – DEN	TUR – CZE	SUI – GER	NOR – POL	FIN – LAT
Wed	7 Nov.	0930	10	GER – POL	ITA – FIN	TUR – DEN	JPN – LAT	SUI – CZE
		1400	11	TUR – LAT	DEN – POL	JPN – FIN	CZE – GER	ITA – NOR
		1830		Tie-Breaker Games (*if required*)				
Thu	8 Nov.	0730		Tie-Breaker Games (*if required*)				
		1200		1 v 2 (*winner qualifies*) **and** 3 v 4 games				
		1630		Loser (1 v 2) v Winner (3 v 4) (*winner qualifies*)				
		2000	**FAREWELL BANQUET** – Old Strand Warehouse					

On the practice day (3 November) each team practices for 12 minutes on each sheet, rotating from A to B to C to D to E. The Umpires will control the practice, and will indicate when to switch from sheet to sheet.

First named teams in each draw have the first practice session. At the conclusion of each team's pre-game practice, one player delivers one stone to the tee at the home end. The team with the better Last Stone Draw (LSD) has the choice of delivering first or second stone in the first end. Also, the first named teams in each draw play the stones with the dark coloured handles, and wear dark coloured upper playing garments, second named teams in each draw play the stones with the light coloured handles, and wear light coloured upper playing garments.

Note: If no tie-breaker games required on Thursday, 8 Nov, playoff games will be at **10:30 and 16:30.**

DAY	DATE	TIME	IMPORTANT EVENTS
Saturday	3 Nov.	1030	Team Meeting – Mirror Hall (main building)
Saturday	3 Nov.	1555	Opening Ceremony – on-ice, just prior to 1st games
Saturday	3 Nov.	1930	Welcome Reception – Lobby Restaurant (main building)
Thursday	8 Nov.	2000	Farewell Banquet – Old Strand Warehouse

2012 세계 휠체어 컬링 예선

3-8 2012년 11월 - KISAKALLIO SPORTS INSTITUTE, LOHJA, FINLAND

일정표

요일	날짜	시간	Draw	경기장A	경기장B	경기장C	경기장D	경기장E
토요일	11월3일	0900	훈련	x	체코	일본	스위스	라트비아
		1030	팀 매칭 - Mirror Hall (본관)					
		1130	훈련	x	핀란드	터키	덴마크	노르웨이
		1300	훈련	영국	x	이탈리아	x	폴란드
		1600	I	체코-일본	스위스-라트비아	핀란드-터키	덴마크-노르웨이	영국-이탈리아
		1930	**개회식** - 레스토랑 로비 (본관)					
일요일	11월4일	0930	2	폴란드-핀란드	영국-일본	노르웨이-체코	터키-이탈리아	덴마크-스위스
		1400	3	라트비아-노르웨이	체코-덴마크	폴란드-스위스	영국-핀란드	일본-터키
		1830	4	덴마크-영국	노르웨이-터키	이탈리아-라트비아	스위스-일본	체코-폴란드
월요일	11월5일	1030	5	스위스-터키	폴란드-이탈리아	덴마크-일본	라트비아-세코	노르웨이-핀란드
		1630	6	일본-이탈리아	핀란드-스위스	영국-노르웨이	폴란드-터키	라트비아-덴마크
화요일	11월6일	0930	7	핀란드-체코	일본-노르웨이	라트비아-폴란드	이탈리아-스위스	터키-영국
		1400	8	노르웨이-스위스	라트비아-영국	체코-이탈리아	핀란드-덴마크	폴란드-일본
		1830	9	이탈리아-덴마크	터키-체코	스위스-영국	노르웨이-폴란드	핀란드-라트비아
수요일	11월7일	0930	10	영국-폴란드	이탈리아-핀란드	터키-덴마크	일본-라트비아	스위스-체코
		1400	11	터키-라트비아	덴마크-폴란드	일본-핀란드	체코-영국	이탈리아-노르웨이
		1830		타이 브레이커 게임 (만약 필요하다면)				
목요일	11월8일	0730		타이 브레이커 게임 (만약 필요하다면)				
		1200		1v2(승리자 자격) 그리고 3v4 게임				
		1630		패배자 (1v2) v 승리자 (3v4) (승리자 자격)				
		2000	**송별회** - Old Strand Warehouse					

연습 날에는 (11월 3일) 경기장 A에서 B에서 C에서 D에서 E에서 돌아가면서. 각각의 팀들이 각각의 경기장에서 12분 동안 연습한다. 심판은 연습을 통제할 것이고, 그리고 각 시트에서 다른 시트로 전환을 지시할 것이다.

각 드로우에서 처음으로 호명된 팀은 첫 번째 연습을 한다. 한 선수가 홈 엔드의 티라인을 향해 스톤을 딜리버리하여 각 팀들의 경기 시작 전 연습을 통한 LSD로 선·후공을 정하고, LSD 기록이 더 우수한 팀이 선공 or 후공을 선택할 수 있고 또한, 첫 번째로 호명된 팀은 어두운색깔의 스톤 핸들과 어두운색의 상의를 입어야 하고, 두 번째로 호명된 팀은 경기마다 밝은색깔의 스톤 핸들과 밝은색의 상의를 입고 경기를 하여야 한다.

주의: 목요일에 타이브레이크 게임이 필요 없게 된다면, 11월 8일 10:30 과 16:30분에 플레이오프 경기를 할 것이다.

요일	날짜	시간	중요한 사건
토요일	11월 3일	10:30	팀 미팅 - Mirror Hall(본관)
토요일	11월 3일	15:55	개막식 - 빙상장에서, 첫 번째 경기 바로 전에
토요일	11월 3일	19:30	리셉션에 오신 걸 환영합니다 - 레스토랑 로비(본관)
목요일	11월 8일	20:00	송별회 - Old Strand Warehouse

TEAM MEETING

The team meeting chaired by the Chief Umpire will be held on Saturday, 3 November 2012 at 1030hrs in the Mirror Room (main building). Attendance is mandatory for all team members and coaches.

The Team Meeting document will be distributed to all participating teams through their Member Associations.

FUNCTIONS

During the event, there will be mandatory functions to be attended by all team members and coaches in team uniforms appropriate to the occasion. Teams are requested not to leave these official functions before team introductions have been made and all speeches and thanks have been given.

Saturday	3 Nov.	1555	Opening Ceremony – on-ice, just prior to 1st games
Saturday	3 Nov.	1930	Welcome Reception – Lobby Restaurant (main building)
Thursday	8 Nov.	2000	Farewell Banquet – Old Strand Warehouse

Opening & Closing Function tickets will be available to all teams and spectators at no charge.

MEDIA RELATIONS

There will be international, national and local media coverage of the event. The WCF and Organising Committee request that players grant interviews as requested by the media. Words of caution however, make certain you do not make reference to any matters you do not wish quoted. If you have a specific complaint about the qualification, please express it to the appropriate official of the WCF, not to the media.

PINS AND BADGES

Prior to the commencement of all round-robin games it is customary for each team member to exchange with his or her opposite competitor a pin, badge or banner representative of his or her club, region or Member Association as a souvenir gift. The teams' Member Association should arrange the required supply of these items.

MEDICAL SERVICES

Medical services will be available.
The Hospital is located in the city of Lohja, about 15 minutes from Kisakallio.

CLASSIFICATION

Assessment of athletes who are not yet classified will take place during team training on Saturday, 3 November 2012.

RULES

The competition will be played under the World Curling Federation rules, as published in the Rules of Curling and the Rules of Competition Booklet (June 2011).

It is the duty of all players and coaches to become fully acquainted with all rules prior to the team meeting.

The final authority for the operation and general conduct of the World Curling Federation events rests with the President of the Federation and her appointee(s).

Competitors should note that the WCF forbids doping and maintains an active policy to prevent the supply and taking of "prohibited substances" to or by players, coaches, Umpires, officials or other agents involved with the conduct of the sport of curling. "Prohibited substances" shall be those substances which shall from

팀 미팅

팀 미팅은 주심의 주최로 토요일, 2012년 11월 3일 10시 30분 Mirror Room(본 건물)에서 진행될 것이다. 모든 팀원과 코치는 무조건 필참해야 한다

팀 미팅 서류는 모든 참가 팀들의 임원 단체를 통해 배분될 것이다.

행사

이벤트 진행 동안, 모든 팀과 코치들은 유니폼을 갖춰 입은 필참 행사가 있을 것이다. 이 행사에 팀들은 자기 소개, 연설, 그리고 감사의 말씀이 끝나 전에 떠나는 것을 자제해주길 바란다.

토요일	11월 3일	15:55	개회식-빙판 위, 첫 번째 게임 시작
토요일	11월 3일	19:30	환영행사- 로비 식당(본 건물)
목요일	11월 8일	20:00	송별식-Old Strand Warehouse

개회식 및 송별식 행사 티켓은 모든 팀과 관람자들에게 무료로 제공될 것이다.

미디어 홍보

경기를 보도하기 위한 국제적, 국가적 그리고 지역적 미디어가 있을 것이다. 세계컬링연맹과 조직위원회는 선수들에게 미디어와의 인터뷰를 요청할 것이다. 선수는 단어 선택에 주의해야 하고, 당신의 말이 인용되기 원하지 않는다면 어느 문제라도 언급하지 않을 것을 분명히 해야 한다, 만약 조직에 대한 불만을 가지고 있다면, 미디어에 말고 세계컬링연맹에 적절하게 표현하기를 부탁한다.

핀과 배지

매 라운드 로빈 경기 시작 전에 선수들은 상대 선수들에게 임원 단체나 자신의 클럽을 상징하는 핀이나 배지, 또한 국가 상징물을 교환하는 것이 관습이다. 팀의 협회는 기념품과 자원을 마련해야 한다.

의료 서비스

의료 서비스는 제공될 것이다.

병원은 키사칼리오(Kisakallio)로부터 약 15분 거리에 있는 로하(Lohja) 시에 있다.

분류

선수의 평가가 아직 이루어지지 않았다면 팀의 연습 시간인 2012년 11월 3일 토요일에 분류할 것이다.

규칙

『컬링과 경쟁의 규칙』책자로 출판된(2011.6) 세계컬링연맹의 규칙을 따를 것이다.

팀 매칭 이전에 모든 규칙을 완벽하게 숙지해 오는 것이 모든 선수들과 코치들의 의무이다. 세계컬링연맹 경기의 작용과 일반적인 수행을 위한 마지막 권한은 연맹의 회장과 지명된 사람에게 책임이 있다. 참가자들은 세계컬링연맹이 도핑을 금하고 컬링의 스포츠의 수행에 관련된 경기자, 코치, 주심, 임원 또는 다른 에이전트에 의해 금지된 물질의 공급과 복용을 막기 위해 엄격한 정책을 시행하고 있는 것에 주의해야 한다. 금지된 물질은 세계반도핑기구에 의해 수시로 준비 목록에 표시되어야 하고 개개인의 육체적 또는 정신적 상태에 대한 영향을 미치는지 그리고 그것에 의해 선수들 또는 임원의 스포츠 수행능력의 영향을 끼치는지 보여주는 물질일 것이다.

time to time appear on lists prepared by the World Anti Doping Agency and which have been shown to affect an individual's physical or mental condition and thereby influence the sporting performance of players or officials.

DOPE TESTING

Dope testing may be carried out during the Qualifier. A copy of the current list of banned substances and methods as issued by the World Anti Doping Agency (WADA) can be found at http://www.worldcurling.org/anti-doping-medical. Any competitors, who are currently taking any medication, which is on the banned list of substances, must firstly seek expert medical advice on the possibility of it being substituted by a comparable substance, which is not on the banned list. **If this is not possible, a Therapeutic Use Exemption (TUE) in respect of the banned substance should have been made by 03 October 2012 (if this has not been done please apply immediately) to** The Secretary General, World Curling Federation, 74 Tay Street, Perth PH2 8NP, Scotland, fax 44 1738 451641. TUE application details should be obtained from http://www.worldcurling.org/anti-doping-medical. The WCF is required by the WADA to follow these procedures. It is therefore extremely important that **ALL ATHLETES** who may participate at WCF events are fully aware of these requirements and also provided with the necessary medical advice.

CRESTING

Your attention is drawn to the enclosed "WCF Cresting Policy".

Please note that submissions of proposed crests, either national or sponsors, must be made to the WCF Secretariat. These submissions should be forwarded either by the Member Association concerned or accompanied by written approval of the Member Association. This is necessary to ensure that advertising on team crests does not conflict with products of major event sponsors, written approval of the WCF is therefore required.

The Event Crests, if provided by the Organising Committee should be attached to the upper left arm of playing garments.

Cresting placement should be the same for all team members on all playing-garments.

No cresting shall be permitted in any other area, or on other items of clothing or curling equipment without prior application to, and approval of the World Curling Federation.

All members of team support staff with On-Ice Accreditation must also adhere to the stated cresting policy.

Each team member shall wear identical uniforms for all games. Each garment: shirt, jacket or sweater, shall have the player's surname, in 2-inch (5cm) letters across the upper back of the garment and the country name, in 2-inch (5cm), or larger letters, across the back above the waist. If desired, a national emblem may also be worn on the back, but only in addition to the country name and should be displayed between the player's surname and the country name. The members of a team shall wear light-coloured shirts when throwing stones with light-coloured handles and team members shall wear dark-coloured shirts when throwing stones with dark handles. Upper playing garments of all team members must be the same colour during the competition. **(n.b. red is classified as a dark colour)**.

When two players have the same surname, the first letter of their given name shall be added to the player's name on the garment. If the first letter is also the same either another initial should be added, or the full or abbreviated given names shown.

All Member Associations shall register the colour of the outer garments, jackets or sweaters, to be used by their teams when competing in World Championships.

도핑 테스트

도핑 테스트는 예선경기 동안 수행할 것이다. 금지된 물질의 현재 목록의 카피와 그리고 세계반도핑기구에 의해 발행된 방법들은 http://www.worldcurling.org/anti-doping-medical에서 확인할 수 있다. 현재 금지된 물질목록에 있는 어떤 약물치료를 받는 선수는 첫 번째로 금지 목록엔 없는 비교할 만한 물질을 대체한 가능성이 있는지 전문의사에게 진단을 받아야 한다. 만약 이것이 불가능하다면, 금지된 물질에 대한 TUE 사무총장, 세계컬링연맹, 74 Tay Street, Perth PH2 8NP, 스코틀랜드, 팩스 44 1738 451641에 2012년 10월 3일 만들어졌어야 한다. (만약 이 작업이 완료되지 않았다면 즉시 신청해라) TUE 적용 세부사항은 http://www.worldcurling.org/anti-doping-medical로부터 얻어야 한다. 세계컬링연맹는 이러한 절차를 따르기 위해 WADA에 의해 요구될 것이다. 그러므로 세계컬링연맹 경기에 참가하는 모든 운동선수는 이러한 요구사항을 완전히 알고 필요한 의학적 경고를 제공해 주는 것이 절대적으로 중요하다.

장식

다음 사항은 '세계컬링연맹 장식 정책'에서 제공한 것이다.

국내, 국외 스폰서 간에 제안된 장식은 모두 세계컬링연맹 사무국에 제출하는 것으로 알아두시길 바란다. 제출서는 연관된 임원 단체나, 아니면 승인 받은 것만 보내야만 한다. 이것은 팀 장식에 대한 홍보와 유명 스폰서 간의 갈등을 초래하지 않기 위한 것이다. 그래서 세계컬링연맹의 승인이 필요한 것이다.

이벤트 장식, 만약 기획 단체에서 제공된다면 선수 복장 왼쪽 팔 위에 부착되어야 한다.
장식 부착은 모든 선수 복장에 동일해야 한다.

장식은 다른 부위 어디든 허락되지 않으며, 다른 복장과 기구 또한 컬링 소품에도 사전 허락이나 세계컬링연맹의 허락 없이는 안 된다.

빙판 승인 단체의 지원 스태프는 공지된 장식 조항에 대해 엄수해야 한다.

각 팀원들은 동일 복장을 착용할 것이다. 각 의상: 셔츠, 재킷 또한 스웨터는, 선수의 성(이름)을 2-인치(5㎝) 복장 등 위에 새겨져 있어야 하며, 또한 국가 이름도 2-인치(5㎝), 아니면 큰 글씨로, 허리 뒤에 새겨야 한다. 만약 원한다면, 등에 국가 상징 부착이 가능하지만, 국가 명칭 다음이며, 선수의 성(이름)과 국가 명칭 사이에 있어야 한다. 또한, 선수들이 밝은색깔 손잡이스톤을 던질 때는 그에 맞게 밝은색깔 복장을 입을 것이며, 색깔이 어두운 손잡이 스톤이면 똑같이 어두운색깔 복장을 갖춰 입어야 한다. 상의 복장 색깔은 대회 기간 동안 선수마다 동일한 색깔이어야 한다(빨간색은 어두운 색깔로 간주한다).

만약 두 선수의 이름이 같은 경우에는, 이름의 첫 철자가 복장에 같이 부착될 것이다. 이름 첫 철자도 만약 같은 상황이면, 두 개의 철자를 새겨도 되고, 아니면 이름을 단축해서 표시 가능하다.

모든 임원 단체는 세계선수권대회에서 참여하는 각 팀이 사용하게 될 겉옷, 잠바 또한 스웨터의 색깔을 등록해야 한다.

CRESTING POLICY FOR WHEELCHAIR CURLING

There are **six** positions for the display of crests and badges on uniforms; allotted areas shall be the following:

- **THE RIGHT CHEST (1) AND UPPER LEFT ARM (1)** will be reserved for the event sponsor of the World Championship or an event crest of the Host Committee. Member Associations will be advised of the preferred placement for these crests.

- **THE LEFT CHEST (1) AND UPPER RIGHT ARM (2)** will be reserved for a team sponsor's crest or Member Association's emblem.

- **SIDE OF THE LEG (1) (between the knee and ankle)** will be reserved for a team sponsor's crest. All team members must wear the crest on the same leg and the crests must be at the same height.

Total crest size (edge to edge) shall not be greater than 10cm (4 inches) or not greater than 100 square centimeters (16 square inches). Only one crest is permitted in each of the six areas stated. All team sponsors' cresting must have the approval of the team's Member Association. A clothing manufacturer's trademark may be displayed provided it is not greater than 20 square centimeters (3.1 square inches) on jackets and trousers and not greater than 6 square centimeters (0.93 square inches) on any other item of clothing, including caps.

Caps
The only logo permitted, in addition to the manufacturer's logo, is either that of the Event, or the athlete's Member Association.

The following cresting and/or logos are permitted on wheelchairs during World Wheelchair Curling Championships:
One sponsor's crest on each wheel (may be different sponsors) with the total crest size per wheel not greater than 200 square centimeters (31 square inches).

Member Association/Country Name & Emblem
These may be displayed on each wheel and may be in addition to a sponsor's crest. There are no size restrictions.

They may also be displayed along with the player's surname on the back of the seat in the same dimensions as shown below for uniforms in the following order. Top: player's surname, middle: emblem, bottom: country.

Manufacturers Trademark
A wheelchair manufacturer's trademark may be displayed on each wheel and on the back of the seat, provided it is not greater than 60 square centimeters (9.3 square inches).

Team or Member Associations sponsors cresting will only be permitted if they advertise companies or organizations that carry out business in the country represented by the team concerned, and do not conflict with any Sponsor of World Championships. Member Associations shall register sponsor names, and business category with a photograph or diagram in actual size with the WCF by **26 October 2012.** The WCF will confirm approval in writing. Every effort will be made to facilitate the acceptance of team sponsor requests. Sponsor names registered later, or not registered, may not be approved by the WCF. Crests that are not approved must be removed from the on-ice uniform and wheelchairs.

휠체어 컬링을 위한 장식 정책

깃장식과 배지 전시를 위한 총 6개의 위치가 있다: 할당된 위치는 아래와 같이:

- **오른쪽 가슴(1) 그리고 왼팔 위쪽(1)** 세계선수권 이벤트 스폰서나, 아니면 개최 의회단 깃 장식을 위해 예비될 것이다. 임원 단체는 이 깃장식에 대한 바람직한 위치를 알 것이다.
- **왼쪽 가슴(1) 그리고 오른팔 위쪽(2)** 팀 스폰서 깃 장식이나 임원 단체의 문장 장식으로 예비될 것이다.
- **다리 옆면(1)(무릎이랑 발목 사이)**팀 스폰서 깃장식으로 예비된다. 또한, 모든 팀 멤버는 깃장식을 같은 다리와 높이에 착용하고 있어야 한다.

깃장식의 전체 크기(모서리에서 모서리까지) 10㎝(4인치)보다 크지 않을 것이며, 또한 100㎠(16제곱인치) 이상이면 안 된다. 언급된 6군데 중에 한 곳만 깃장식이 가능하다. 모든 팀 스폰서 장식은 팀들의 임원 단체로부터 허가받아야 한다. 또한 옷 제조업자 상표도 착용할 수 있으나, 대신 재킷이나 바지에 20㎠(3.1제곱인치) 이상 크지 않으며, 모자를 포함한 다른 의상의 6㎠(0.93인치)보다 크지 않으면 기재가 가능하다.

모자

허가되는 상표는, 제조업을 포함해서, 이벤트에 관련되거나, 선수들의 임원 단체 상표만이 허락된다.

아래에 언급된 깃장식/상표는 세계 휠체어 컬링 대회 동안 휠체어에 기제가 가능한 조항이다.
한 바퀴에 하나의 스폰서 깃장식(다른 스폰서 가능)을 하며 장식의 전체 크기가 200㎠(31제곱인치) 이상이 아니어야 한다.

임원단체/국가 이름 및 상징

한 바퀴마다 표시 가능하며, 스폰서 깃장식으로 추가된다. 사이즈 제한은 없다.

아래 유니폼에 보인 것과 같이 뒷부분에 동일한 크기로 선수 성(이름)과 같이 표시할 수 있으며 순서는 이와 같다. 상단 부분: 성(이름), 중간 부분: 상징, 하단 부분: 국가.

제조업자 상징

휠체어 제조업 상징이 각 바퀴랑 좌석 뒤에 표시할 수 있으며, 60제곱㎠(9.3제곱인치) 이상의 크기 아니면 된다.

팀이나, 임원 단체의 스폰서 장식은 핀란드 내에서 사업 중인 기업이나, 단체에 대한 홍보를 하면서, 세계 스폰서 대회(SWC) 규정과 겹치지 않으면 허락된다. 임원 단체는 2012년 10월 26일까지 스폰서 성명과 업종을 사진이나 실제 크기의 도표를 첨부하여 세계컬링연맹에 등록해야 한다. WFC는 글로 승인을 확인할 것이다. 모든 팀 스폰서 요청 승인이 이뤄지도록 가능한 한 모든 노력을 할 것이다. 추후의 스폰서 등록, 혹은 등록 안 되는 경우는 WFC로부터 승인 못 받을 수 있다. 허가받지 않은 깃장식은 빙상장 유니폼과 휠체어로부터 제거해야 한다.

PASSPORTS
All persons entering Finland must be in possession of a valid passport.

TRAVEL
Kisakallio is located 30 minutes northwest of Helsinki by the fresh water lake in the tranquil forest of Lohja region. Transfer from Helsinki Airport to Kisakallio and back is included in the Team Accommodation Package Price. Please provide the Organising Committee with your exact travel times by 3 October 2012 so that they can arrange your pick-up.

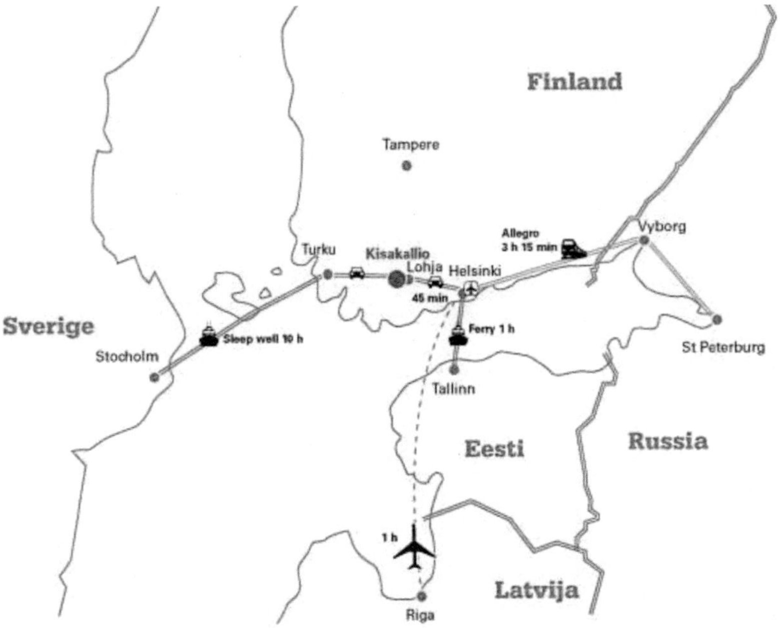

INSURANCE
All team members and officials are responsible for their own travel and medical insurance.

ACCOMMODATION
An Accommodation booking form is distributed to Member Associations. Those forms have to be returned to the Organising Committee by 3 October 2012 to guarantee your booking. The participating Member Associations concerned are responsible for the cost. Should you have any questions please contact Lauri Ikävalko (lauri.ikavalko@kisakallio.fi).

MEALS
Kisakallio restaurant is located in the main building, about 2 minutes away from the ice hall or accommodation.

The accommodation cost includes breakfast and either lunch or dinner. The cost of the other meal (either lunch/dinner) will be 10 Euros per person. An evening snack is available from the restaurant at the cost of 6 Euros per person.

여권

핀란드로 입국하는 모든 이는 유효한 여권을 소지하고 있어야 한다.

찾아오는 길

키사칼리오는 로하 지역 고요한 숲 인근에 있는 헬싱키(Helsinki)에서 북서 30분 거리에 있다. 헬싱키 공항에서 키사칼리오로 오고가는 왕복권을 TAP(Team Accommodation Package: 팀 동반 패키지)에 포함되었다. 픽업 시간을 수월하게 정하기 위해 2012년 10월 3일까지 OG(조직 위원회)에 신청하기 바란다.

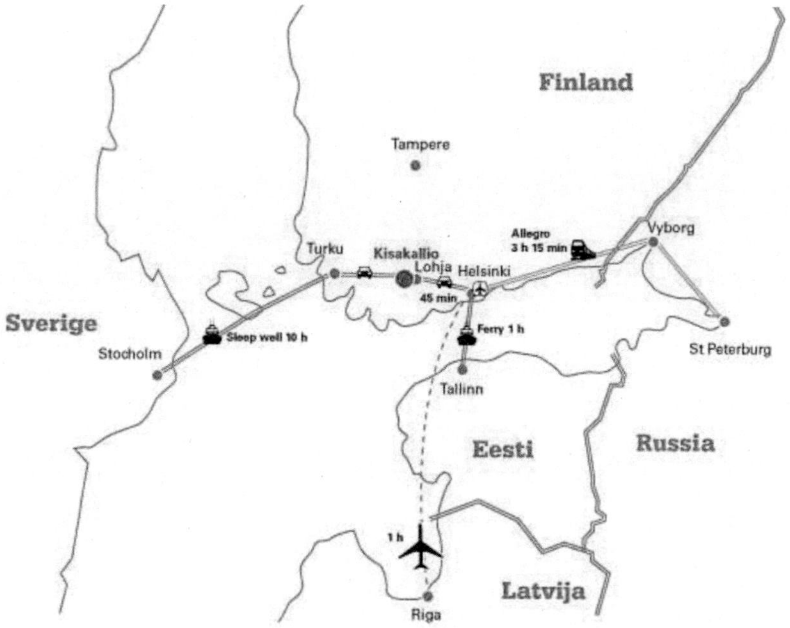

보험

모든 팀 인원과 관리자들은 개인의 여행와 의료보험에 책임 있다.

숙박

숙밥 신청 서류는 임원 단체에 배급이 된다. 예약을 위해서는 2012년 10월 3일까지 조직 위원회에 제출해야 한다. 비용은 참여하는 임원 단체에서 부담할 것이다. 문의 사항이 있을 시에는 Lauri Ikävalko에게 연락해야 한다(lauri.ikavalko@kisakallio.fi). .

식사

키사칼리오 식당은 숙소와 얼음 홀 2분 거리인 본 건물에 있다.

숙박 비용은 아침과 점심 또는 저녁 식사를 포함한다. 다른 식사(점심/저녁)의 비용은 인당 10유로가 될 것이다. 저녁 식사는 인당 6유로의 비용으로 레스토랑에서 할 수 있다.

MEAL TIMES

Breakfast	07:00 to 09:00
Lunch	10:30 to 13:30 (extended on Mon. to suit draw)
Dinner	16:00 to 19:00 (extended on Mon. to suit draw)
Evening Snack	20:00 to 22:00

LAUNDRY

The hotel has laundry and dry cleaning services @ 5 Euros/laundry bag. Further details will be available at the reception.

LOCAL CURRENCY

Currency rates of exchange are (approx.)

1.00 EUR	=	1.20	SFr.
	=	1.21	US$
	=	95.00	JPY
	=	25.00	CZK
	=	2.20	TRY
	=	7.50	DKK

There is no ATM cash machine in Kisakallio, the nearest would be 4km away. Credit cards are accepted.

POWER ADAPTERS

Electricity is supplied at an alternating current of 230V/50Hz (European plug).

MAIL

A postcard to Finland and anywhere in the world costs €0.75.

COUNTRY DIALING CODES

Dialing into Finland:	00358
Emergencies:	dial 112 (police, ambulance, fire)

TIPPING

In Finland, tips are not expected and given mainly if the service exceeds your expectations, e.g. to hotel staff, taxi drivers, or waiters.

WEATHER

Local weather may be found at: www.ilmatieteenlaitos.fi. You are in Finland - dress for the cold.

식사시간

아침	07:00~09:00
점심	10:30~13:30 (월요일에는 연장. 정장 착용)
저녁	16:00~19:00 (월요일에는 연장. 정장 착용)
오후 간식	20:00~22:00

세탁

이 호텔은 5유로/빨래 가방(유로마다/한 가방). 더 자세한 사항은 추후 환영식때 공지할 것이다.

지역 환율

교환의 환율 수치는 대략적인 수치이다.

1.00EUR(유로)	=	1.20 SFr
	=	1.21 US$
	=	95.00 JPY
	=	25.00 CZK
	=	2.20 TRY
	=	7.50 DKK

키사칼리오 인근에는 ATM이 없다. 그나마 가까운 건 4㎞ 거리에 있다. 신용카드는 언제든지 가능하다.

전기 어댑터

전기는 230V/50Hz의 전류로 번갈아 공급되고 있다.

우편물

핀란드와 세계 어디든지 보낼 수 있는 엽서는 0.75EU(유로)

지역 국번

핀란드 00358

긴급 112(경찰, 병원, 소방)

팁

핀란드에서는 보통 팁이 의무가 아니며, 주로 기대치 이상의 대접을 받았을 때 한다. 예) 호텔 직원, 택시, 웨이터

IMPORTANT INFORMATION

International Embassies:

-	Czech Republic:	Armfeltintie 14 , 00150 Helsinki , Tel: +358 9 171 169
-	Denmark:	Keskuskatu 1A, 00101 Helsinki, Tel: +358 9 6841050
-	Germany:	Krogiuksentie 4, 00340 Helsinki, Tel: +358 9 458 580
-	Italy:	Itäinen puistotie 4A, 00140 Helsinki, Tel: +358 9 6811280
-	Japan:	Eteläranta 8, 00130 Helsinki, Tel: +358 9 686 0200
-	Latvia:	Armfeltintie 10, 00150 Helsinki, Tel: +358 9 4764 7244
-	Norway:	Rehbinderintie 17, 00150 Helsinki, Tel: +358 9 686 0180
-	Poland:	Armas Lindgrenintie 21, 00570 Helsinki, Tel: +358 9 684 8077
-	Switzerland:	Uudenmaankatu 16A, 00120 Helsinki, Tel: +358 9 6229 500
-	Turkey:	Puistokatu 1BA3, 00140 Helsinki, Tel: +358 9 6811 030

Water

The people of Finland are extremely proud of their local water. In fact, they would even boast that they have better tasting water compared to other water bottle companies in the world. Some countries resort to bottled water as compensation for their lack of potable water supply. Finland, on the other hand, has the lowest rate in the use of bottled water. You ask: "Is the water safe to drink in Finland?" Definitely, yes.

BASIC FINNISH

Hello:	Hei
Goodbye:	Näkemiin
Yes:	Kyllä
No:	Ei
Thank you:	Kiitos
Excuse me:	Anteeksi
Hotel:	Hotelli
Room:	Huone
Passport:	Passi
Airport:	Lentokenttä
Train station:	Rautatieasema
Bus station:	Bussiasema
Ticket:	Lippu
Water:	Vettä
Milk:	Maito
Coffee:	Kahvi
Bread:	Leipä

Finnish Numbers
1: yksi, 2: kaksi, 3: kolme, 4: neljä, 5: viisi, 6: kuusi, 7: seitsemän, 8: kahdeksan, 9: yhdeksän, 10: kymmenen

중요한 정보

국제 대사관

- 체코슬로바키아 Armfeltintie 14 , 00150 Helsinki , Tel: +358 9 171 16
- 덴마크 Keskuskatu 1A, 00101 Helsinki, Tel: +358 9 6841050
- 독일 Krogiuksentie 4, 00340 Helsinki, Tel: +358 9 458 580
- 이탈리아 Itäinen puistotie 4A, 00140 Helsinki, Tel: +358 9 6811280
- 일본 Eteläranta 8, 00130 Helsinki, Tel: +358 9 686 0200
- 라트비아 Armfeltintie 10, 00150 Helsinki, Tel: +358 9 4764 7244
- 노르웨이 Rehbinderintie 17, 00150 Helsinki, Tel: +358 9 686 0180
- 폴란드 Armas Lindgrenintie 21, 00570 Helsinki, Tel: +358 9 684 8077
- 스위스 Uudenmaankatu 16A, 00120 Helsinki, Tel: +358 9 6229 500
- 터키 Puistokatu 1BA3, 00140 Helsinki, Tel: +358 9 6811 030

물(식수)

핀란드 사람들은 자기 나라 물에 대한 자부심이 매우 높다. 심지어, 자기 나라 물이 세계 어느 가공 물 회사들의 물보다 더 맛있다고 할 정도이다. 어떤 국가들은 식수 부족으로 인해 가공된 물을 만들어서 마신다. 하지만 핀란드에서는 가공된 물의 식용도는 제일 낮은 것으로 나타났다. 그래서 "핀란드 물은 마시기에 안전한가요?"라고 물으면 당연히 "예."이다.

기본 핀란드어

안녕하세요	Hei
안녕히 가세요	Nakemiin
예	Kylla
아니요	Ei
감사합니다	Kiitos
실례합니다	Anteeksi
호텔	Hotelli
방	Huone
여권	Passi
공항	Lentokentta
기차역	Rautatieasema
버스역	Bussiasema
티켓	Lippu
물	Vetta
우유	Maito
커피	Kahvi
빵	Leipa

48. WCF ICE TECHNICIAN'S AGREEMENT

WORLD CURLING FEDERATION

WCF ICE TECHNICIAN'S AGREEMENT

Role of the Ice Technician:

- An Ice Technician must be professional and dedicated to providing and maintaining optimum ice conditions in order to allow the sport to be played to the highest level.
- The Ice Technician must have a sound knowledge of the game and treat all those involved with the competition with courtesy and respect.
- The Ice Technician must commit to the competition the required number of working hours to ensure that ice conditions are optimal. All draws must be able to start on time.
- It must be remembered that a competition may be judged by the quality of the ice conditions. To that end the Ice Technician is a vitally important person in any competition and as such it is their responsibility to ensure that the best ice conditions are provided for the athletes at all times throughout the competition.

Code of Conduct for Ice Technicians:

Ice Technicians are in a position of trust and responsibility and as such the following code of ethics should be followed:

- An Ice Technician must be impartial in respect of all participating competitors, but they should be prepared to converse with athletes and coaches on a general level (i.e. non-specific information). The Ice Technician can give more detailed information about the ice conditions to the Chief Umpire and the WCF Stone and Technical Controller (WCF STC, currently Leif Ohman, Richard Harding, Keith Wendorf or WCF Technical Delegate).
- The Chief Ice Technician should be the only person to answer media questions about ice conditions. Remember that there is no such thing as an "off the record" comment, so be careful what is said.
- A good working relationship between the athletes, coaches, other officials, media and site personnel is expected. Respect everyone's job assignment, roles and duties.
- Never put yourself in a position, real or perceived, of being partial in any situation.
- Never become involved in any betting in a competition where you are working as an Ice Technician.
- Consumption of alcoholic beverages during a competition should be done in moderation. Alcoholic beverages may not be consumed during a game being worked by an Ice Technician. The WCF Director of Competitions / Technical Delegate may suspend any Ice Technician for violating basic common sense with alcohol, or other items in the code of conduct.
- Comments about any aspect of ice making and the competition should only be discussed amongst the Ice Technicians – not in the presence of other people or media.

48. 세계컬링연맹 경기 기술자 동의서

세계컬링연맹 경기 기술자 동의서

경기 기술자의 역할:

- 아이스 기술자는 선수들이 높은 수준의 경기를 선보일 수 있도록 최고의 얼음 상태를 유지하는 데 전념한다.
- 아이스 기술자는 경기에 대한 지식을 갖추어야 하고, 모든 선수들에게 공손함과 존중을 표하면서 대하여야 한다.
- 아이스 기술자는 경기 시간 동안 최적의 얼음 상태를 유지하도록 하여 선수들에게 제공하는 것이 필수고, 모든 경기는 제시간에 시작할 것이다.
- 얼음 상태 수준에 따라 경기의 결과가 좌우될 수 있다는 것을 명심해야 한다. 아이스 기술자들은 어느 경기에서든 극도로 중요한 사람들이고, 최고의 얼음을 선수들에게 제공하는 것은 그들의 책임이다.

기술자들의 행동강령:

기술자들은 믿음과 책임이 중요한 역할로서 아래의 행동강령을 따라야 한다:

- 아이스 기술자들은 모든 선수들에게 공정하고 존중해야 하고, 그들은 선수나 코치들과 일반적인 얘기를 나눌 수 있는 준비를 해야 한다(예: 구체적이지 않은 정보). 아이스 기술자는 주심과 세계컬링연맹 스톤 관리자에게 아이스 상태에 대한 정확한 정보를 줄 수 있어야 한다(세계컬링연맹 STC는 현재 Leif Ohman, Richard Harding, Keith Wendorf or 세계컬링연맹 기술적 대표).
- 오직 주아이스 기술자만이 얼음 상태에 대한 미디어의 질문에 대답할 수 있다. 그들에게 "비공개한다."와 같은 대답은 없으므로 말할 때 조심하는 것을 명심하여야 한다.
- 선수들이나 코치들, 다른 직원들, 미디어 그리고 현장 직원들과 좋은 관계로 지낼 것을 기대한다. 모두의 직업과 역할, 의무를 존중해라.
- 어느 상황에서 불리한 입장이 되었다면 사실로 인지되어도 절대 자신을 불리한 위치로 만들지 마라.
- 아이스 기술자는 자신이 어디서 일하든 어느 경기의 베팅에도 관여해서는 안 된다.
- 아이스 기술자는 경기하는 동안 음주는 적당히 해야 한다. 아이스 기술자로 일하게 되면 음주는 금지될 수 있다. 세계컬링연맹 경기 위원장과 기술적 대표는 아이스 기술자에게 기본적인 감각에 위반되는 알코올도 금지할 수 있고 그 외에 다른 행동도 금지할 수 있다.
- 얼음 만드는 것에 대한 언급과 경기와 관련된 얘기는 오직 아이스 기술자와 상의하여야만 한다. - 특정한 사람이나 미디어가 참여해서는 안 된다.

- The WCF will set the on-ice dress code for all Ice Technicians. An Ice Technician should wear appropriate attire at all Event functions (i.e. – no blue jeans). The Field of Play clothing shall be black pants and a special jacket (supplied by the Organising Committee or the WCF). Whenever possible, the Chief Ice Technician's jacket should be marked with Chief Ice Technician and similar for the Deputy Chief Ice Technician. Outside the curling facility (public places) the official clothing should not be worn, unless it is to go directly from the venue to the place of residence.
- A neat and clean personal appearance and proper conduct is essential at all times.
- Ice Technicians should ensure that they have had enough rest so that their minds are fresh and alert. In order to present the best impression during games, Ice Technicians should be seated or standing, not leaning against the boards. Ice Technicians should not be in the Field of Play without reason during games (e.g. - should not be in the Field of Play taking pictures).
- Ice Technicians should uphold the principles of the ice making system and the philosophies of the WCF at all times, but maintain a degree of flexibility to avoid confrontation with the Organising Committee, teams, WCF Executive Board and the media.
- Ice Technicians should never become more than casually involved socially with any specific team or athlete during the competition. There should be full disclosure to the WCF if there is a personal or business relationship with an athlete or coach. It is acceptable to speak with and be around teams socially, but Ice Technicians should be careful not to be found in a position of spending an excessive amount of time with one team or player.
- During the competition the Chief Ice Technician and crew should be at the venue in enough time to prepare the ice for every game and practice. The ice crew must follow the Chief Ice Technician's work schedule. In the absence of the Chief Ice Technician, the Deputy Chief Ice Technician will be in charge and assume the duties of the Chief Ice Technician.
- The Chief Ice Technician is responsible for the WCF Ice Technician Equipment Boxes. An inspection of the boxes must be done at the start of every competition. If a box is not properly packed, or there are missing items, this must be reported to the WCF TD. At the conclusion of the competition, the boxes must be properly packed and ready for shipment. The equipment boxes will be inspected by the WCF and the cost of any missing items will be deducted from the Chief Ice Technician's honorarium. The WCF will supply documents that list the contents of each box, the proper usage of the boxes, and details on how to correctly pack the boxes.
- The Chief Ice Technician must submit a report to the WCF Director of Competitions within 3 weeks of the conclusion of the competition.
- Disciplinary action for an Ice Technician will be determined and administered by the WCF Discipline Committee (minimum of three persons: WCF President or Vice President; one Executive Board Member or Secretary General; and the WCF Director of Competitions or WCF Technical Delegate). Ice Technicians who do not follow the code of conduct and the agreement stated below may not be considered for future WCF competitions.

WCF's Definition of Competition Ice:

The ice should have a movement and speed that gives advantage to the player's skill and also gives the guarantee of an interesting game.

The WCF requests the following Ice Conditions:

Curl between 4 and 5 feet (no more, no less) and with aggressive movement without "dive" at the end.
The speed should be between 24-26 seconds (no more, no less) hog line to tee line.
The surface should be keen and easy to sweep.

The above conditions should remain throughout the duration of the competition.

- 세계컬링연맹에서 아이스 기술자들에게 빙상장용 옷을 줄 것이다. 아이스 기술자들은 모든 행사에 적절한 옷을 입어야 한다(예: 청바지 금지). 현장에서의 옷은 검은 바지와 특별한 재킷을 입어야 한다(세계컬링연맹 조직위원회에서 지원해줄 것이다). 가능하다면 주기술자들 재킷 뒤에 주아이스 기술자라고 표시하고 부아이스기술자들에게 비슷하게 하라고 한다. 컬링장 밖에서(공공장소)는 바로 집 가는 경우를 제외하고 공식 복장은 착용을 금한다.
- 깔끔하고 깨끗한 용모와 적절한 행동은 언제나 필수다.
- 아이스 기술자들은 신선하고 기민한 마음가짐을 가져야 하므로 충분한 휴식을 보장받아야 한다. 경기 중에 최상의 상태를 유지하기 위해, 아이스 기술자들은 앉거나 서있어야 하며, 게시판에 기대어서는 안 된다. 아이스 기술자들은 이유 없이 경기 중에 경기장에 있어서는 안 된다. (예 - 경기장에서 사진을 찍고 있어선 안 된다)
- 아이스 기술자들은 얼음 제작 시스템의 기초와 세계컬링연맹의 철학을 항상 유지해야 하지만 조직위와 팀들과 세계컬링연맹 이사회와 미디어와의 대립을 피하기 위해 유연한 자세를 가져야 한다.
- 아이스 기술자들은 어떤 특정한 선수와 특정한 팀에게 대회 기간 동안 일반적인 정도 이상으로 엮여서는 안 된다. 만약 개인적 혹은 사업적으로 특정 선수와 감독과의 관계가 있다면 세계컬링연맹에 전부 공개해야 한다. 주변의 팀과 사회적으로 이야기를 나눌 순 있지만, 아이스 기술자는 과도한 시간을 한 팀 혹은 선수와 보내는 것을 주의하여야 한다.
- 대회 기간 동안 최고 아이스 기술자와 팀은 모든 경기와 연습을 위해 해당 장소에 준비할 충분한 시간을 가져야 한다. 아이스 팀은 최고 아이스 기술자의 업무 시간에 따라야 한다. 주아이스 기술자가 부재 시, 부아이스 기술자가 최고 아이스 기술자의 의무를 이행해야 한다.
- 최고 아이스 기술자는 세계기술연맹의 기술 장비 상자들에 대한 책임이 있다. 만약 장비 상자가 충분히 들어있지 않거나 잃어버린 물건이 있으면 세계컬링연맹에 보고하여야 한다. 시합의 결과에서 상자들은 충분히 들어있어야 하고 장비들이 준비되어있어야 한다. 장비 상자들은 세계컬링연맹에 의해 점검받아야 하며 잃어버린 장비에 대한 비용은 최고 아이스 기술자의 사례비에서 공제된다. 세계컬링연맹은 각 박스의 내용물과 각 박스의 사용법과 세부사항 그리고 박스가 어떻게 올바르게 싸여야 하는지에 대한 문서를 제공할 것이다.
- 최고 아이스 기술자는 세계컬링연맹의 시합 지도자에게 최소 3주 전에 시합의 결과에 대해 보고서를 제출해야 한다.
- 아이스 기술자에 대한 징계는 세계컬링연맹의 징계위원회에 의해 결정되고 징계위원회에서 권한을 가지고 있다 (최소한 3인으로 구성: 세계컬링연맹 회장 혹은 연맹 부회장; 위원회 회원 한 명 혹은 사무총장; 세계컬링연맹 시합 지도자 혹은 세계컬링연맹 기술대표). 행동강령과 언급된 협정을 따르지 않은 아이스 기술자들은 다가올 세계컬링연맹 대회들에서 고려되지 않을 수 있다.

세계컬링연맹의 빙상에 대한 정의:

얼음은 동작과 속도에서 선수의 기술들을 발휘하는 데 도움을 주어야 하고 흥미로운 게임을 진행하도록 보장되어야 한다.

세계컬링연맹은 빙질에 대해 아래의 사항을 요구한다:

스톤의 컬이 더 많거나 적지 않게 4-5피트 정도로 해야 하고(더 많거나 적지 않게) 끝에 가서 웨이트가 갑자기 떨어지지 않고 던진 속도로 예측 가능해야 한다. 속도는 호그 라인에서 티 라인까지 24에서 26초 정도(그 이상 혹은 그 이하)이어야 한다. 표면은 예리하고 스위핑하기 쉬워야 한다.

위의 조건은 대회 기간 동안 유지되어야 한다.

Agreement Points:

1. The Ice Technician accepts the Role of Ice Technician and agrees to follow the Code of Conduct.

2. The Ice Technician agrees to make ice to the best of his or her ability to match the WCF definition and conditions of competition ice as defined above.

3. The WCF will support the Ice Technician by ensuring that the stones provided for the Competition allow these conditions to be met.

4. The WCF will ensure the facility meets the technical requirements that the WCF requires for hosting WCF competitions.

5. Ice Technicians are not permitted to maintain the running surfaces on WCF stones without prior agreement and control from WCF.

6. The stone movement should be checked by the ice technicians and a WCF Stone and Technical Controller (WCF STC, currently Leif Ohman, Richard Harding, Keith Wendorf or WCF Technical Delegate) prior to the start of the competition (i.e. - before the practice).

7. If the above specifications regarding ice conditions are not being achieved due to either ice or stones, maintenance on the running surface of the stones can be done by the appointed Chief Ice Technician (CIT), but only under supervision from the WCF STC. Any procedure carried out shall be recorded by the CIT and WCF STC.

8. If stones other than WCF competition stones are being used, and the stones need to be maintained to meet the WCF's definition of competition ice, the WCF and the owner of the stones must give approval before any maintenance of the running surface can be carried out, and the WCF STC must be present.

9. If stones other than WCF competition stones are being used, and the required WCF specifications cannot be reached because of problems with these stones and the CIT is not allowed to maintain the stones by the owner, this will not be considered a failure on the part of the Chief Ice Technician.

Competition(s) & Position: ______________________Honorarium: US$ ___

______________________ Honorarium: US$ ___

Read and agreed: Name: ______________________

Signature: ____________________

Date: ______________________

협정 요점:

1. 아이스 기술자들은 아이스 기술자의 역할을 받아들이고 행동 강령에 동의한다.
2. 아이스 기술자는 세계컬링연맹의 규정된 정의와 시합 상태에 맞게 그 혹은 그녀의 능력에서 최고의 얼음을 만들 것에 동의한다.
3. 세계컬링연맹은 대회 상황의 조건을 충족시키는 스톤을 제공하는 것을 보장함으로써 아이스 기술자들을 지원할 것이다.
4. 세계컬링연맹은 연맹이 주최하는 대회에서 연맹의 기술적 요구에 충족하는 장소를 보장할 것이다.
5. 아이스 기술자들은 세계컬링연맹의 우선적 협정과 통제 없는 연맹의 스톤들로 활주면을 유지할 것을 허가치 않는다.
6. 스톤의 움직임은 우선적으로 시합시작 전에 아이스 기술자들과 세계컬링연맹 스톤과 기술 조정자들(세계컬링연맹 STC, 현재 Leif Ohman, Richard Harding, Keith Wendorf 혹은 세계컬링연맹 기술 대표)에 의해 점검된다. (예 - 연습 전)
7. 만약 빙질에 관하여 얼음이나 스톤 때문에 사양이 충족되지 않는다면, 스톤의 활주면 보존은 최고 아이스 기술자에 의해 약속되지만 세계컬링연맹 STC의 감독하에서만 가능하다. 다른 어떤 절차 진행도 CIT 혹은 세계컬링연맹 STC에 의해 기록될 것이다.
8. 만약 세계컬링연맹 시합의 스톤 외에 다른 스톤들이 사용될 경우 그 스톤들은 세계컬링연맹의 얼음 규정을 충족해야 하며 세계컬링연맹과 스톤들의 주인은 어떤 활주면에서도 사용가능하다는 허가서를 제출해야 하며, 세계컬링연맹 STC가 입회해야만 한다.
9. 만약 스톤들이 세계컬링연맹 시합용 스톤 외에 다른 스톤이 사용되고 그 스톤들이 세계컬링연맹의 사양에 도달하지 못하는 경우와 CIT가 소유주에게 스톤의 유지를 허락치 않은 상황이라면, 이 상황은 최고 아이스 기술자의 잘못으로 판단치 않을 것이다.

대회(들) & 위치: ______________________________사례금: US$ __________

______________________________사례금: US$ __________

읽었고 동의함: 이름: ______________________________

서명: : ______________________________

날짜: : ______________________________

49. CARE OF CURLING STONES

1. The running edge of a curling stone is prepared to a detailed specification and must be protected at all times from coming into contact with any abrasive surface, however fine. Placing the stones on pavement or any similar surface will contaminate the running edge with minute particles of abrasive dust and could alter the performance of individual stones.

2. Grease, oil or any other viscous liquid will, if it comes in contact with the running edge, enter the molecular structure of the granite and affect performance. Keep clear of all contaminants. Also avoid placing stones on top of ice rink surround barriers when removing from the ice.

3. When transporting stones, place a clean piece of cardboard under each stone at all times.

4. Curling stones are intended to strike other stationary stones that are on a low friction surface (ice). Stones should not be directed at each other from opposite directions. This doubles the striking momentum and doubles the force exerted on the striking band, which may cause damage to the striking band or even fractures in the body of the stone.

5. Stones are supplied in matched pairs. If the stone handles are removed, note which handle belongs to which stone, so that when they are reassembled they will be correctly matched.

6. If you need to substitute a stone it is best to substitute a pair of stones rather than a single stone. Use the substitute pair of stones as the lead player's stones, playing them for a few ends to break them in.

7. Every stone is numbered to ensure accurate records of each stone.

8. When transporting stones in a vehicle, remember that each stone weighs 18kg. Ensure they are firmly wedged against movement caused by accelerating, braking or cornering. An 18kg projectile can cause serious damage to vehicles and people.

49. 컬링 스톤 관리

1. 컬링 스톤의 모서리는 자세한 사양으로 준비되어야 하고 어떤 거친 면에서도 항상 양호하도록 준비되어야 한다. 통로나 혹은 어떤 유사한 장소에도 스톤이 위치할 땐 아주 작은 거친 먼지에도 오염될 수 있고 각각의 스톤의 움직임을 변화시킬 수 있다.

2. 미끄러운 것, 기름 혹은 어떤 끈적거리는 액체로, 만약 모서리에 닿았을 때, 화강암 분자구조에 들어올 수 있다. 모든 오염물들을 깔끔히 하라. 또한 빙상에서 스톤을 제거할 때 아이스링크 위쪽 벽 근처에 두는 것을 피하라.

3. 스톤들을 옮길 때, 항상 모든 스톤 아래에 판지 같은 것을 위치하라.

4. 컬링 스톤들로 다른 멈춰있는 스톤을 때리려 시도할 때 작은 금이 갈 수 있다(얼음). 스톤들은 다른 방향에 곧바로 접촉하도록 하지 말라. 이것은 운동량을 2배로 늘리고 부딪치는 부분의 힘을 2배로 늘리며, 이것은 부딪치는 부분에 피해를 입히거나 스톤의 몸체에 작은 금을 만들 수 있다.

5. 스톤은 맞는 짝이 요구된다. 만약 스톤의 손잡이가 제거했을 때, 어느 손잡이가 어느 스톤에 속해 있었는지 기록하고, 그리하여 그것들을 조립할 때 서로 맞게 조립되도록 하라.

6. 만약 스톤의 교체가 필요할 땐 하나씩 교환하는 것보다 한 쌍의 스톤을 교체하는 것이 최선이다. 리드 플레이어의 스톤들을 교체에 사용하고, 그것들로 몇 엔드의 게임을 해서 길들여라.

7. 모든 스톤들은 각각의 정확한 기록을 보장하기 위해 번호를 매겨라.

8. 이동수단으로 스톤들을 옮길 때, 각각의 스톤이 18kg인 것을 기억하라. 그것들을 고정해 가속, 감속, 코너링 때 움직임이 배제된 것을 확실히 하라. 18kg의 발사체는 차량들이나 사람들에게 심각한 피해를 일으킬 수 있다.

50. DEALING WITH THE MEDIA

GUIDELINES FOR PLAYER INTERVIEWS

1. Post-game interviews may be conducted outside the Field of Play (FOP) at a designated location, adjacent to the FOP. Media Relations Officer(s) (**MRO**) on-site will advise of a Mixed-Zone (interview area) between the FOP exit and athletes changing rooms.

2. Athletes may only exit the FOP via the designated exit and through the Mixed Zone.

3. Although not compulsory, all athletes should acknowledge interview requests in the Mixed Zone area. If they do not wish to conduct an interview, athletes must inform the MRO or media representative politely.

4. While any game is in progress, all interviews will be conducted away from the FOP.

5. While a game is in progress, flash or extra lights will not be permitted in the interview area adjacent to the FOP.

6. When all games are completed, interviews and the use of flash and extra lighting may be allowed within the FOP subject to the Chief Umpire's approval, but not on the ice surface.

7. Specific interview requests should be given to the CU before the start of the sixth end (round robin) or eighth end (post round robin) so that players can be advised to go to the interview area before going to their changing room.

8. Specific interviews will take precedence over general interviews in the designated area. Post-game interviews for TV should take precedence.

9. It will be presumed that all junior athletes have permission to speak with the media. Junior players will be informed of this and the interview procedures at the Team Meeting. At this point, athletes or coaches should identify any concerns or restrictions with media activity.

10. Any athletes or coaches who have concerns or would like advice in relation to media interviews should contact the event MRO.

50. 언론 통제(관리)

선수 인터뷰 가이드라인(지침)

1. 경기 전 인터뷰는 지정된 위치의 경기장 밖이나 경기장에서 인접한 곳에서 수행될 수 있다. 그곳의 언론 관련 직원들에게 경기장 출구와 탈의실 사이에 있는 혼합 지역(인터뷰 지역)에 있도록 충고하라.

2. 선수들을 지정된 출구를 경유하여 혼합 지역으로만 나가도록 하라.

3. 비록 강제적이진 않지만, 모든 선수들은 혼합 지역에서 인터뷰 요청을 받는 것을 알아야 한다. 만약 그들이 인터뷰를 하고 싶지 않다면, 선수들은 언론 관련 직원이나 언론 대표에게 정중히 알려야 한다.

4. 어떤 경기든 진행되는 동안은, 모든 인터뷰는 경기장 밖에서 진행될 것이다.

5. 경기가 진행되는 동안은, 플래시 혹은 어떤 추가적인 조명도 경기장에 가까운 인터뷰 지역에서는 허가되지 않을 것이다.

6. 모든 경기가 끝났을 때, 주심이 인정하는 한도 내에서, 인터뷰들과 플래시나 다른 추가적인 조명이 허가될 수 있지만, 빙상에서는 불가능하다.

7. 특정 인터뷰 요청은 여섯 번째 엔드(round robin) 혹은 여덟 번째 엔드(post round robin) 전에 주심에게 제출하여야 한다. 그래서 선수들이 탈의실에 가기 전에 인터뷰 지역으로 갈 수 있도록 충고받도록 해야 한다.

9. 모든 주니어 선수들은 언론과 이야기하기 전에 허가가 있어야 한다고 가정한다. 주니어 선수들에게 이것들을 알리고 인터뷰는 팀 미팅에서 진행한다. 이 부분에서, 선수들이나 감독들은 언론 활동에서 어떤 걱정 혹은 제한된 점에 대해 인식해야 한다.

10. 걱정되는 부분이나 언론 활동에서 조언을 받고 싶은 선수들 혹은 감독들은 언론 관련 직원들과 접촉해야 한다.

51. MEDIA INTERVIEWS

The only Umpire who ever talks to the media is the Chief Umpire and only when a particular situation or incident makes a statement necessary. If the WCF MRO is onsite for the event, he/she should be informed and aware of all media requests to talk to the Chief Umpire. The listed guidelines should be followed when giving media interviews:

1. The number one item to remember when talking to the media is that "nothing is off the record". Anything you say to a reporter at any time may be used by the reporter in a story.

2. Ensure you know exactly what you are going to say about the situation at hand. Do not let the interviewer side track you to another issue or put words in your mouth.

3. Remember how to say "no" – not every question must be answered. If a reporter requests confidential information, say no, directly and POLITELY.

4. You may even turn the question into an opportunity to make a positive statement.

5. Make your answers clear, short and to the point. Do not be afraid to leave the interviewer with dead air. It is the reporter who will look bad – not you.

6. If you are working with a "scrum" of reporters, once you feel you have made your point and there is really nothing further that can be added, excuse yourself and leave, again, politely.

7. Should a situation involve any sort of a conflict with a player, be very careful not to get into a situation of making any comments about the player other than to suggest what procedure is to be followed to handle the situation.

8. If the WCF Media Relations Officer is available at an event, the Chief Umpire should liaise with the MRO regarding procedures ahead of any media interviews.

51. 언론 인터뷰

언론과 대화할 수 있는 유일한 심판은 주심이고 특정한 상황 혹은 사건에 대해서 필요한 언급만 할 수 있다. 만약 세계컬링연맹의 언론 관련 직원이 행사를 위해 현장에 있다면, 그 혹은 그녀가 알릴 것이고 주심에 대한 언론의 요청에 대해 알려주어야 한다. 언론 인터뷰를 진행할 때 목록화한 가이드라인을 따라야 한다.

1. 언론과의 인터뷰 때 첫 번째로 기억해야 할 것은 "비공개란 없다."이다. 당신이 기자에게 말하는 어떤 시점에 어떤 것을 말하든 그것은 기사에서 기자에 의해 쓰일 수 있다.
2. 어떤 상황에 대해서 말할 것인지 정확히 알아라. 인터뷰어가 다른 측면에서 다른 주제에 대해 말하거나 당신의 입에서 나오도록 놔두지 말라.
3. 어떻게 "아니오."라고 말하는지 기억하라. - 모든 질문에 답할 필요는 없다. 만약 기자가 은밀한 정보를 요구한다면, 직접적이고 정중하게 "아니오."라고 말하라.
4. 당신이 긍정적인 언급으로 만들 기회가 있다면 질문을 돌려라.
5. 답변은 깔끔하고 짧게 요점만 하라. 인터뷰어가 방송중단에 처하는 것을 두려워하지 마라. 나쁘게 보이는 것은 기자지 당신이 아니다.
6. 만약 당신이 기자들이 밀치락달치락하는 와중에 있다면, 당신이 느낀 당신의 요점을 말해 주고 더 이상 하지 말고, 양해를 구하고 정중하게 다시 떠나라.
7. 다른 선수와 어떤 종류의 대립을 포함하는 상황에 있을 때, 그 선수에 대한 언급은 최대한 신중하게 할 것이며 상황을 다룰 수 있는 방향으로 진행되도록 제안하라.
8. 만약 세계컬링연맹 직원이 그 행사에 있다면, 주심은 어떤 언론 인터뷰의 진행에 관해서도 언론 관련 직원에게 연결되도록 해야 한다.

52. WCF CODE OF CONDUCT FOR PHOTOGRAPHERS

All photographers must be identified with an appropriate MEDIA accreditation

The World Curling Federation (WCF) has put these regulations in place to ensure the smooth operation of photographers accredited for WCF events.

Generally, photographers are allowed onto the Field of Play (FOP) during curling events and can shoot from:

- a position between the hog lines (*starting about 3 metres/10 feet inside each hog line)* on the carpeted areas separating the sheets of ice
- the corners of the arena
- behind the lower corners of the scoreboards signs

In all cases, this is provided that you are not obscuring the vision of spectators, blocking the scoreboard, in the way of the players or are a particular visual distraction to the WCF host broadcaster World Curling TV (WCTV) or Rights-Holding TV Broadcasters (RHBs).

Photography Rules:

1. **Flash photography is not allowed.**

2. **Please turn mobile/cell phone off before entering the Field of Play (FOP).** Silent or vibrate settings are permitted.

3. **Photographers are not allowed on the ice surface at any time**.

4. Photographers are requested to **wear dark clothing** and to **wear shoes that have only been worn indoors or shoe covers** whilst at work on the FOP.

5. Photographers must **photograph from a sitting/squatting/kneeling position,** not a standing or lying position. They must move along the walkway at appropriate intervals in order not to consistently block the view of the same spectators.

6. Photographers must **always walk** and not run inside the FOP.

7. **When preparing to move either along a walkway or across the end of a sheet – photographers are to be reminded that other games may be going on at the same time. The must ensure they look down both adjacent sheets to ensure that no player is in the process of delivery.** If one is, then they must await the completion of the delivery before moving.

8. When crossing the end, photographers must **cross behind the scoreboard**, not in front.

9. Photographers must **be mindful of any WCTV or RHB camera**, which may also be on the same walkway.

10. When a player is about to deliver a stone, photographers must be behind him/her or between the hog lines.

11. Photographers must be made aware that the WCTV or RHB cameras may move along a walkway or to a different walkway during any draw. They are expected to cooperate with any request regarding the moving of cables, cameras, etc.

52. 세계컬링연맹의 사진사에 대한 행동강령

모든 사진사들은 정확한 언론 승인을 받아야만 한다.

세계컬링연맹은 세계컬링연맹의 행사에서 원활한 진행을 위하여 이 규제를 둔다. 일반적으로, 사진사들은 경기장 내에서 컬링 경기 동안 허가받고 아래 상황에서 촬영이 가능하다.:

- 호그 라인들 사이(대략 각각의 호그 라인에서 3미터 혹은 10피트 이내) 얼음과 떨어진 카펫이 깔린 지역
- 경기장 구석들
- 점수판 아래 낮은 코너들

이것은 관람객들의 시야를 가리거나, 점수판을 가리거나, 선수들이나 세계컬링연맹이 관리하는 WCTV 혹은 RHB의 특별한 시야를 분산시키지 않는 모든 경우에 제공된다.

촬영 수칙:

1. 플래시 촬영 불가.
2. 경기장 출입 시 휴대폰 전원 종료. 무음이나 진동은 허용.
3. 사진사는 어떠한 경우에도 빙판에 가는 것은 불가하다.
4. 사진사들은 어두운 옷을 입기를 바라며 경기장 내에서 일하는 동안 실내화나 신발 커버를 사용해 주기를 요청한다.
5. 사진사들은 앉거나 쪼그려 앉거나 무릎을 꿇은 자세로 촬영해야 하며, 서있거나 누워있는 자세로는 촬영할 수 없다. 그들은 관객들의 시야를 지속적으로 막지 않도록 지정된 시간에 통로로만 움직여야 한다.
6. 사진사들은 경기장 내에서 걷기만 해야 하며 뛰면 안 된다.
7. 통로나 깔개의 가장자리를 통해 이동을 준비할 때 - 사진사들은 동시에 다른 경기들이 진행되고 있다는 것을 명심해야 한다. 가장 확신해야 할 점은 그들이 지정된 깔개 위를 지나갈 때 그곳에 딜리버리를 진행 중인 선수가 없어야 한다는 것이다. 만약에 있다면, 움직이기 전에 선수의 딜리버리가 끝날 때까지 기다려야 한다.
8. 엔드를 가로질러 갈 때, 사진사들은 점수판 앞이 아닌 뒤쪽으로 이동해야 한다.
9. 사진사들은 WCTV 혹은 RHB의 카메라를 염두에 두어야 하고, 이는 같은 통로에 있을 수 있다.
10. 선수들이 스톤을 딜리버리하고 있을 때, 사진사들은 그 혹은 그녀의 뒤나 호그 라인 앞에 있어야 한다.
11. 사진사들은 어떤 드로우 중에도 WCTV나 RHB 카메라 쪽 통로 혹은 다른 통로로 이동해야 한다는 것을 알아야 한다.
12. 준결승과 결승에선, 촬영 장소에 대한 특별한 지시가 발행된다. 각 회사별로 한 명의 사진사만이 지정된 카펫 지역이나 사진사를 위한 통로에 위치할 수 있다. 같은 회사의 다른 사진사들은 지정되지 않은 통로 뒤쪽이나 경기장 측면에 위치해야 한다. 특정한 사진사들은 점수판 뒤쪽의 핵심 위치에 자리하는 것도 허가된다.
13. 사진사들은 선수권 트로피에 대한 촬영을 결승전 이전에 할 수 있다.
14. 특정 행사에선 완장 정책이 시행될 수도 있다.

이 규제들을 따르는 것에 실패한다면 당신들의 언론에 대한 허가를 즉각 철회하는 결과를 낳을 수 있다.

12. **For the semi-final and final, special instructions will be issued on photography locations. Only one photographer per affiliation will be allowed onto the carpeted area/walkway designated for photographers** located adjacent to the game sheet. All other photographers from the same affiliation must position themselves on a non-adjacent walkway behind or to the side of the playing area. *Certain photographers may also be allowed a key position behind the scoreboard.*

13. Photography instructions regarding the presentation of the championship trophy will be issued prior to the final.

14. For certain events an armband policy may be implemented.

Failure to comply with these regulations may result in the immediate withdrawal of your media accreditation.

53. PHOTOGRAPHING - THINGS TO WATCH FOR

Competition: Team names are posted on the scoreboards.

Pre-game action: Prior to the start of each draw (round of games), each team receives practice time on the sheet of ice it will be competing on, usually starting 30 minutes before game time. The final minutes before the official start of competition are used for team introductions and final preparation of the ice.

A game of curling: A game usually last 10 ends. An 'end' usually lasts 15 minutes. The action goes down and back, from one end of the sheet to the other, hence the name 'ends'. Games going to '10 ends' will finish at the 'home end'. However, teams can concede at any point after 6 ends in round robin games and 8 ends in play-off and medal games. Watch the scoreboard and if a team is losing badly look for players shaking hands and conceding the game early after the last stones have been delivered in an end.

Last stones may not be delivered: If a team needs two points to win, and has no stones in scoring position with only one stone remaining to play, the game will end without last stones being delivered.

Field of Play personnel will try not to obstruct your sightlines. However, they must perform their duties and will occasionally interfere with your photography.

53. 촬영 - 주의점

시합: 팀 명은 점수판에 나온다.

경기 전 행동: 각각의 드로우(게임의 라운드)를 진행하기 전에, 각각의 게임은 게임 시작 전에 보통 30분 정도 연습할 시간을 받는다. 공식적인 대회가 시작되기 직전 마지막 몇 분간은 팀의 도입과 얼음에 대한 준비를 위해 사용된다.

컬링 경기: 경기는 보통 10엔드로 진행된다. 각각의 엔드는 15분간 진행된다. 한쪽에서 다른 쪽으로 오가는 것을 '엔드'라고 한다. 경기는 '10엔드'까지 진행되며 '홈 엔드'에서 끝난다. 하지만, 팀들은 6엔드 이후에 패배를 인정할 수 있고 플레이오프와 메달 게임에선 8엔드에 패배를 인정할 수 있다. 점수판을 보고 만약 팀이 심하게 지고 있다면 그 엔드의 마지막 스톤을 딜리버리한 후에 손을 흔들면서 패배를 인정하는 선수들을 찾을 수 있다.

마지막 스톤들은 딜리버리가 되지 않을 수도 있다.: 만약 팀이 2점 차로 이기고 있고, 점수 지역 내에 스톤이 없는 채로 경기할 수 있는 스톤이 하나만 남아 있다면, 그 게임은 마지막 스톤을 딜리버리하지 않은 채로 끝난다.

경기장 내 직원들은 당신들의 시선을 방해하지 않으려 노력할 것이다. 하지만 그들은 그들의 의무를 이행하고 때때로 촬영을 방해할 수도 있다.

54. SOCIAL MEDIA COMMUNICATIONS

Athletes and coaches are responsible for their own social media communications, regardless if they are run by third parties such as agents, Member Association Media Officers or other individuals for example.

Social Media communication includes posts on Facebook, tweets on Twitter, updates on blogs or websites or any other form of online/digital communication, which will be deemed as public communication. Copying posts and retweeting inappropriate content will also be considered punishable under WCF Rules of Curling Rule R16. Inappropriate Behaviour.

Any posts relating to race, faith, disability, sexual orientation or which are interpreted as inappropriate comments directed towards ITOs, athletes or coaches, should be brought to the attention of the Chief Umpire.

The Chief Umpire should immediately inform the Director of Competitions who will then decide whether or not the case should be referred to the WCF Competitions Commission. Collectively the Chief Umpire, the Director of Competitions and, if referred to, the WCF Competitions Commission, will decide whether direct action is required to be taken by the WCF.

Punishment for such communications includes a formal warning for minor infractions and the relevant MA will be notified. For serious infractions the perpetrator will be immediately suspended from present and/or future competition.

Individuals found in breach of these rules will be asked to immediately remove the communication and apologise immediately thereafter on the social media outlet.

Athletes and coaches are advised to download and read the WCF's Social Media Guidelines which are available in the **Resources** section of the WCF website and contact a Media Relations Officer on site if they have any further questions.

Social Media (Policy for Officials)

Tweets and texts have replaced conversations and phone calls. They take only as long as a few keystrokes on an iPhone or Blackberry made in the heat of the moment, and are available to millions of people for an indefinite time.

The lesson for officials is the same as for everyone else: assume that nothing in social media is private, and post or tweet only things that they would be willing to have read by anyone, including other officials, players, coaches and fans.

People expect officials to be fair and impartial, and speaking in glowing or harsh terms about a specific player, coach or team may bring under question your ability to be objective.

The safest approach is to never make public comments about coaches, teams, players, games and other officials. If you wouldn't say it publicly, don't post it. The Umpire's job is to officiate games, not to talk about them.

54. 소셜 미디어 커뮤니케이션

만약 예를 들어, 에이전트나 MAMO 혹은 다른 개인적인 제3의 모임에 개의치 않고 운영했을 때, 선수들과 감독들은 그들 스스로의 소셜 미디어 커뮤니케이션에 책임이 있다. 소셜 미디어 커뮤니케이션은 페이스북에 글을 게시하고, 트위터에 글을 올리고, 블로그를 업데이트하거나, 다른 어떤 온라인 혹은 디지털 커뮤니케이션들 따위의 공공의 커뮤니케이션이라고 여겨지는 것들을 포함한다. 글을 퍼오거나 적절치 않은 내용물을 리트윗하는 것은 또한 세계컬링연맹의 제정한 컬링 규칙하에서 처벌할 수 있다고 판단할 수 있다.

R16. 부적절한 행동

인종, 진실, 장애, 성적 성향 혹은 그와 관련된 게시물들은 ITOs를 향한 부적절한 발언으로 선수들 혹은 감독들에게 이해되며 주심에게 경고를 받는다.

주심은 즉시 이 사건을 세계컬링연맹 시합 위원회에 올릴지 말지 결정할 시합의 지도자에게 알린다. 주심이 총괄해서, 시합의 지도자와 협의 후 만약 올린다면, 세계컬링연맹 시합 위원회에 세계컬링연맹이 즉각적인 행동을 할 것을 요청한다. 이런 커뮤니케이션에서의 처벌은 사소한 잘못의 경우 일반적인 경고로 끝나고 관련 MA에 알린다. 심각한 잘못은 가해자는 즉시 지금의 시합 혹은 미래의 시합에서 출전 정지된다.

이런 규칙들을 위반한 것이 알려진 개인들은 즉시 커뮤니케이션을 제거하도록 요청받고 소셜미디어에 즉시 사과하도록 요청받는다.

선수들과 감독들은 세계컬링연맹 홈페이지에 있는 자원들 섹션에서 볼 수 있는 소셜 미디어 가이드라인들을 다운받고 읽으라고 충고하고 만약 질문이 있다면 현장에서 언론 관련 직원들과 접촉하도록 충고한다.

소셜 미디어(공식 정책)

대화나 전화 통화는 트위터나 게시물로 대체되었다. 그들은 아이폰이나 블랙베리에서 몇 번의 타자를 치는 순간 히트하고 무기한의 시간 동안 수백만 명의 사람들이 접근 가능하다.

공적인 교육은 모두에게 같다.: 소셜 미디어에 개인적인 것이라곤 없다고 가정하고 게시하거나 트윗한 것들은 다른 직원, 선수들, 감독들, 팬들은 포함한 그 누구도 읽을 수 있다는 것을 알아야 한다.

사람들이 직원들이 공정하고 극찬받거나 특정 선수나 감독 혹은 팀에게 가혹하게 말하길 바라는 점이 당신의 능력에 객관적인 질문을 가져올지도 모른다.

가장 안전한 접근은 감독들, 팀들, 선수들, 다른 직원들에 대해 공식적인 그 어떤 언급도 하지 않는 것이다. 만약 당신이 어떤 것도 공식적으로 말하고 싶지 않다면, 게시하지 마라. 심판의 일은 경기에 대한 공무를 수행하는 것이지, 그것에 대해 이야기하는 것이 아니다.

55. CURLING

Curling is a sport played on ice between two 4-player teams. Each player throws two stones alternating with his/her counterpart on the opposing team. When all 16 stones have been played, the 'end' is complete and a point is scored for every stone nearer to the centre of a target ('house') than any stone of the opposing team. Only stones in the house count towards the score, and only one team can score per end. Play then resumes in the opposite direction and the team that scored in the previous end delivers the first stone. A game consists of 8 or 10 ends and the team scoring the most points wins.

EQUIPMENT: Stones weigh about 20 kg and are made of granite. Curling shoes have one sliding foot and one gripping foot. The brushes can be made of hog hair, horse hair or synthetic material.

SWEEPING: Proper sweeping melts the top of the ice forming a thin layer of water which reduces friction between the stone and the ice. This allows the stone to travel further and straighter.

THE ICE: After the ice has been levelled as much as possible, fine water droplets are sprinkled over it (pebbling). The underside of the stone glides over these frozen pebbles.

DELIVERY: A rotation is applied to the handle of a stone just prior to release, which determines the direction the stone moves or "curls" as it slides down the ice. The turn applied makes the stone rotate in a clockwise or counter-clockwise direction. The 'skip' or team captain determines the shot to be played and indicates the shot while positioned in the house at the far end of the ice. The player delivering the stone pushes off from a fixed support ('hack'), and aims at the skip's brush. The stone must be released before the near hog line and pass the far-end hog line to be in play. If a stone touches the side lines or passes the far-end back line it is removed from play. The other two team members follow the stone and are ready to sweep if necessary.

STRATEGY: Curling is often described as chess on ice. Basic strategy involves trying to score two or more points when your team has last stone, keeping the centre of the sheet open. Without last stone you try and control the centre of the sheet and hope to 'steal' a point.

SPIRIT OF CURLING: One of the most important aspects of Curling is sportsmanship. Games always begin and end with all players shaking hands, and fair play and proper etiquette, both on and off the ice, are strongly emphasized.

MEMBERS: As of 2012 there are 49 Member Associations of the World Curling Federation (WCF).

MORE INFORMATION: The website of the WCF www.worldcurling.org contains full details of the Rules of Curling and Rules of Competition.

55. 컬링

컬링은 빙판 위에서 4명의 선수가 한 팀을 이룬 두 팀이 경기하는 스포츠다. 각각의 선수들은 2개의 스톤을 번갈아가며 반대쪽 팀을 향해 던지는 경기다. 16개의 스톤이 플레이 되었을 때, '엔드'가 끝나며 상대의 스톤보다 타켓의 중심(하우스)에 가까운 모든 스톤의 개수가 점수가 된다. 하우스에서 가까운 스톤만 점수가 되며, 한 엔드에 한 팀만이 점수를 획득할 수 있다. 전 엔드에서 스톤을 딜리버리해서 점수를 딴 팀이 먼저 경기를 재개한다. 한 게임은 8엔드 혹은 10엔드까지 지속되며 가장 많은 포인트를 획득한 팀이 승리한다.

장비: 스톤들의 무게는 약 20kg에 육박하며 화강암으로 만들어졌다. 컬링 신발 한쪽은 슬라이딩하고 한쪽은 잡는 발이다. 빗자루는 돼지털이나 말털 혹은 인조털로 만들어져있다.

스위핑: 적당한 스위핑은 얼음 윗부분을 녹여 얇은 물의 층을 만들고 이것이 스톤과 얼음 사이의 마찰을 줄인다. 이것이 스톤이 더 멀리 더 곧게 나가도록 한다.

얼음: 얼음이 가능한 한 층을 많이 만들면, 좋은 작은 물방울들을 그 위에 뿌린다(페블링). 스톤의 아랫부분은 이들 얼음 페블을 미끄러진다.

딜리버리: 회전은 스톤에서 손을 놓기 직전에 결정되고 이는 스톤의 이동 방향 혹은 '컬'하여 얼음 위를 미끄러져가는 방향을 결정한다. 회전은 시계 방향이나 시계 반대 방향으로 스톤을 돌게 한다. '스킵' 혹은 팀의 주장이 얼음의 끝에 있는 하우스에서 샷의 방향을 결정하고 지시한다. 선수는 스톤을 고정된 형태로 밀고('핵') 스킵의 브러시 방향을 조준한다. 스톤은 호그 라인 근처 이전에 놓여야 하고 반대 호그 라인을 지나가야 인플레이 된다. 만약 스톤이 사이드 라인에 닿거나 뒤쪽 끝 선을 지나갈 경우 이 스톤은 경기에서 제거된다. 다른 팀의 두 멤버는 스톤을 따라가면서 필요하다면 스윕할 준비를 한다.

전략 :컬링은 빙판 위의 체스라고 종종 묘사된다. 기본 전략은 당신의 팀이 마지막 스톤을 가졌을 때 2점 혹은 그 이상의 점수를 얻기 위해 시도하는 것이고, 센터를 지키는 것이다. 마지막 스톤 없이 당신은 시도하고 중심을 조절해서 점수를 훔치기를 바란다.

컬링의 정신: 컬링의 가장 중요한 측면은 스포츠맨십이다. 경기는 항상 모든 선수의 악수로 시작과 끝을 맺고 공정한 경기 그리고 적절한 에티켓이 양쪽 모두에게 크게 강조된다.

회원국:2012년 기준으로 세계컬링연맹에는 49개국이 회원국으로 가입해 있다.

더 많은 정보: 세계컬링연맹의 웹사이트 www.worldcurling.org는 컬링의 룰과 시합의 룰에 대한 모든 세부사항을 포함하고 있다.

56. CURLING HISTORY

Curling has been described as the `Roarin' Game`, the `roar` coming from the noise of a granite stone as it travels over the ice. The exact origins of the game, however, are unclear, lost in the mists of time.

Paintings by a 16th Century Flemish Artist, Pieter Bruegel (1530-1569) portrayed an activity similar to curling being played on frozen ponds. The first written evidence appeared in Latin, when in 1540, John McQuhin, a notary in Paisley, Scotland, recorded in his protocol book a challenge between John Sclater, a monk in Paisley Abbey and Gavin Hamilton, a representative of the Abbot. The report indicated that Sclater threw a stone along the ice three times and asserted that he was ready for the agreed contest.

What is clear, however, is that what may have started as an enjoyable pastime of throwing stones over ice during a harsh Northern European winter, has evolved into a popular modern sport with its own World Championships attracting large television audiences.

Curling in its early days was played on frozen lochs and ponds – a pastime still enjoyed in some countries when weather permits – but all National and International competitive curling competitions now take place in indoor rinks with the condition of the ice carefully temperature controlled.

It is also clear that the first recognised Curling Clubs were formed in Scotland, and during the 19th Century the game was `exported` wherever Scots settled around the world in cold climates, most notably at that time in Canada, USA, Sweden, Switzerland, Norway and New Zealand.

The first Rules were drawn up in Scotland, and they were formally adopted as the `Rules in Curling` by the Grand Caledonian Curling Club which was formed in Edinburgh in 1838 and became the sports Governing Body. Four years later, following a demonstration of curling on the ballroom floor of Scone Palace near Perth by the Earl of Mansfield during a visit by Queen Victoria, the Queen was so fascinated by the game that in 1843 she gave permission for the Club's name to be changed to the Royal Caledonian Curling Club (RCCC).

It is recorded that international curling events were staged in the 19th century in Europe and North America, but it was not until the first Olympic Winter Games at Chamonix in 1924 that any form of official International competition took place for Men's teams. Great Britain defeated Sweden and France in what is now accepted by the International Olympic Committee (IOC) as Curling's Olympic debut with medals awarded.

In 1932 at Lake Placid, curling again was listed but this time as a demonstration sport at the Winter Olympics, and Canada was a winner over the United States in a two-country competition in which each country entered four Men's teams.

Another 25 years passed before a meeting was held in Edinburgh in 1957 to consider the formation of an international organisation which would be required in order to apply for Olympic medal status. No progress was documented, but two years later, in 1959, Scotland and Canada reached a major milestone by launching the Scotch Cup series between their national men's curling champions.

Interest in other countries was generated, and the USA (1961), Sweden (1962), Norway and Switzerland (1964), France (1966) and Germany (1967) expanded the Scotch Cup entry. The 1959-67 results now are recognised in the curling history of the Men's World Championship.

The success of the Scotch Cup series led to another attempt, in March 1965, to create a global administration. The Royal Caledonian Curling Club (Scotland) convened a meeting in Perth, Scotland, and six countries (Scotland, Canada, USA, Sweden, Norway and Switzerland) agreed to a proposal to form an international committee of the Royal Club, to be called the International Curling Federation (ICF).

The following year, in March, 1966, in Vancouver, Canada, a draft constitution for the ICF was considered by seven countries (France was added to the original six), and the Federation was declared to be established as of 1 April 1966.

56. 컬링의 역사

컬링은 'roarin' Game'으로 묘사되는데, 'roar'은 스톤이 얼음 위를 가르는 소리에서 나온 말이다. 하지만 정확한 게임의 기원은 불확실하게 시간 속에 잊혀졌다.

16세기 플랑드르 미술가, Pieter Bruegel (1530-1569)은 얼음 호수에서 컬링 경기를 하는 그림을 그렸다. 첫 문헌상 언급은 1540년 공증인 John Mcquhin이 스코틀랜드 페이즐리에서 그의 책 초고에 라틴어로 페이즐리 에비의 수도승 John Sclater와, 수도원장 Gavin Hamilton의 대결을 기록했다. 그 기록에는 Sclater가 스톤을 얼음을 따라 세 번 던졌고 그가 대회에 나갈 준비가 되었다고 주장했다고 쓰여 있다.

하지만, 분명한 것은, 북유럽의 혹독한 겨울 동안 돌 던지는 즐거운 취미 활동에서 시작되었다는 것이고 세계선수권이 TV의 많은 관중들을 끌어들이면서 대중적인 스포츠로 발전되었다는 것이다.

초기의 컬링은 호수나 연못 등에서 경기했다. - 여전히 몇몇 국가에선 날씨가 가능할 때 취미로 즐긴다. - 하지만 모든 국가적이고 세계적인 컬링 대회들은 실내 링크에서 조심스럽게 조절된 온도 상태에서 경기한다.

또한, 첫 번째 컬링 클럽은 스코틀랜드에서 만들어진 것이 알려졌고 19세기, 추운 기후를 가진 세계 곳곳에 정착한 스코틀랜드인들이 수출했고 그중 가장 두드러진 것이 캐나다, 미국, 스웨덴, 스위스, 노르웨이, 뉴질랜드였다.

첫 규칙은 스코틀랜드에서 만들어졌고 1838년 에딘버러에서 만들어진 그랜드 칼레도니안 컬링 클럽에서 '컬링의 규칙'으로 공식 채택되었으며 공식 경기가 열렸다. 4년 뒤, 빅토리아 여왕이 방문하고 있는 동안 맨필드의 얼옆 펄쓰 근처에 있는 스콘 궁궐의 무도회장에서 아래의 설명이 나왔고, 여왕은 게임에 매우 큰 매력을 느껴 1843년에 로열 칼레도니안 컬링 클럽이라는 이름을 허가해서 바꾸게 되었다.

19세기 유럽과 북아메리카에서 세계적인 컬링 행사가 있었다는 기록은 있지만 1924년 샤모니 동계 올림픽에서 처음으로 남성팀의 공식적 국제대회가 진행되었다. 영국은 스웨덴과 프랑스를 꺾고 IOC에서 컬링의 올림픽 데뷔 메달을 수상했다.

1932년 플래시드 레이크 올림픽에서 컬링은 다시 동계 올림픽에 들어왔고 4인 남성 팀 경기에서 미국을 꺾고 캐나다가 승리했다.

25년이 지난 후 에딘버러에서 올림픽 메달에 적용하기 위해 국제조직의 결성이 필요하다고 고려되었다. 진행은 기록되지 않았지만 2년 뒤, 1959년에 스코틀랜드와 캐나다가 그들의 남자 컬링팀들 사이에 선수권을 시작함으로써 중요한 단계에 도달했다. 다른 국가들의 관심이 증가했고, 미국(1961), 스웨덴(1962), 노르웨이와 스위스(1964), 프랑스(1966) 그리고 독일(1967)년이 스카치 컵의 엔트리를 확장시켰다. 1959-67년의 성과로 남성 컬링 세계선수권이 컬링의 역사로 인정받는다.

스카치 컵 시리즈의 성공은 1965년 3월에 새로운 시도를 낳는데, 세계적인 관리조직의 결성이다. 로열 칼레도니안 컬링 클럽(스코틀랜드)이 스코틀랜드, 퍼쓰에서 회의를 소집했고 6개 국가(스코틀랜드, 캐나다, 미국, 스웨덴, 노르웨이, 스위스)가 로열 클럽의 국제 위원회가 제안한 형태에 동의함으로써, 국제컬링연맹으로 불리게 되었다(ICF).

이듬해, 1966년 3월 캐나다 밴쿠버에서, ICF의 규칙 원안이 7개국(기존 6개국에 프랑스가 추가됨)에 의해 고려되었고, 연맹은 1966년 4월 1일에 설립을 선언하였다.

The constitution was approved in March 1967, at Perth, and a set of rules for international competition was proposed. At the Federation's annual meeting in 1968 in Pointe Claire, Quebec, these rules were adopted, but are subject to amendment and revision each year.

Also in 1968, the Air Canada Silver Broom replaced the Scotch Cup, and it was sanctioned as the World Curling Championship. In 1975, the Federation endorsed the World Junior Men's Curling Championship, in 1979 the Ladies' Curling Championship; and in 1988, the World Junior Ladies' Curling Championship. The four events were combined into two in 1989 at Milwaukee, Wisconsin, and Markham, Ontario, and became known as the World Curling Championships (WCC) and the World Junior Curling Championships (WJCC).

The Constitution had a significant adjustment in 1982, when the Federation was declared an independent entity and approved as the governing body for curling in the world, while the Royal Caledonian Curling Club was acknowledged as the Mother Club of Curling.

In 1991, the name of the Federation was changed to the World Curling Federation (WCF).

Curling was a demonstration sport for a second and third time at the Winter Olympics of 1988 (Calgary) and 1992 (Albertville) for teams of Men and Women.

On 21 July 1992, at its session in Barcelona, Spain, the International Olympic Committee granted official medal status to Men's and Women's Curling, to take effect no later than the Winter Olympic Games of 2002, with an option for 1998 at Nagano, Japan. During the meeting of the IOC Executive Board held on 19-22 June 1993 in Lausanne, the Organising Committee of the Nagano Olympic Winter Games (NAOC '98) officially agreed to include Curling in the programme of the XVIII Olympic Winter Games, 1998. Eight teams for men and women participated in Nagano, and this was increased to ten for the Salt Lake City Olympic Winter Games of 2002.

At the Semi-Annual General Assembly of the Federation in Leukerbad, Switzerland, in December 1993, a revised Constitution was adopted. This included changes to the Management Structure. The revised structure became operational following the election of the Executive Board at the Annual General Assembly in Oberstdorf, Germany, in April 1994.

From 1966 to 1994, the administration of the ICF and WCF was the responsibility of employees of the RCCC. Following the adoption of the revised Constitution, the WCF set up its own Head Office and Secretariat in Edinburgh, Scotland in 1994.

At the Semi-Annual General Assembly of the Federation in Grindelwald, Switzerland, in December 1995, a completely re-written Constitution was adopted in order to comply with Swiss law following the Federation's registration in that country. In May 2000, the WCF Secretariat moved from Edinburgh to Perth, Scotland.

The first World Wheelchair Curling Championship was held in January 2002 and in March that year, the International Paralympic Committee granted official medal status to Wheelchair Curling for mixed gender teams. The Organising Committee of the Torino Paralympic Winter Games 2006 agreed to include Wheelchair Curling in its programme.

Other international events introduced in 2002, included World Senior Championships for Men and Women, and the Continental Cup, a competition run along the same lines as the Ryder Cup in Golf, with North America (Canada & USA) versus the Rest of the World, with twelve men and twelve women in each team competing in various curling disciplines.

In 2003, Curling was featured in the programmes of the World University Winter Games and the Asian Winter Games for the first time.

In 2005, the World Men's and Women's Championships were separated once again, and held in different parts of the world. Also that year the European Youth Olympic Festival introduced a curling competition for Junior men and women between 15 and 18 years of age.

법안은 1967년 3월 퍼쓰에서 승인되었고 국제대회의 규칙이 제안되었다. 연맹의 연간 회의는 퀘벡의 Pointe Clair에서 규정으로 채택되었고, 매년 개정되고 있다.

또한 1968년 Air Canada Silver Broom에서 스카치 컵을 대체하고 세계 컬링 선수권으로 인가받았다. 1975년에 연맹은 세계 주니어 남성 컬링 선수권을 승인했고, 1979년엔 여성 컬링 선수권을; 1988년엔 세계 주니어 여성 컬링 선수권을 승인했다. 4개의 행사는 1989년 위스콘신, 밀워키와 온타리오, 마크함에서 2개로 합쳐졌고 세계 컬링 선수권과 세계 주니어 컬링 선수권이 되었다.

1982년에 법이 수정되었고 연맹이 독립체임을 선언하였을 때 세계 컬링의 이사회가 승인되었고, 로열 칼레도니아 컬링 클럽이 컬링 클럽의 모체로 인정받았다. 1991년 연맹의 이름은 세계컬링연맹으로 바뀌었다.

1988년(캘거리)와 1992년(알베르빌) 동계 올림픽에서 남성과 여성 컬링이 두 번과 세 번, 시범 종목으로 채택되었다.

1992년 7월 2일 스페인 바르셀로나에서 IOC는 공식적으로 남성과 여성 컬링에 메달을 수여했고, 머지않아 2002년 동계 올림픽에서 효과를 보였고, 1998년 일본 나가노에서도 선택되었다. 로잔에서 1993년 6월 19일에서 22일까지 열린 IOC 이사회 미팅에서 나가노 동계 올림픽 조직위(NAOC '98)는 공식적으로 컬링을 18번째 동계 올림픽 종목으로 승인했다. 남성, 여성 8개 팀이 나가노에 참가했고, 2002년 솔트 레이크 시티 동계 올림픽에서는 10개 팀으로 늘어났다. 스위스의 로이커바트에서 1993년 12월에 열린 회의에서 개정된 법안이 채택되었다. 관리구조의 변화를 포함한 것이었다. 개정된 구조는 독일의 오버스트도르프에서 1994년 4월에 연간 회의에서 이사회의 선출과 함께 활용할 준비가 됐다.

1966년부터 1994년까지 ICF와 세계컬링연맹의 관리직은 RCCC의 직원들이 책임을 져왔다. 채택된 개정 법안에 따르면, 세계컬링연맹은 스스로의 본부를 가지고 1994년 스코틀랜드 에딘버러에 사무국을 세웠다.

1995년 12월 스위스 그린델발트에서 열린 반기 회의에서 완전히 새롭게 쓰인 법으로 연맹의 스위스 법을 따르는 대신 개정되었다. 2000년 5월 세계컬링연맹 사무국은 에딘버러에서 스코틀랜드 퍼쓰로 이전했다. 2002년 1월 첫 세계 휠체어 컬링대회가 열렸고 그해 3월, 국제 패럴림픽 위원회에서 남녀혼성팀에게 공식메달을 수여했다.

2006년 토리노 패럴림픽 조직위에서 휠체어 컬링을 프로그램에 넣는 것을 동의했다. 다른 국제 대회는 2002년부터 열린 남녀 세계 시니어 선수권 골프의 라이더 컵처럼 북아메리카(캐나다&미국) 대 전 세계가 붙는 대륙간컵이 있다. 12명의 남성과 12명의 여성이 각자의 다양한 팀에서 훈련을 받고 있다.

2003년 컬링은 세계 동계 유니버시아드와 동계 아시안 게임에서 처음 채택되었다.

2005년 세계 남자, 여자 선수권이 다시 한 번 분리되었고 세계의 다른 지역에서 열렸다. 또한 그해 유럽 유스 올림픽 축제에서 15세에서 18세까지의 남성과 여성 주니어들을 위한 컬링 대회가 열렸다.

The growth of the sport in Asia was recognized with the World Women's Championship held in Aomori, Japan, in 2007 and Gangneung, Korea, in 2009.

In 2008 the first World Mixed Doubles Curling Championship was staged in Vierumäki, Finland. Mixed doubles curling marks a break from traditional curling, as teams are comprised of two players – one male and one female. The Championship has grown from strength to strength and is now an annual fixture on the WCF calendar.

There are currently 49 WCF Member Associations.

아시아 지역에서 이 스포츠의 성장은 2007년 일본 아오모리와 2009년 대한민국 강릉에서 열린 여자 세계선수권 대회로 인식되었다.

2008년 핀란드 비에루마키에서 첫 혼합복식(믹스더블) 세계선수권이 열렸다. 혼합(믹스더블)은 컬링 전통의 파괴를 나타내는 것으로, 팀은 두 선수 - 한 명의 남자와 여자로 구성된다.

선수권대회는 날로 성장해서 이제는 매년 WCF 달력에 표기되고 있다.

현재 WCF 회원국으로 49개국이 있다.

Olympic Winter Games

In Nagano, Japan in 1998, the Men's Olympic Curling Gold Medal went to Switzerland who overcame Canada in the final with the Canadians taking the first Women's gold against Denmark.

In the Salt Lake City Olympics in 2002, the curling event featured 10 teams of men and women, an increase from 8 in Japan. The Norwegian men's team and the women's team from Great Britain won gold medals.

The 2006 Olympic Games were held in Torino, Italy with the gold medals going to the Canadian men and Swedish women.

The 2010 Olympics were held in Vancouver, Canada with the gold medals going again to the Canadian men and Swedish women.

The 2014 Olympics will be held in Sochi, Russia.

The Olympic Curling Competition in Sochi in 2014 will be comprised of 10 teams for Men and Women.

• The top 7 Associations (excluding Russia) who have collected the most qualifying points from the World Women's Curling Championships (WWCCs) and the World Men's Curling Championships (WMCCs) held in 2012 and 2013 will qualify.

• Any eligible Association that earned qualification points at the 2012 or 2013 WCCs, or participated at the 2011 WCCs, who do not qualify for the 2014 Olympic Winter Games as the host, or as one of the top 7 Associations, may enter the new Olympic Qualification Event (OQE) which will be run by the WCF in December 2013.

• The top two teams from the OQE also qualify their Association (National Olympic Committee) for the 2014 Olympic Winter Games. Points are awarded according to final ranking of the 12 participating teams in WCCs as follows: 14 – 12 – 10 – 9 – 8 – 7 – 6 – 5 – 4 – 3 – 2 – 1

* Russia as host country for the 2014 Olympic Winter Games has guaranteed qualification.

** Great Britain qualification points gained by Scotland at World Championships.

To ensure that every Member Association of the World Curling Federation (currently 49) is provided with an opportunity to secure an Olympic place, zonal qualifying competitions open to all members are held each year as required for entry to the World Championships.

The Curling Associations of England, Scotland and Wales are all individual members of the WCF and thereby eligible to compete in World Championships should they qualify. The points issue is resolved by an agreement whereby only Scotland is allocated Olympic points towards qualification for Great Britain.

World Curling Championships and the Olympic Qualification Event determine if a country qualifies to play in the Olympics. National Olympic Committees (NOCs) in conjunction with the Member Associations of the WCF each devise their own system of team selection which varies from country to country. The traditional method, still favoured by the majority, involves established teams of 4 athletes, plus 1 reserve, competing in a series of qualifying competitions, culminating in a final Olympic Trial for the `cream` of the country's teams.

Some NOCs favour a squad system whereby a number of individual athletes are selected at least one year in advance for special training with the final decision on the 5 to represent their country being made by the team management – a method employed by Great Britain in 2010.

동계 올림픽 게임

1998년 일본 나가노에서 열린 올림픽 컬링 종목 남자부는 스위스 팀이 결승에서 캐나다를 이기고 금메달을 획득했다. 또한 여자부 결승에선 캐나다 팀이 덴마크를 상대로 첫 여자부 금메달을 획득했다.

일본에서 열린 올림픽에서 컬링은 남녀 8팀이 출전했지만, 2002년 제19회 솔트레이크시티 동계 올림픽에서는 컬링 경기가 남, 녀 10팀이 출정하도록 규정되어 일본 나가노 올림픽에서의 8팀으로부터 2팀을 늘렸고, 노르웨이 남자팀과 영국 여자팀이 금메달을 차지했다.

이탈리아 토리노에서 개최된 2006년 올림픽에서는 캐나다 남자팀과 스웨덴 여자팀이 정상에 도달했다.

캐나다 벤쿠버에서 열린 2010년 올림픽에서는 또다시 캐나다 남자팀과 스웨덴 여자팀이 정상에 도달했다.

2014년 올림픽은 러시아 소치에서 열릴 예정이다. 2014년에 소치에서 열릴 올림픽 컬링 시합은 남, 녀 각각 10팀으로 구성될 것이다.

러시아를 제외하고, 2012년, 2013년에 개최된 남녀 세계 컬링선수권대회에서 많은 자격 포인트를 모은 7개의 국가가 참가자격을 얻게 된다.

2012년 또는 2013년 세계선수권에서 자격 포인트를 획득했거나, 2014년 동계올림픽에 참가국으로서 자격이 없는 2011년 세계선수권대회의 참가국이었거나, 7개의 상위연맹국 중의 한 국가로서 자격이 부여된 국가는 2013년 12월에 세계컬링연맹에 의해 운영될 새로운 올림픽 예선에선 등록할 수 있다.

예선상위 두 팀 또는 그들의 협회(국가 올림픽위원회)에 2014년 동계 올림픽 출전 자격이 주어진다.

포인트는 세계 컬링 선수권대회에서 12개 참가 팀의 최종 순위에 따라 이와 같이 수여된다.

: 14 - 12 - 10 - 9 - 8 - 7 - 6 - 5 - 4 - 3 - 2 - 1

* 개최국으로서 러시아는 2014년 동계 올림픽에 출전 자격을 얻는다.

** 영국의 취득 포인트는 세계선수권대회에서 스코틀랜드에 의해 얻어졌다.

세계컬링연맹의 모든 회원국(현재 49개국)을 확인하는 것은 올림픽이 열리는 장소에서 안전할 기회를 제공받는 것이며, 모든 회원국에서 열리는, 지역의 인정(허가)받은 경기는 세계선수권의 참가 신청을 채움으로써 매년 열린다.

잉글랜드, 스코틀랜드, 웨일즈의 컬링협회는 세계컬링연맹의 개별적인 구성국이고, 그러므로 각각의 출전 자격이 있는 세계선수권대회에서 경쟁할 자격이 주어진다.

포인트 문제는 스코트랜드만이 영국에 올림픽 포인트가 할당됨에 따라, 동의를 받고 해결되었다.

WCC와 OQE는 각 나라들이 올림픽에 참가할 조건이 되는지 결정한다.

세계컬링연맹의 회원국들과 협력하여, 국가 올림픽 위원회는 국가마다 다른 그들만의 팀 선택 시스템을 고안한다.

여전히 다수결에 의해 지지되는 전통적인 방식은, 4명의 선수와 1명의 후보 선수를 더해 구성된 팀을 포함하여, 인정(허가)받은 경기에서 연속하여 경쟁하여 국가대표팀의 발탁을 위한 최종 올림픽 선발전에서 끝나는 것이다.

몇몇의 국가 올림픽 위원회들은 선수단 시스템을 선호한다. 많은 개별적인 선수들이, 그들의 국가를 대표하는 다섯 명의 선수에 대한 최종 결정이 팀 경영진(감독)에 의해 정해진 채로, 특별 훈련을 목적으로 적어도 1년 전에는 발탁된다. - 2010년에 영국이 활용한 방법이다.

57. LIST OF FORMS

Entry Forms (sent out by WCF Office)

- Covering Letter
- Release Agreement
- Health Information
- Doping Control
- Doping Control – Appendix I
- Doping Control – Parent/Guardian Consent
- Alcohol Consumption Policy
- Biographical Information – Athlete
- Biographical Information – Coach
- Event Entry Form
- Team Entry
- Registration for Americas Challenge
- Sportsmanship Award (WMCC, WWCC, WJCC)(sent to Chief Umpire)

Competition Forms

- Original Team Line-Up Form
- Original Team Line-Up Form WMDCC
- Game Team Line-Up Form
- Change of Team Line-Up Form
- Last Stone Draw (LSD)
- Draw Shot Challenge (DSC)
- Draw Shot Challenge Summary Form
- On-Ice Official's Scorecard
- Game Timing Form
- Violation Chart
- Play-Off Game Information
- Stone Selection
- Stone Selection WMDCC
- Stone Feedback Form
- Team Playing Uniforms
- Order of Delivery in WMDCC
- Wheelchair-Stone Selection
- Officiating Report Sheet
- Officiating Summary Sheet
- Special Meetings
- Evening Practice Schedule (pre-allocated)
- Procedure Evening Practice During Round Robin
- Evening Practice Reservation Form (2)
- Hog-Line Violation
- Summary Seating Coach Bench
- Summary Seating Coach Bench WMDCC
- WCF Dress Code
- WMDCC Placing Point Chart

57. 양식 리스트

참가 신청서 (세계컬링연맹 사무국으로부터 발송된)

- 첨부서
- 동의서
- 건강 정보
- 도핑 검사(조절)
- 도핑 검사 - 부록1
- 도핑 검사 - 부모/보호자 동의서
- 음주량 정책
- 약력 - 선수용
- 약력 - 코치용
- 경기 참가 신청서
- 팀 엔트리
- 미국 대회 출전을 위한 등록
- 주심으로부터 전송된 (세계 남녀/주니어 선수권대회) 스포츠맨십 대회

수상 형식

경기 형식

- 기존 팀 라인업 형식
- 세계 혼성(4인믹스) 컬링 선수권대회 기존 팀 라인업 형식
- 게임 팀 라인업 형식
- 변경된 팀 라인업 형식
- Last Stone Draw(LSD)
- Draw Shot Challenge(DSC)
- DSC 요약 형식
- 빙상 위 공식 득점표
- 게임 타이밍 형식
- 위반표
- 동점 결승 경기 정보
- 스톤 선택
- 세계 혼성(4인믹스) 컬링 선수권대회에서의 스톤 선택
- 스톤 피드백 형식
- 팀플레이 복장
- 세계 혼성(4인믹스) 컬링 선수권대회 딜리버리 순서
- 휠체어-스톤 선택법
- 공무 수행 기록표
- 공무 집계표
- 특별 회의
- 미리 할당된 저녁 연습 스케줄
- 라운드 로빈(각 팀이 참가 팀 모두와 경기하는 방식) 때 저녁 연습 형식
- 예약 형식(2)
- 호그 라인 위반
- 코치의 지도 범위 요약
- 세계 혼성(4인믹스) 컬링 선수권대회에서의 코치 지도 범위 요약
- 세계컬링연맹 복장 규정
- 세계 남녀혼성 컬링 선수권대회 점수 배치표

58. ENTRY FORMS (WCF Office)

WORLD _____ CURLING CHAMPIONSHIP

Venue:
Date:

The following forms must be returned to the Secretariat, 74 Tay Street, Perth, PH2 8NP, Scotland
Email: info@worldcurling.org

WCF Release Agreement
Each competitor, including alternate, along with the President/Secretary of his Curling Association, must complete and sign the WCF Release Agreement. Failure to return this document will result in disqualification.

Biographical Information
Biographical information for each competitor, including alternate and coach, must be completed and returned to the Secretariat, World Curling Federation **by Email** info@worldcurling.org. These forms should be checked by a national official to ensure the information is relevant, and confined to factual details.

Team Photograph
The Host Committee requests that each team provides two copies of a **coloured** photograph showing the team and fifth player, head and shoulders only. The size should be approximately 13cm x 9cm. They request that the photograph, as you look at it, is, from left to right: skip, third player, second player, lead and alternate. Please also enclose players' names stating playing position (FIRST NAME FOLLOWED BY FAMILY NAME), either typed or clearly printed. There should be no advertising in the background and players should be standing shoulder to shoulder in matching jackets. The team photographs should be submitted in Electronic form (**.jpg** file) to ____________ **by** _________ **or earlier if available**. If it is not possible to send by Email please mail (use express courier if necessary to meet deadline date) to ______________________

FORMS TO BE TAKEN TO CHAMPIONSHIPS

Health Information Sheet

Each competitor, including alternate, must complete the Health Information Sheet. **This is a very confidential document which must be handed to the Chief Umpire at the team meeting.**

58. 세계컬링연맹 공식 참가 신청서

세계 컬링 선수권

장소:

날짜:

아래의 양식은 사는 사무국장 Tay 씨께 보내져야 한다, 74 Tay Street, Perth, PH2 8NP, Scotland Email: info@worldcurling.org

세계컬링연맹 동의서

회장/총무와 함께 후보를 포함한 각 선수들은 세계컬링연맹에 대한 동의서를 작성하고 서명해야 한다.

자료를 제출하지 않으면 자격이 박탈된다.

약력

후보를 포함한 각 선수와 코치의 약력은 세계컬링연맹 사무국 Email info@worldcurling.org에 제출되어야 한다.

이 형식은 내용이 적절한지 공식적으로 보장되어야 하고 세부사항까지 국한된다.

팀 사진

개최국 위원회는 팀 멤버와 5번째 선수(후보)의 머리 - 어깨까지 보이는 컬러 사진 2장을 각 팀별로 요구한다.

사진 사이즈는 대략 13㎝×9㎝여야 한다. 위원회가 필요한 사진은 당신이 알다시피 왼쪽에서 오른쪽 순서대로: 스킵, 써드, 세컨, 리드, 후보 순이다.

이름, 성 순으로 선수들의 이름 또한 써서 붙여주시기 바란다. (자필이나 프린트 둘 다 됨)

사진 배경엔 광고가 없어야 하며 선수들끼리는 맞춰 입은 옷을 입고 어깨끼리 맞닿아 있어야 한다.

이 팀 사진은 (.jpg file) ___________ 이나 _________ 로 가능한 빨리 제출되어야 한다.

이메일로 못 보내면 _____________________일까지 등기로 보내라. (마감날짜까지 도착해야 한다)

자료는 선수권대회로 전달된다.

건강 기록서

후보를 포함한 각 선수는 건강 기록을 필히 제출해야 한다. 이것은 팀 미팅 때 주심에게 비밀리에 전달될 것이다.

World ____ Curling Championship

WCF RELEASE AGREEMENT

MEMBER ASSOCIATION____

I certify that the following players: (PLEASE PRINT)

Delivery Order	Name	Please indicate Position of Skip
Fourth		
Third		
Second		
Lead		
Alternate		

will represent ________________________ in the World _____ Curling Championship, and that each is a member in good standing and eligible under the Rules of the World Curling Federation to represent ______________________________ Curling Association

President/Secretary's name: ________________ Signature: ______________________

Release Agreement

The members of the ___________________________ team, listed above, and entered in the World _____ Curling Championship, __________, ________ hereby give irrevocable consent to the World Curling Federation and the Organising Committee of the World ___ Curling Championship, to reproduce, display and use their names, photographs, or other likenesses, in connection with reports, promotion, advertising and publicity without restriction, about and on behalf of the World _____ Curling Championship, issued, produced or authorised by the WCF and/or the Organising Committee of the World _____ Curling Championship. By signing below, we acknowledge having read and agreed to this waiver.

Fourth __________________________ Third ________________________

Second __________________________ Lead ________________________

Alternate __________________________ Date: ________________________

Please return to: The Secretariat, World Curling Federation, 74 Tay Street, Perth, PH2 8NP, Scotland by ________. Email: info@worldcurling.org: Tel: 44 1738 451630

세계선수권대회

세계컬링연맹 양도 계약서

회원국 ________________________________

나는 아래의 선수들을 보증한다.: (프린트하여라)

딜리버리 순서	이름	스킵의 포지션을 적어주세요
포스		
써드		
세컨		
리드		
후보		

는 대표할 것이다.__________________________ 세계 컬링 선수권대회에서, 각각의 선수는 회원 자격이 있고 세계컬링연맹이가 수여한다.

__________________________ 컬링협회를 대표하여

회장/총무 이름: ________________ 서명: ________________

동의서

위에 기재되었고 ____ 컬링 세계선수권대회에 참가한 __________________________ 의 팀 멤버는, ________, ______ 이에 동의하고 세계컬링연맹과 세계 ___컬링 선수권대회가 전적으로 동의한다. 재사용하려면 세계 _____ 컬링 선수권대회에 대한 선수들의 이름과 세계컬링연맹 그리고/또는 세계_____ 컬링 선수권대회 조직 위원회에 의해 발행, 제작 및 위임된 사진 관련 자료, 광고나 규제에 적합한 홍보가 이루어져야 한다.

아래에 서명함으로써 위의 계약서 내용을 읽고 동의한다.

포스 ________________________ 써드 ____________________

세컨 ________________________ 리드 ____________________

후보 ________________________ 날짜 ____________________

회신해 주십시오.: 사무국, 세계컬링연맹, 74 Tay Street, Perth, PH2 8NP, Scotland by ________, Email:info@worldcurling.rg: 전화: 44 1738 451630

World _____ Curling Championship
Venue:
Date:

HEALTH INFORMATION FORM

Member Association: ______________________________

Name ______________________________ Date of Birth: ________________________

Address: ______________________________ Telephone No.________________________

____

Health Insurance Company Name ____

Policy or Identification Number____

If you have any active medical problems at present, please explain:________________________

If you are under a physician's care at present, please explain:____________________________
Note: Special attention should be paid to the WCF Anti-Doping policy as random drug-testing may be carried out at this competition. It is important that all medications, however trivial, taken before the competition are reported.

If you have a history of any of the following, please explain:

Heart condition ______________________ Diabetes__________________________

Allergies __________________________ Bleeding conditions____________________

Psychiatric Illnesses __________________ Operations_________________________

Asthma or Shortness of Breath ____________________ Epilepsy ____________________

List Current Medication ____

____

In the event of an emergency, please notify:__________________________________

Address: ____

Telephone: ________________________ Relationship________________________

Signature: ________________________ Date______________________________

This form should be placed in a sealed envelope marked 'Health Information Form' and ensure that your Coach hands it to the Chief Umpire at the team meeting.

세계선수권대회
장소:
날짜:

건강 정보 형식

협회 구성원: ____________________

이름 ____________________ 출생일 ____________________

주소: ____________________ 전화번호 ____________________

건강 보험 회사 이름 ____________________

주민등록번호 ____________________

현재 건강에 이상이 있거나 질병이 있을 경우 적어라. ____________________

현재 의사의 진료를 받는 경우 적어라.
세계선수권대회 도핑 정책은 랜덤 테스트이며 이 대회에 참가하기 위해 참여해야한다. 대회가 공지된 후부터의 모든 의약품이 중요하다.
다음과 같은 질병이 있었을 경우 꼭 기재하라.

심장 질환 ____________________ 당뇨병 ____________________

알레르기 ____________________

정신질환 ____________________ 수술 이력 ____________________

천식/ 호흡곤란 ____________________ 간질 ____________________

현재 복용약 기재 ____________________

비상 시 알아야 할 것 :

주소: ____________________

전화번호: ____________________ 관계 ____________________

서명: ____________________ 날짜 ____________________

이 자료는 '건강 정보 양식' 봉투에 동봉되어 팀 코치가 팀 미팅의 주심에게 준 것에 동의된다.

World ____ Curling Championship

DOPING CONTROL

To whom it may concern (parent/guardian)

Competitors under 18 years of age during the competition must return the Letter of Consent to the World Curling Secretariat on or before _________.

Your child has qualified to participate in the World _____ Curling Championship, _______. To be eligible to compete, he/she must be prepared, if selected by random choice, to go to the medical control centre at the venue in order to provide a specimen of urine for analysis by the accredited drug-testing laboratory.

The samples are collected in private under observation by a sampling officer of the same sex, and your child may be accompanied to the doping-control station by a parent, coach or official.

Your permission is required in order that this testing may take place at the World _____ Championships, 20__.

Failure to give this permission will mean that your child will not be able to compete in the Championships.

The results of all laboratory findings will be reported to the individual concerned and to the respective Member Association.

If you concur with this, please ensure that the Parent/Guardian's Consent Form is signed and returned to the WCF Secretariat.

세계선수권대회

도핑 검사

관계자분께(부모/대리인)

18세 이하의 선수들은 대회 기간 동안 반드시 세계컬링연맹 사무국이나 이전 ____________ 의 동의서를 회신해야 한다.

당신의 자녀(선수)가 세계선수권에 참가할 자격을 얻어 경쟁하기 위해서는, 그/그녀(선수)는 반드시 (동의서가) 준비되어야 하며, 무작위 선택으로 공인된 약물 실험실에 가서 오줌 샘플을 제공하기 위해 가야 한다.

그 샘플들은 같은 성별의 샘플 담당 직원에 감시 아래 수집되고, 자녀는 부모, 코치나 대리인에 의해 도핑 관리실에 동반할 수 있다.

당신의 승인은 이 테스트(도핑 검사)가 20________년 세계 ____________ 선수권에서 시행되는 것에 따라서 요구된다.

승인을 회답하지 않는 것은 당신의 자녀가 선수권에 참가하지 못할 것임을 의미할 것이다.

실험 자료의 모든 결과는 협회 멤버를 존중하기 위해 개인 비밀을 보장할 것이다.

만약 당신이 위에 동의한다면, 부모님/보호자의 동의 서약서가 서명되었고, 세계컬링연맹 사무국으로 회신되었음을 확실히 해주길 바란다.

WORLD CURLING FEDERATION

Appendix I to the Anti-Doping Rules of the World Curling Federation

______________________ **CURLING CHAMPIONSHIPS**

Acknowledgement and Agreement

I, as a member of ________________ Member Association and a participant in the ________________ Curling Championships 20___, hereby acknowledge and agree as follows:

1. I have received and had an opportunity to review the WCF Anti-Doping Rules.

2. I consent and agree to comply with and be bound by all of the provisions of the WCF Anti-Doping Rules, including but not limited to, all amendments to the Anti-Doping Rules and all International Standards incorporated in the Anti-Doping Rules.

3. I acknowledge and agree that ________________Member Association and WCF have jurisdiction to impose sanctions as provided in the WCF Anti-Doping Rules.

4. I also acknowledge and agree that any dispute arising out of a decision made pursuant to the WCF Anti-Doping Rules, after exhaustion of the process expressly provided for in the WCF Anti-Doping Rules, may be appealed exclusively as provided in Article 13 of the WCF Anti-Doping Rules to an appellate body for final and binding arbitration, which in the case of International Level Athletes is the Court of Arbitration for Sport.

5. I acknowledge and agree that the decisions of the arbitral appellate body referenced above shall be final and enforceable, and that I will not bring any claim, arbitration, lawsuit or litigation in any other court or tribunal.

6. I have read and understand this Acknowledgement and Agreement.

____________ Date	______________________ Print Name (Last Name, First Name)
____________ Date of Birth (Day/Month/Year)	______________________ Signature (or, if a minor, signature of legal guardian)

세계컬링연맹

세계컬링연맹 반도핑 규정의 부록 1

_______________________ 컬링선수권

인지 및 동의

I, ______________ 회원국의 멤버로서, ______________ 20____년 세계 컬링 선수권대회의 참가자로서, 인지 및 동의한다.

1. 나는 (규정을 명시)받았고, 세계컬링연맹의 반도핑 규정을 다시 볼 기회를 가지고 있다.
2. 나는 (규정에)동의하고, 이에 따를 것에도 동의한다. 그리고 세계컬링연맹에서 공급하는 모든 반도핑 규정에 얽매여, 반도핑 규정의 모든 개정이나 모든 반도핑 규정의 국제적인 규격의 주식회사에 포함되지만, 그에 제한되지 않겠다.
3. 나는 ______________ 회원국과 세계컬링연맹이 제공된 세계컬링연맹 반도핑 규정에 의해 제재를 가하는 관할권을 가지고 있다는 것을 인지하고 동의한다.
4. 나는 또한 세계컬링연맹의 반도핑 규정으로부터 특별히 제공되는 과정의 소진 이후에, 세계컬링연맹의 상소기구나 구속력이 있는 조정에서 반도핑 규정의 13가지 조항에 제공됨으로써 배타적으로 호소될 수도 있어, 국제적 수준의 선수들이 스포츠 중재 재판소의 경우에 해당한다는 것을 세계컬링연맹의 반도핑 규정에 따라 만들어진 결과로 발생하는 어떤 분쟁이라 인지하고 동의한다.
5. 나는 위에서 참조되는 상소 중재 기구의 중재 결과가 마지막일 수 있고, 시행할 수 있으며, 어떠한 불평이나 중재, 소송을 다른 법정이나 재판소에서 하지 않을 것을 인정하고 동의한다.
6. 나는 이 인지와 동의(조항들)를 읽고 이해했다.

__________   ____________________

날짜   성명 (성, 이름)

__________   ____________________

생일   서명 (혹은, 만약 미성년자라면, 법적 보호자가 (일/달/연도)에 서명)

World ___ Curling Championship

DOPING CONTROL

PARENT/GUARDIAN CONSENT FOR DRUG TESTING

I have read the document regarding drug testing and give permission for my child/ward to participate in dope testing procedures, if selected. I agree to abide by the doping regulations

Competitor's Name____

(Please print)

Member Association:____

Parent / Legal Guardian: ____

(Please print)

Signed: ____

Address: ____

____

Telephone number: ____

Mobile Telephone number: ____

Email address: ____

Date: ____

Please return to: The Secretariat, World Curling Federation, 74 Tay Street, Perth, PH2 8NP, Scotland by ___________. Email *info@worldcurling.org*

세계컬링연맹

도핑 검사

부모 / 보호자 동의서

나는 선발되면 도핑테스트에 관한 자료를 읽고 제 자녀/피보호자의 도핑 테스트 과정 가운데 함께 참여할 것을 허가한다. 나는 도핑 규정 준수에 동의한다.

선수 이름: ____

(프린트하여라)

협회 구성원: ____

부모/법정 보호자: ____

(프린트하여라)

서명: ____

주소: ____

자택 전화번호: ____

핸드폰 번호: ____

Email 주소: ____

날짜: ____

회신해 주십시오.: 사무국, 세계컬링연맹, 74 Tay Street, Perth, PH2 8NP, Scotland by____________. Email:info@worldcurling.rg:

20__ World Junior Curling Championships

Location:

WCF ALCOHOL CONSUMPTION POLICY

The World Curling Federation (WCF), with the approval of all Member Associations, has an Alcohol Consumption Policy. This policy demands that there will be no alcohol consumed by any athletes participating in the 20__ World Junior Curling Championships.

The responsibility to enforce this zero alcohol consumption policy rests with the Member Associations and their players, coaches and Team Leaders. If WCF personnel see an infraction, a report will be filed with the WCF Executive Board for follow-up action. The penalties may include the exclusion of athletes and coaches from future WCF events (period determined by the WCF Executive Board in liaison with the Member Association).

This policy applies during the entire length of the Championship, from arrival in _____ to departure, and must be adhered to in all public and private locations.

The undersigned agree that they have read this document and will abide by this policy.

Member Association: ______________________________ ☐ Jr. Men ☐ Jr. Women

	(PLEASE PRINT)	(SIGNATURE)
Skip	____________________	____________________
Third	____________________	____________________
Second	____________________	____________________
Lead	____________________	____________________
Alternate	____________________	____________________
Team Coach	____________________	____________________

Please return to:* *The Secretariat, World Curling Federation, 74 Tay Street, Perth, PH2 8NP, Scotland, by ______________. Email:* Info@worldcurling.org; *Tel: 44 1738 451630

세계컬링연맹

20____ 세계 주니어 컬링 선수권대회

지역:

세계선수권대회 음주량 정책

세계컬링연맹(WCF)는 협회 전원의 동의와 함께 음주량 정책을 시행한다. 이 정책은 20 _______ 세계주니어선수권대회에 참여하는 모든 선수가 금주해야 한다는 내용이다.

알코올 농도 0 (금주)에 대한 이 책임은 협회 멤버와 각 선수들, 코치들, 팀 리더들이 함께 진다.

만약 세계컬링연맹 직원들이 위반한 것을 적발할 경우, 세계컬링연맹 중역이사회에서 후속 조치에 대한 보고서를 첨부할 것이다.

그 처벌은 향후 열릴 선수 세계컬링연맹 대회에 선수들과 코치들의 박탈이 포함될 것이다.

(기간은 협회 멤버와 함께 세계컬링연맹 중역이사회의 연락에 의해 결정됨)

이 정책은 선수권대회 전체 기간 동안 적용되며, ____에 도착한 이후로부터 공적, 사적인 자리에서도 고수되어야 한다.

서명인은 이 문서를 읽고 이 정책에 준수할 것에 동의한다.

회원국: ______________________________ ☐ Jr. Men ☐ Jr. Women

	(프린트하여라)	(서명)
스킵	____________	____________
써드	____________	____________
세컨	____________	____________
리드	____________	____________
후보	____________	____________
팀 코치	____________	____________

회신해 주십시오.: 사무국, 세계컬링연맹, 74 Tay Street, Perth, PH2 8NP, Scotland by ________.
Email:info@worldcurling.rg:

World _____ Curling Championship

Biographical Information - Athlete

PLEASE PRINT CLEARLY

Member Association:	
First Name:	
Family Name:	
Other names (nickname, known as) :	
Position on Team:	
Name of Coach:	
Age:	
Date of Birth dd/mm/yyyy:	
Birthplace:	
Home Address:	
Telephone Numbers:	Home: Cell:
Email Address:	
Year started curling:	
Years on team:	
Curling Club – Name & City:	
Delivery (left/right hand):	
Height/Weight:	
Education	
Occupation:	
Employer:	
Marital status:	
Spouse's name:	
Children (Names & Age)	
Famous Curling Relatives & their major achievements or honours	
Hobbies:	
Other Sports:	

Best Results of Curling Career:

Championship/Year	Position	Final Rank

Best 3 Results this Season:

Championship/Year	Position	Final Rank

Earlier World Championships & World Junior Championships:

Championship/Year	Position	Final Rank

Please return to: The Secretariat, World Curling Federation, 74 Tay Street, Perth, PH2 8NP, Scotland by _______.
Email info@worldcurling.org

세계 컬링 선수권대회

개인 정보 - 선수

깨끗하게 인쇄하여라.

회원국		
이름:		
성(姓):		
기타 이름(별명, 알려져 있는 별칭 등):		
팀 내 포지션(역할):		
코치 성명:		
나이:		
생년월일: 일/월/연도		
태어난 곳:		
집 주소:		
전화번호 :	휴대폰 번호:	집 번호:
이메일 주소:		
컬링을 시작한 해:		
컬링 팀에 소속된 기간:		
컬링 팀 - 이름 & 지역:		
딜리버리(왼손/오른손 사용):		
학력:		
직업:		
고용주:		
결혼 여부:		
배우자의 이름:		
자녀(이름 & 나이):		
유명한 컬링 동료 & 그들의 주요 성과 또는 업적:		
취미:		
다른 스포츠:		

컬링 업적 중 최고 성과:

대회/연도	포지션(역할)	최종 순위

이번 시즌 내 최고 성적~3위까지의 결과:

대회/연도	포지션(역할)	최종 순위

이전 세계선수권 & 주니어 세계선수권:

대회/연도	포지션(역할)	최종 순위

World _____ Curling Championship

Biographical Information – Coach

PLEASE PRINT CLEARLY

Member Association		
First Name:		
Family Name:		
Other names (nickname, known as):		
Coach to: (Men or Women)		
Date of Birth: dd/mm/yyyy		
Birthplace:		
Home Address:		
Telephone Numbers	**Home:**	**Cell:**
Email Address:		
Year started curling:		
Years Coaching Team:		
Curling Club – Name & City:		
Education		
Occupation:		
Employer:		
Marital status:		
Spouse's name:		
Children (Names & Age)		
Hobbies:		
Other Sports:		

Coach in Past Championships:

Championship	Year	Final Ranking

Please return to: The Secretariat, World Curling Federation, 74 Tay Street, Perth, PH2 8NP, Scotland by _______.
Email info@worldcurling.org

세계 컬링 선수권대회

개인 정보 - 코치

깨끗하게 인쇄하여라.

회원국	
이름:	
성(姓):	
기타 이름(별명, 알려져 있는 별칭 등):	
코치의 성별: (남성 혹은 여성)	
생년월일: 일/월/연도	
태어난 곳:	
집 주소:	
전화번호 :	휴대폰 번호: 집 번호:
이메일 주소:	
컬링을 시작한 해:	
컬링 팀에 소속된 기간:	
컬링 팀 - 이름 & 지역:	
학력:	
직업:	
고용주:	
결혼 여부:	
배우자의 이름:	
자녀(이름 & 나이):	
취미:	
다른 스포츠:	

코치의 과거 경력

대회	연도	최종 순위

사무국으로 회신 부탁드림. 세계컬링연맹(World Curling Federation) 74 Tay Street, Perth, PH2 8NP, Scotland by ________. Email info@worldcurling.org

WORLD CURLING FEDERATION

74, Tay Street, Perth PH2 8NP, Scotland
Tel. 44 1738 451630 Fax. 44 1738 451641
Email: info@worldcurling.org

WORLD _____ CURLING CHAMPIONSHIPS 20__
Venue________
Date__________

ENTRY

Please check Appropriate box(es)

MEN	
WOMEN	
NO ENTRY BEING MADE	

MEMBER ASSOCIATION:	
CONTACT NAME:	
ADDRESS:	
TELEPHONE NO:	
FAX NO:	
EMAIL ADDRESS:	

Team Names Enclosed ☐

Team Names return will be sent by (date) ______________________________

Return this form to WCF Secretariat at the above address by ___________at the latest.
Email info@worldcurling.org

WORLD ____________ CURLING CHAMPIONSHIPS 20_______

장소______________

날짜______________

출전선수

적절한 곳에 표시하시오.

남성	
여성	
만들어진 출전 명단이 없음	

회원국	
이름	
주소	
전화번호	
팩스번호	
이메일 주소	

참가자 이름 포함 ☐

제출 마감 날짜 (date) ______________________________

이 양식을 최소한 ________________________ 까지 위 주소로 WCF 사무국으로 제출해야 한다.

이메일: info@worldcurling.org

74, Tay Street, Perth PH2 8NP, Scotland
Tel. 44 1738 451630 Fax. 44 1738 451641
Email: info@worldcurling.org

WORLD _____ CURLING CHAMPIONSHIPS 20__
Venue________
Date__________

MEMBER ASSOCIATION ____

PARTICIPANTS NAMES

MEN	DATE OF BIRTH D/M/Y		WOMEN	DATE OF BIRTH D/M/Y
		SKIP		
		THIRD		
		SECOND		
		FIRST		
		ALTERNATE		
		COACH		

MEMBER ASSOCIATION:	
CONTACT NAME:	
ADDRESS:	
TELEPHONE NO:	
FAX NO:	
EMAIL ADDRESS:	

Return this form to WCF Secretariat at the above address along with the entry form by _________________, if names known by then. If not, return separately as soon as possible after that date. Email: info@worldcurling.org

WORLD ____________ CURLING CHAMPIONSHIPS 20_______

장소 ____________________

날짜 ____________________

회원국 ____

참가자 이름

남성	생년월일		여성	생년월일
		스킵		
		써드		
		세컨		
		리드		
		후보		
		코치		

회원국:	
이름:	
주소:	
전화 번호:	
팩스 번호:	
이메일 주소:	

이 양식을 출전명단 양식과 함께 위 주소로 WCF 사무국으로______________________까지 제출하시오. 만일 그렇지 않을 경우, 기한 후에도 최대한 빨리 개별로 제출하시오.

이메일: info@worldcurling.org

74, Tay Street, Perth PH2 8NP, Scotland
Tel. 44 1738 451630; Email. info@worldcurling.org

AMERICAS CHALLENGE COMPETITION

REGISTRATION FORM FOR ENTRY

WORLD WOMEN'S CURLING CHAMPIONSHIP 20__ ☐
Date____ Venue_____

WORLD MEN'S CURLING CHAMPIONSHIP 20__ ☐
Date____ Venue_____

WORLD JUNIOR CURLING CHAMPIONSHIPS 20__
Date____ Venue_____ **MEN** ☐

WOMEN ☐

Please tick appropriate boxes

Member Association ______________________________

This registration form confirms that a challenge for entry to the competition/s indicated above is being made ☐ / accepted ☐

Contact Name ______________________________

Address ______________________________

____

____

Telephone ______________________________

Fax ______________________________

Email ______________________________

Please return this form to the WCF Secretariat, by email to ***info@worldcurling.org*** or by fax +44 1738 451641 by _______ at the latest.

AMERICAS CHALLENGE COMPETITION

출전명단 등록 양식

WORLD WOMEN'S CURLING CHAMPIONSHIP 20 ______ ☐

날짜____________ 장소__________________

WORLD MEN'S CURLING CHAMPIONSHIP 20 ______ ☐

날짜____________ 장소__________________

WORLD JUNIOR CURLING CHAMPIONSHIP 20 ______

날짜____________ 장소__________________

남자 ☐

여자 ☐

적절한 곳에 표시하시오.

회원국 ____

위에 명시된 시합에 나갈 도전 출전 명단을 확인하는 이 등록 양식은 현재 만드는 중이다 □ / 수락 중이다 □

이름 ____

주소 ____

____

____

전화번호 ____

팩스번호 ____

이메일 ____

이 양식은 이메일 info@worldcurling.org 또는 팩스 +44 1738 451641 으로 적어도 _______까지 WCF 사무국으로 반환하시오.

WORLD JUNIOR WOMEN'S CURLING CHAMPIONSHIP 20__

SPORTSMANSHIP AWARD

Association: __________

All Participants are invited to nominate a fellow competitor who, in their view, has best exemplified the traditional values of skill, honesty, fair play, sportsmanship and friendship during these Championships. The Award will be presented at the Awards Ceremony. Players are not allowed to vote for a member of their own team.

PERSON NOMINATED - ______________________________

PLAYING FOR TEAM - ______________________________

Please return this card to the Chief Umpire at the end of the round robin

WORLD JUNIOR WOMEN'S CURLING CHAMPIONSHIP 20__

SPORTSMANSHIP AWARD

Association: __________

All Participants are invited to nominate a fellow competitor who, in their view, has best exemplified the traditional values of skill, honesty, fair play, sportsmanship and friendship during these Championships. The Award will be presented at the Awards Ceremony. Players are not allowed to vote for a member of their own team.

PERSON NOMINATED - ______________________________

PLAYING FOR TEAM - ______________________________

Please return this card to the Chief Umpire at the end of the round robin

WORLD JUNIOR WOMEN'S CURLING CHAMPIONSHIP 20__

SPORTSMANSHIP AWARD

Association: __________

All Participants are invited to nominate a fellow competitor who, in their view, has best exemplified the traditional values of skill, honesty, fair play, sportsmanship and friendship during these Championships. The Award will be presented at the Awards Ceremony. Players are not allowed to vote for a member of their own team.

PERSON NOMINATED - ______________________________

PLAYING FOR TEAM - ______________________________

Please return this card to the Chief Umpire at the end of the round robin

WORLD JUNIOR WOMEN'S CURLING CHAMPIONSHIP 20__

SPORTSMANSHIP AWARD

Association: __________

All Participants are invited to nominate a fellow competitor who, in their view, has best exemplified the traditional values of skill, honesty, fair play, sportsmanship and friendship during these Championships. The Award will be presented at the Awards Ceremony. Players are not allowed to vote for a member of their own team.

PERSON NOMINATED - ______________________________

PLAYING FOR TEAM - ______________________________

Please return this card to the Chief Umpire at the end of the round robin

WORLD JUNIOR WOMEN'S CURLING CHAMPIONSHIP 20____

스포츠 정신상

회원국: ________________

모든 참가자들은 이 대회 기간 중에 자신들의 관점에서 기술, 정직, 공정성, 스포츠맨 정신, 동료애와 같은 가치들을 가장 잘 보여준 상대 선수 한 명을 지명 초대합니다. 수상은 시상식에서 발표될 예정입니다. 선수들은 자신의 팀의 일원에게 투표를 할 수 없습니다.

지명 선수 - ________________________________

소속 팀 - ________________________________

이 카드는 라운드 로빈이 끝나면 심판장에게 제출해주시길 바랍니다.

WORLD JUNIOR WOMEN'S CURLING CHAMPIONSHIP 20____

스포츠 정신상

회원국: ________________

모든 참가자들은 이 대회 기간 중에 자신들의 관점에서 기술, 정직, 공정성, 스포츠맨 정신, 동료애와 같은 가치들을 가장 잘 보여준 상대 선수 한 명을 지명 초대합니다. 수상은 시상식에서 발표될 예정입니다. 선수들은 자신의 팀의 일원에게 투표를 할 수 없습니다.

지명 선수 - ________________________________

소속 팀 - ________________________________

이 카드는 라운드 로빈이 끝나면 심판장에게 제출해주시길 바랍니다.

WORLD JUNIOR WOMEN'S CURLING CHAMPIONSHIP 20____

스포츠 정신상

회원국: ________________

모든 참가자들은 이 대회 기간 중에 자신들의 관점에서 기술, 정직, 공정성, 스포츠맨 정신, 동료애와 같은 가치들을 가장 잘 보여준 상대 선수 한 명을 지명 초대합니다. 수상은 시상식에서 발표될 예정입니다. 선수들은 자신의 팀의 일원에게 투표를 할 수 없습니다.

지명 선수 - ________________________________

소속 팀 - ________________________________

이 카드는 라운드 로빈이 끝나면 심판장에게 제출해주시길 바랍니다.

WORLD JUNIOR WOMEN'S CURLING CHAMPIONSHIP 20____

스포츠 정신상

회원국: ________________

모든 참가자들은 이 대회 기간 중에 자신들의 관점에서 기술, 정직, 공정성, 스포츠맨 정신, 동료애와 같은 가치들을 가장 잘 보여준 상대 선수 한 명을 지명 초대합니다. 수상은 시상식에서 발표될 예정입니다. 선수들은 자신의 팀의 일원에게 투표를 할 수 없습니다.

지명 선수 - ________________________________

소속 팀 - ________________________________

이 카드는 라운드 로빈이 끝나면 심판장에게 제출해주시길 바랍니다.

WORLD JUNIOR MEN'S CURLING CHAMPIONSHIP 20__

SPORTSMANSHIP AWARD

Association: __________

All Participants are invited to nominate a fellow competitor who, in their view, has best exemplified the traditional values of skill, honesty, fair play, sportsmanship and friendship during these Championships. The Award will be presented at the Awards Ceremony. Players are not allowed to vote for a member of their own team.

PERSON NOMINATED - ______________________________

PLAYING FOR TEAM - ______________________________

Please return this card to the Chief Umpire at the end of the round robin

WORLD JUNIOR MEN'S CURLING CHAMPIONSHIP 20__

SPORTSMANSHIP AWARD

Association: __________

All Participants are invited to nominate a fellow competitor who, in their view, has best exemplified the traditional values of skill, honesty, fair play, sportsmanship and friendship during these Championships. The Award will be presented at the Awards Ceremony. Players are not allowed to vote for a member of their own team.

PERSON NOMINATED - ______________________________

PLAYING FOR TEAM - ______________________________

Please return this card to the Chief Umpire at the end of the round robin

WORLD JUNIOR MEN'S CURLING CHAMPIONSHIP 20__

SPORTSMANSHIP AWARD

Association: __________

All Participants are invited to nominate a fellow competitor who, in their view, has best exemplified the traditional values of skill, honesty, fair play, sportsmanship and friendship during these Championships. The Award will be presented at the Awards Ceremony. Players are not allowed to vote for a member of their own team.

PERSON NOMINATED - ______________________________

PLAYING FOR TEAM - ______________________________

Please return this card to the Chief Umpire at the end of the round robin

WORLD JUNIOR MEN'S CURLING CHAMPIONSHIP 20__

SPORTSMANSHIP AWARD

Association: __________

All Participants are invited to nominate a fellow competitor who, in their view, has best exemplified the traditional values of skill, honesty, fair play, sportsmanship and friendship during these Championships. The Award will be presented at the Awards Ceremony. Players are not allowed to vote for a member of their own team.

PERSON NOMINATED - ______________________________

PLAYING FOR TEAM - ______________________________

Please return this card to the Chief Umpire at the end of the round robin

WORLD JUNIOR WOMEN'S CURLING CHAMPIONSHIP 20____
스포츠 정신상

회원국: ____________

모든 참가자들은 이 대회 기간 중에 자신들의 관점에서 기술, 정직, 공정성, 스포츠맨 정신, 동료애와 같은 가치들을 가장 잘 보여준 상대 선수 한 명을 지명 초대합니다. 수상은 시상식에서 발표될 예정입니다. 선수들은 자신의 팀의 일원에게 투표를 할 수 없습니다.

지명 선수 - ____________________________________

소속 팀 - ____________________________________

이 카드는 라운드 로빈이 끝나면 심판장에게 제출해주시길 바랍니다.

WORLD JUNIOR WOMEN'S CURLING CHAMPIONSHIP 20____
스포츠 정신상

회원국: ____________

모든 참가자들은 이 대회 기간 중에 자신들의 관점에서 기술, 정직, 공정성, 스포츠맨 정신, 동료애와 같은 가치들을 가장 잘 보여준 상대 선수 한 명을 지명 초대합니다. 수상은 시상식에서 발표될 예정입니다. 선수들은 자신의 팀의 일원에게 투표를 할 수 없습니다.

지명 선수 - ____________________________________

소속 팀 - ____________________________________

이 카드는 라운드 로빈이 끝나면 심판장에게 제출해주시길 바랍니다.

WORLD JUNIOR WOMEN'S CURLING CHAMPIONSHIP 20____
스포츠 정신상

회원국: ____________

모든 참가자들은 이 대회 기간 중에 자신들의 관점에서 기술, 정직, 공정성, 스포츠맨 정신, 동료애와 같은 가치들을 가장 잘 보여준 상대 선수 한 명을 지명 초대합니다. 수상은 시상식에서 발표될 예정입니다. 선수들은 자신의 팀의 일원에게 투표를 할 수 없습니다.

지명 선수 - ____________________________________

소속 팀 - ____________________________________

이 카드는 라운드 로빈이 끝나면 심판장에게 제출해주시길 바랍니다.

WORLD JUNIOR WOMEN'S CURLING CHAMPIONSHIP 20____
스포츠 정신상

회원국: ____________

모든 참가자들은 이 대회 기간 중에 자신들의 관점에서 기술, 정직, 공정성, 스포츠맨 정신, 동료애와 같은 가치들을 가장 잘 보여준 상대 선수 한 명을 지명 초대합니다. 수상은 시상식에서 발표될 예정입니다. 선수들은 자신의 팀의 일원에게 투표를 할 수 없습니다.

지명 선수 - ____________________________________

소속 팀 - ____________________________________

이 카드는 라운드 로빈이 끝나면 심판장에게 제출해주시길 바랍니다.

WORLD WOMEN'S CURLING CHAMPIONSHIP 20__

FRANCES BRODIE AWARD

Association: __________

All Participants are invited to nominate a fellow competitor who, in their view, has best exemplified the traditional values of skill, honesty, fair play, sportsmanship and friendship during these Championships. The Award will be presented at the Awards Ceremony. Players are not allowed to vote for a member of their own team.

PERSON NOMINATED - ______________________________

PLAYING FOR TEAM - ______________________________

Please return this card to the Chief Umpire at the end of the round robin

WORLD WOMEN'S CURLING CHAMPIONSHIP 20__

FRANCES BRODIE AWARD

Association: __________

All Participants are invited to nominate a fellow competitor who, in their view, has best exemplified the traditional values of skill, honesty, fair play, sportsmanship and friendship during these Championships. The Award will be presented at the Awards Ceremony. Players are not allowed to vote for a member of their own team.

PERSON NOMINATED - ______________________________

PLAYING FOR TEAM - ______________________________

Please return this card to the Chief Umpire at the end of the round robin

WORLD WOMEN'S CURLING CHAMPIONSHIP 20__

FRANCES BRODIE AWARD

Association: __________

All Participants are invited to nominate a fellow competitor who, in their view, has best exemplified the traditional values of skill, honesty, fair play, sportsmanship and friendship during these Championships. The Award will be presented at the Awards Ceremony. Players are not allowed to vote for a member of their own team.

PERSON NOMINATED - ______________________________

PLAYING FOR TEAM - ______________________________

Please return this card to the Chief Umpire at the end of the round robin

WORLD WOMEN'S CURLING CHAMPIONSHIP 20__

FRANCES BRODIE AWARD

Association: __________

All Participants are invited to nominate a fellow competitor who, in their view, has best exemplified the traditional values of skill, honesty, fair play, sportsmanship and friendship during these Championships. The Award will be presented at the Awards Ceremony. Players are not allowed to vote for a member of their own team.

PERSON NOMINATED - ______________________________

PLAYING FOR TEAM - ______________________________

Please return this card to the Chief Umpire at the end of the round robin

WORLD WOMEN'S CURLING CHAMPIONSHIP 20_____
프랑스 브로디 상

회원국: ________________

모든 참가자들은 이 대회 기간 중에 자신들의 관점에서 기술, 정직, 공정성, 스포츠맨 정신, 동료애와 같은 가치들을 가장 잘 보여준 상대 선수 한 명을 지명 초대합니다. 수상은 시상식에서 발표될 예정입니다. 선수들은 자신의 팀의 일원에게 투표를 할 수 없습니다.

지명 선수 - ____

소속 팀 - ____

이 카드는 라운드 로빈이 끝나면 심판장에게 제출해주시길 바랍니다.

WORLD WOMEN'S CURLING CHAMPIONSHIP 20_____
프랑스 브로디 상

회원국: ________________

모든 참가자들은 이 대회 기간 중에 자신들의 관점에서 기술, 정직, 공정성, 스포츠맨 정신, 동료애와 같은 가치들을 가장 잘 보여준 상대 선수 한 명을 지명 초대합니다. 수상은 시상식에서 발표될 예정입니다. 선수들은 자신의 팀의 일원에게 투표를 할 수 없습니다.

지명 선수 - ____

소속 팀 - ____

이 카드는 라운드 로빈이 끝나면 심판장에게 제출해주시길 바랍니다.

WORLD WOMEN'S CURLING CHAMPIONSHIP 20_____
프랑스 브로디 상

회원국: ________________

모든 참가자들은 이 대회 기간 중에 자신들의 관점에서 기술, 정직, 공정성, 스포츠맨 정신, 동료애와 같은 가치들을 가장 잘 보여준 상대 선수 한 명을 지명 초대합니다. 수상은 시상식에서 발표될 예정입니다. 선수들은 자신의 팀의 일원에게 투표를 할 수 없습니다.

지명 선수 - ____

소속 팀 - ____

이 카드는 라운드 로빈이 끝나면 심판장에게 제출해주시길 바랍니다.

WORLD WOMEN'S CURLING CHAMPIONSHIP 20_____
프랑스 브로디 상

회원국: ________________

모든 참가자들은 이 대회 기간 중에 자신들의 관점에서 기술, 정직, 공정성, 스포츠맨 정신, 동료애와 같은 가치들을 가장 잘 보여준 상대 선수 한 명을 지명 초대합니다. 수상은 시상식에서 발표될 예정입니다. 선수들은 자신의 팀의 일원에게 투표를 할 수 없습니다.

지명 선수 - ____

소속 팀 - ____

이 카드는 라운드 로빈이 끝나면 심판장에게 제출해주시길 바랍니다.

WORLD MEN'S CURLING CHAMPIONSHIP 20__

COLLIE CAMPBELL MEMORIAL AWARD

Association: __________

All Participants are invited to nominate a fellow competitor who, in their view, has best exemplified the traditional values of skill, honesty, fair play, sportsmanship and friendship during these Championships. The Award will be presented at the Awards Ceremony. Players are not allowed to vote for a member of their own team.

PERSON NOMINATED - ________________________________

PLAYING FOR TEAM - ________________________________

Please return this card to the Chief Umpire at the end of the round robin

WORLD MEN'S CURLING CHAMPIONSHIP 20__

COLLIE CAMPBELL MEMORIAL AWARD

Association: __________

All Participants are invited to nominate a fellow competitor who, in their view, has best exemplified the traditional values of skill, honesty, fair play, sportsmanship and friendship during these Championships. The Award will be presented at the Awards Ceremony. Players are not allowed to vote for a member of their own team.

PERSON NOMINATED - ________________________________

PLAYING FOR TEAM - ________________________________

Please return this card to the Chief Umpire at the end of the round robin

WORLD MEN'S CURLING CHAMPIONSHIP 20__

COLLIE CAMPBELL MEMORIAL AWARD

Association: __________

All Participants are invited to nominate a fellow competitor who, in their view, has best exemplified the traditional values of skill, honesty, fair play, sportsmanship and friendship during these Championships. The Award will be presented at the Awards Ceremony. Players are not allowed to vote for a member of their own team.

PERSON NOMINATED - ________________________________

PLAYING FOR TEAM - ________________________________

Please return this card to the Chief Umpire at the end of the round robin

WORLD MEN'S CURLING CHAMPIONSHIP 20__

COLLIE CAMPBELL MEMORIAL AWARD

Association: __________

All Participants are invited to nominate a fellow competitor who, in their view, has best exemplified the traditional values of skill, honesty, fair play, sportsmanship and friendship during these Championships. The Award will be presented at the Awards Ceremony. Players are not allowed to vote for a member of their own team.

PERSON NOMINATED - ________________________________

PLAYING FOR TEAM - ________________________________

Please return this card to the Chief Umpire at the end of the round robin

WORLD MEN'S CURLING CHAMPIONSHIP 20____
콜리 캠벨 기념상

회원국: ______________

모든 참가자들은 이 대회 기간 중에 자신들의 관점에서 기술, 정직, 공정성, 스포츠맨 정신, 동료애와 같은 가치들을 가장 잘 보여준 상대 선수 한 명을 지명 초대합니다. 수상은 시상식에서 발표될 예정입니다. 선수들은 자신의 팀의 일원에게 투표를 할 수 없습니다.

지명 선수 - ______________________________

소속 팀 - ______________________________

이 카드는 라운드 로빈이 끝나면 심판장에게 제출해주시길 바랍니다.

WORLD MEN'S CURLING CHAMPIONSHIP 20____
콜리 캠벨 기념상

회원국: ______________

모든 참가자들은 이 대회 기간 중에 자신들의 관점에서 기술, 정직, 공정성, 스포츠맨 정신, 동료애와 같은 가치들을 가장 잘 보여준 상대 선수 한 명을 지명 초대합니다. 수상은 시상식에서 발표될 예정입니다. 선수들은 자신의 팀의 일원에게 투표를 할 수 없습니다.

지명 선수 - ______________________________

소속 팀 - ______________________________

이 카드는 라운드 로빈이 끝나면 심판장에게 제출해주시길 바랍니다.

WORLD MEN'S CURLING CHAMPIONSHIP 20____
콜리 캠벨 기념상

회원국: ______________

모든 참가자들은 이 대회 기간 중에 자신들의 관점에서 기술, 정직, 공정성, 스포츠맨 정신, 동료애와 같은 가치들을 가장 잘 보여준 상대 선수 한 명을 지명 초대합니다. 수상은 시상식에서 발표될 예정입니다. 선수들은 자신의 팀의 일원에게 투표를 할 수 없습니다.

지명 선수 - ______________________________

소속 팀 - ______________________________

이 카드는 라운드 로빈이 끝나면 심판장에게 제출해주시길 바랍니다.

WORLD MEN'S CURLING CHAMPIONSHIP 20____
콜리 캠벨 기념상

회원국: ______________

모든 참가자들은 이 대회 기간 중에 자신들의 관점에서 기술, 정직, 공정성, 스포츠맨 정신, 동료애와 같은 가치들을 가장 잘 보여준 상대 선수 한 명을 지명 초대합니다. 수상은 시상식에서 발표될 예정입니다. 선수들은 자신의 팀의 일원에게 투표를 할 수 없습니다.

지명 선수 - ______________________________

소속 팀 - ______________________________

이 카드는 라운드 로빈이 끝나면 심판장에게 제출해주시길 바랍니다.

59. COMPETITION FORMS

COMPETITION: ______________________________

DATE / LOCATION: ______________________________

ORIGINAL TEAM LINE-UP FORM

TEAM: ______________________________ MEN: ☐ WOMEN: ☐

(Delivering Order)	FIRST NAME	FAMILY NAME	L/R	TC
FOURTH				
THIRD				
SECOND				
LEAD				
ALTERNATE				

SKIP		
VICE-SKIP		

TEAM COACH			
2nd TEAM OFFICIAL			
TRANSLATOR			

SIGNATURE	
PHONE / ROOM NUMBER (IN CASE OF EMERGENCY)	

NOTE:

L/R - Indicate if the player delivers with the left or right hand.
TC – Indicate which person (1) is the Team Contact person (off the ice) for the Umpires.
For every game the order can be changed using the Game Team Line-up form.
The Original Team Line-Up will be used for the "curling history", the presentation of the team and the medal ceremony.
Only the players, team coach and the 2nd team official or translator listed on this form will be allowed access to the coaches' bench (maximum three persons).

59. 대회 양식

대회: ____________________

날짜/장소: ____________________

공식라인업 양식

팀: ____________________ 남성: ☐ 여성: ☐

딜리버리 순서	이름	성	L/R	TC
Fourth				
Third				
Second				
Lead				
후보				

스킵		
바이스 스킵		

감독			
코치			
통역사			

서명	
전화/방 번호(응급상황에 대비해)	

추신:

L/R- 선수가 왼손 투구인지 오른손 투구인지 표시하기.

TC- 심판에게 연락할 팀원(얼음 밖의)을 표시하기.

모든 게임의 선수명단은 게임 팀 라인업 양식을 사용해 바꿀 수 있다.

선발 팀 라인-업은 '컬링 역사', 팀 발표와 메달 수여식에 사용될 것이다.

오직 이 양식에 올라간 선수, 감독과 코치 또는 통역사만이 벤치를 사용할 수 있다. (최대 3명)

COMPETITION: ______________________________

DATE / LOCATION: ______________________________

ORIGINAL TEAM LINE-UP FORM WMDCC

TEAM:

	FIRST NAME	FAMILY NAME	L/R	TC
FEMALE				
MALE				

TEAM COACH				
TRANSLATOR (where required)				

SIGNATURE	
PHONE / ROOM NUMBER (IN CASE OF EMERGENCY)	

NOTE:

L/R - Indicate if the player delivers with the left or right hand.
TC – Indicate which person (1) is the Team Contact person (off the ice) for the Umpires.
The Original Team Line-Up will be used for the "curling history", the presentation of the team and the medal ceremony.
Only the team coach and translator listed on this form will be allowed access to the coaches' bench.

대회: ____

날짜/장소: ____

공식라인업 양식 WMDCC

팀: ______________________________

	이름	성	L/R	TC
여성				
남성				

코치			
통역사			

서명	
전화/방 번호(응급상황에 대비해)	

추신:

L/R- 선수가 왼손 투구인지 오른손 투구인지 표시하기.

TC- 심판에게 연락할 팀원(얼음 밖의)을 표시하기.

모든 게임의 선수명단은 게임 팀 라인업 양식을 사용해 바꿀 수 있다.

선발 팀 라인-업은 '컬링 역사', 팀 발표와 메달 수여식에 사용될 것이다.

오직 이 양식에 올라온 코치와 통역사만이 코치 벤치를 사용할 수 있다.

COMPETITION: ______________________________

DATE / LOCATION: ______________________________

GAME TEAM LINE-UP FORM

TEAM: ______________________________ MEN: ☐ WOMEN: ☐

DATE: ______________ **TIME**: ______________ **SHEET**: ______

(Delivering Order)	FIRST NAME	FAMILY NAME
FOURTH		
THIRD		
SECOND		
LEAD		
ALTERNATE		

SKIP		
VICE-SKIP		

TEAM COACH		

SIGNATURE	

NOTE:

L/R - Indicate if the player delivers with the left or right hand.
This form to be given to an Umpire 15 minutes before the start of the first pre-game practice.

대회: ______________________________

날짜/장소: ______________________________

경기라인업 양식

팀: ______________________________ 남성: ☐ 여성: ☐

날짜: ____________ 시간: ____________ 시트: ____________

딜리버리 순서	이름	성
Fourth		
Third		
Second		
Lead		
후보		

스킵		
바이스 스킵		

코치		

서명	

추신:

L/R- 선수가 왼손 투구인지 오른손 투구인지 표시하기.

이 양식은 첫 시합 연습 시작하기 15분 전에 주심에게 전달해야 한다.

COMPETITION: ____

DATE / LOCATION: ____

CHANGE OF TEAM LINE-UP FORM

TEAM: ______________________________ MEN: ☐ WOMEN: ☐

DATE: __________________ **TIME**: ______________ **SHEET**: _____

CHANGE OF LINE-UP AT THE BEGINNING OF END: ☐

(New Delivery Order)	FIRST NAME	FAMILY NAME
FOURTH		
THIRD		
SECOND		
LEAD		
ALTERNATE		

SKIP		
VICE-SKIP		

SIGNATURE	

NOTE:

L/R - Indicate if the player delivers with the left or right hand.
This form to be given to the Chief or Deputy Chief Umpire before the alternate will be allowed into the Field of Play.

대회: ______________________________

날짜/장소: ______________________________

변경라인업 양식

팀: ______________________________ 남성: ☐ 여성: ☐

날짜: ____________ 시간: ____________ 시트: ____________

시작할 때 진용 변경: ☐

변경한 순서	이름	성
Fourth		
Third		
Second		
Lead		
후보		

스킵		
바이스 스킵		

서명	

추신:

L/R- 선수가 왼손 투구인지 오른손 투구인지 표시하기.

이 양식은 후보 선수가 경기장 플레이를 허락받기 전에 주심 또는 부심에게 전달되어야 한다.

COMPETITION: ____________________

DATE / LOCATION: ____________________

LAST STONE DRAW (LSD)

DATE: ____________________ **TIME**: ____________________

SHEET: ____________ ROUND: ____________ MEN: ☐ WOMEN: ☐

Team	Player	**Last Stone Draw (LSD)**	Toss Required Yes / No	Last Stone First End (LSFE)
		cm		
		cm		

SHEET: ____________ ROUND: ____________ MEN: ☐ WOMEN: ☐

Team	Player	**Last Stone Draw (LSD)**	Toss Required Yes / No	Last Stone First End (LSFE)
		cm		
		cm		

SHEET: ____________ ROUND: ____________ MEN: ☐ WOMEN: ☐

Team	Player	**Last Stone Draw (LSD)**	Toss Required Yes / No	Last Stone First End (LSFE)
		cm		
		cm		

SHEET: ____________ ROUND: ____________ MEN: ☐ WOMEN: ☐

Team	Player	**Last Stone Draw (LSD)**	Toss Required Yes / No	Last Stone First End (LSFE)
		cm		
		cm		

SHEET: ____________ ROUND: ____________ MEN: ☐ WOMEN: ☐

Team	Player	**Last Stone Draw (LSD)**	Toss Required Yes / No	Last Stone First End (LSFE)
		cm		
		cm		

Stones so close to the Tee that they cannot be measured = 0.0 cm
Stones completely outside of the House = 185.4 cm

대회: ______________________________

날짜/장소: ______________________________

라스트스톤 드로우(LSD)

날짜: ____________________ 시간: ____________________

시트: ______________ 라운드: ______________ 남성: ☐ 여성: ☐

팀	선수	라스트스톤 드로우 (LSD)	토스 필요 여부 예/아니오	라스트스톤 퍼스트엔드(LSFE)
		cm		
		cm		

시트: ______________ 라운드: ______________ 남성: ☐ 여성: ☐

팀	선수	라스트스톤 드로우 (LSD)	토스 필요 여부 예/아니오	라스트스톤 퍼스트엔드(LSFE)
		cm		
		cm		

시트: ______________ 라운드: ______________ 남성: ☐ 여성: ☐

팀	선수	라스트스톤 드로우 (LSD)	토스 필요 여부 예/아니오	라스트스톤 퍼스트엔드(LSFE)
		cm		
		cm		

시트: ______________ 라운드: ______________ 남성: ☐ 여성: ☐

팀	선수	라스트스톤 드로우 (LSD)	토스 필요 여부 예/아니오	라스트스톤 퍼스트엔드(LSFE)
		cm		
		cm		

시트: ______________ 라운드: ______________ 남성: ☐ 여성: ☐

팀	선수	라스트스톤 드로우 (LSD)	토스 필요 여부 예/아니오	라스트스톤 퍼스트엔드(LSFE)
		cm		
		cm		

측정 불가능할 정도로 티에 가까운 스톤들 =0.0cm
완전히 하우스 밖에 있는 스톤들 =185.4cm

COMPETITION: ______________________________

DATE / LOCATION: ______________________________

DRAW SHOT CHALLENGE (DSC)

TEAM: ____________	**TEAM**: ____________	**TEAM**: ____________
Men: ☐ Women: ☐	Men: ☐ Women: ☐	Men: ☐ Women: ☐
SHEET # : ________	SHEET # : ________	SHEET # : ________
Player 1: ________ cm	Player 1: ________ cm	Player 1: ________ cm
Player 2: ________ cm	Player 2: ________ cm	Player 2: ________ cm
Player 3: ________ cm	Player 3: ________ cm	Player 3: ________ cm
Player 4: ________ cm	Player 4: ________ cm	Player 4: ________ cm
TOTAL: ________ cm	**TOTAL**: ________ cm	**TOTAL**: ________ cm
TEAM: ____________	**TEAM**: ____________	**TEAM**: ____________
Men: ☐ Women: ☐	Men: ☐ Women: ☐	Men: ☐ Women: ☐
SHEET # : ________	SHEET # : ________	SHEET # : ________
Player 1: ________ cm	Player 1: ________ cm	Player 1: ________ cm
Player 2: ________ cm	Player 2: ________ cm	Player 2: ________ cm
Player 3: ________ cm	Player 3: ________ cm	Player 3: ________ cm
Player 4: ________ cm	Player 4: ________ cm	Player 4: ________ cm
TOTAL: ________ cm	**TOTAL**: ________ cm	**TOTAL**: ________ cm

Stones so close to the Tee that they cannot be measured = 0.0 cm
Stones completely outside of the House = 185.4 cm
If teams have identical cumulative scores, the team with the best single result, and if that is the same the second best result, etc. will be ranked higher.

Umpire: ______________________________ **Date:** ______________

대회: ____________________

날짜/장소: ____________________

드로우 샷 챌린지(DSC)

팀: ______ 남자: ☐ 여자: ☐ 시트#: ______ 선수1: ______ cm 선수2: ______ cm 선수3: ______ cm 선수4: ______ cm **TOTAL**: ______ cm	**팀**: ______ 남자: ☐ 여자: ☐ 시트#: ______ 선수1: ______ cm 선수2: ______ cm 선수3: ______ cm 선수4: ______ cm **TOTAL**: ______ cm	**팀**: ______ 남자: ☐ 여자: ☐ 시트#: ______ 선수1: ______ cm 선수2: ______ cm 선수3: ______ cm 선수4: ______ cm **TOTAL**: ______ cm
팀: ______ 남자: ☐ 여자: ☐ 시트#: ______ 선수1: ______ cm 선수2: ______ cm 선수3: ______ cm 선수4: ______ cm **TOTAL**: ______ cm	**팀**: ______ 남자: ☐ 여자: ☐ 시트#: ______ 선수1: ______ cm 선수2: ______ cm 선수3: ______ cm 선수4: ______ cm **TOTAL**: ______ cm	**팀**: ______ 남자: ☐ 여자: ☐ 시트#: ______ 선수1: ______ cm 선수2: ______ cm 선수3: ______ cm 선수4: ______ cm **TOTAL**: ______ cm

측정 불가능할 정도로 티에 가까운 스톤들 =0.0cm

완전히 하우스 밖에 있는 스톤들 =185.4cm

만약 팀의 누적 점수가 같거나 팀 내 최고 결과마저 같다면 두 번째 좋은 결과가 더 높은 순위가 된다.

심판: ____________________ 날짜: ____________________

COMPETITION: ______________________________

DATE / LOCATION: ______________________________

DRAW SHOT CHALLENGE(DSC) SUMMARY FORM

Stones so close to the Tee that they cannot be measured = 0.0 cm
Stones completely outside of the House = 185.4 cm

TEAM						
LSD Game # 1						
LSD Game # 2						
LSD Game # 3						
LSD Game # 4						
LSD Game # 5						
LSD Game # 6						
LSD Game # 7						
LSD Game # 8						
LSD Game # 9						
LSD Game # 10						
LSD Game # 11						
TOTAL						
Result to deduct =						
FINAL TOTAL						
AVERAGE = DSC						

TEAM						
LSD Game # 1						
LSD Game # 2						
LSD Game # 3						
LSD Game # 4						
LSD Game # 5						
LSD Game # 6						
LSD Game # 7						
LSD Game # 8						
LSD Game # 9						
LSD Game # 10						
LSD Game # 11						
TOTAL						
Result to deduct =						
FINAL TOTAL						
AVERAGE = DSC						

Ranked # 1		Ranked # 5		Ranked # 9	
Ranked # 2		Ranked # 6		Ranked # 10	
Ranked # 3		Ranked # 7		Ranked # 11	
Ranked # 4		Ranked # 8		Ranked # 12	

Umpire: ______________________________ **Date:** ____________________

대회: ______________________________

날짜/장소: ______________________________

드로우 샷 챌린지(DSC) 요약 양식

측정 불가능할 정도로 티에 가까운 스톤들 =0.0㎝
완전히 하우스 밖에 있는 스톤들 =185.4㎝

팀						
LSD 게임#1						
LSD 게임#2						
LSD 게임#3						
LSD 게임#4						
LSD 게임#5						
LSD 게임#6						
LSD 게임#7						
LSD 게임#8						
LSD 게임#9						
LSD 게임#10						
LSD 게임#11						
TOTAL						
결과 공제						
FINAL TOTAL						
평균=DSC						
팀						
LSD 게임#1						
LSD 게임#2						
LSD 게임#3						
LSD 게임#4						
LSD 게임#5						
LSD 게임#6						
LSD 게임#7						
LSD 게임#8						
LSD 게임#9						
LSD 게임#10						
LSD 게임#11						
TOTAL						
결과 공제						
FINAL TOTAL						
평균=DSC						

순위 #1		순위 #5		순위 #9	
순위 #2		순위 #6		순위 #10	
순위 #3		순위 #7		순위 #11	
순위 #4		순위 #8		순위 #12	

심판: ______________________ 날짜: ______________________

COMPETITION: ____________________

DATE / LOCATION: ____________________

ON-ICE OFFICIAL'S SCORECARD

SHEET: __________ MEN: ☐ WOMEN: ☐

DATE: ____________________ **TIME**: ____________________

START TIME: ____________________ **FINISH TIME**: ____________________

TEAM -														
ENDS	LSFE	1	2	3	4	5	6	7	8	9	10	11	12	TOTAL
TEAM -														

TEAM: __________

Team Time-Out		End #	Stone #
	1st		
	2nd	1st Extra	
	3rd	2nd Extra	

TEAM: __________

Team Time-Out		End #	Stone #
	1st		
	2nd	1st Extra	
	3rd	2nd Extra	

Hog Line Violations		End #	Stone #
	1st		
	2nd		
	3rd		
	4th		

Hog Line Violations		End #	Stone #
	1st		
	2nd		
	3rd		
	4th		

Other Violations	Type	End #	Stone #

Other Violations	Type	End #	Stone #

SKIP NAME: ____________________ **SIGNATURE**: ____________________

SKIP NAME: ____________________ **SIGNATURE**: ____________________

ON-ICE OFFICIAL: ____________________ **SIGNATURE**: ____________________

대회: ______________________________

날짜/장소: ______________________________

얼음 위 심판의 점수카드

시트: ______________ 남성: ☐ 여성: ☐

날짜: ______________ 시간: ______________

시작 시간: ______________ 종료 시간: ______________

팀-														
ENDS	LSFE	1	2	3	4	5	6	7	8	9	10	11	12	TOTAL
팀-														

팀: ______________ 팀: ______________

팀 타임아웃		End#	스톤#
	1st		
	2nd	1st 추가	
	3rd	2nd 추가	

팀 타임아웃		End#	스톤#
	1st		
	2nd	1st 추가	
	3rd	2nd 추가	

호그 라인 위반		End#	스톤#
	1st		
	2nd		
	3rd		
	4th		

호그 라인 위반		End#	스톤#
	1st		
	2nd		
	3rd		
	4th		

다른 위반	유형	End#	스톤#

다른 위반	유형	End#	스톤#

스킵 이름: ______________ 날짜: ______________

스킵 이름: ______________ 날짜: ______________

얼음 위 심판: ______________ 날짜: ______________

COMPETITION: ______________________________

DATE / LOCATION: ______________________________

GAME TIMING FORM

DATE: ____________________ DRAW: ____________________

SHEET: ____________________ START-TME: ____________________

Team: (Dark)		
Actual Clock Time at the completion of end:		Time-Out
End 1		
End 2		
End 3		
End 4		
End 5		
End 6		
End 7		
End 8		
End 9		
End 10		
Extra-End		
Extra-End		

Team: (Light)		
Actual Clock Time at the completion of end:		Time-Out
End 1		
End 2		
End 3		
End 4		
End 5		
End 6		
End 7		
End 8		
End 9		
End 10		
Extra-End		
Extra-End		

Notes: ______________________________

____

____

____

Timing Official: ____________________ Signature: ____________________

대회: ____________________

날짜/장소: ____________________

경기 시간 양식

날짜: ____________________ 드로우: ____________________

시작 시간: ____________________ 종료 시간: ____________________

팀 : (어두운색)		
실제 경기 종료 시간		타임아웃
End 1		
End 2		
End 3		
End 4		
End 5		
End 6		
End 7		
End 8		
End 9		
End 10		
Extra End		
Extra End		

팀 : (어두운색)		
실제 경기 종료 시간		타임아웃
End 1		
End 2		
End 3		
End 4		
End 5		
End 6		
End 7		
End 8		
End 9		
End 10		
Extra End		
Extra End		

노트: ____________________

타임 심판: ____________________ 서명: ____________________

COMPETITION: ____________________

DATE / LOCATION: ____________________

WHEELCHAIR GAME TIMING FORM

DATE: ____________________ DRAW: ____________________

SHEET: __________CLOCKS SET AT **68 Minutes** START-TME: ____________________

Team: (Dark)		
Actual Clock Time at the completion of:		Time-out
End 1		
End 2		
End 3		
End 4		
End 5		
End 6		
End 7		
End 8		
Extra End		
Extra End		

Team: (Light)		
Actual Clock Time at the completion of:		Time-out
End 1		
End 2		
End 3		
End 4		
End 5		
End 6		
End 7		
End 8		
Extra End		
Extra End		

(10 minutes per team for each extra end)

Notes: ____________________

Timing Official: ____________________ Signature: ____________________

대회: ______________________________

날짜/장소: ______________________________

휠체어 경기 시간 양식

날짜: ____________________ 드로우: ____________________

시트: ______________ 시계를 68분에 맞춤 시작 시간: ______________

팀 : (어두운색)		
실제 경기 종료 시간		타임아웃
End 1		
End 2		
End 3		
End 4		
End 5		
End 6		
End 7		
End 8		
End 9		
End 10		

Extra End		
Extra End		

팀 : (어두운색)		
실제 경기 종료 시간		타임아웃
End 1		
End 2		
End 3		
End 4		
End 5		
End 6		
End 7		
End 8		
End 9		
End 10		

Extra End		
Extra End		

(각각의 엑스트라 엔드마다 10분씩)

노트: ______________________________

타임 심판: ____________________ 서명: ____________________

COMPETITION: ______________________________

DATE / LOCATION: ______________________________

VIOLATION CHART

Draw	Team	Player	End	Stone	Violation	Action

D – Dumping
H – Hog Line
WP – Wrong Position
WS – Wrong Sweeper
BP – Body Prints
O – Other

PWS – Played Wrong Stone
M – Movement
RP – Readiness to Play
FGZ – Free Guard Zone
EA – Equipment Abuse

SP – Snow Ploughing
POT – Played Out Of Turn
TS – Touched Stone
T – Timing
DC – Dress Code

Observer: ______________________ Signature: ______________________

대회: ______________________________

날짜/장소: ______________________________

위반 차트

드로우	팀	선수	엔드	스톤	위반 내용	행동

D-덤핑
H-호그 라인
WP-잘못된 포지션
WS-잘못된 스위퍼
BP-인체 흔적
O-그 외

PWS-잘못 위치된 스톤
M-무브먼트
RP-플레이할 준비
FGZ-프리가드 존
EA-장비 남용

SP-제설차
POT-차례위반
TS-스톤터치
T-타이밍
DC-드레스코드

관찰자: ______________________ 서명: ______________________

COMPETITION: ____________________

DATE / LOCATION: ____________________

PLAY-OFF GAME INFORMATION

MEN ☐ WOMEN ☐ TEAM ☐

GAME BEING PLAYED: ____________________

GAME INFORMATION:

DATE OF GAME: ____________________

GAME TIME: ____________________

GAME SHEET: ____________________

TEAMS: ____________________ V ____________________

LAST STONE 1ST END: ____________________

STONE SELECTION: DARK: __________ LIGHT: __________

PRACTICE TIME(S): ____________________

____

MINIMUM ENDS TO BE PLAYED: __________

ANY SPECIAL PRE- OR POST-GAME ACTIVITIES: ____________________

____

END OF THE GAME PROCEDURES: ____________________

____

대회: ____________________

날짜/장소: ____________________

플레이오프 게임 정보

남자: ☐ 여자: ☐ 팀: ☐

플레이된 게임: ____________________

게임 정보

게임 날짜: ____________________

게임 시트: ____________________

팀: ____________________ V ____________________

라스트 스톤 1st END: ____________________

스톤 선택: 어두운색: ____________________ 밝은색: ____________________

연습 팀: ____________________

____

플레이되어야 하는 최소 엔드: ____________________

특별한 전후 게임 활동: ____________________

____

게임 절차의 엔드: ____________________

____

PAGE PLAY-OFF GAMES SUMMARY:

1 v 2 ____________________ v____________________

1st Choice: ____________________ Day & Time: ________________________

Ice: ______________ Last stone 1st end:___________________

STONE COLOR: RED______________________________ YELLOW_____________________________

---

3 v 4 ____________________ v____________________

1st Choice: ____________________ Day & Time: ________________________

Ice: ______________ Last stone 1st end:_____________________

STONE COLOR: RED______________________________ YELLOW_____________________________

SEMI-FINAL ____________________ v____________________

1st Choice: ____________________ Day & Time: ____________________________

Ice: ______________ Last stone 1st end: _______________________

STONE COLOR: RED______________________________ YELLOW_____________________________

BRONZE ____________________ v____________________

1st Choice: ____________________ Day & Time: ____________________________

Ice: ______________ Last stone 1st end:_______________________

STONE COLOR: RED______________________________ YELLOW_____________________________

GOLD ____________________ v______________________

1st Choice: ____________________ Day & Time: ___________________________

Ice: ______________ Last stone 1st end: ______________________

STONE COLOR: RED______________________________ YELLOW____________________________

플레이오프 게임 요약

1V2 ______________________ V ______________________

1st 선택: ______________________ 날짜 / 시간: ______________________

얼음: ______________________ 라스트 스톤 1st 엔드: ______________________

스톤 색: 빨강 ______________________ 노랑 ______________________

3V4 ______________________ V ______________________

1st 선택: ______________________ 날짜 / 시간: ______________________

얼음: ______________________ 라스트 스톤 1st 엔드: ______________________

스톤 색: 빨강 ______________________ 노랑 ______________________

SEMI-FINAL ______________________ V ______________________

1st 선택: ______________________ 날짜 / 시간: ______________________

얼음: ______________________ 라스트 스톤 1st 엔드: ______________________

스톤 색: 빨강 ______________________ 노랑 ______________________

BRONZE ______________________ V ______________________

1st 선택: ______________________ 날짜 / 시간: ______________________

얼음: ______________________ 라스트 스톤 1st 엔드: ______________________

스톤 색: 빨강 ______________________ 노랑 ______________________

GOLD ______________________ V ______________________

1st 선택: ______________________ 날짜 / 시간: ______________________

얼음: ______________________ 라스트 스톤 1st 엔드: ______________________

스톤 색: 빨강 ______________________ 노랑 ______________________

COMPETITION: ______________________________

DATE / LOCATION: ______________________________

STONE SELECTION

TEAM: ______________________________ MEN: ☐ WOMEN: ☐

GAME: ______________________________

DATE: ______________ **TIME:** ______________ **ICE:** __________

STONE COLOUR: ______________________________

SELECTED FROM SHEETS: ______ or ______ or ______ or ______ or ______

Stone Selection	From Sheet	Stone Number
1.		
2.		
3.		
4.		
5.		
6.		
7.		
8.		
Reserve		

TEAM'S SIGNATURE: ______________________________

NOTE:

The Chief Umpire will designate the sheets from which the stones may be selected.
Stone handles may not be changed from one stone to another stone.
This form has to be handed to the Chief Umpire a minimum of 15 minutes prior to the start of the first pre-game practice.

STONES CHECKED BEFORE START OF PRE-GAME PRACTICE

TEAM'S SIGNATURE: ______________________________

대회: ____

날짜/장소: ____

스톤 선택

팀: ____________________ 남성: ☐ 여성: ☐

게임 : ____

날짜: ______________ 시간: ______________ 얼음: ______________

스톤 색: ____

시트 선택: __________ or __________ or __________ or __________ or __________

스톤 선택	시트	스톤 넘버
1.		
2.		
3.		
4.		
5.		
6.		
7.		
8.		
reserve		

팀 서명: ______________________________

노트:

주심은 어떤 스톤이 선택될지 시트를 결정한다.
스톤 핸들은 한 스톤으로부터 다른 스톤으로 바뀔 수 없다.
이 서식은 적어도 첫 연습게임 15분 전에 주심에게 전달해야 한다.

연습게임 시작 전 스톤이 체크됨

팀 서명: ______________________________

COMPETITION: ______________________________

DATE / LOCATION: ______________________________

STONE SELECTION WMDCC

TEAM: ______________________________

GAME: ______________________________

DATE: ____________ **TIME:** ____________ **ICE:** ________

STONE COLOUR: ______________________________

SELECTED FROM SHEETS: ______ or ______ or ______ or ______ or ______

Stone Selection	From Sheet	Stone Number
1.		
2.		
3.		
4.		
5.		
6.		

TEAM'S SIGNATURE: ______________________________

NOTE:

The Chief Umpire will designate the sheets from which the stones may be selected.
Stone handles may not be changed from one stone to another stone.
This form has to be handed to the Chief Umpire a minimum of 15 minutes prior to the start of the first pre-game practice.

STONES CHECKED BEFORE START OF PRE-GAME PRACTICE

TEAM'S SIGNATURE: ______________________________

대회: ____________________

날짜/장소: ____________________

스톤 선택

팀: ____________________

게임 : ____________________

날짜: __________ 시간: __________ 얼음: __________

스톤 색: ____________________

시트 선택: ________ or ________ or ________ or ________ or ________

스톤 선택	시트	스톤 넘버
1.		
2.		
3.		
4.		
5.		
6.		

팀 서명: ____________________

노트:

주심은 어떤 스톤이 선택될지 시트를 결정한다.
스톤 핸들은 한 스톤으로부터 다른 스톤으로 바뀔 수 없다.
이 서식은 적어도 첫 연습게임 15분 전에 주심에게 전달해야 한다.

연습게임 시작 전 스톤이 체크됨

팀 서명: ____________________

COMPETITION: ____

DATE / LOCATION: ____

STONE FEEDBACK FORM

The World Curling Federation is currently working to optimise the stone sets which are used at their Events. To be able to try and get the best possible sets, the feedback of the participating teams is requested and will be treated in the strictest confidence.

TEAM: ________________________________

Sheet	Stone #	Colour	Problems with a stone: please give as much detail as possible

THANK YOU

Please return to:
Chief Umpire or WCF Technical Delegate
or Keith Wendorf or Richard Harding

대회: ______________________________

날짜/장소: ______________________________

스톤 피드백 서식

세계컬링연맹은 현재 이벤트에 사용되는 스톤 세트를 최적화하기 위해 노력하고 있다. 시도하고 최상의 세트를 얻을 수 있으려면, 참가 팀의 피드백이 요구되고 엄격한 비밀로 취급된다.

팀: ______________________________

시트	스톤	색깔	스톤의 결함: 가능한 자세히 기록

감사합니다

주심이나 WCT 기술 대표
혹은 Keith Wedorf나 Richard Harding
에게 제출해 주십시오

COMPETITION: ______________________________

DATE / LOCATION: ______________________________

TEAM PLAYING UNIFORMS

MEN: ☐ WOMEN: ☐

TEAM	Colour of DARK Jacket	Colour of DARK Shirt	Colour of LIGHT Jacket	Colour of LIGHT Shirt

Umpire: ______________________________ Date: ______________________________

대회: ____________________

날짜/장소: ____________________

팀 경기 유니폼

남성: ☐ 여성: ☐

팀	어두운 재킷	어두운 셔츠	밝은 재킷	밝은 셔츠

심판: ____________________ 날짜: ____________________

COMPETITION: ______________________________

DATE / LOCATION: ______________________________

ORDER OF DELIVERY IN WMDCC

END	DARK STONES (RED)	LIGHT STONES (YELLOW)
1		
2		
3		
4		
5		
6		
7		
8		
9		
10		

Mark **M** = Male
Mark **F** = Female

Umpire: ______________________ Date: ______________________

대회: ______________________________

날짜/장소: ______________________________

WMDCC의 오더 순서

엔드	어두운 스톤(빨강)	밝은 스톤(노랑)
1		
2		
3		
4		
5		
6		
7		
8		
9		
10		

M표식 = 남성
F표식 = 여성

심판: ______________________ 날짜: ______________________

Wheelchair - Stone Selection					
TEAM			TEAM		
	R/L	RED		R/L	YELLOW
1st Player Stone - 1			1st Player Stone - 1		
1st Player Stone - 2			1st Player Stone - 2		
2nd Player Stone - 1			2nd Player Stone - 1		
2nd Player Stone - 2			2nd Player Stone - 2		
3rd Player Stone - 1			3rd Player Stone - 1		
3rd Player Stone - 2			3rd Player Stone - 2		
4th Player Stone - 1			4th Player Stone - 1		
4th Player Stone - 2			4th Player Stone - 2		

휠체어-스톤 선택					
팀			팀		
	R/L	빨강		R/L	노랑
첫 번째 선수 스톤-1			첫 번째 선수 스톤-1		
첫 번째 선수 스톤-2			첫 번째 선수 스톤-2		
두 번째 선수 스톤-1			두 번째 선수 스톤-1		
두 번째 선수 스톤-2			두 번째 선수 스톤-2		
세 번째 선수 스톤-1			세 번째 선수 스톤-1		
세 번째 선수 스톤-2			세 번째 선수 스톤-2		
네 번째 선수 스톤-1			네 번째 선수 스톤-1		
네 번째 선수 스톤-2			네 번째 선수 스톤-2		

EVENT: ______________________________

OFFICIATING REPORT SHEET

GENDER & DRAW:	
SHEET:	
NAME OF UMPIRE/OFFICIAL:	

	RED STONES	**YELLOW STONES**
TEAM		
LSD		
LAST STONE FIRST END		
FINAL SCORE		
NUMBER OF ENDS PLAYED		
TEAM TIME OUT (end & stone #)		
TIME REMAINING END OF GAME		
MEASURES/DECISIONS (include whether FGZ, biter, shot, 2nd shot, etc.)		
OFFICIAL'S TIME OUTS (reason + end & stone #)		
HOGLINE VIOLATIONS (end & stone #)		
FGZ VIOLATIONS (end & stone #)		
HANDLE MALFUNCTION (end & stone # with 'outcome')		
TOUCHED RUNNING STONE (end & stone # with 'outcome')		
DISPLACED STATIONARY STONE (end & stone # with 'outcome')		
WRONG COLOUR DELIVERED (end & stone # with 'outcome')		
DRESS CODE VIOLATIONS		
OTHER RULINGS/ COMMENTS/INCIDENTS (end & stone # if applicable)		

경기: ______________________________

공식 레포트 시트

성별&드로우:			
시트:			
심판/주심 이름			
	빨간 스톤		**노란 스톤**
팀			
LSD			
라스트 스톤 퍼스트 엔드			
최종 점수			
엔드 플레이어의 넘버			
팀 타임아웃(엔드&스톤)			
게임의 남은 엔드			
측정/결정			
심판의 타임아웃			
호그 라인 위반			
FGZ 위반			
핸들 고장			
스톤 터치			
잘못 위치된 스톤			
드레스코드 위반			
다른 판정/코멘트/사건 (엔드 & 스톤 #)			

EVENT: ______________________________

OFFICIATING SUMMARY SHEET

	NUMBER	DETAIL
MEASURES (include whether FGZ, biter, shot, 2nd shot, etc.) & DECISION		___ v ___ - draw # - end - stone
HOGLINE VIOLATIONS		
FGZ VIOLATIONS		
TOUCHED RUNNING STONE		
DISPLACED STATIONARY STONE		
WRONG COLOUR THROWN		
DRESS CODE VIOLATIONS		___ v ___ - draw # - end - athlete
HANDLE MALFUNCTION		___ v ___ - draw # - end - stone # colour - outcome:

이벤트: ____________________

공식 레포트 시트

	넘버		디테일
측정(FGZ, biter, shot, 2nd shot 등 포함)& 결과			v -드로우# -엔드-스톤
호그 라인 위반			
FGZ 위반			
스톤 터치			
잘못 위치된 스톤			
잘못 던져진 스톤 색깔			
드레스 코드 위반			v -드로우# -엔드-선수
핸들 불량			v -드로우# -엔드-스톤#색깔-결과

WORLD CURLING FEDERATION

SPECIAL MEETING

The World Curling Federation asks all interested team and national coaches, team leaders, etc. to attend a special meeting to discuss ______________________________

We would appreciate hearing your ideas and comments.

Date: ______________________________

Location: ______________________________

Attending: ______________________________

____

____

WORLD CURLING FEDERATION

특별한 만남

세계컬링연맹은 모든 팀들, 코치들, 팀 리더 등에게 ______________________________ __________를 논의하기 위한 특별한 만남을 요구한다.

우리는 당신들의 생각과 비판을 듣는 것에 대해 감사할 것이다.

날짜: ____

장소: ____

참석자: ____

____

____

COMPETITION: ____________________

DATE / LOCATION: ____________________

EVENING PRACTICE SCHEDULE (PRE-ALLOCATED)

Date	Time	Sheet A	Sheet B	Sheet C	Sheet D
	0-10 min.				
	10-20 min.				
	20-30 min.				
	30-40 min.				
	40-50 min.				
	50-60 min.				
	0-10 min.				
	10-20 min.				
	20-30 min.				
	30-40 min.				
	40-50 min.				
	50-60 min.				
	0-10 min.				
	10-20 min.				
	20-30 min.				
	30-40 min.				
	40-50 min.				
	50-60 min.				
	0-10 min.				
	10-20 min.				
	20-30 min.				
	30-40 min.				
	40-50 min.				
	50-60 min.				
	0-10 min.				
	10-20 min.				
	20-30 min.				
	30-40 min.				
	40-50 min.				
	50-60 min.				

대회: ______________________________

날짜/장소: ______________________________

야간 연습 일정
(할당되기 전)

날짜	시간	A석	B석	C석	D석
	0-10분				
	10-20분				
	20-30분				
	30-40분				
	40-50분				
	50-60분				
	0-10분				
	10-20분				
	20-30분				
	30-40분				
	40-50분				
	50-60분				
	0-10분				
	10-20분				
	20-30분				
	30-40분				
	40-50분				
	50-60분				
	0-10분				
	10-20분				
	20-30분				
	30-40분				
	40-50분				
	50-60분				
	0-10분				
	10-20분				
	20-30분				
	30-40분				
	40-50분				
	50-60분				

COMPETITION: ______________________________________

DATE / LOCATION: __________________________________

EVENING PRACTICE - GUIDELINES (PRE-ALLOCATED)

First practice session starts approx. 5 minutes after the end of the last game of the day.

1. Each practice session is to be used only by the team to whom it has been assigned.

2. If a session is not being used, the next team assigned to that sheet may use that time slot instead of the one to which they were originally assigned.

3. Teams may use the sheets only for the number of times they will play the next day – if they play once, they will have only one practice sessions even if there are sessions to which no team is assigned.

4. If a team does not want to use their practice session(s), please inform the officials.

대회: ______________________________

날짜/장소: ______________________________

야간 연습 지침서
(할당되기 전)

첫 번째 연습 시간은 그날 마지막 게임 종료 후 약 5분간 시작한다.

1. 각 연습 시간은 할당되어 있는 팀에 의해서만 사용된다.

2. 만약 연습 시간이 사용되지 않은 경우, 그 시트에 할당된 다음 팀은 원래 할당된 팀 대신에 그 시간을 사용할 수도 있다.

3. 팀은 그들이 다음날 연습 횟수에 대해서만 시트를 사용할 수 있다. 그들이 만약 한번 연습한다면, 그들은 할당된 시간이 있다 하더라도 한 번의 연습 시간을 가질 것이다.

4. 팀이 연습 시간을 사용하지 않는 경우, 임원에게 알려주어야 한다.

COMPETITION: ____________________

DATE / LOCATION: ____________________

PROCEDURE

EVENING PRACTICE DURING ROUND ROBIN

Start time:

- Approximately 5 minutes after the last game of the day, as soon as the Ice Technician finishes cleaning and pebbling the slide paths.
- Only during the round robin portion of the draw. For teams in tie-breakers or playoff games, the practice times will be decided by the Chief Umpire.

Practice Length:

- 4 sessions - 15 minutes each (10 minutes for Mixed Doubles).

Ice access criteria:

- The only persons permitted in the Field of Play for these practices will be the players, the team coach, and a maximum of one other team official or translator (maximum of 7 people), all in proper uniform.
- No person may participate in more than 2 sessions per evening.

Practice schedule:

- Posted by the Chief Umpire at ______ hrs.

At ______ hrs:

- Teams may reserve 1 session on any sheet.
- Teams may reserve a combined men and women's session, but this joint practice will count as one full training session for both genders.

At ______ hrs:

- Teams may reserve a 2nd session.
- No team may practice on the same sheet twice on the same evening.
- An Association may not reserve 2 consecutive sessions on the same sheet.

At ______ hrs:

- Reservation list comes down and no more sheets can be booked.

Team Penalty for failure to use a reserved practice session:

Reservations for that team may not be made until ______ hrs each day.

대회: ____

날짜/장소: ____

절차
리그전이 진행될 동안의 야간 연습

시작 시간:

- 그날 마지막 게임 종료 후 거의 5분간, 얼음담당자는 슬라이드 경로의 청소와 페블링을 마친다.
- 리그전이 무승부일 때. 연장전이나 결승전을 치르는 팀에게 주어지는 연습 시간은 최고 심판에 의해 결정된다.

연습 시간:

- 4번 - 각각 15분 (믹스 더블은 10분)

얼음 접근 조건:

- 이러한 연습에서 경기장에 들어올 수 있는 유일한 사람은 단복을 입은 선수, 코치, 팀의 관계자나 통역사 (최대 7명)이다.
- 저녁마다 2번 이상의 연습에 참여할 수 있는 선수는 없다.

연습 일정:

- ______________시에 심판장에 의해 게시된다.

______________시:

- 팀은 시트에 하나의 시간을 예약할 수 있다.
- 팀은 남자와 여자의 시간을 예약할 수 있지만 공동 연습은 남녀 모두에 대한 하나의 전체 시간으로 간주된다.

______________시:

- 팀은 두 번째 시간을 예약할 수 있다.
- 팀은 같은 날 저녁에 같은 시트를 두 번 예약할 수 없다.
- 협회는 같은 시트에 연속으로 2번 예약할 수 없다.

______________시:

- 예약 목록이 결정되면 더 이상 시트를 예약할 수 없다.

예약된 연습 시간을 사용하지 않아 발생한 문제에 대한 팀의 불이익:
그 팀의 예약은 매일 ______________시까지 이루어질 수 없다.

COMPETITION: ______________________ DATE: ______________

TIME	SHEET A	SHEET B	SHEET C	SHEET D
SESSION # 1 START: 5 minutes after the end of the last game	Men ☐ Women ☐ **TEAM:**	Men ☐ Women ☐ **TEAM:**	Men ☐ Women ☐ **TEAM:**	Men ☐ Women ☐ **TEAM:**
SESSION # 2 START: 20 minutes after the end of the last game	Men ☐ Women ☐ **TEAM:**	Men ☐ Women ☐ **TEAM:**	Men ☐ Women ☐ **TEAM:**	Men ☐ Women ☐ **TEAM:**
SESSION # 3 START: 35 minutes after the end of the last game	Men ☐ Women ☐ **TEAM:**	Men ☐ Women ☐ **TEAM:**	Men ☐ Women ☐ **TEAM:**	Men ☐ Women ☐ **TEAM:**
SESSION # 4 START: 50 minutes after the end of the last game	Men ☐ Women ☐ **TEAM:**	Men ☐ Women ☐ **TEAM:**	Men ☐ Women ☐ **TEAM:**	Men ☐ Women ☐ **TEAM:**

Each practice session is 15 minutes. Please indicate your Association (3 letter code) as well as Men and/or Women.

대회: ______________________ 날짜: ______________

시간	시트A	시트B	시트C	시트D
세션#1 시작: 마지막 게임 종료 후 5분	남자□ 여자□ 팀 :	남자□ 여자□ 팀 :	남자□ 여자□ 팀 :	남자□ 여자□ 팀 :
세션#2 시작: 마지막 게임 종료 후 20분	남자□ 여자□ 팀 :	남자□ 여자□ 팀 :	남자□ 여자□ 팀 :	남자□ 여자□ 팀 :
세션#3 시작: 마지막 게임 종료 후 35분	남자□ 여자□ 팀 :	남자□ 여자□ 팀 :	남자□ 여자□ 팀 :	남자□ 여자□ 팀 :
세션#4 시작: 마지막 게임 종료 후 50분	남자□ 여자□ 팀 :	남자□ 여자□ 팀 :	남자□ 여자□ 팀 :	남자□ 여자□ 팀 :

각 연습 시간은 15분이다. 남자/여자뿐만 아니라 협회(3문자코드)를 표시해주시기 바란다.

COMPETITION: ____________________ DATE: ____________

TIME	SHEET A	SHEET B	SHEET C	SHEET D	SHEET E
SESSION # 1 START: 5 minutes after the end of the last game	Men ☐ Women ☐ **TEAM:**	Men ☐ Women ☐ **TEAM:**	Men ☐ Women ☐ **TEAM:**	Men ☐ Women ☐ **TEAM:**	Men ☐ Women ☐ **TEAM:**
SESSION # 2 START: 20 minutes after the end of the last game	Men ☐ Women ☐ **TEAM:**	Men ☐ Women ☐ **TEAM:**	Men ☐ Women ☐ **TEAM:**	Men ☐ Women ☐ **TEAM:**	Men ☐ Women ☐ **TEAM:**
SESSION # 3 START: 35 minutes after the end of the last game	Men ☐ Women ☐ **TEAM:**	Men ☐ Women ☐ **TEAM:**	Men ☐ Women ☐ **TEAM:**	Men ☐ Women ☐ **TEAM:**	Men ☐ Women ☐ **TEAM:**
SESSION # 4 START: 50 minutes after the end of the last game	Men ☐ Women ☐ **TEAM:**	Men ☐ Women ☐ **TEAM:**	Men ☐ Women ☐ **TEAM:**	Men ☐ Women ☐ **TEAM:**	Men ☐ Women ☐ **TEAM:**

Each practice session is 15 minutes. Please indicate your Association (3 letter code) as well as Men and/or Women.

대회: ______________________ 날짜: ______________

시간	시트A	시트B	시트C	시트D	시트E
세션#1 시작: 마지막 게임 종료 후 5분	남자□ 여자□ 팀 :	남자□ 여자□ 팀 :	남자□ 여자□ 팀 :	남자□ 여자□ 팀 :	남자□ 여자□ 팀 :
세션#2 시작: 마지막 게임 종료 후 20분	남자□ 여자□ 팀 :	남자□ 여자□ 팀 :	남자□ 여자□ 팀 :	남자□ 여자□ 팀 :	남자□ 여자□ 팀 :
세션#3 시작: 마지막 게임 종료 후 35분	남자□ 여자□ 팀 :	남자□ 여자□ 팀 :	남자□ 여자□ 팀 :	남자□ 여자□ 팀 :	남자□ 여자□ 팀 :
세션#4 시작: 마지막 게임 종료 후 50분	남자□ 여자□ 팀 :	남자□ 여자□ 팀 :	남자□ 여자□ 팀 :	남자□ 여자□ 팀 :	남자□ 여자□ 팀 :

각 연습 시간은 15분이다. 남자/여자뿐만 아니라 협회(3문자코드)를 표시해주시기 바란다.

COMPETITION: ____________________

DATE: ____________________ TIME: ____________________

Ice	Team	Player	End 1	End 2	End 3	End 4	End 5	End 6	End 7	End 8	End 9	End 10	End 11	End 12	Score
		1.													
		2.													
		3.													
		4.													
		1.													
		2.													
		3.													
		4.													

Ice	Team	Player	End 1	End 2	End 3	End 4	End 5	End 6	End 7	End 8	End 9	End 10	End 11	End 12	Score
		1.													
		2.													
		3.													
		4.													
		1.													
		2.													
		3.													
		4.													

OK - ✓ CLOSE - / HOG LINE VIOLATION - X NOT PLAYED - O

OFFICIAL'S NAME: ____________________ SIGNATURE: ____________________

대회: ______________________________

날짜: ______________________________ 시간: ______________________________

Ice	팀	선 수	End 1	End 2	End 3	End 4	End 5	End 6	End 7	End 8	End 9	End 10	End 11	End 12	점수
		1.													
		2.													
		3.													
		4.													
		1.													
		2.													
		3.													
		4.													

Ice	팀	선 수	End 1	End 2	End 3	End 4	End 5	End 6	End 7	End 8	End 9	End 10	End 11	End 12	점수
		1.													
		2.													
		3.													
		4.													
		1.													
		2.													
		3.													
		4.													

확인 - ✓ 종료 - / 호그 라인 위반 - X 진행 안 함 - O

담당자 이름 : ______________________________ 서명 : ______________________________

COMPETITION: ______________________________
DATE / LOCATION: ______________________________

SUMMARY – SEATING COACH BENCH

Men: ☐ Women: ☐

Team	1st Team Official	2nd Team Official	Alternate Player

대회: ____________________

날짜, 장소: ____________________

요약 - 코치 좌석

남자: ☐ 여자: ☐

팀	첫 번째 관계자	두 번째 관계자	대체 선수

COMPETITION: ______________________________

DATE / LOCATION: ______________________________

SUMMARY – SEATING COACH BENCH WMDCC

Team	Team Official	Translator (where required)

대회: ____________________

날짜, 장소: ____________________

요약 - WMDCC 코치 좌석

팀	팀 관계자	통역가(필요한 곳에)

WCF - DRESS CODE

ITEMS	POLICY
SHOES	No restrictions, personal preference
SOCKS	If worn under the pants, no restrictions
LEG WARMERS	Includes socks worn over the pants, same for the complete team
PANTS/TROUSERS	Same logos/crests/colour, can be different brands
BELTS	If showing, all the same
KILTS	Same colour or tartan, same colour of tights, can be a team mixture of kilts and pants
UNDERSHIRTS	Can be visible (long sleeves under short sleeves) but outfit must have colour coordination
SHIRTS	Can be tucked in or out
VESTS	Okay, must have colour coordination (name, Association, etc.), one or more can wear
JACKETS	As per WCF guidelines, Association, player's name, etc.
TWO-TONE JACKETS	Predominately one colour, but can have an accent colour
HOODED JACKETS	Hood cannot be showing, rolled up or tucked inside
HATS	One or more can wear, more than 1 all the same, peaks forward, logos = Assn. or the Event
SCARVES	One or more can wear, more than 1 all the same
HEAD & WRIST BANDS	One or more can wear, more than 1 all the same, large logos = Association or the Event
JEWELLERY	No restrictions, personal preference
GLOVES	No restrictions, personal preference
BRACES	Cannot be visible, worn under a shirt or jacket

WCF - 복장 규정	
아이템	**정책**
신발	제약 없음, 개인적 선호.
양말	바지 아래 신으면 제약 없음.
레그 워머	바지 위에 덧신는 양말 포함해서 팀 전체가 같아야 한다.
바지	같은 로고/장식/색깔, 다른 브랜드 사용 허용.
벨트	밖으로 보인 면 모두 같아야 한다.
킬트	짙은 색, 같은 색 타이츠, 팀은 킬트와 팬츠를 섞어 입어도 된다.
속셔츠	밖으로 보일 수 있음(짧은 팔옷 속에 긴팔옷 입기). 그러나 옷은 반드시 동등한 색이어야 한다.
셔츠	안이나 밖으로 나올 수 있음.
조끼	사용허가, 반드시 동등한 색(이름, 협회 등), 하나 또는 그 이상을 입을 수 있음
재킷	세계컬링연맹 가이드라인에 따라서 협회, 선수 이름
두 가지 톤 재킷	한 가지 색이 우세해야 하나 강조 색을 가질 수 있다.
후드 재킷	후드는 보여서 안 되며 안쪽으로 넣어야 한다.
모자	하나 이상 쓸 수 있고 하나 이상은 반드시 같은 색이어야 하고 뾰족한 부분이 앞으로 향하게 해야 한다.
스카프	하나 이상 쓸 수 있고 하나 이상은 같은 색이어야 한다.
머리, 손목 밴드	하나 이상 쓸 수 있고 하나 이상은 같은 색이어야 하며, 협회는 큰 로고여야 한다.
액세서리	제약 없음, 개인적 선호.
장갑	제약 없음, 개인적 선호.
팔찌	보이지 않게 셔츠나 재킷 아래 찬다.

The Placing-Point we are using for this draw is:

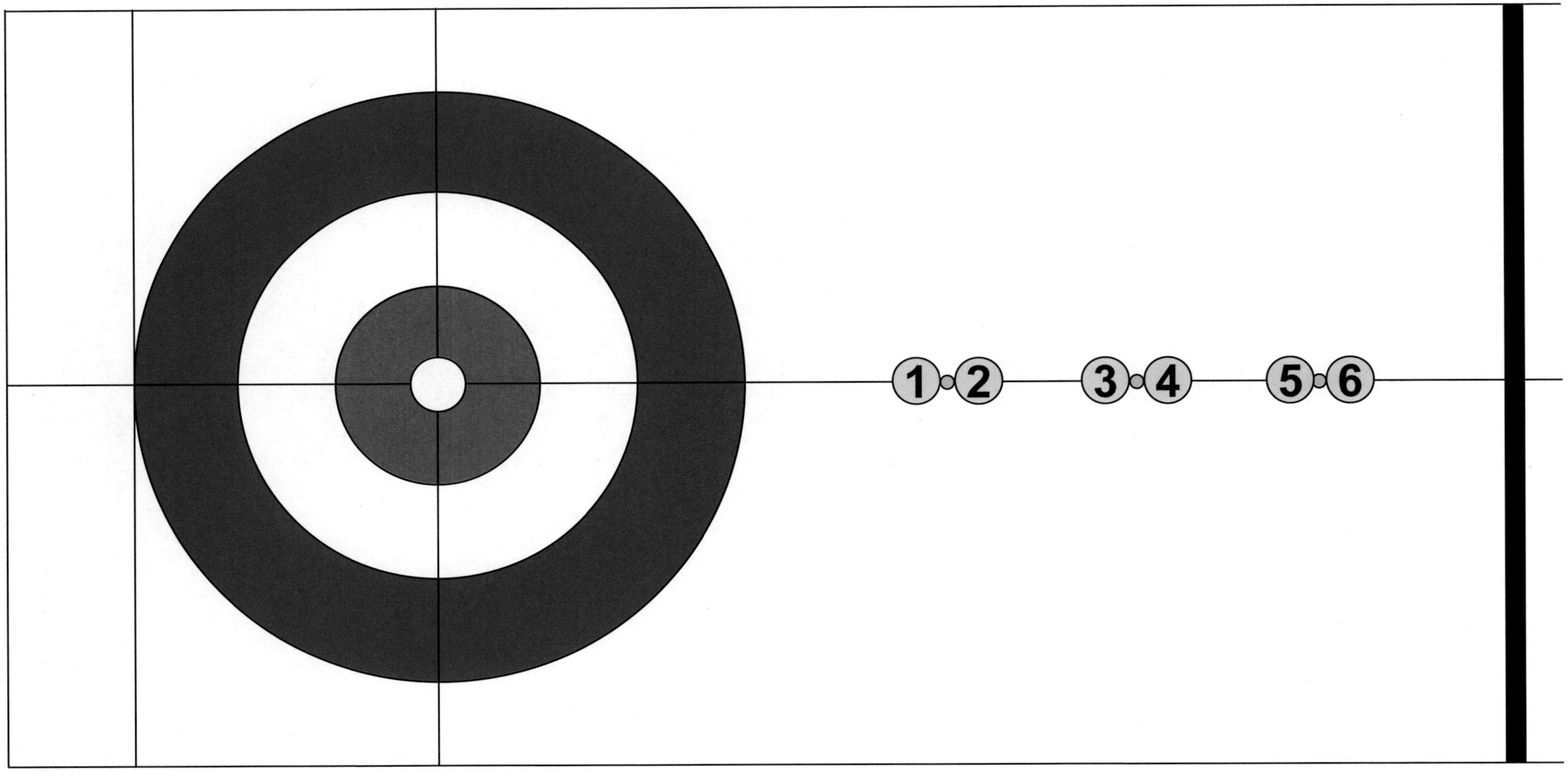

위치

이 그림은 우리가 사용하는 포인트를 나타낸다.

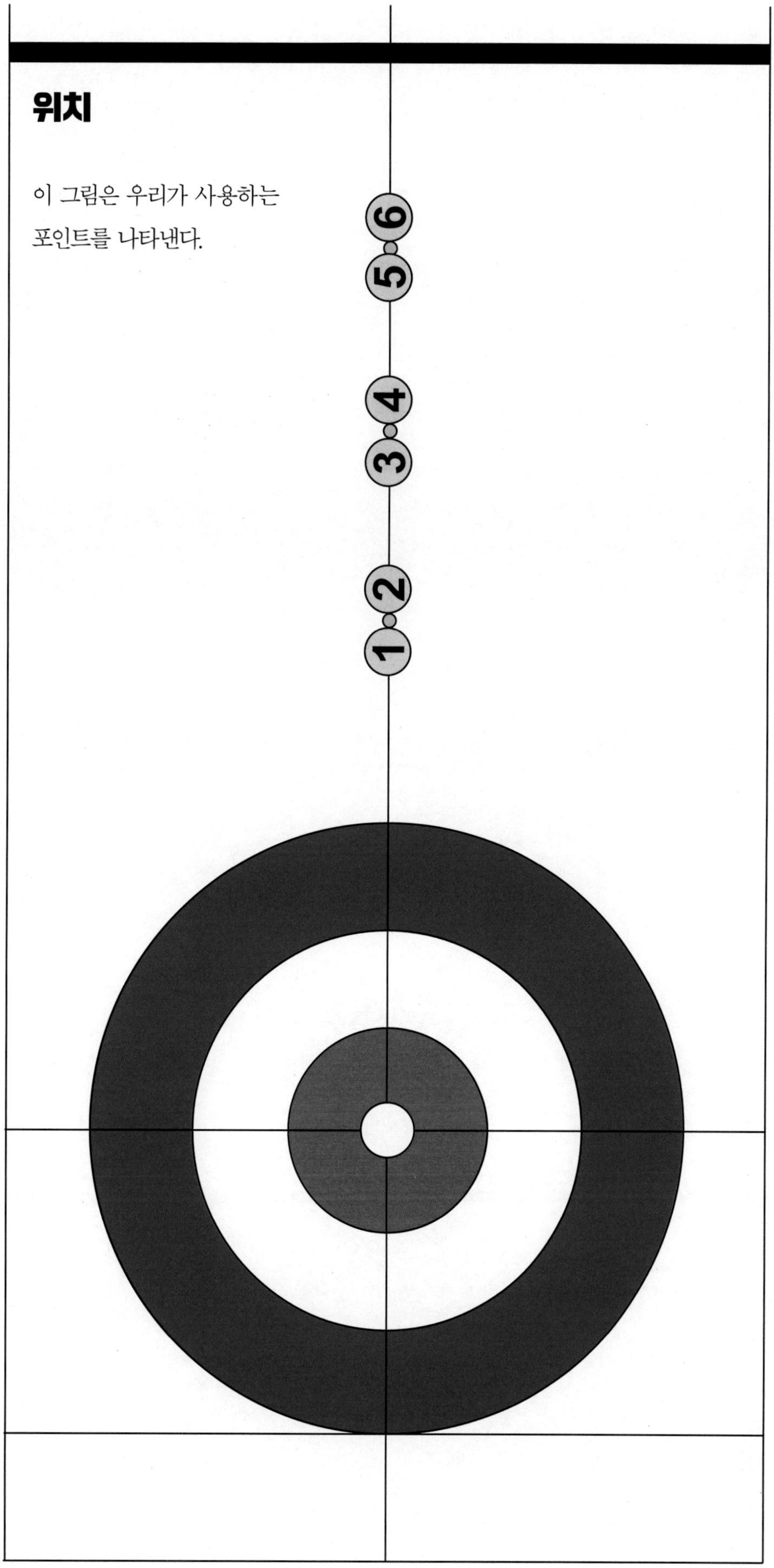

OLYMPIC WINTER SPORT

THE RULES OF CURLING

and

Rules of Competition

October 2017

THE SPIRIT OF CURLING

Curling is a game of skill and of tradition. A shot well executed is a delight to see and it is also a fine thing to observe the time-honoured traditions of curling being applied in the true spirit of the game. Curlers play to win, but never to humble their opponents. A true curler never attempts to distract opponents, nor to prevent them from playing their best, and would prefer to lose rather than to win unfairly.

Curlers never knowingly break a rule of the game, nor disrespect any of its traditions. Should they become aware that this has been done inadvertently, they will be the first to divulge the breach.

While the main object of the game of curling is to determine the relative skill of the players, the spirit of curling demands good sportsmanship, kindly feeling and honourable conduct.

This spirit should influence both the interpretation and the application of the rules of the game and also the conduct of all participants on and off the ice.

REVIEW PROCESS

The Rules of Curling and the Rules of Competition will be reviewed by the World Curling Federation (WCF) Competitions & Rules Commission on an annual basis. Member Associations may submit in writing suggestions for this review to the Secretariat by 15 May. The proposals will be discussed at the WCF Annual Congress and then voted upon at the WCF Annual General Assembly.

WCF MISSION STATEMENT

To be the world's favourite Olympic / Paralympic Winter team sport.

WCF SECRETARIAT
3 Atholl Crescent
Perth PH1 5NG, Scotland
Tel: +44 1738 451 630 Fax: +44 1738 451 641
info@worldcurling.org www.worldcurling.org

TABLE OF CONTENTS

Page

October 2017 / Review Process / WCF Mission Statement

Table of Contents

The Rules of Curling:
R1. Sheet
R2. Stones
R3. Teams
R4. Position of Players
R5. Delivery
R6. Free Guard Zone (FGZ)
R7. Sweeping
R8. Touched Moving Stones
R9. Displaced Stationary Stones
R10. Equipment
R11. Scoring
R12. Interrupted Games
R13. Wheelchair Curling
R14. Mixed Curling
R15. Mixed Doubles Curling
R16. Prohibited Substances
R17. Inappropriate Behaviour

Rules of Competition:
C1. General
C2. Participating Teams
C3. Uniforms / Equipment
C4. Pre-Game Practice
C5. Length of Games
C6. Game Timing
C7. Team Time-Outs / Technical Time-Outs
C8. Stone Assignment / LSD
C9. Team Ranking Procedure / DSC
C10. Umpires

Competitions – the Playdown Systems
Qualification - World Championships Men & Women
Qualification - World Junior Championships(WJCC)
World Mixed Doubles(WMDCC)
World Seniors & World Mixed
Pacific-Asia Curling Championships(PACC)
European Curling Championships(ECC)
Qualification System – the Americas Zone
Minimum Standards, Eligibility
Play-off Systems
Quarter-Finals Play-off System
Dress Code
Glossary of Terms

THE RULES OF CURLING

These rules apply to any game or competition to which they are made applicable by the curling organisation having jurisdiction.

R1. SHEET

(a) The length of the ice sheet from the inside edges of the back boards is 45.720 metres (150 feet). The width of the sheet from the inside edges of the side lines is a maximum of 5.000 m. (16 ft. 5 inches). This area is delineated by lines drawn, or by dividers placed on the perimeter. If the size of an existing facility will not permit these measurements, then the length may be reduced to a minimum of 44.501 m. (146 ft.), and the width to a minimum of 4.420 m. (14 ft. 6 in.).

(b) At each end of the sheet there are clearly visible parallel lines in the ice from side line to side line as follows:

- (i) the tee line, 1.27 cm. (1/2 in.) maximum width, placed so that the centre of the line is 17.375 m. (57 ft.) from the middle of the sheet.
- (ii) the back line, 1.27 cm. (1/2 in.) maximum width, placed so that the outside edge is 1.829 m. (6 ft.) from the centre of the tee line.
- (iii) the hog line, 10.16 cm. (4 in.) in width, placed so that the inside edge is 6.401 m. (21 ft.) from the centre of the tee line.
- (iv) the centre line, 1.27 cm. (1/2 in.) maximum width, joins the midpoints of the tee lines and extends 3.658 m. (12 ft.) beyond the centre of each tee line.
- (v) the hack line, 0.457 m. (1 ft. 6 in.) in length and 1.27 cm. (1/2 in.) maximum width, is placed parallel to the tee line, at each end of the centre line.
- (vi) the courtesy line, 15.24 cm. (6 in.) in length and 1.27 cm. (1/2 in.) maximum width, is placed 1.219 m. (4 ft.) outside and parallel to the hog lines, on each side of the sheet.

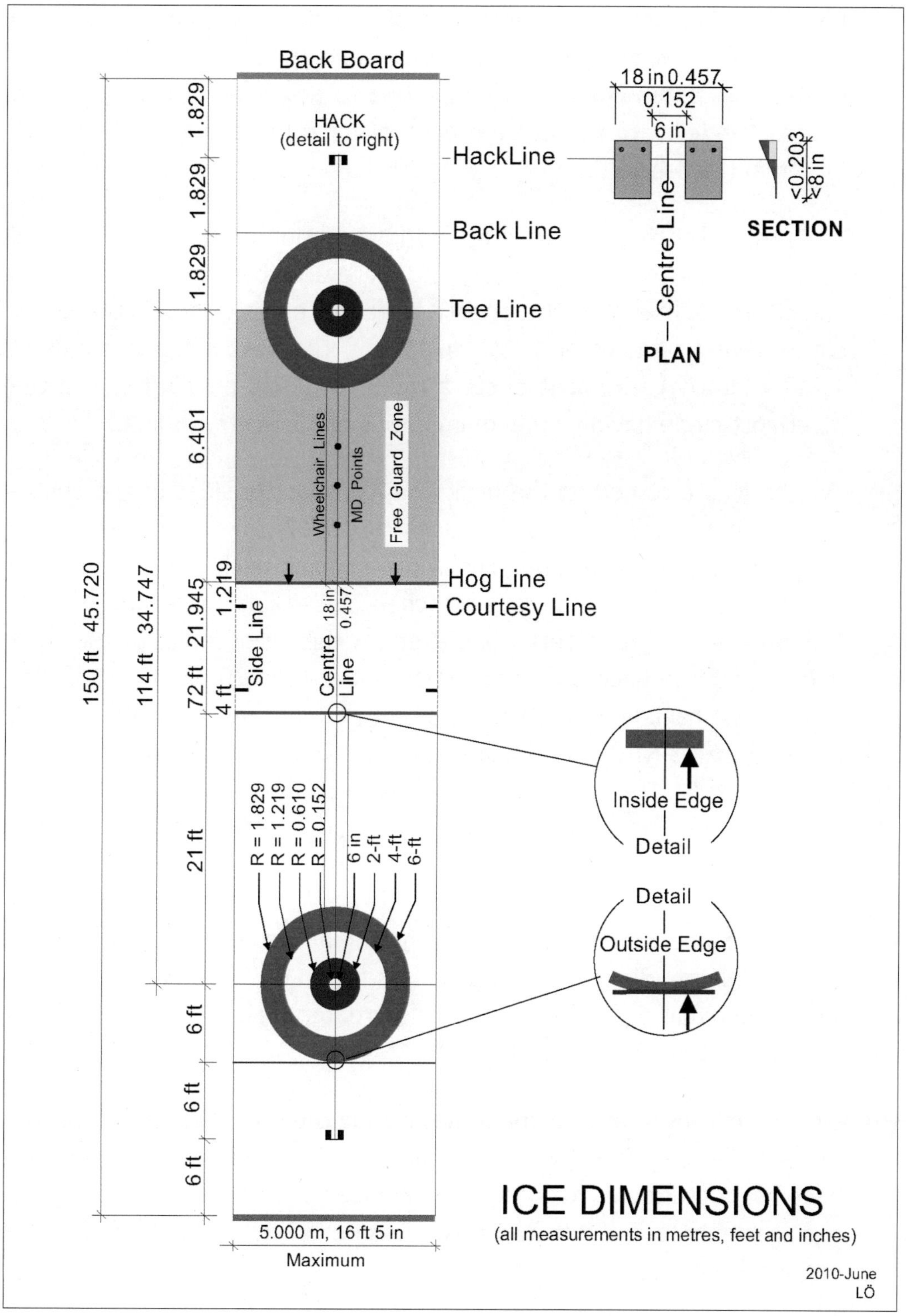
Back Board
HACK
(detail to right)
HackLine
Back Line
Tee Line
Hog Line
Courtesy Line
Wheelchair Lines
MD Points
Free Guard Zone
Side Line
Centre Line
18 in
0.457
1.829
1.829
1.829
6.401
1.219
150 ft 45.720
114 ft 34.747
72 ft 21.945
4 ft
21 ft
6 ft
6 ft
6 ft
R = 1.829
R = 1.219
R = 0.610
R = 0.152
6 in
2-ft
4-ft
6-ft
18 in 0.457
0.152
6 in
Centre Line
PLAN
<0.203
<8 in
SECTION
Inside Edge
Detail
Detail
Outside Edge
5.000 m, 16 ft 5 in
Maximum
ICE DIMENSIONS
(all measurements in metres, feet and inches)
2010-June
LÖ

(c) For wheelchair events, at each end of the sheet, 2 thin (i.e. - wool) wheelchair lines are placed parallel to and on opposite sides of the centre line, extending from the hog line to the outermost edge of the nearest circle, with the outside edge of each line being 0.457 m. (18 in.) from the centre line.

(d) A centre hole (tee) is placed at the intersection of each tee line and centre line. With the tee as centre, there are four concentric circles placed at each end of the sheet, with the outer edge of the outer circle having a radius of 1.829 m. (6 ft.), the next circle a radius of 1.219 m. (4 ft.), the next circle a radius of 0.610 m. (2 ft.), and the innermost circle having a minimum radius of 15.24 cm. (6 in.).

(e) Two hacks are placed on the hack line, on opposite sides of the centre line, with the inside edge of each hack 7.62 cm. (3 in.) from the midpoint of the centre line. The width of each hack shall not exceed 15.24 cm. (6 in.). The hack is attached to suitable material, and the inside edge of that material is placed on the inside edge of the hack line so that the hack does not extend more than 20.32 cm. (8 in.) in front of the hack line. If the hack is recessed into the ice, this is not to be more than 3.81 cm. (1.5 in.) in depth.

R2. STONES

(a) A curling stone is of circular shape, having a circumference no greater than 91.44 cm. (36 in.), a height no less than 11.43 cm. (4.5 in.), and a weight, including handle and bolt, no greater than 19.96 kg. (44 lbs.) and no less than 17.24 kg. (38 lbs.).

(b) Each team uses a set of eight stones having the same handle colour and individually identified by visible markings. If a stone is damaged and becomes unsuitable for play, a replacement stone is used. If a replacement stone is not available, a stone previously delivered in the end is redelivered.

(c) If a stone is broken in play, the teams use the "Spirit of Curling" to decide where the stone(s) should be placed. If agreement cannot be reached, the end will be replayed.

(d) If a stone rolls over while in motion, or comes to rest on its side or top, it is removed from play immediately.

(e) Should a handle completely separate from a stone during delivery, the delivering player has the option of either allowing the play to stand, or of redelivering the stone after any displaced stones have been replaced to their positions prior to the incident taking place.

(f) A stone that does not come to rest completely beyond the inside edge of the hog line at the playing end is removed from play immediately, except when it strikes another stone, in which case it remains in play.

(g) A stone that completely crosses the outside edge of the back line at the playing end is removed from play immediately.

(h) A stone that touches a divider or a side line is removed from play immediately and is prevented from entering adjacent sheets.

(i) A stone may be measured only visually until the last stone of the end has come to rest, except to determine if a stone is in play, or, prior to playing the second, third, or fourth stone of an end, to determine if a stone is in the Free Guard Zone.

(j) Teams are not to make alterations to, nor place any object on or over, their game stones.

R3. TEAMS

(a) A team is composed of four players. Each player delivers two stones, in consecutive order in each end, while alternating with an opponent.

(b) A team declares its delivery rotation, and the skip and vice-skip positions, prior to the start of a game and maintains that rotation and those positions throughout that game subject to (d) (ii). A team that deliberately changes its delivery rotation, or positions, during a game will forfeit the game, unless it was done when bringing in an alternate player.

(c) If a player is missing at the start of a game, the team may either:

(i) start the game with three players, the first two players delivering three stones each, and the third player delivering two stones, in which case the missing player may enter the game in the declared delivery rotation and position at the start of an end; or

(ii) start the game using a qualified alternate.

(d) Where a player is unable to continue to play in a game, the team may either:

(i) continue play with the remaining three players, in which case the player who left the game may re-enter only at the start of an end. A player may leave and return to a game only one time in any game; or

(ii) bring in a qualified alternate at the beginning of an end, in which case the delivery rotation and the skip and vice-skip positions may be changed (the revised rotation of play applying for the remainder of that game), and the replaced player may not re-enter the game.

(e) A team may not play with fewer than three players, all players delivering all their allocated stones in each end.

(f) In competitions where alternates are allowed, only one alternate can be registered and used in that competition. If there is a violation, the offending team will forfeit the game.

(g) If a player delivers the first allocated stone of an end and is unable to deliver the second allocated stone, the following is the procedure for the remainder of that end. If the player is the:

(i) first player, the second player delivers the stone.
(ii) second player, the first player delivers the stone.
(iii) third player, the second player delivers the stone.
(iv) fourth player, the third player delivers the stone.

(h) If a player whose turn it is to deliver is unable to deliver both of the allocated stones during an end, the following is the procedure for the remainder of that end. If the player is the:
(i) first player, the second player delivers three stones, then the third player delivers three stones, then the fourth player delivers the last two stones.
(ii) second player, the first player delivers three stones, then the third player delivers three stones, then the fourth player delivers the last two stones.
(iii) third player, the first player delivers the first stone of the third player, then the second player delivers the second stone of the third player, then the fourth player delivers the last two stones.
(iv) fourth player, the second player delivers the first stone of the fourth player, then the third player delivers the second stone of the fourth player.

R4. POSITION OF PLAYERS

(a) Non-Delivering Team:
(i) During the process of delivery, the players take stationary positions along the side lines between the courtesy lines. However:
1) the skip and/or vice-skip may take stationary positions behind the back line at the playing end, but must not interfere with the choice of place of the skip or vice-skip of the delivering team.
2) the player who is to deliver next may take a stationary position to the side of the sheet, behind the hacks, at the delivery end.

(ii) The non-delivering team players must not take any position, nor cause any motion, which could obstruct, interfere with, distract or intimidate the delivering team. If such an action occurs, or an external force distracts a player during delivery, that player has the option of allowing the play to stand, or of redelivering the stone after all displaced stones have been replaced to their positions prior to the violation taking place.

(b) Delivering Team:

(i) The skip, or the vice-skip when it is the skip's turn to deliver, or when the skip is not on the ice, is in charge of the house.

(ii) The player in charge of the house is positioned inside the hog line, with at least one foot/wheel on the ice surface of the playing end of the team's sheet, while the team is in the process of delivery.

(iii) The players who are not in charge of the house or delivering a stone take positions to sweep.

(iv) Any improper position of players will result in the delivered stone being removed from play, and any displaced stones shall be replaced, by the non-offending team, to their positions prior to the violation taking place.

R5. DELIVERY

(a) Unless predetermined, or decided by the Last Stone Draw (LSD), the teams opposing each other in a game shall use a coin toss to determine which team delivers the first stone in the first end. This order of play shall be maintained until one team scores, after which the team that most recently scored delivers the first stone in any subsequent end.

(b) Unless predetermined, the team playing the first stone of the first end has the choice of stone handle colour for that game.

(c) Right-handed deliveries are delivered from the hack on the left of the centre line and left-handed deliveries are delivered from the hack on the right of the centre line. A stone delivered from the wrong hack is removed from play, and any displaced stones are replaced, by the non-offending team, to their positions prior to the violation taking place.

(d) A stone must be clearly released from the hand before it reaches the hog line at the delivery end. If the player fails to do so, the stone is immediately removed from play by the delivering team.

(e) If a hog line violation stone is not immediately removed and strikes another stone, the delivered stone is removed from play by the delivering team, and any displaced stones are replaced, by the non-offending team, to their positions prior to the violation taking place.

(f) A stone is in play, and considered delivered, when it reaches the tee line (hog line for wheelchair curling) at the delivery end. A stone that has not reached the relevant line may be returned to the player and redelivered.

(g) All players must be ready to deliver their stones when their turns come, and not take an unreasonable amount of time to play.

(h) If a player delivers a stone belonging to the opposing team, that stone is allowed to come to rest, and is then replaced by a stone belonging to the delivering team.

(i) If a player delivers a stone out of proper rotation, the end continues as if the mistake had not occurred. The player who missed a turn delivers the last stone for that team in that end. If it cannot be determined which player delivered out of proper rotation, the player who delivered the first stone in the end for that team delivers the last stone for that team in that end.

(j) If a player inadvertently delivers too many stones in one end, the end continues as if the mistake had not occurred and the number of stones allocated to the last player of the offending team shall be reduced accordingly.

(k) If a team delivers two stones in succession in the same end:

(i) the second stone is removed and any displaced stones replaced, by the non-offending team, to their positions prior to the violation taking place. The player who delivered the stone played by mistake, redelivers it as the last stone for the team in that end.

(ii) should the infraction not be discovered until after the delivery of a subsequent stone, the end is replayed.

(l) If the wrong team delivers the first stone of an end:

(i) if the error is discovered after only the first stone has been delivered, the end shall be replayed.

(ii) if the error is discovered after the 2nd stone of the end has been delivered, play continues as if the error had not occurred.

R6. FREE GUARD ZONE (FGZ)

(a) A stone that comes to rest between the tee line and the hog line at the playing end, excluding the house, is deemed to be within an area designated as the FGZ. Also, stones that are in play, on or before the hog line, after striking stones in the FGZ, are deemed to be in the FGZ.

(b) If, prior to the delivery of the fifth stone of an end, a delivered stone causes, either directly or indirectly, an opposition stone to be moved from the FGZ to an out-of-play position, then the delivered stone is removed from play, and any displaced stones are replaced, by the non-offending team, to their positions prior to the violation taking place. (*effective 1 October 2018 the 5 stone FGZ will be implemented*)

R7. SWEEPING

(a) The sweeping motion can be in any direction (it need not cover the entire width of the stone), must deposit no debris in front of a moving stone, and must finish to either side of the stone.

(b) A stationary stone must be set in motion before it can be swept. A stone set in motion by a delivered stone, either directly or indirectly, may be swept by any one or more of the team to which it belongs anywhere in front of the tee line at the playing end.

(c) A delivered stone may be swept by any one or more of the delivering team anywhere in front of the tee line at the playing end.

(d) No player may ever sweep an opponent's stone except behind the tee line at the playing end, and may not start to sweep an opponent's stone until it has reached the tee line at the playing end.

(e) Behind the tee line at the playing end, only one player from each team may sweep at any one time. This may be any player of the delivering team, but only the skip or vice-skip of the non-delivering team.

(f) Behind the tee line, a team has first privilege of sweeping its own stone, but it must not obstruct or prevent its opponent from sweeping.

(g) If a sweeping violation occurs, the non-offending team has the option of allowing the play to stand, or of placing the stone, and all stones it would have affected, where they would have come to rest had the violation not occurred.

R8. TOUCHED MOVING STONES

(a) Between the tee line at the delivery end and the hog line at the playing end:

(i) If a moving stone is touched, or is caused to be touched, by the team to which it belongs, or by their equipment, the touched stone is removed from play immediately by that team. A double-touch by the person delivering the stone, prior to the hog line at the delivering end, is not considered a violation.

(ii) If a moving stone is touched, or is caused to be touched, by an opposition team, or by its equipment, or is affected by an external force:

1) If the stone was the delivered stone, it is redelivered.

2) If the stone was not the delivered stone, it is placed where the team to which it belongs reasonably considers it would have come to rest had it not been touched.

(b) Inside the hog line at the playing end:

(i) If a moving stone is touched, or is caused to be touched, by the team to which it belongs, or by its equipment, all stones are allowed to come to rest, after which the non-offending team has the option to:

1) remove the touched stone, and replace all stones that were displaced after the infraction to their positions prior to the violation taking place; or

2) leave all stones where they came to rest; or

3) place all stones where it reasonably considers the stones would have come to rest had the moving stone not been touched.

(ii) If a moving stone is touched, or is caused to be touched, by an opposition team, or by its equipment, all stones are allowed to come to rest, after which the non-offending team places the stones where it reasonably considers the stones would have come to rest, had the moving stone not been touched.

(iii) If a moving stone is touched, or is caused to be touched, by an external force, all stones are allowed to come to rest, and then placed where they would have come to rest if the incident had not occurred. If the teams cannot agree, the stone is redelivered after all displaced stones have been replaced to their positions prior to the violation taking place. If agreement on those positions cannot be reached, the end is replayed.

(c) Last Stone Draw (LSD) stones:

(i) If a member of the delivering team touches a moving stone, or causes it to be touched, the stone will be removed and recorded as 199.6 cm (6 ft. 6.5 in.).

(ii) If a member of the non-delivering team touches a moving stone, or causes it to be touched, the stone will be redelivered.

(iii) If an external force touches a moving stone, or causes it to be touched, the stone will be redelivered.

(d) If a moving stone is touched by a stone deflecting off the sheet dividers, the non-delivering team shall place the stone where it reasonably considers the stone would have come to rest had the moving stone not been touched.

R9. DISPLACED STATIONARY STONES

(a) If a stationary stone which would have had no effect on the outcome of a moving stone is displaced, or caused to be displaced, by a player, it is replaced, by the non-offending team, to their positions prior to the violation taking place.

(b) If a stationary stone which would have had no effect on the outcome of a moving stone is displaced, or caused to be displaced, by an external force, it is replaced, with agreement of the teams, to its position prior to the violation taking place.

(c) If a stone which would have altered the course of a moving stone is displaced, or caused to be displaced, by a player, all stones are allowed to come to rest and then the non-offending team has the option to:

(i) leave all stones where they came to rest; or

(ii) remove from play the stone whose course would have been altered, and replace any stones that were displaced after the violation to their positions prior to the violation taking place; or

(iii) place all stones in the positions the team reasonably considers they would have come to rest had a stone not been displaced.

(d) If a stone which would have altered the course of a moving stone is displaced, or caused to be displaced, by an external force, all stones are allowed to come to rest, and are then placed in the positions in which they would have come to rest had a stone not been displaced. If the teams cannot agree, the stone is redelivered after all displaced stones have been replaced to their positions prior to the violation taking place. If agreement on those positions cannot be reached, the end is replayed.

(e) If a displacement is caused by stones deflecting off the sheet dividers, the stones are replaced, by the non-delivering team, to their positions prior to the violation taking place.

(f) Last Stone Draw (LSD) Stones:

(i) If a member of the delivering team displaces a stationary stone, or causes it to be displaced, before the official completes the measurement, the stone will be removed and recorded as 199.6 cm (6 ft. 6.5 in.).

(ii) If a member of the non-delivering team displaces a stationary stone, or causes it to be displaced, before the official completes the measurement, the stone is replaced, by the delivering team, to its position prior to the violation taking place.

(iii) If an external force displaces a stationary stone, or causes it to be displaced, before the official completes the measurement, the stone is replaced, by the delivering team, to its position prior to the violation taking place.

R10. EQUIPMENT

(a) No player shall cause damage to the ice surface by means of equipment, hand prints, or body prints. The procedure will be:
1st incident = 1st official on-ice warning, repair damage.
2nd incident = 2nd official on-ice warning, repair damage.
3rd incident = repair damage and remove player from the game.

(b) No equipment shall be left unattended anywhere on the ice surface.

(c) Teams must not use electronic communication equipment, or any device to modify the voice, during a game. With the exception of stopwatches that are limited to providing 'time' data only, the use of electronic devices during the games, which provide information to players on the field of play, are forbidden.

(d) When a properly functioning electronic hog line device is being used:

(i) The handle must be properly activated so that it is functioning during the delivery, or it will be considered a hog line violation stone.

(ii) A glove or mitt must not be worn on the delivery hand during the delivery of a stone. If there is a violation, the delivered stone shall be removed from play, and any displaced stones shall be replaced, by the non-offending team, to their positions prior to the violation taking place.

(e) The use of a delivery stick shall be restricted as follows:

(i) The delivery stick may not be used in any WCF competition or qualifying event, except wheelchair events.

(ii) Players choosing to deliver with a delivery stick must use that device for the delivery of all their stones during the entire game.

(iii) The stone must be delivered along a straight line from the hack to the intended target.

(iv) The stone must be clearly released from the delivery stick before either foot of the player delivering the stone has reached the tee line at the delivery end. A stone is in play, and considered delivered, when it reaches the hog line at the delivery end.

(v) A delivery stick shall not convey any mechanical advantage other than acting as an extension of the arm/hand.

(vi) If a stick delivery violation occurs, the delivered stone shall be removed from play, and any displaced stones shall be replaced, by the non-offending team, to their positions prior to the violation taking place.

R11. SCORING

(a) The result of a game is decided by a majority of points at the completion of the scheduled ends of play, or when a team concedes victory to its opponent, or when one team is arithmetically eliminated, provided the minimum number of ends has been completed. A team that has been arithmetically eliminated may finish the current end but no new end may be started. However, if a team is arithmetically eliminated in the last end of a game, the game should stop when this occurs and the end will not be finished. If the score is tied at the completion of the scheduled ends, play continues with extra end(s) and the team that scores first wins the game.

(b) At the completion of an end (when all stones have been played), a team scores one point for each of its own stones located in or touching the house that are closer to the tee than any stone of the opposition.

(c) The score of an end is decided when the skips or vice-skips in charge of the house agree upon the score. If stones that may have affected the points scored in an end are displaced prior to that decision, the non-offending team receives the benefit that might have accrued from a measurement.

(d) When determining the score of an end, if teams cannot visually decide which stones are closer to the tee, or whether a stone is touching the house, a measuring device is used. Measurements are taken from the tee to the nearest part of the stone. The person in charge of the house from each team is allowed to observe any measurement that is made by a measuring device.

(e) If two or more stones are so close to the tee that it is impossible to use a measuring device, the determination is made visually.

(f) If a decision cannot be reached, either visually or with a measuring device, the stones are considered equal, and:

  (i) If the measure was to determine which team scored in the end, the end is blanked.

  (ii) If the measure was to determine additional points, only the stones closer to the tee are counted.

(g) Should an external force cause the displacement of stones that would have affected the score prior to agreement of the score, the following applies:

  (i) If the displaced stones would have determined which team scored in an end, the end is replayed.

  (ii) If a team secured a point(s), and the displaced stone(s) would have determined if an additional point(s) was scored, that team has the option of replaying the end or of keeping the point(s) already secured.

(h) A team concedes a game only when it is the delivering team. When a team concedes the game before the completion of an end, the score of the end is determined at that time, in the following manner:

(i) If both teams still have stones to be delivered, "X"s are placed on the scoreboard.

(ii) When only one team has delivered all of its stones:

1) If the team that delivered all its stones has stone(s) counting, no points are given, "X"s are placed on the scoreboard unless the points are required to determine the outcome.

2) If the team that did not deliver all its stones has stone(s) counting, these points are given and placed on the scoreboard.

3) If no stones are counting, "X"s are placed on the scoreboard.

(i) If a team is not available to start a game at the designated time, the following takes place:

(i) If the delay of the start of play is 1-15 minutes, then the non-offending team receives one point, and will have choice of first or second stone in the first end of actual play; one end is considered completed.

(ii) If the delay of the start of play is 15-30 minutes, then the non-offending team receives one additional point, and choice of first or second stone in the first end of actual play; two ends are considered completed.

(iii) If play has not started after 30 minutes, then the non-offending team is declared the winner by forfeit.

(j) The final score of a forfeited game is recorded as "W - L" (win - loss).

R12. INTERRUPTED GAMES

If for any reason, a game is interrupted, the game recommences where play was stopped.

R13. WHEELCHAIR CURLING

(a) Stones are delivered from a stationary wheelchair.

(b) When the stone is delivered between the hack and the outermost edge of the top of the house at the delivery end, the chair must be positioned so that at the start of the delivery the stone is positioned on the centre line. When the stone is delivered between the outermost edge of the top of the house and the hog line at the delivery end, the chair must be positioned so that at the start of the delivery the entire width of the stone is within the wheelchair lines.

(c) During delivery, the feet of the player delivering the stone must not touch the ice surface and the wheels of the chair must be in direct contact with the ice.

(d) The delivery of the stone is undertaken by the conventional arm/hand release or by the use of an approved delivery stick. Only head assemblies used during the 2017 World Wheelchair Curling Championship will be allowed to be used during the 2017/18 season in WCF controlled Wheelchair Curling events, including the 2018 Paralympic Winter Games.

Stones must be clearly released from the hand or stick before the stone reaches the hog line at the delivery end.

(e) A stone is in play when it reaches the hog line at the delivery end. A stone that has not reached the hog line at the delivery end may be returned to the player and redelivered.

(f) Sweeping is not permitted.

(g) If a delivery violation occurs, the delivered stone shall be removed from play, and any displaced stones shall be replaced, by the non-offending team, to their positions prior to the violation taking place.

(h) For WCF wheelchair competitions, each on-ice team must have four players delivering stones and must be comprised of both genders at all times during games. A team violating this rule will forfeit the game.

(i) All games will be scheduled for 8 ends.

R14. MIXED CURLING

(a) Each team shall have two male and two female players and the male and female players must deliver stones alternately (M, F, M, F - or - F, M, F, M). No alternate players are permitted.

(b) If a team plays with three players, the alternate gender order of delivery must be maintained (M, F, M - or - F, M, F). If this occurs while a game is in progress, the delivery rotation can be changed to meet this criterion.

(c) The skip and vice-skip can be anyone in the team, but they must be from opposite genders.

(d) All Mixed games are scheduled for 8 ends.

(e) The team is allowed one coach and one other team official. Only those two persons may sit on the designated coach bench.

R15. MIXED DOUBLES CURLING

(a) A team is composed of two players, one male and one female. Alternate players are not allowed. A team must forfeit any game(s) in which it fails to have both players playing for the entire game. One coach and one other team official will be allowed for each team.

(b) The scoring shall be the same as in a regular game of curling. The "positioned" stones that are placed prior to the beginning of each end are eligible to be counted in the scoring.

(c) Each game will be scheduled for 8 ends.

(d) Each team shall deliver 5 stones per end. The player delivering the team's first stone of the end must also deliver the team's last stone of that end. The other team member shall deliver the team's second, third and fourth stones for that end. The player delivering the first stone can change from end to end.

(e) No stone in play, including the "positioned" stones and those in the house, can be moved to an out-of-play position prior to the delivery of the fourth stone of an end (the fourth delivered stone is the first stone that can remove any stone from play). If there is a violation, the delivered stone shall be removed from play, and any displaced stone(s) shall be replaced, by the non-offending team, to their positions prior to the violation taking place.

(f) Prior to the start of every end, one team shall place its "positioned" stone at the playing end of the sheet in one of two positions, designated A and B. The opponent's "positioned" stone shall then be placed in whichever position (A or B) remains vacant. The location of these positions shall be as follows:

(i) Position A: Placement so that the stone is bisected by the centre line and is either immediately in front of or immediately behind one of 3 points in the ice. The points are placed on the centre line (see diagram):

1) at the mid-point between the hog line and the outermost edge of the top of the house.
2) 0.915 m. (3 feet) from the mid-point closer to the house.
3) 0.915 m. (3 feet) from the mid-point closer to the hog line.

Based on the ice conditions, when no event official is available to make the decision, the teams shall determine the specific placement for each sheet for Position A to be used prior to the start of the pre-game practice and that same placement must be used for the entire game.

(ii) Position B: Placement so that the stone is bisected by the centre line and is in the back of the 4-foot circle. The back edge of the stone is aligned with the back edge of the 4-foot circle (see diagram).

(iii) Power Play: Once per game, each team, when it has the decision on the placement of the “positioned” stones, can use the “Power Play” option to position those two stones. The in-house stone (B), which belongs to the team with last stone in that end, is placed on either side of the house with the back edge of the stone touching the tee line, at the point where the 8-foot and 12-foot circles meet. The guard stone (A) is positioned to the same side of the sheet, the same distance that was determined for the centre guards (see diagram). The “Power Play” option cannot be used in extra ends.

Figure No. 1 - Centre Guard

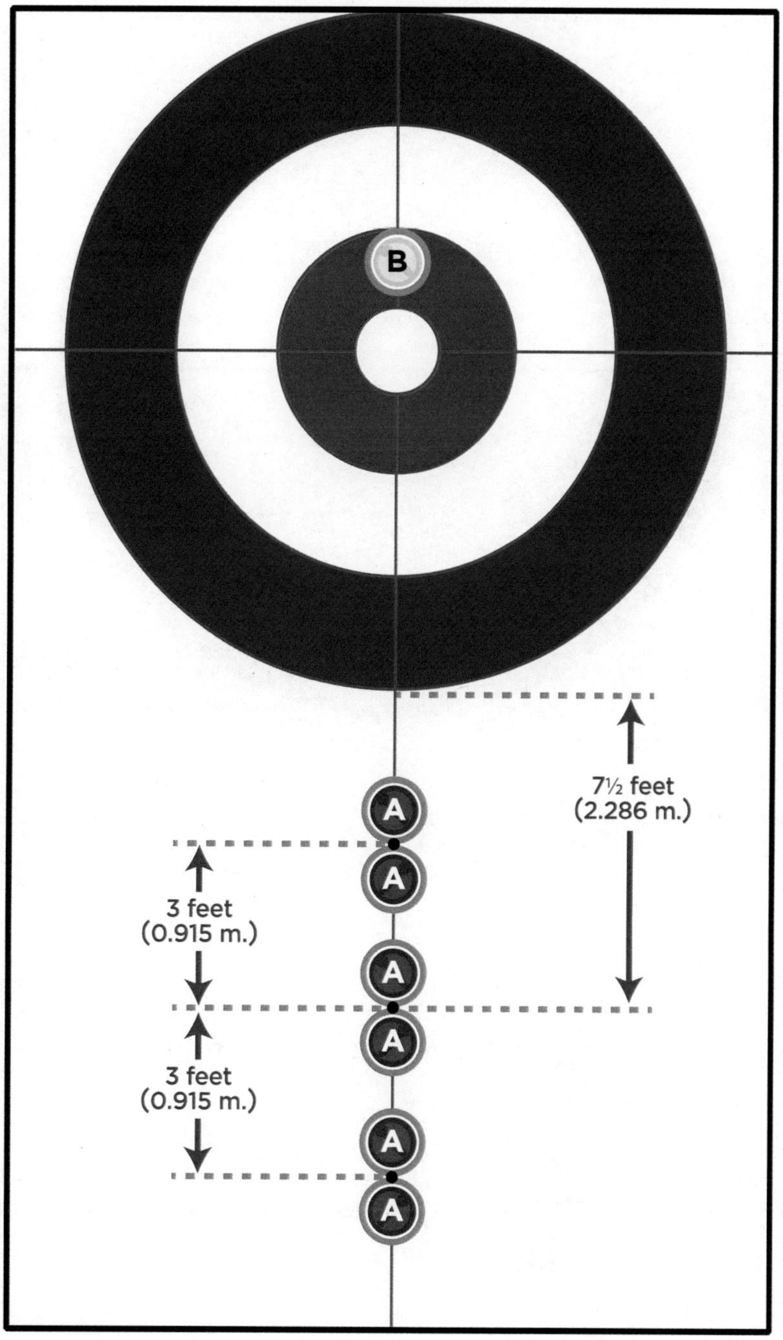

Figure No. 2 - Power Play Option

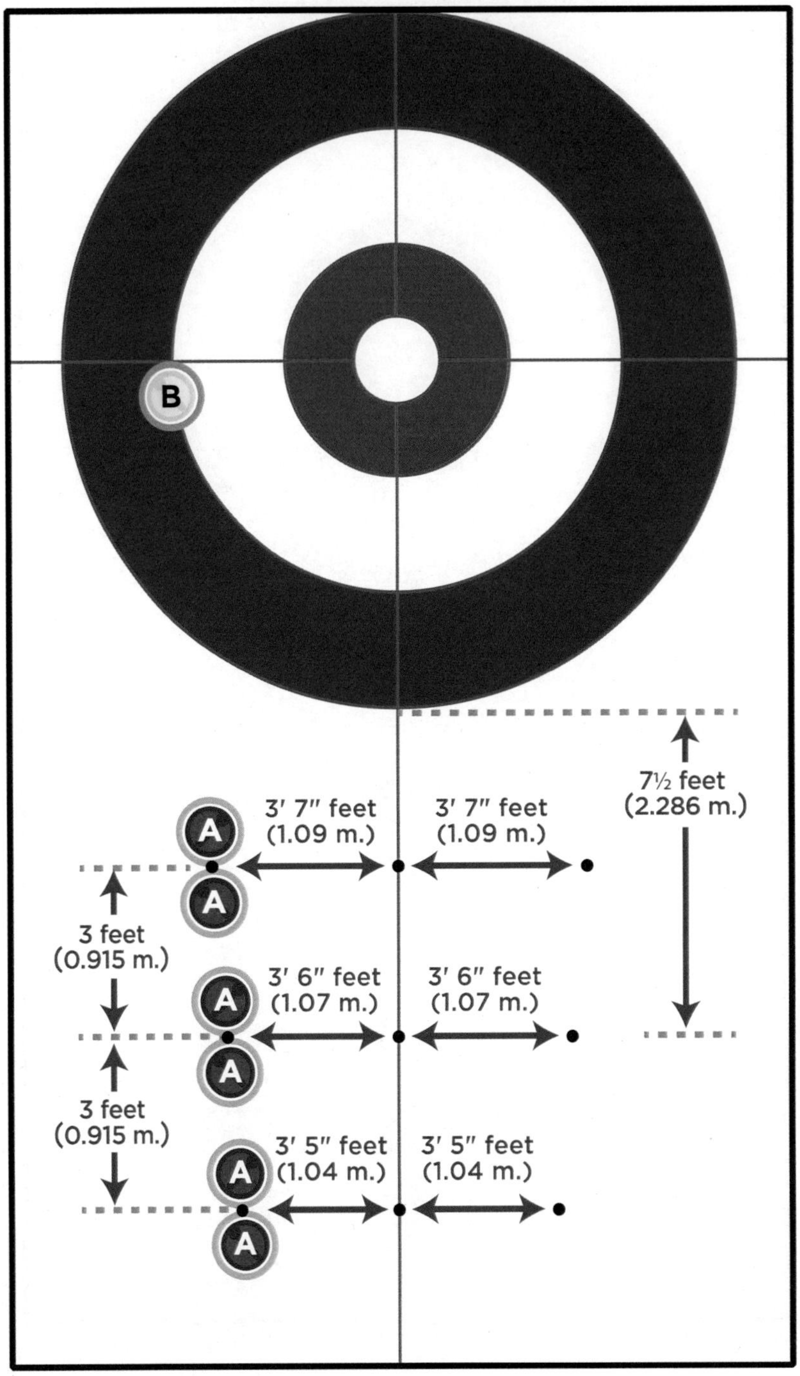

(g) The team having the decision on the placement of the "positioned" stones shall be:

(i) Teams opposing each other in the game shall use the Last Stone Draw (LSD) to determine which team has the decision in the first end. The team with the lesser LSD distance shall have the decision on the placement.

(ii) Following the first end, the team that did not score shall have the decision on the placement.

(iii) If neither team scores in an end, the team that delivered the first stone in that end shall have the decision on placement in the next end.

(h) The team whose "positioned" stone is placed in Position A (in front of the house) shall deliver the first stone in that end, and the team whose "positioned" stone is placed in Position B (in the house) shall deliver the second stone in that end.

(i) While the team is in the process of delivery, the non-delivering player may be anywhere on the ice surface of the team's sheet. After delivery, either or both players may sweep their delivered stone and any stones set in motion that belong to their team anywhere in front of the tee line at the playing end. This applies during all of the team's delivered stones, including the LSD.

(j) If a delivery violation occurs, the delivered stone shall be removed from play, and any displaced stones shall be replaced, by the non-offending team, to their positions prior to the violation taking place. Should the infraction not be discovered until after the delivery of a subsequent stone, play continues as if the infraction had not occurred, however, the player that delivered the first stone of the end can deliver a maximum of two stones in that end.

R16. PROHIBITED SUBSTANCES

The use of all performance-enhancing drugs, without therapeutic exemption, whether taken knowingly or otherwise, is unethical and prohibited. If such use occurs the player(s) will be disqualified from the competition, their Member Association will be notified, and it could lead to further suspension.

R17. INAPPROPRIATE BEHAVIOUR

Improper conduct, foul or offensive language, equipment abuse, or wilful damage on the part of any team member is prohibited. Any violation may result in suspension of the offending person(s) by the curling organisation having jurisdiction.

RULES OF COMPETITION

C1. GENERAL

(a) The rules of play for WCF competitions are the current rules of the World Curling Federation (WCF). If there are any modifications, these are explained during the Team Meeting.

(b) The dates of the WCF competitions are determined by the Executive Board of the WCF.

(c) The playing and event schedules are determined by the WCF in consultation with the Host Committee.

(d) Smoking, including e-smoking devices, within the confines of the competition area at WCF competitions is prohibited.

(e) The WCF Anti-Doping rules and procedures, which meet the requirements of the World Anti-Doping Agency are applicable, and published in the WCF Anti-Doping Pamphlet.

(f) Any variation from the recommended sheet measurements must be approved by the WCF.

(g) For WCF Championships, gold medals are awarded to the first placed team, silver medals to the second placed team, and bronze medals to the third placed team. The 5 players (2 for Mixed Doubles, 4 for Mixed) and their coach, receive medals, if they are in attendance and fulfil their team obligations, and are allowed on the podium. For the Olympic Winter Games, Youth Olympic Games and the Paralympic Winter Games, only the players receive medals and are allowed on the podium.

C2. PARTICIPATING TEAMS

(a) Each team is designated by its Association/Federation.

(b) If a designated team is unable or unwilling to participate, the Association/Federation involved nominates another team.

(c) The teams for each event must be declared at least 14 days prior to the start of the competition. Notification of a replacement must be done by the end of the team meeting.

(d) All players at a WCF competition must be bona fide members in good standing of their Associations/Federations.

(e) To be eligible to play in the World Junior Curling Championships (WJCC) and qualifying events, a player must be less than 21 years of age by the end of the 30th day of June of the year immediately preceding the year in which the championship is to take place.

(f) To be eligible to play in the World Senior Curling Championships (WSCC) and qualifying events, a player must be not less than 50 years of age by the end of the 30th day of June of the year immediately preceding the year in which the championship is to take place.

(g) To be eligible to play in the World Wheelchair Curling Championship (WWhCC) and qualifying events, a player must have substantial demonstrable impairments in leg/gait function and use a wheelchair for daily mobility, or qualify within the eligibility criteria.

(h) All players and their coach must attend the Team Meeting. Failure to do so, without approval of the Chief Umpire, results in the forfeit of the last stone advantage for that team in its first game. Only the team players, one coach, a Team Leader, and a translator if necessary, are allowed to attend. For teams in post round robin play, one or two team members (players and/or coach) must attend the play-off meetings, or the team will lose the choices (first or second practice, colour of stones, etc.) to which they would normally be entitled.

(i) The team delivery rotation, skip and vice-skip positions, alternate player, and coach are listed on the original team line-up form, and submitted to the Chief Umpire at the end of the Team Meeting. The team leader / national coach / translator, if appropriate, are also listed. A game team line-up form (paper or electronic) must be submitted to the Chief Umpire at least 15 minutes prior to the pre-game practice to either confirm the original team line-up or to indicate a change.

(j) A team must start a competition with four players (two for Mixed Doubles) delivering stones. A team will forfeit each game at the start of the competition, until it can start a game with four qualified players. In extenuating circumstances, and with approval from a panel of three persons (WCF Director of Competitions or Representative, event Technical Delegate, event Chief Umpire) a team may be allowed to start a competition with three players. If required, an appeal would be heard by the WCF President or his/her representative.

(k) While a game is in progress, the coach, the alternate player, and all other team officials are prohibited from communicating with their team or being within the playing area except during specifically designated breaks or a team time-out. This restriction applies to all verbal, visual, written, and electronic communication, including any attempt to signal for the implementation of a team time-out. The coach, the alternate player, and one team official may participate in the pre-event and the pre-game practices, but may not communicate with their team during the LSD. During the game, there shall be no unauthorised communications or broadcasts of any sort from the coach bench to anyone who is not sitting in that designated area. Coaches and other team personnel sitting on the coach bench cannot watch or listen to broadcasts. For any violation, the offending person will be removed from the coach's bench for that game.

(l) For the purpose of identification to the media and to the public, teams are referred to by the name under which their Association/Federation competes, and by the name of the skip.

C3. UNIFORMS / EQUIPMENT

(a) All team members wear identical uniforms and appropriate footwear when accessing the field of play for games or practice sessions. The team wears light-coloured shirts and playing jackets/sweaters when assigned stones with light-coloured handles, and wears dark-coloured shirts and playing jackets/sweaters when assigned stones with dark-coloured handles. The colour of these garments shall be registered with the WCF prior to the start of each competition. The team coaches/officials must wear a team or national uniform whenever accessing the field of play. Red is considered to be a dark colour.

(Effective 1 October 2018, unless otherwise approved by the WCF, a light-coloured uniform will be predominantly white or yellow in colour. Approval for any alternative colour must be requested at least 8 weeks prior to an event or may be requested at the start of a season for multiple events.)

(b) Each shirt and jacket/sweater has the player's surname, in 5.08 cm. (2-in.) or larger letters, across the upper back of the garment, and the name under which their Association/Federation competes, in 5.08 cm. (2-in.) or larger letters, across the back above the waist. If desired, a national emblem may also be worn on the back, but only in addition to the name under which the Association/Federation competes, and displayed between that name and the player's surname. When two or more team members have the same surname, the first letter(s) of their given names are also displayed.

(c) Advertising is permitted on a player's clothing or equipment strictly in accordance with the current guidelines issued by the WCF. The WCF may, in its sole discretion, forbid the use of any clothing or equipment that it feels is unacceptable or unsuitable for WCF competition play. The WCF Dress Code is contained within this book.

(d) A player or coach with an improper uniform shall be denied access to the field of play and the coach bench.

(e) Each player must declare an approved sweeping device at the start of a game, and only that player can use that device for sweeping during the game. Penalty: If a player sweeps with another person's sweeping device the stone shall be removed from play.

(f) Players may not change their brush heads during a game, unless the Chief Umpire grants special permission. Penalty: If a change is made without permission, the team will forfeit the game.

(g) If an alternate player comes into a game, that player must use the brush head of the player being replaced. Penalty: If a new brush head is brought into the game, the team will forfeit the game.

(h) All field of play equipment used at WCF competitions must meet WCF Equipment Standards, as defined and published on the WCF website. Reasons for equipment being considered non-approved include, but not restricted to: damage to the ice surface, non-conformance with existing rules or standards (i.e. - electronic communication devices), performance testing results that give an unfair advantage, failing to register equipment with the WCF office by the deadline date.

(i) The penalty for using equipment in WCF competitions that does not conform to standards for Competition Equipment established by the WCF:
(i) First team offence during a competition - the player is disqualified from the competition and the team forfeits the game.
(ii) Second team offence during a competition - the team is disqualified from the competition and all players are not permitted to play in WCF competitions for a 12-month period.

C4. PRE-GAME PRACTICE

(a) Prior to the start of every game at WCF competitions, each team is allowed a pre-game practice on the sheet on which it will be playing.

(b) The time and duration of the pre-game practice is given at the Team Meeting.

(c) The schedule for pre-game practices during the round robin will be predetermined as much as possible, based on the criterion that each team has first and second practice an equal number of times. For the round robin games where this cannot be predetermined the winner of a coin toss will have the choice of first or second practice.

(d) In post round robin games, when the Last Stone First End has been pre-determined, the team delivering the last stone in the first end practices first.

(e) If the Chief Ice Technician deems it necessary, the ice will be cleaned, and the slide path re-pebbled, after the pre-game practice.

C5. LENGTH OF GAMES

(a) In competitions in which 10 ends are scheduled, a minimum of 6 ends must be completed in round robin games, and 8 ends must be completed in play-off games.

(b) In competitions in which 8 ends are scheduled, a minimum of 6 ends must be completed.

C6. GAME TIMING

(a) Each team shall receive 38 minutes of thinking time for a 10-end game and 30 minutes of thinking time for an 8-end game (38 minutes in wheelchair curling, 22 minutes in mixed doubles curling). This time is recorded, and visible to the teams and coaches, throughout the game.

(b) When a team delays the start of a game, the thinking time allotted to each team is reduced by 3 minutes 45 seconds (4 minutes 45 seconds in wheelchair curling, 2 minutes 45 seconds in mixed doubles curling) for each end which was considered completed (Rules of Curling R11(i) apply).

(c) When extra ends are required, the game clocks are reset and each team receives 4 minutes 30 seconds of thinking time for each extra end (6 minutes in wheelchair curling, 3 minutes in mixed doubles curling).

(d) The game and each end starts when the allotted break time expires. The delivering team's game clock will not run during the start of the game/end unless that team is delaying the start (no forward motion from the hack, or the stone not released from the delivery stick), then its game clock will be started. If there is no delay, the first game clock to start in each end will be that of the team delivering the second stone.

(e) Once all of the criteria below are met, the non-delivering team becomes the delivering team, and its game clock is started:

(i) all stones have come to rest or have crossed the back line; and

(ii) stones that are displaced due to violations by the delivering team, and require repositioning, are returned to their positions prior to the violation; and

(iii) the playing area has been relinquished to the other team, the person in charge of the house has moved behind the back line and the deliverer and sweepers have moved to the sides of the sheet.

(f) A team's game clock stops once the stone has reached the tee line (hog line in wheelchair curling) at the delivery end.

(g) A team delivers stones only when its game clock is running or scheduled to be running. Any violation results in the stone being redelivered after any displaced stones have been returned, by the non-offending team, to their positions prior to the violation. The time clock of the offending team will start as soon as any displaced stones have been repositioned and will stop when the redelivered stone reaches the tee line (hog line for wheelchair curling) at the delivering end.

(h) If stones need to be repositioned due to a violation caused by an external force both game clocks are stopped.

(i) Game clocks are stopped at any time an umpire intervenes.

(j) After the teams have agreed on the score for an end, a break occurs, when neither game clock is running. If a measurement is required, the break begins at the completion of that measurement. The length of the break between ends, which may vary due to television requirements or to other external factors, is determined for each competition and explained at the Team Meeting. When a break is of 3 minutes or more, the teams are informed when 1 minute of the break remains. Teams should not deliver the first stone of the next end until less than 10 seconds of the break time remains. The delivering team's game clock will start at the conclusion of the break unless the player is in the process of delivery. The length of the break will normally be:

  (i) 1 minute at the completion of each end, except as noted in (j)(ii). In Mixed Doubles, when players are responsible for placing the stationary stones before each end, 30 seconds will be added to the time between ends.

  Teams cannot meet, or communicate in any way, with a coach, the alternate player or any other team official.

  (ii) 5 minutes at the completion of the end that defines the halfway point in the game. Teams are allowed to meet, within the playing area, with any player and team official that is authorised to be on the coach bench for that game.

(k) If a player is allowed to redeliver a stone, the umpire decides if the time required is to be deducted from the game time for that team.

(l) If an end is to be replayed, the game clocks are reset to the time recorded at the completion of the previous end.

(m) If an umpire determines that a team is unnecessarily delaying a game, the umpire notifies the skip of the offending team and, after that notification, if the next stone to be delivered has not reached the tee line (hog line in wheelchair curling) at the delivery end within 45 seconds, the stone is removed from play immediately.

(n) Each team must complete its part of a game within the time given, or forfeit the game. If a stone reaches the tee line (hog line in wheelchair curling) at the delivery end before time expires, the stone is considered delivered in time.

(o) A team whose clock has run due to a timing error (wrong clock running) will have double the agreed error time added back to its clock.

(p) A team whose time clock did not run due to a timing error (no clock running) will not have time deducted from its time clock, but the appropriate amount of time will be added to the other team's time clock.

C7. TEAM TIME-OUTS / TECHNICAL TIME-OUTS

(a) Team time-outs will be allowed at all WCF events, with or without time clocks being used.

(b) Each team may call one 60 second team time-out during each game and one 60 second team time-out in each extra end.

(c) Procedures for a team time-out are as follows:

(i) Only the players on the ice may call a team time-out.

(ii) Team time-outs may be called by any on-ice team player only when that team's game clock is running. Players signal a team time-out by using a "T" hand signal.

(iii) A team time-out (when the game clock is stopped) starts as soon as the time-out is called and consists of 'travel time' to get to the team plus 60 seconds. The amount of travel time will be determined at each event by the Chief Umpire, and is given to all teams, whether or not they have a coach, and whether or not a coach is coming to the field of play.

(iv) Only one person, who is sitting in the designated coaching area and a translator, if required, of the team that called the team time-out is allowed to meet with the team. This person, or persons if a translator is required, must use the designated route to the team. Where walkways are beside the sheet, that person must not stand on the playing ice surface.

(v) The team is notified when there are 10 seconds remaining in the team time-out.

(vi) When the team time-out has expired, the person(s) from the coach's bench must stop conferring with the team and leave the playing area immediately.

(d) A technical time-out may be called by a team to request a ruling, for an injury or in other extenuating circumstances. Game clocks will be stopped during technical time-outs.

C8. STONE ASSIGNMENT / LAST STONE DRAW

(a) The team listed first in the draw schedule for the round robin games will play the stones with the dark-coloured handles; the team listed second will play with the stones with the light-coloured handles.

(b) For games requiring Last Stone Draws (LSD), at the conclusion of each team's pre-game practice, two stones will be delivered to the tee at the home end, by different players – the first stone with a clockwise and the second with a counter-clockwise rotation. A player (alternate) that delivers an LSD stone does not have to play in that game. Sweeping is allowed (except in wheelchair curling). In Mixed curling each gender must deliver one stone, but the team selects the sweepers independent of their gender.

The first stone will be measured and removed from play before the second stone is delivered. The distances recorded for each stone will be added together to give the team its LSD total for that game. The team with the lesser LSD total will have the choice of delivering the first or second stone in the first end of that game. If the LSD totals for both teams are the same, the individual LSD stones are compared and the best non-equal LSD has the choice of delivering first or second stone in the first end. When both teams have the exact same individual LSD stone distances, a coin toss will be used to determine that choice.

(c) LSD distances will be measured and recorded in the following manner:

(i) All single measurements will be from the tee to the nearest part of the stone, but the LSD distances will be displayed in centimetres as the distance from the tee to the centre of the stone.

(ii) The official radius to be used in WCF championships is 14.2 cm.

(iii) To any result measured, the radius of 14.2 cm has to be added. This means that the distance for stones not in the house is 185.4 cm + 14.2 cm = 199.6 cm.

(iv) Stones covering the tee will be measured from two locations (holes) at the edge of the 4ft circle. These two locations make a 90-degree angle with the centre hole and are 0.61 m (2 feet) from the centre hole.

(d) The number of LSD stones, and the number of clockwise and counter-clockwise deliveries for each player, will be determined at each competition depending upon the number of games in the round robin. Based on the Original Team Line-up form, the four players (2 in Mixed Doubles) have to fulfil the minimum number of LSD deliveries. If there is a violation where the minimum requirements are not fulfilled, the appropriate LSD(s) will be recorded as 199.6 cm.

(i) LSD stones delivered by the alternate can be combined at the end of the round robin with only one other player, so that this player fulfils the minimum required number of LSD stones.

(ii) Where a team plays an entire event with only 3 players, the LSD stone requirements of the missing player are shared equitably amongst the other players.

(iii) Where a team starts a competition with a complete team but then, for any reason, a player cannot fulfil their minimum LSD requirements, the maximum of 199.6cm will be recorded for each of their missed LSD stones.

Round robin games	Number of LSD stones	Minimum for each player
4	8	2 stones, 1 clockwise + 1 counter-clockwise
5	10	2 stones, 1 clockwise + 1 counter-clockwise
6	12	2 stones, 1 clockwise + 1 counter-clockwise
7	14	3 stones, minimum 1 clockwise + minimum 1 counter-clockwise
8	16	3 stones, minimum 1 clockwise + minimum 1 counter-clockwise

9	18	4 stones, 2 clockwise + 2 counter-clockwise
10	20	4 stones, 2 clockwise + 2 counter-clockwise
11	22	4 stones, 2 clockwise + 2 counter-clockwise

(e) For Mixed Doubles each player delivers an equal number of clockwise and counter-clockwise LSD stones. If there are an odd number of games a variation of one rotation per player has to occur.

(f) When round robin play (one group) is used at WCF competitions, with each competing team playing all other teams, first stone in the first end of post round robin games is determined as follows:

(i) The team with the better win/loss record has the choice of playing first or second stone in the first end.

(ii) If the teams have the same win/loss record, the winner of their round robin game has the choice of playing first or second stone in the first end.

(iii) Notwithstanding (i) and (ii), for competitions that use the Page play-off system, the team that wins the 1 versus 2 game has the choice of delivering the first or second stone in the first end of the gold medal game; the team that loses the semi-final game has the choice of delivering the first or second stone in the first end of the bronze medal game.

(g) At WCF competitions when teams play a round robin in separate groups, for the play-off game(s) if the teams are from the same group C8 (f) will be used, and if the teams are from different groups, the team with the lesser DSC has choice of either the first or second practice or the stone handle colour. Then regular LSD procedures (without minimum requirements), will determine which team has the choice of delivering the first or second stone in the first end.

(h) In post round robin games where the team delivering the first stone in the first end has been pre-determined, the team delivering the first stone of the first end has the choice of stone handle colour.

C9. TEAM RANKING PROCEDURE / DRAW SHOT CHALLENGE

(a) During the round robin portion of a competition, teams with the same win-loss record will be listed alphabetically, by their three-letter code, and ranked equal.

(b) The following criteria (in order) will be used to rank the teams at the completion of the round robin:

(i) Teams will be ranked according to their win/loss record;

(ii) If two teams are tied, the team that won their round robin game will be ranked higher;

(iii) Where three or more teams are tied, the record of the games between the tied teams shall provide the ranking (should this procedure provide a ranking for some teams but not all, then the record of the games between the remaining teams that are still tied shall determine the ranking);

(iv) For all remaining teams, whose ranking cannot be determined by (i) or (ii) or (iii), ranking is determined using the Draw Shot Challenge (DSC). The DSC is the average distance of all the individual Last Stone Draw stones, which were delivered by a team during the round robin.

Where there is more than one group and these groups are of differing sizes, to ensure the DSC is calculated in the same way, only the LSDs from the first 'equal number' of games will be used.

Where a total of 11 or fewer individual stones will be considered, the single least favourable result is automatically eliminated when calculating the average distance. Where more than 11 individual stones will be considered, the two least favourable results will be eliminated when calculating the average distance.

The team with the lesser DSC receives the higher ranking. If the DSCs are equal then the team with the best non-equal counting LSD receives the higher ranking. In the case where all counting LSDs are equal the team ranked higher in the WCF World Rankings is ranked higher.

(v) When teams compete in different groups and do not qualify for the play-offs, the final ranking will be determined by comparing the DSCs from the teams in all groups with the same ranking, with the best DSC being ranked highest.

(vi) In events where a single loss eliminates a team from the competition, teams eliminated during the same session will be listed alphabetically, by their three-letter code, and ranked equal.

(c) When teams are tied for a play-off position, team(s) shall be eliminated without playing an extra game, as tie-breaker games will not be played.

(d) When teams are tied for a challengeable position, team(s) can avoid the challengeable position without winning an extra game, as tie-breaker games will not be played.

(e) When teams are tied for a relegation position, team(s) can avoid or be placed in a relegation position without playing an extra game, as tie-breaker games will not be played.

C10. UMPIRES

(a) The WCF appoints a Chief Umpire and the Deputy Chief Umpire(s) for every WCF competition. These officials should include both men and women. Officials are approved by their respective Associations/ Federations.

(b) The umpire determines any matter in dispute between teams, whether or not the matter is covered by the rules.

(c) An umpire may intervene at any time during a competition, and give directions concerning the placement of stones, the conduct of players and adherence to the rules.

(d) The Chief Umpire, when authorised, may intervene at any time in any game and give such directions concerning the conduct of the game as is considered proper.

(e) An umpire may delay a game for any reason and determine the length of the delay.

(f) All matters pertaining to the rules are adjudicated by an umpire. In the event that there is an appeal against an umpire's decision, the decision of the Chief Umpire is final.

(g) The Chief Umpire may eject a player, coach or team official from a game for what is considered to be unacceptable conduct or language. The ejected person must leave the competition area and take no further part in that game. When a player is ejected from a game, an alternate player may not be used in that game, for that player.

(h) The Chief Umpire may recommend to the curling organisation having jurisdiction the disqualification, or suspension, of any player, coach or team official from present or future competitions.

COMPETITIONS – THE PLAYDOWN SYSTEMS

Olympic Winter Games (OWG) – Men & Women

- 10 teams for each gender… 1 team from the Host National Olympic Committee (NOC) + 7 teams from the NOCs which gained the most qualification points from the two previous Men's and Women's World Curling Championships + 2 teams from the Olympic Qualification Event (OQE) which is open to teams which played in any of the four previous Men's or Women's World Curling Championships and did not gain sufficient qualification points to directly qualify for the OWG. Also, the third-place teams from the PACC events held during the Olympic cycle will be allocated a spot in the Olympic Qualification Event, if they have not already qualified by their participation in the WCCs.
- Teams placed in one group, playing a round robin to establish the top four ranked teams.

Play-off System: Semi-finals with 1 v 4 and 2 v 3; winners play in the final (for the gold and silver medals), losers play in the bronze medal game.

Olympic Winter Games (OWG) – Mixed Doubles

- 8 teams… 1 team from the Host National Olympic Committee (NOC) + 7 teams from the NOCs which gained the most qualification points from the two previous World Mixed Doubles Curling Championships.
- Teams placed in one group, playing a round robin to establish the top four ranked teams.

Play-off System: Semi-finals with 1 v 4 and 2 v 3; winners play in the final (for the gold and silver medals), losers play in the bronze medal game.

Paralympic Winter Games (PWG) – Mixed Gender Teams

- 12 teams… 1 team from the Host National Paralympic Committee (NPC) + 11 teams from the NPCs which gained the most qualification points from the three previous World Wheelchair Curling Championships.
- Teams placed in one group, playing a round robin to establish the top four ranked teams.

Play-off System: Semi-finals with 1 v 4 and 2 v 3; winners play in the final (for the gold and silver medals), losers play in the bronze medal game.

Winter Youth Olympic Games (YOG)

- The National Olympic Committees (NOCs) will collect points from the two previous World Curling Federation's World Junior Curling Championships (WJCC) and World Junior-B Curling Championships (WJBCC). In the event that a specific Challenge event is needed for the Americas, it will be added to the qualification timeline.

The first 16 Mixed teams will be selected (based on the highest number of points accumulated) in the manner shown below, and the last 8 teams will be selected using the WCF Junior World Rankings and alternating between genders:

- 1 team guaranteed to the host National Olympic Committee (NOC)
- 2 teams from North America
- 1 team from South America
- 3 teams from Asia
- 1 team from Oceania
- 8 teams from Europe

The points shall be awarded on the following basis:

WJCC	WJBCC
1st = 20 points	1st = awarded at WJCC
2nd = 18 points	2nd = awarded at WJCC
3rd = 17 points	3rd = awarded at WJCC
4th = 16 points	4th = 5 points
5th = 15 points	5th = 4 points
6th = 14 points	6th = 3 points
7th = 13 points	7th = 2 points
8th = 12 points	8th = 1 points
9th = 11 points	
10th = 10 points	

World Curling Championships - Men (WMCC) & Women (WWCC)

- 13 teams (qualification process explained on Page 49).
- Teams placed in one group, playing a round robin to establish the top six ranked teams.

Play-off System: The teams ranked 1st and 2nd get a bye to the semi-finals. The teams ranked 3rd to 6th play in qualification games (3 v 6 and 4 v 5). The winners of those qualification games advance to the semi-finals, with the 1st ranked team playing the lowest ranked winner (e.g. - 6th) and the 2nd ranked team playing the other team. The winners of the semi-finals play in the gold medal game, the losers of the semi-final play in the bronze medal game.

World Junior Curling Championships (WJCC) - Junior Men & Junior Women

- 10 teams for each gender... 1 team from the Host Association/Federation, top 6 highest ranked Association/Federation from the previous year's WJCC and top 3 teams from the previous WJBCC.
- Teams placed in one group, playing a round robin to establish the top four ranked teams.

Play-off System: Semi-finals with 1 v 4 and 2 v 3; winners play in the final (for the gold and silver medals), losers play in the bronze medal game.

World Junior-B Curling Championships (WJBCC) - Junior Men & Junior Women

- Open to junior teams from all WCF Member Associations that have not already qualified for the next WJCC. Three teams will qualify from this event.
- If 1-10 teams enter they will be placed in one group, playing a round robin to establish the top four ranked teams.

Play-off System: Semi-finals with 1 v 4 and 2 v 3; winners play in the final (for the gold and silver medals), losers play in the bronze medal game.

- If more than 10 teams enter they will be placed into groups which meet the schedule requirements. The groups play a round robin to establish the teams required for the quarter-final play-offs.

Play-off System: At the end of the round robin series there must be a ranking for 1st, 2nd, 3rd and 4th (if two groups); 1st, 2nd and 3rd (if three groups); 1st and 2nd (if four groups).

Where there are three groups the 1st and 2nd ranked teams qualify directly for the quarter-finals, as well as the 3rd ranked team with the best Draw Shot Challenge (DSC) result. The other two 3rd ranked teams play a qualification game to decide the last team entered into the quarter-finals.

The winners of the quarter-finals play in the semi-finals.

The losers of the semi-finals play in the Bronze Medal game.

The winners of the semi-finals play in the Gold Medal game.

Winter University Games (WUG) - Men & Women University Students

- 10 teams for each gender... 1 team from the Host Association + 9 teams according to FISU entry regulations.
- Teams placed in one group, playing a round robin to establish the top four ranked teams.

Play-off System: Semi-finals with 1 v 4 and 2 v 3; winners play in the final (for the gold and silver medals), losers play in the bronze medal game.

World Wheelchair Curling Championship (WWhCC) - Mixed Gender Teams

- 12 teams ... 1 team from the Host Association + 8 teams from the Associations which qualified from the previous WWhCC + 3 teams from the Associations which qualified through the World Wheelchair-B Curling Championship (WWhBCC).
- Teams placed in one group, playing a round robin to establish the top six ranked teams.

Play-off System: The top two teams will progress to the semi-final stages with the four next highest ranked teams playing in qualification games (3v6 and 4v5). The winners of these games then progress to the semi-finals. The semi-finals will be played as follows: the team ranked 1st will play the lowest ranked team left following the qualification games, the team ranked 2nd will play the highest ranked team left following the qualification games.

World Wheelchair-B Curling Championship (WWhBCC) - Mixed Gender Teams

- Open to teams from Associations that have not already qualified for the next WWhCC. Three teams will qualify from this event.
- If 1-10 teams enter they will be placed in one group; if more than ten teams enter they will be placed in two groups. The group(s) play a round robin to establish the teams required for the play-offs.

Play-off System:
a) if one group: Semi-finals with 1 v 4 and 2 v 3; winners play in the final (for the gold and silver medals), losers play in the bronze medal game. The medal winning teams qualify for the next WWhCC.
b) if two groups: 1st place in both groups qualify for the semi-finals; qualification games A2 v B3 and A3 V B2 winners qualify for semi-finals; Semi-finals: If 2 teams from each group then A1 plays the B qualifier and B1 plays the A qualifier. If 3 teams from one group then the 1st ranked team of that group plays the 3rd ranked team from the same group, and the 1st ranked team of the other group plays the 2nd ranked team from the group that qualified 3 teams.

The medal winning teams qualify for the next WWhCC.

World Mixed Doubles Curling Championship (WMDCC)

Open number of entries (qualification process and play-off system explained Page 50-51)

World Mixed Curling Championship (WMxCC)

Open number of entries (qualification process and play-off system explained Page 51)

World Senior Curling Championships (WSCC) - Men & Women

Open number of entries (qualification process and play-off system explained Page 51)

Pacific-Asia Curling Championships (PACC) - Men & Women

Open to teams from the Pacific-Asia Curling Zone (qualification process and play-off system explained on Page 52).

QUALIFICATION - WORLD CHAMPIONSHIPS MEN & WOMEN

For the 2018 World Men's and Women's Championships there are 13 teams, selected in this manner:

- 2 American Zone (including host)
- 3 Pacific-Asia Zone
- 8 European Zone

Effective for the 2019 World Men's and Women's Championships there are 13 teams, selected in this manner:

- 2 American Zone (including host) *
- 2 Pacific-Asia Zone (including host) *
- 8 European Zone (including host) *
- 2 World Qualification Event

  *Zone with last place team at the previous WCC loses one guaranteed spot

Effective for the 2019 World Men's and Women's Championships there will be a World Qualification Event (WQE):

8 teams entered and two (2) qualify for the next World Championship

Teams - 1 Host + 1 Americas + 2 Pacific-Asia + 4 Europe

QUALIFICATION - WORLD JUNIOR CHAMPIONSHIPS (WJCC)

All Zones	1 team	To the Host Association / Federation.
	6 teams	The top six (6) teams, excluding the host, from the previous WJCC.
	3 teams	The top three (3) teams from the previous WJBCC.

WORLD MIXED DOUBLES (WMDCC)

- An Association's team is made up of curlers who are bona fide members of that Association and who fulfil the eligibility criteria for playing for that Association.
- The World Curling Federation reserves the right to adjust the system of play.

ENTRIES	PLAYING SYSTEM	PLAY-OFFS	FINAL RANKINGS
1-10 Entries	**ONE** Group Round robin + Play-offs	Olympic play-off system with top four teams as shown in the chart on page 59	Teams ranked 1- 10 as per WCF ranking procedure
11- 20 Entries **Group-A** 1,4,5,8,9,12,13, 16,17,20 **Group-B** 2,3,6,7,10,11,14, 15,18,19 Rankings from the previous 3 years. MAs that did not play in those events will be ranked (at the end of the list) according to the WCF World Ranking	**TWO** Groups Group round robins to determine top 3 teams in each group + Qualification games, semi-finals and medal games	Top teams qualify for the semi-finals; qualification games A2 v B3 and A3 v B2 to determine last teams in the semi-finals	Teams in each group will be ranked as per WCF ranking procedure DSC results are used for the final ranking of the teams that did not qualify for the play-offs, when comparing teams with the same rank but from a different group Final ranking will be established from 1 - 20
21-30 Entries **Group-A** 1,6,7,12,13,18, 19,24,25,30 **Group-B** 2,5,8,11,14,17, 20,23,26,29 **Group-C** 3,4,9,10,15,16, 21,22,27,28 Rankings from the	**THREE** Groups Group round robins to determine the top 3 teams in each group + One qualification game to determine the last team in the quarter-finals + Quarter-finals, semi-finals and medal games	Quarter-finals as shown in the chart on page 60 When qualification games are played, the losers will be ranked equal and listed alphabetically by 3-letter country code. When quarter-final games are played, the	Teams in each group will be ranked as per WCF ranking procedure DSC results are used for the final ranking of the teams that did not qualify for the play-offs or the qualification games, when comparing teams with the same rank but from a different group

previous 3 years. MAs that did not play in those events will be ranked (at the end of the list) according to the WCF World Ranking.		losers will be ranked equal (5th) and listed alphabetically by 3-letter country code.	Final ranking will be established from 1 – 30
31+ Entries (For example) **Group-A** 1,8,9,16,17,24,25,32, 33,40 **Group-B** 2,7,10,15,18,23,26,31, 34,39 **Group-C** 3,6,11,14,19,22,27,30, 35,38 **Group-D** 4,5,12,13,20,21,28,29, 36,37 Rankings from the previous 3 years. MAs that did not play in those events will be ranked (at the end of the list) according to the WCF World Ranking.	**FOUR or FIVE** Groups Group round robins to determine the top 4 teams in each group + If 4 groups, the top 4 teams advance to the 1/8 finals. If 5 groups, the top three teams qualify directly for the 1/8 finals, as well as the 4th ranked team with the best DSC result. + 1/8 finals, 1/4 finals, semi-finals and medal games	The playoff system is based on 16 teams and ranking is clearly established by games for 12 teams; after losing games the other 4 teams will be ranked equal (13th) and listed alphabetically by 3-letter country code.	Teams in each group will be ranked as per WCF ranking procedure DSC results are used for the final ranking of the teams that did not qualify for the play-offs, when comparing teams with the same rank but from a different group Final ranking will be established from 1 – 31+

WORLD SENIORS (WSCC) & WORLD MIXED CURLING CHAMPIONSHIP (WMxCC)

- An Association's team is made up of curlers who are bona fide members of that Association and who fulfil the eligibility criteria for playing for that Association.
- The format of these "open" enter championships are worked out to give every team the chance to win the Championship and to play as many games as possible. Teams will be advised of the playing system in the Team Meeting Documents, prior to the start of play.
- The World Curling Federation reserves the right to adjust the system of play depending on the number of entries and the sheets of ice available.

PACIFIC-ASIA CURLING CHAMPIONSHIPS (PACC)

Qualification – World Curling Championships (WCC)

World Curling Federation (WCF) determines the System of Play

One to Four teams qualifying:

ENTRIES	PLAYING SYSTEM	PLAY-OFFS	QUALIFICATION
6 or fewer Entries	One group Double round robin to determine top 4 teams + Play-offs	Olympic play-off system with top four teams as shown in the chart on page 59	Depending on the number of teams qualifying for the WCCs, the teams are selected in this order: Gold, Silver, Bronze and 4th place. Teams ranked as per WCF ranking procedure
7 or more Entries	One group Single round robin to determine top 4 teams + Play-offs		

EUROPEAN CURLING CHAMPIONSHIPS (ECC)

- The European Curling Championship qualifies European teams to the World Curling Championships.
- For the 2018 World Men's and Women's Championships: Europe receives 8 places.
- Effective for the 2019 World Men's and Women's Championship: 8 guaranteed European Zone places (including host), however, if the Zone has the last place team at the previous WCC it loses one guaranteed spot.
- "ECC World Challenge" - the last team from A-Division to qualify plays a best-of-three challenge against the winner of the B-Division (if either of those teams are the host of the next WCC the next team in line will play the challenge). The winner qualifies for the WCC.
- The World Curling Federation reserves the right to adjust the system of play. In the event of no entries for the C-Division, B9 + B10 Women and B15 + B16 Men remain in the B-Division.

ENTRIES	PLAYING SYSTEM	PLAY-OFFS	FINAL RANKINGS
A Division **Men and Women** **10 Teams** **A1 - A8** **+ B1 + B2** Rankings taken from the previous ECC	One Group: Round robin to determine top 4 teams + Play-offs	Olympic play-off system with top four teams as shown in the chart on page 59	Teams ranked A1- A10 as per WCF ranking procedure. **A9 + A10 are relegated to B Division for next ECC** The last team from A-Division to qualify plays winner B1 in World Challenge - best of three games
B Division **Women** **10 Teams** **A9 + A10** **+ B3 - B8** **+ C1 + C2** Rankings taken from the previous ECC	One Group: Round robin to determine top 4 teams + Play-offs	Olympic play-off system with top four teams as shown in the chart on page 59	Teams ranked B1- B10 as per WCF ranking procedure. **B1 + B2 are promoted to A Division for next ECC** **B9+B10 are relegated to C Division** Winner B1 plays the last team from A-Division to qualify in World Challenge - best of three games
B Division **Men** 16 teams **A9 + A10** **+ B3 - B14** **+ C1 + C2** Rankings taken from the previous ECC	Two Groups of 8 teams: Group round robins to determine top 3 teams + Play-offs	1st ranked teams advance directly to the semi-finals; A2 v B3 and A3 v B2 to determine last teams in semi-finals. For the semi-finals: If 2 teams from each group then A1 plays the B qualifier and B1 plays the A qualifier. If 3 teams from one group then the 1st ranked team of that group plays the 3rd ranked team from the same group, and the 1st ranked team of the other group plays the 2nd ranked team from the	Teams ranked B1- B16 as per WCF ranking procedure. **B1 + B2 are promoted to A Division for next ECC** **B15 + B16 are relegated to C Division** Winner B1 plays the last team from A-Division to qualify in World Challenge - best of three games

		group that qualified 3 teams. The relegation for the ECC B-Division men is determined in the following manner: MA7 v MB7 - winner is not relegated and MA8 v MB8 - loser is relegated Loser (MA7 v MB7) v winner (MA8 v MB8) - winner is not relegated, loser is relegated There is no tie-breaker game(s) before those relegation games and the ranking is solely done by the results of the round robin.	
C Division **Men** **B15+B16**+ other entries **C Division** **Women** **B9+B10**+ other entries	**ONE** Group if 11 or less teams and **TWO** groups if 12 or more teams. Group round robin + Play-offs	Ranking determined for 1st to 4th place 1 v 2 winner gold medal and qualifies for ECC-B and 3 v 4 game. Loser 1 v 2 plays winner 3 v 4, winner silver medal and qualifies for ECC-B loser bronze medal.	Teams ranked as per WCF ranking procedure. **C1 + C2 are promoted to B-Division for next ECC**

QUALIFICATION SYSTEM - THE AMERICAS ZONE

CHALLENGE EVENT

The 2nd ranked Americas Zone Association from the previous WCC, provided they are not hosting the next Championship, will be subject to any "challenges" that might come from other Associations in the Americas Zone.

If the 2nd ranked Association is hosting the next Championship, then the other Americas Zone Association from the previous Championship will be subject to any "challenges" which might come from other Associations in the Americas Zone.

The Challenge Event will have the following criteria:

1. The Association that is subject to the challenge will be determined at the conclusion of each WCC based upon the final rankings, and also considering which Association has been awarded the right to host the next WCC.

2. Other Associations in the Americas Zone that wish to challenge for a place in the WCC must submit a registration form to the WCF Secretariat by the deadline date of 31 July of the year preceding the next WCC. By the same date the Association that is subject to the challenge must also submit a registration form to the WCF Secretariat to show they are willing to host and participate in the challenge event. The registration forms will be sent by the WCF to the Americas Zone Associations prior to 1 May.

3. If there is only one Association that registered by the deadline date, then that Association is automatically qualified for the next WCC. If no teams register, the vacant spot will be given to the European or Pacific Zone in a manner determined by the WCF Executive Board.

4. The Association that is being challenged will host the challenge event. The venue and the dates of the event must be approved by the WCF prior to 31 October of the year preceding the next WCC.

5. The challenge event must be played during the month of January preceding the next WCC, unless another suitable date is agreed between the WCF, host and challengers.

6. Any Association that must host more than one challenge is not required to have those challenges at the same venue and same dates.

7. The Chief Umpire and Chief Ice Technician are appointed by the Host Association, subject to the approval of the WCF. The Host Association is responsible for their expenses.

8. Each Association involved in a WCC challenge is responsible for the Per Diem and accommodation expenses for its own teams and officials.

9. The WCF will not reimburse any travel expenses for the WCC challenge.

Playing System:

Two teams registered - a “best-of-five” series
Day One - Team Meeting + Official Training + 1 game
Day Two - 2 games
Day Three - 2 games (if required)

Three teams registered - a “double round robin”
Day One - Team Meeting + Official Training + Games 1 v 2 and 1 v 3
Day Two - Games 2 v 3 and 1 v 2 and 1 v 3
Day Three - Game 2 v 3

Four teams registered - a “double round robin”
Day One - Team Meeting + Official Training + Draws 1 and 2
Day Two - Draws 3 and 4 and 5
Day Three - Draw 6

Five or six teams registered - a “single round robin” and a 1 v 2 play-off
Day One - Team Meeting + Official Training + Draws 1 and 2
Day Two - Draws 3 and 4 and 5
Day Three -the 1 v 2 play-off

Time table:

- Conclusion of WCCs - challenged Associations declared
- 1 May - prior to this date registration forms sent out by WCF Secretariat
- 31 July - deadline date for registration (forms returned to the WCF Secretariat)
- 31 October - prior to this date the hosting venue and dates approved by WCF
- January (or agreed date) - the Challenge

MINIMUM STANDARDS

Required by Member Associations for Entry into World Curling Championships

1. **Curling Season:** A minimum of three months.

2. **Standard of Play:** The World Curling Federation may judge if the standard of play of a Member Association is adequate to enter the World Curling Championships.

3. **Qualification:** No Member Association, whose Annual Subscription and arrears to the World Curling Federation are not paid by 1 September of any year, is eligible to enter the World Curling Championships the following year.

ELIGIBILITY

1. Athletes are a national of the country they are representing - their residence can be anywhere.

   or

   Athletes are a resident of the country they are representing for a period of at least two consecutive years immediately prior to the start of the competition.

2. If an athlete has represented a country in any WCF competition, or played in an international qualifier for a WCF competition, that athlete may not represent another country in any WCF competition or WCF international qualifier until the athlete fulfils one of the above criteria **AND** a period of two consecutive years has elapsed.

3. This eligibility does not apply to competing in the Olympic / Paralympic Winter Games, which are governed by the regulations of the International Olympic / Paralympic Committee.

4. The WCF Executive Board shall resolve any dispute relating to the determination of the WCF Member Association that an athlete may represent in a WCF competition.

PLAY-OFF SYSTEMS

OLYMPIC PLAY-OFF SYSTEM

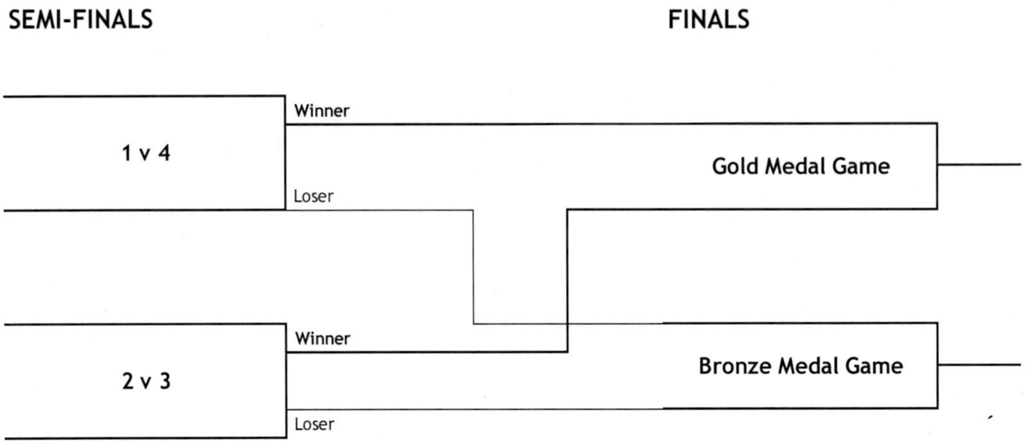

PAGE PLAY-OFF SYSTEM

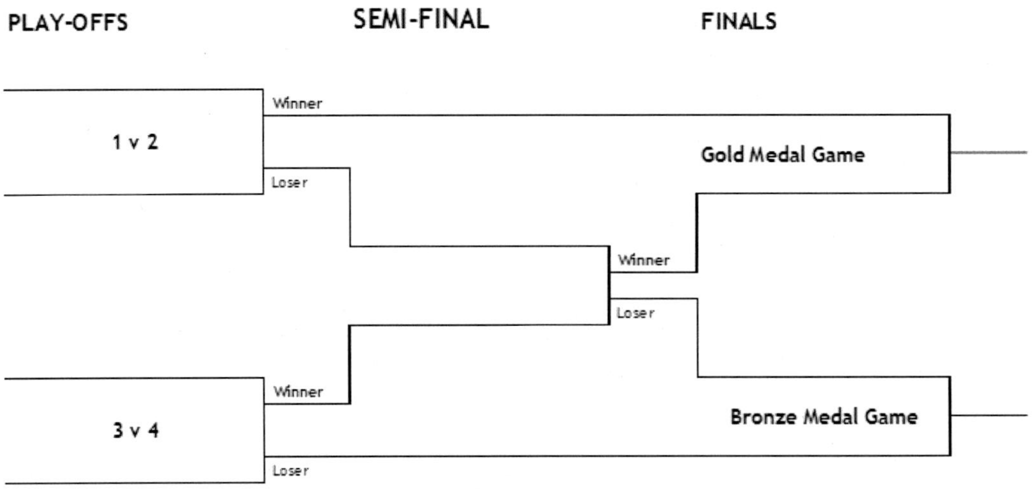

QUARTER-FINALS PLAY-OFF SYSTEM

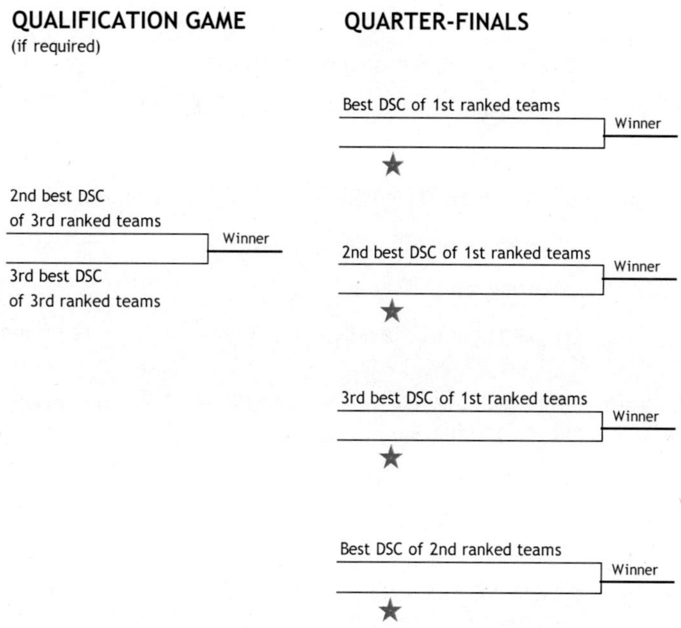

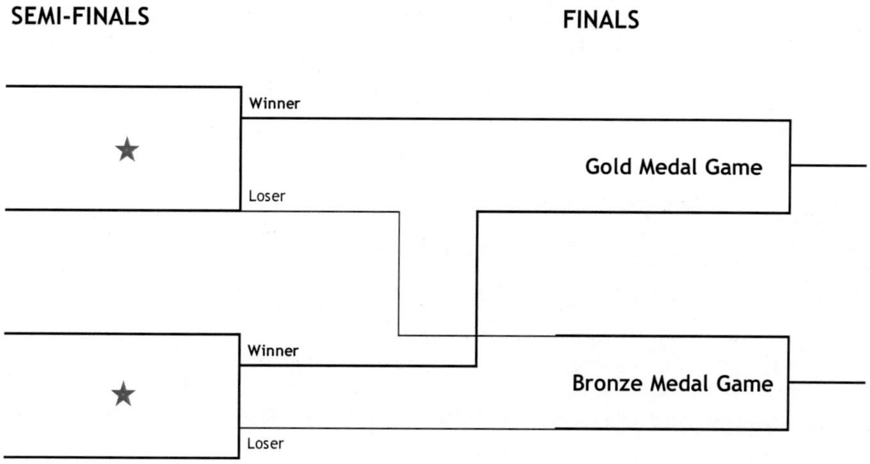

★ Where possible, opponents will be selected on the basis of not having teams from the same group compete against each other. If necessary, the opponents will be determined by a "draw from the hat" (random selection) at the post round robin team meeting.

DRESS CODE

Items	Policy
Shoes	No restrictions, personal preference
Socks	If worn under the trousers, no restrictions
Leg Warmers	Includes socks worn over the trousers, same for the complete team
Trousers	Same logos/crests/colour, can be different brands
Shorts	Not allowed in WCF competitions
Belts	If showing, all the same
Skirts	Matching colour, same colour of tights, can be a team mixture of skirts and trousers
Undershirts	Can be visible (long sleeves under short sleeves) but outfit must have colour coordination
Shirts	Can be tucked in or out
Vests	Okay, must have colour coordination (name, Association, etc.), one or more can wear
Jackets	As per WCF guidelines, Association, player's name, etc. Predominately one colour, but can have an accent colour
Hooded Jackets	Hood cannot be showing, rolled up or tucked inside
Hats	One or more can wear, more than 1 all the same, peaks forward, logos = Association or the Event. Applies to the team and persons on the coach bench
Scarves	One or more can wear, more than 1 all the same
Head & Wrist Bands	One or more can wear, more than 1 all the same, large logos = Association or the Event
Jewellery	No restrictions, personal preference
Gloves	No restrictions, personal preference
Braces	Cannot be visible, worn under a shirt or jacket
Crests	No previous event crests are allowed Approval of sponsor crests has to be sought or renewed for each event

GLOSSARY OF TERMS

Alternate	A registered, non-playing member of the team who is eligible to substitute for one of the competing players.
Arithmetically Eliminated	The status of a team that has a combined total of stones left to be delivered and/or remaining in play that is less than the number needed to produce either a tie or a win.
Away End	The end of the sheet to which the first stone of a game is delivered.
Back Board / Bumper	Material (e.g. foam or wood) placed at the end (perimeter) of each sheet of ice.
Back House Weight	The speed given to a stone at delivery so that it will just reach the back of the house.
Back Line	A line at the back of the house, extending across the width of the sheet, which is parallel to and located 1.829 m. (6 ft.) from each tee line.
Back of the House	The area within the house that lies between the tee line and the back line.
Biter	A stone that just touches the outer edge of the outside circle of the house.
Blank End	An end resulting in no score for either team.
Bonspiel	A curling competition or tournament.
Brush (Broom)	See definition: Sweeping Device.
Brush Head	The part of the brush that comes in contact with the ice surface when sweeping.
Button	The small circle at the centre of the house.
Burned Stone	A stone in motion touched by a player or any part of a player's equipment.
Centre Line	The line dividing the playing surface down the middle. It joins the midpoints of the tee lines and extends 3.658 m. (12 ft.) beyond the centre of each tee line.
Circles	See definition: House.
Competition	Any number of teams playing games to determine a winner.
Come Around	A shot that curls behind another stone.
Counter	Any stone in or touching the house and is considered a potential point.
Courtesy Line	A line indicating where the sweepers from the non-delivering team are allowed to stand in order to ensure that an umpire can view the hog line and to prevent distraction of a delivering player.
Curl	The curved path of a stone as it travels down the sheet of ice.

Debris	Any substance, including frost, snow or material originating from brushes, shoes or clothing.
Delivery End	The end of the sheet from which the stones are being delivered.
Delivering Team	The team that is currently in control of the playing area, and scheduled to deliver the next stone.
Delivery	The motion a player makes when playing a curling stone.
Delivery Stick	A device that attaches to the handle of the stone and acts as an extension of the arm/hand during the delivery process.
Displaced Stone	A stationary stone that has been moved to a new location.
Divider	Material (e.g. foam or wood) used to separate the sheets of curling ice.
Double Take-out	A stone that removes two of the opponent's stones from play.
Draw	A stone which stops inside or in front of the house.
Draw Shot Challenge (DSC)	The calculation made by taking the average distance of the Last Stone Draws (LSD), excluding the least favourable LSD(s), and used, if required, to assist in the determination of ranking after a round robin.
Draw Weight	The momentum required for a delivered stone to reach the house at the playing end.
Electronic Hog Line Device	A device that indicated if a stone was released by a player before the stone reached the hog line at the delivery end.
End	A portion of a curling game that is completed when each team has thrown eight stones and/or the score has been decided.
Equipment	Anything that is worn or carried by a player.
Extra End	An additional end played to break a tie at the end of regulation play.
External Force	An occurrence not caused by either team.
First Player	The first curler on a team to deliver two stones in each end.
Fourth Player	The fourth curler on a team to deliver two stones in each end.
Free Guard Zone (FGZ)	The area at the playing end, between the hog line and the tee line, but excluding the house.
Freeze	A form of a draw shot that stops directly up against another stone.
Front House Weight	The momentum required for a delivered stone to reach the front part of the house at the playing end.
Forfeit	If a team cannot start or continue a game the other team will win that game. The final game score will be recorded as W-L.
Game	Two teams playing a specified number of ends to determine a winner.
Guard	A stone that is placed in a position so that it may protect another stone.

Hack	The foot-hold at each end of the ice which is used by players (except wheelchair curlers) to start the delivery of a curling stone.
Hack Line	A small line 0.457 m. (1 ft. 6 in.) parallel to the tee line, at each end of the centre line.
Hack Weight	The momentum required for a delivered stone to reach the hack at the playing end.
Handle	The part of a curling stone that a player grips in order to deliver.
Hammer	A term used to describe the stone that will be the last stone delivered in that end.
Heavy	A stone delivered with a greater speed than necessary.
Hit	A take-out. Removal of a stone from the playing area by hitting it with another stone.
Hit and Roll	A stone that knocks an opponent's stone out of play, and then rolls to another position in play.
Hog Line	A line extending across the width of the sheet that is parallel to and located 6.40 m. (21 ft.) from each tee line.
Hog Line Violation	A stone that is removed from play for the end, because it was not released before it reached the hog line at the delivery end.
Hogged Stone	A stone that is removed from play for the end, because after being delivered, it did not come to rest completely beyond the inside edge of the hog line at the playing end.
Home End	The end of the sheet from which the first stone of a game is delivered.
House	The area within the concentric circles at each end of the sheet.
Hurry	A command, which instructs players to sweep harder.
Ice Surface	The complete ice area that is within the perimeters of the curling sheet.
In the Process of Delivery	The sequence of play that begins when the delivering player is in position to start the delivery and concludes when the stone is released.
In-turn	The rotation applied to the handle of a stone by a right-handed curler, which causes the stone to rotate in a clockwise manner, for left-handed curlers it is a counter-clockwise rotation.
Last Stone Draw (LSD)	A contest conducted at the conclusion of a team's pre-game practice in which each team delivers two stones by different players, the first stone with a clockwise and the second with a counter-clockwise rotation, to the tee at the home end. The resulting distances are measured and used to determine which team has the choice of delivering the first or second stone in the first end.
Lead	The first player on a team to deliver two stones in each end.
Measuring Device	An instrument that determines which stone is closer to the centre of the house (Tee), or whether a stone is in the house.

Moving Stone	A stone in motion either from a delivery or from being struck by another stone.
Original Position of a Stone	The location on the ice where a stone rested prior to its being displaced.
Out-of-play Position	The location of a stone that is not in play (e.g. one which has touched a side line, or crossed the back line).
Out-turn	The rotation applied to the handle of a stone by a right-handed curler, which causes the stone to rotate in a counter-clockwise manner, for left-handed curlers it is a clockwise rotation.
Pebble	The water droplets applied to a sheet of ice before commencing play. These droplets freeze, which then reduces the friction between the ice and the stones.
Peel	A shot designed to remove a guard.
Playing End	The end of the sheet to which the stones are being delivered.
Point	At the completion of an end, one is awarded to a team for each of its own stones located in or touching the house that is closer to the tee than any stone of the opposition.
Port	An opening, or gap, between stones.
Positioned Stones	In Mixed Doubles games, the two stones that are placed in designated positions prior to the start of each end.
Power Play	In Mixed Doubles games, the team that has the decision on the placement of the "positioned" stones, can one time in a game place the stones in designated positions to the side of the sheet instead of the designated centre positions.
Raise	A type of draw which bumps forward another stone.
Raise Take-out	A delivered stone hits a stationary stone, which then starts to move and it hits a third stone out of play.
Rings	See definition: House.
Rock	See definition: Stone.
Roll	The sideways movement of a curling stone after it has struck a stationary stone.
Rotation	The direction of turn of a stone (clockwise or counter-clockwise).
Round Robin	A competition in which each team plays all the other teams in their group.
Score	The number of points received by a team in an end.
Scoring	A team scores one point for each of its stones that is within the house and closer to the tee than any stone of the opposing team.
Second Player	The second curler on a team to deliver two stones in each end.
Sheet	The specific ice surface upon which a curling game is played.
Shot (stone or rock)	At any time during an end, the stone closest to the tee.
Side Line	A line placed at the side (perimeter) of each sheet of ice.

Skip	The player who directs play for the team.
Slider	Slippery material placed on the sole of the sliding shoe, which makes it easier to slide on the ice.
Spare	See definition: Alternate.
Stationary Stone	A stone in play which is not in motion.
Stone	Also known as a rock, a curling stone is made of granite and is delivered by the players in a curling game.
Stone Set in Motion	A stationary stone hit by another stone which causes it to move.
Sweeping	The action of moving a broom or brush back and forth in front of the path of a moving stone to clean or polish the ice surface.
Sweeping Device	A device used by players to sweep/clean the ice.
Swingy Ice	The condition of the ice or stones causing the stones to have excessive curl.
Take-out	Removal of a stone from the playing area by hitting it with another stone.
Team	Four players competing together. A team may include a fifth player (to act as an alternate) and a coach. Mixed Doubles have one male and one female player, and may include a coach.
Team Time-out	A 60 second on-ice meeting between a team and their coach.
Technical Time-out	Stoppage of play called by a team or umpire for a ruling, injury, or in other extenuating circumstances, etc.
Tee	The exact centre of the house.
Tee Line	A line extending across the width of the sheet that passes through the centre of the house parallel to the hog line and backline.
Third Player	The third curler on a team to deliver two stones in each end.
Tie-breaker	A game that is played to break a tied ranking at the end of the round robin.
Top of the House	The area within the house that lies between the hog line and the tee line.
Umpire	The person(s) responsible for the conduct of the game in accordance with the rules.
Vice-Skip (Mate or Acting Skip)	The player who directs play for the team when it is the skip's turn to deliver.
Weight	The amount of force/speed given to the stone during the delivery.
Wheelchair Lines	Two lines that run from the hog line to the outermost edge of the nearest circle of the house. Wheelchair curlers are allowed to start their delivery with the stone placed between these lines.